William A. Van Roo, S.J.: MAN THE SYMBOLIZER

Analecta Gregoriana

Cura Pontificiae Universitatis Gregorianae edita
Vol. 222. Series Facultatis Theologiae: Sectio A, n. 23

WILLIAM A. VAN ROO, S. J.

MAN THE SYMBOLIZER

GREGORIAN UNIVERSITY PRESS
ROME 1981

WILLIAM A. VAN ROO, S. J.

MAN THE SYMBOLIZER

GREGORIAN UNIVERSITY PRESS
ROME 1981

IMPRIMI POTEST

Romae die 17 februarii 1981

R. P. Urbanus Navarrete, S.I.
Rector Universitatis

Con approvazione del Vicariato di Roma
in data 10 marzo 1981

ISSN: 0066-1376

TIP. P. U. G. - ROMA

TABLE OF CONTENTS

which had been on one of my shelves for years, awaiting the
attention which it deserved and at last received. I have published a long article setting forth Cassirer's thought, along with
that of Susanne Langer, and giving my critical evaluation.[2]
For any reader interested in such a full exposition and critique
I can only refer to that article. Here I shall indicate briefly
some significant features of Cassirer's thought, and some of the
further questions which occurred to me as I considered it.

Cassirer projected a vast extension and re-working of the
Kantian critique of knowledge. His scope was the study of
the whole range of the formative function of the human spirit
or consciousness, from perception through all of the modes of
concept formation in myth, religion, common sense language,
and art, as well as in science. His purpose was the elaboration
of what he called a phenomenology of human consciousness,
which was to be a sort of prolegomenon to a full philosophy
of human culture.

His whole theory rests on his conception of the dynamic
structure of human consciousness. We can approach his notion
by considering his formulation of the problem of representation.
It is this: "... how can a finite and particular sensory content
be made into the vehicle of a general spiritual 'meaning'?"[3]
A definite law, a specific principle of aesthetic formation, is at
work. Sensory particulars do not stand by themselves. They
are articulated in a conscious whole, from which they take their
qualitative meaning. Every particular content of consciousness
is situated in a network of diverse relations, and the representation of the whole in the particular content is an original process
which belongs to the very essence of consciousness. The basic
relations are those of space, time, thing-attribute, and cause.
They run through all of the formative operations of conscious·
ness, and in perception and all kinds of concept formation
these same relations are found in varying modalities. It is this
sameness of relations which constitutes the unity of consciousness. The general structural laws of consciousness are given
in each of its contents, for this is the nature of a content of
consciousness: it exists only in so far as it immediately goes
beyond itself in various directions of synthesis. Consciousness
of the moment contains references to temporal succession. Con-

---

    [2] WILLIAM A. VAN ROO, S.J., "Symbol According to Cassirer and
Langer," *Gregorianum* 53 (1972) 407-486; 615-677.
    [3] *Philosophy of Symbolic Forms*, vol. I, p. 93.

INTRODUCTION

On June 15, 1970 I was writing page 144 of the typescript of a book to be entitled *The Christian Sacrament*. Three fourths of the way down the page I stopped. I was treating the sacrament as a symbol, and suddenly I felt as if I held a handful of dust, scholastic dust. The old definitions and distinctions, and the pedagogical illustrations, seemed utterly inadequate, and I wondered what others had to say about symbols and symbolism. Taking the challenge of my own question, I began a quest which has resulted in this book.

I could not suspect what lay in store for me, how many further questions I should have to face, and how many times I should have to expand my modest original project to take in kinds of symbols which I had not planned to treat. For some time I planned to devote half of this book to the exposition and critical evaluation of some of the works which seemed to me to be especially important, and which would serve to locate my effort in relation to known positions in the field. Life is too short to read such books, let alone to write them. I have abandoned that project, and I limit myself in the body of this book to setting forth my own thought, which has taken shape slowly at first in tentative elaborations of elements, than with a steady, inexorable development as I carried out the long, sustained reflection.

To provide some introduction which may set my thought against the background of the work of other thinkers whom I found most helpful and most stimulating, I shall sketch the following: (1) four well-known positions; (2) the whole field as I envision it; (3) my scope and method.

Four Well-known Positions

Early in my search for significant works I realized the portance of Ernst Cassirer's *Philosophy of Symbolic Fo*

---

[1] Ernst Cassirer, *The Philosophy of Symbolic Forms*, 3 volumes lated by Ralph Manheim (New Haven and London: 1953, 1955, 1'

sciousness of the point contains references to space as the sum and totality of all possible designations of position.

Usually Cassirer does not differentiate sign and symbol, nor does he give a single definition of either. These are some of his characteristic quasi-definitions or descriptions: "... [The] sign is no mere accidental cloak of the idea, but its necessary and essential organ. It serves not merely to communicate a complete and given thought-content, but is an instrument, by means of which this content develops and fully defines itself. The conceptual definition of a content goes hand in hand with its stabilization in some characteristic sign ..." [4] A sign is a means of representation,[5] a basic instrument of representation.[6] Signs are representatives of objects.[7] A symbolic sign is a means of representation of a concept.[8] Cassirer gives the concept symbol a broad meaning, to "... encompass the totality of those phenomena in which the sensuous is in any way filled with meaning, in which a sensuous content, while preserving the mode of its existence and facticity, represents a particularization and embodiment, a manifestation and incarnation of a meaning ..." [9]

With these basic concepts of consciousness, its formative functions, and the symbols which are its products, Cassirer worked out an intelligible account of a vast body of data regarding myth, ordinary language in its development from intuitive beginnings toward scientific symbols, and scientific knowledge. His treatment of religion is unsure, and he did not work out an account of the art symbol; but his project is open to a full phenomenology of human culture.

I should recognize three merits in Cassirer's work: his insistence on the formative function of consciousness; his insight into the similarity of function running through all types of symbol-making; and his illustration of continuity in the gradual development of symbols from intuitive and mythic beginnings to the most refined scientific and mathematical symbols. Limited as Cassirer's achievement may be, it affords a strong argument for taking *symbol* in a very broad sense. Surely there is need for considerable differentiation of symbols, but there is a great advantage in embracing all symbols in a wide-ranging theory.

---

4 *Ibid.*, vol. I, p. 86.
5 *Ibid.*, vol. III, p. 136.
6 *Ibid.*, vol. III, p. 479.
7 *Ibid.*, vol. III, p. 45.
8 *Ibid.*, vol. III, p. 337.
9 *Ibid.*, vol. III, p. 93.

Every one is understood better if it is located within the whole field.

Most of the serious defects in Cassirer's thought, and most of the pressing further questions, regard the severely restricted neo-kantian intellectual world within which he operated. When I say that Cassirer gave an intelligible account, I should add that his account is intelligible only if one admits his philosophical principles. Only a kantian would find his account satisfying. For any independent thinker several further questions arise, and a far more ample field must be explored and charted intellectually.

Cassirer sought the intelligible principles, the a priori, which would account for the range of symbolic forms. I should say that he discovered and accounted for only one pair of the many intelligible principles which are needed. The pair are the correlative sets of functions and forms. The analogous likeness of functions and forms through the whole realm of symbolizing from myth to science is the unity of "consciousness". "Subjectivity" for Cassirer is "... a totality of functions, out of which the phenomenon of the world and its determinate order of meaning is actually built up for us ...": [10] the building up of consciousness [11] and the building up of the world [12] coincide. Cassirer's world is a kantian phenomenal world. For him its outer limit is the flow of sensory experience; to that chaotic mass of impressions perception first gives form, [13] and it is the function of knowledge to build up and constitute the object, not as an absolute object but as a phenomenal object, conditioned by this very function. [14] For Cassirer, "... we still remain in a world of 'images'... image-worlds whose principles and origin are to be sought in an autonomous creation of the spirit. Through them alone we see what we call 'reality,' and in them alone we possess it: for the highest objective truth that is accessible to the spirit is ultimately the form of its own activity. In the totality of its own achievements, in the knowledge of the specific rule by which each of them is determined and in the consciousness of the context which reunites all these special rules into *one* problem and one solution: in all this, the human

---

[10] *Ibid.*, vol. III, p. 50.
[11] *Ibid.*, vol. III, p. 203.
[12] Cf. *ibid.*, vol. III, pp. 50, 221, 276.
[13] Sf. *ibid.*, vol. II, p. 35; vol. III, pp. 155, 221-222.
[14] *Ibid.*, vol. III, pp. 4-5.

spirit now perceives itself and reality. True, the question of what, apart from these spiritual functions, constitutes absolute reality, the question of what the 'thing in itself' may be in *this* sense, remains unanswered, except that more and more we learn to recognize it as a fallacy in formulation, an intellectual phantasm ..." [15]

What, then, are the limitations of Cassirer's account of symbols, and what further questions arise? First, he limits his consideration to the cognitive function of symbols: there are further questions to be answered concerning emotive, volitional, and motor aspects of symbolizing and of symbols. Second, even in treating the cognitive function, he works out a phenomenology of functions and forms, but not a full theory of knowledge: further questions regard such a theory which could account for the process of knowledge in which symbols are elaborated. Third, consistently with his philosophical principles and method, he rules out any question of things in themselves, or of the subject in itself. Cassirer himself recognized that consciousness is treated differently in metaphysics, epistemology, and empirical psychology; but he was concerned only with what he called pure phenomenology. Further questions arise for anyone who does not accept the same limitations of his reflection upon human operations and the human way of being, within which symbolizing and symbols can be understood. Finally, Cassirer's consideration of only some aspects of the process of formation of symbols within consciousness raises questions concerning the situation of the person living in the world, engaged in the interplay of persons and things, and affecting the interpersonal world by his symbols.

Susanne Langer, inspired in part by Cassirer, gave a highly personal account of a wide range of symbols,[16] and then made her principal contribution in her treatment of the art symbol.[17] I should say that these elements of her thought have a special bearing on a general theory of symbol: her conceptions of sign and symbol, her conception of the art symbol, her distinction of discursive and non-discursive or presentational symbols, and

---

[15] *Ibid.*, vol. I, p. 111.

[16] SUSANNE K. LANGER, *Philosophy in a New Key* (second edition, New York: 1951).

[17] *Feeling and Form* (New York: 1953), with some further developments in *Mind: An Essay on Human Feeling*, vol. I (Baltimore and London: 1967).

her differentiation of the arts in terms of their primary illusion and basic abstraction.[18]

Langer distinguishes between sign, symptom, and symbol.[19] *Sign* is a general term, denoting any vehicle of meaning. A *signal* is a particular kind of sign, indicating the existence—past, present, or future—of a thing, event, or condition. There are two kinds: natural and artificial. A natural sign [= signal, in this context] "... is part of a greater event, or of a complex condition, and to the experienced observer it signifies the rest of that situation of which it is a notable feature. It is a *symptom* of a state of affairs." Artificial signs are not part of a condition of which they naturally signify the remainder, but their logical relation to their objects is the same as that of natural signs.[20]

Unlike a signal, a *symbol* does not evoke action appropriate to the presence of its object. It is not a proxy for its object. Symbols are "... *vehicles for the conceptions of objects.* To conceive a thing or situation is not the same thing as to 'react toward it' overtly, or to be aware of its presence. In talking *about* things we have conceptions of them, not the things themselves; and *it is the conceptions, not the things, that symbols directly 'mean'...*"[21] A symbol is an instrument of thought.[22] A concept is all that a symbol really conveys.[23] A symbol is any device whereby we are enabled to make an abstraction.[24] The artistic symbol, *qua* artistic, negotiates insight.[25] A symbol is used to articulate ideas of something we wish to think about, and until we have a fairly adequate symbolism we cannot think about it.[26] For example, "... the function of music is not stimulation of feeling, but expression of it; and furthermore, not the symptomatic expression of feelings that beset the composer but

---

[18] I gave an ample exposition of her thought and some critical evaluation in my article already cited, "Symbol According to Cassirer and Langer," *Gregorianum* 53 (1972) 407-486; 615-677; and a brief account and further reflection in another article: "Symbol in Art and Sacrament," in *Symbolisme et théologie* (*Studia Anselmiana*, 64) 151-171, parts of which I am incorporating here.

[19] In *Philosophy in a New Key* there is some ambiguity: *sign* here is both a general term and a particular term with the meaning later assigned to *signal*. See the preface to the second edition, pp. v-vi.

[20] *Ibid.*, pp. 58-59.

[21] *Ibid.*, p. 61.

[22] *Ibid.*, p. 63.

[23] *Ibid.*, p. 70.

[24] *Feeling and Form*, p. xi.

[25] *Ibid.*, p. 22.

[26] *Ibid.*, p. 28.

a symbolic expression of the forms of sentience as he understands them. It bespeaks his imagination of feeling rather than
his own emotional state, and expresses what he *knows about*
the so-called 'inner life'..." [27] As an image, a symbol, the work
of art is the bearer of an idea. [28]

Art is "... the creation of forms symbolic of human feeling."
The art symbol expresses the artist's knowledge of human feeling.
Its essential quality is significant form, expressive form: by a
likeness of form, of structure, the art work expresses the artist's
insight into the form or structure of human feeling. Significant
form is the secret not only of effectiveness in expression, but
also of beauty.

The art work is abstract, detached from the rest of the
world, so that it gives the impression of otherness, of being
a sheer image, a semblance. Its abstraction is achieved, however, not by generalization, but by the deliverance of an individual form from all that is irrelevant: it incarnates human
feeling in a symbol which has far greater expressive power than
the reality of daily life.

Human feeling has a very complex dynamic pattern, whose
form is elusive in actual experience. It has an inner dynamism
for which we have no simple image, such as we have for visually
perceived forms, for colors, or for sound patterns. The art
symbol articulates the forms of human feeling by projecting
them in images which hold them and present them for contemplation. It presents a semblance of feeling, a virtual form,
symbolic of the elusive forms of feeling.

Detached from its physical environment, the art work creates
the impression of an illusion: the illusion of being a sheer image.
Thus a painting presents an illusion, a virtual object: what is
really there is a surface smeared with paint. It is by the variety
of their primary illusions that the arts are differentiated. Corresponding to the primary illusion of every art is the basic
abstraction by which that illusion is created. [29]

---

[27] *Ibid.*, p. 28.

[28] *Ibid.*, p. 47.

[29] The notions of primary illusion and basic abstraction, and of
their roles in a theory of art, are Langer's. In her treatment of the
individual art symbols in *Feeling and Form*, however, she does not always
indicate clearly what are the primary illusion and the basic abstraction,
nor distinguish between them. Thus, regarding the plastic arts, she does
not distinguish consistently. In pictorial art, the scene is indicated as
both the primary illusion (pp. 86, 89, 92) and the basic abstraction (p. 94).
In her account of architecture the ethnic domain is said to be both the

The art symbol is non-discursive, or presentational, or meta-phorical. It differs from discursive from in these ways: (1) though it is composed of elements, it cannot be broken up into basic units with independent meanings: it has no vocabulary, nor a technique of combination which could be called properly a syntax; (2) there can be no dictionary of meanings for the elements of a work of art, nor any definition of one symbol in terms of another; (3) the art symbol is simply not translatable.

When the art symbol is said to be presentational, the meaning is this: it presents an individual object, without general reference. Its laws are those of the imagination. Its role is to articulate knowledge which cannot be rendered discursively, because it concerns experiences which are not formally amenable to discursive projection: rhythms of life, organic, emotional, and mental, which are not simply periodic, but endlessly complex, composing together the dynamic pattern of feeling.

I find Langer's work rich and stimulating, suggesting several further questions. Although *Feeling and Form* has as its sub-title *A Theory of Art Developed from Philosophy in a New Key*, Langer disclaims any effort to work out a general theory, and her reflections on the individual arts surely do not constitute such a theory. These are some of the matters which call for further development: (1) the distinction between sign, signal, symptom, and symbol still calls for a general account of how all of them originate, and they can be understood better if they are held within one general theory of symbolizing or signifying; (2) the account of symbol is limited to its cognitive function, and needs a complementary treatment of other dimensions; (3) Langer provides no theory of knowledge, much less a philosophy of man, which could situate symbolizing and symbols in their intelligible field; (4) the distinction between discursive and non-discursive or presentational symbols brings out some striking differences, and it serves to distinguish fairly satisfactorily plastic arts on the one hand and scientific or philosophical

---

primary illusion and the basic abstraction (pp. 94, 97, 100). In music, the primary illusion is said to be "... the sonorous image of passage, abstracted from actuality to become free and plastic and entirely perceptible ..." (p. 133), and in another place, "... the semblance of this vital, experiential time ..." (p. 109). The first of the texts which I have quoted seems to suggest that the sonorous image of passage is also the basic abstraction. As far as I have been able to determine, Langer nowhere states explicitly what she regards as the basic abstraction in music.

discourse on the other; but it imposes some forced interpretation of many symbols in which language is involved; the criteria for the differentiation of the arts are blurred, and I have attempted another basic differentiation of symbols in this work.

Paul Ricoeur surely is one of the best-known and most influential of the philosophers who have dealt with symbolism. His own work is extensive, and a considerable literature has formed about his thought. Quite frankly, I have not attempted to work through all of Ricoeur's thought, much less the many studies devoted to it. I have studied his basic work, *Philosophie de la volonté*, and his study of Freud,[30] enough, I believe, to mark my relationship to his position, and to continue the development of my own thought with an awareness of some of our differences.

I limit myself here to two elements of Ricoeur's thought, and mark the differences which can help to situate my work in relation to his. One is his notion of symbol. The other is his contribution to a philosophy of man, especially in his volume on the voluntary and the involuntary.

Ricoeur takes symbol in a very narrow, strictly defined sense. He rejects Cassirer's definition of symbolic form as too broad, though he recognizes its advantages. His objection is that, if we take *symbol* in the broad sense as Cassirer did, "... we no longer have a word to designate the group of signs whose intentional texture calls for a reading of another meaning in the first, literal, and immediate meaning. As I see it the problem of the unity of language cannot validly be posed until a fixed status has been assigned to a group of expressions that share the peculiarity of designating an indirect meaning in and through a direct meaning and thus call for something like a deciphering, i.e. an interpretation, in the precise sense of the word. To mean something other than what is said—this is the symbolic function.

"... In every sign a sensory vehicle is the bearer of a signifying function that makes it stand for something else. But I will not say that I interpret the sensory sign when I understand what it says. Interpretation has to do with a more complicated intentional structure: a first meaning is set up which intends something, but this object in turn refers to something else which is intended only through the first object.

---

[30] PAUL RICOEUR, *Philosophie de la volonté* [Tome] I. *Le Volontaire et l'involontaire*; [Tome] II. I. *L'Homme faillible*; II. II. *La Symbolique du mal* (Paris: 1963); *Freud and Philosophy. An Essay on Interpretation*, translated by DENIS SAVAGE (New Haven and London: 1970).

"... I deliberately restrict the notion of symbol to double- or multiple-meaning expressions whose semantic texture is correlative to the work of interpretation that explicates their second or multiple meanings." [31]

"... I have decided to define, i.e. limit, the notions of symbol and interpretation through one another. Thus a symbol is a double-meaning linguistic expression that requires an interpretation, and interpretation is a work of understanding that aims at deciphering symbols ...." [32]

As Ricoeur recognized the advantages of Cassirer's usage, so I recognize the advantages of his. The problem for me is that we do not have enough words to go around, and I prefer a sense of *symbol* even broader than that of Cassirer. Ricoeur encloses a well-defined intellectual world with his correlative notions of symbol and interpretation. I have two difficulties with his choice. First, what he calls symbols are to be found in continuity with many other "signs", and they can be understood better if they are located in the larger realm. We can take *symbol* in a broader sense, to allow for the whole realm, and differentiate clearly within it. Second, his explicit concern is with only the cognitive intentionality of symbols. For reasons which I find compelling, it is necessary to consider a blend of intentional functions in many symbols: not only cognitive, but also emotive, volitional, and motor.

No one can command in this matter. I simply indicate that I have made a different choice, and I suggest that my meaning is to be grasped from the context of my thought.

Although Ricoeur's major work is entitled *Philosophy of the Will*, and his impressive work on Freud is an essay on interpretation, he has made a great contribution to the eventual development of a full philosophy of man. I have found this element of his work stimulating. When Ricoeur sets forth his personal reflections, he is at his best, in my judgment. What may make his work forbidding for many, and what surely imposes a difficult—if not impossible—task of interpretation of his text is his propensity for weaving into his discourse elements taken from the thought of other philosophers. Since every such element ought to be considered in its own context, and Ricoeur's interpretation of every text could itself be open to critical evaluation, one would have to devote a lifetime or

---

[31] RICOEUR, *Freud*, pp. 11-13.
[32] *Ibid.*, p. 9.

more to the works of a great number of other philosophers in order to read Ricoeur and evaluate his thought. For this reason I find it unreasonable to attempt a discussion of his positions. In my own work in this book I attempt to develop my own thought in a coherent discourse, and I ask only that it be regarded as one man's work. I acknowledge the richness and profundity of Ricoeur's thought, but I make no effort here to set it forth, much less to evaluate it critically.

Concerning Merleau-Ponty I shall say least, thought he is the thinker who stimulated me most and occasioned much of my own reflection. One could say that he devoted a life-time to exploring and charting what had become for many a no-man's land between idealism or transcendental philosophy and empiricism. His reflection on structures of human experience suggested to me the task which I had to perform in order to come to a deeper understanding of symbols, symbolizing, and man the symbolizer. I devoted most of my work on Merleau-Ponty to his two great books, *The Phenomenology of Perception* and *The Structure of Behavior*.[33] I could not attempt here an exposition of his thought, nor an indication of particular elements which I regard as significant, much less a critical evaluation. I should say that some of my thought in this book could be understood better against the ground of Merleau-Ponty's work, but I should have to add that I could not indicate a single element which has passed from his into mine. His struggle, and his achievement, inspired me to an effort which had to be mine. As I read him, I was aware that not a single philosophical term in his discourse could fit in the same sense or cluster of senses into my own thought. Yet I feel greatly indebted to him, and I acknowledge the debt gratefully.

THE FIELD

One can come to understand what a symbol is, and formulate a fairly adequate definition of symbol, in so far as one can locate it in the full field in which it is found, and establish the network of relationships in which it is somehow intelligible.

---

[33] MAURICE MERLEAU-PONTY, *Phénoménologie de la perception* (Paris: 1945); in English, *Phenomenology of Perception*, translated by COLIN SMITH (London and New York: 1962). *La Structure du comportement*, third edition (Paris: 1953) in English, *The Structure of Behavior*, translated by ALDEN L. FISHER (Boston: 1963).

To begin with, however, one must have some sense of what we are trying to understand better, some nominal definition which enables us to recognize the range of symbols, all of which in various ways are recognizable as symbols.

I should take this as a preliminary nominal definition: *a human work in which the sensuous is somehow meaningful.* That is a formula broad enough to include all of the kinds of symbols which Cassirer and Langer, for example, have treated or proposed for treatment. In all of them there is question of a human work: the product of some human formative process, from perception through all kinds of conception and shaping of any sensuous medium, within the symbolizer or external to him. It is broad enough to go beyond Cassirer's and Langer's concerns, beyond the realm of the merely cognitive, to include other kinds of intentionality: emotive, volitional, and motor.

The range of symbols, then, extends from perception through memory and imagination and all forms of conception and embodiment of conception in some formed sensuous medium. It includes bodily expression and gesture, language, art works, scientific and philosophical concept and mathematical symbol. It includes the symbols which figure in dreams as well as those in waking consciousness. It includes the meaningful sensuous which is predominantly cognitive, or emotive, or volitional, or motor, and which may involve any blend of several intentionalities.

When we seek to understand *symbol*, then, we are seeking to understand what is common to all of these examples of a meaningful sensuous. For the present, I take *sensuous* as a noun: as we can speak of *the* sensuous, I refer here merely to *a* meaningful sensuous. In the course of our reflection we shall seek to determine more accurately what a symbol is.

If that suffices for the present as a nominal definition, and if our indication of the range of symbols is sufficient to show the variety of what we would call symbols, then how do we go about indicating the *field* within which the meaningful sensuous is to be understood, within which significant intelligible relationships are to be determined?

The total field is the universe of being, within which persons and things are in continual interplay. In a special way, the relevant field is the total interpersonal world, within which symbolizing occurs, and symbols function.

More particularly, the first significant setting within which symbolizing and symbols can be understood is that of the total personal setting of the symbolizer. Symbols occur within the realm of conscious, intentional operations, in full waking consciousness or in dream. The creation and use of symbols, therefore, calls for a reflection upon human conscious, intentional operations: how and why they are discerned, how they are interrelated, how they are involved in symbol-making and symbol-using. Since no symbolizing occurs in the private world of an individual, both symbol-making and symbol-using can be understood only in the setting of an interpersonal world, of persons in community. Moreover, if we are to take account of all symbols which are found in human experience, we must be ready to open our reflection to the structure and function of symbols which are involved in an interpersonal world which is not merely human, but transcendent: religious symbols involving man and God.

Furthermore, other significant relationships are based upon the functions of symbols: how they affect the symbolizer and other persons.

What is involved in all this is analogous to the process by which we can understand any individual symbol. It is understood only as it is integrated in a whole, as it stands as figure against ground, as it is in its total significant setting. What is true of any individual symbol is true at another level of reflection on symbol generally, as a human work, and symbolizing as a human operation. Symbolizing and symbols can be understood only as they are located in the total intelligible structure of human being and operation, personal and interpersonal. Consequently this reflection on symbolizing and symbol must take the form of a contribution to a basic understanding of the human mode of being and operating, personal and interpersonal.

SCOPE AND METHOD

My scope in this work is philosophical. Although I am a theologian, and the occasion of this work was a theological problem, I have worked seriously in philosophy for over forty years. I shall not enter here into my conception of the relationship between the two fields of knowledge. I simply affirm that my aim here is to reach a deeper understanding of human being and operation. I do point out at times further questions which would require a consideration of properly theological data, and which call for a properly theological treatment. I do so because I start with reflection on actual human experience, and many men and women witness to actual experience which involves relationship with God. An account of the properly human way of being and operating must be open to the possibility of moving on to such a further consideration. A theory of man must be capable of accounting for further experiences which are also experiences of men and women who do not cease to be human when they encounter God.

My scope is philosophical, but I do not attempt to elaborate a full philosophy or basic knowledge of human being. I should say that what I have done in this book raises a number of further questions, and the dynamics of the thought would propel me or another thinker to work out the answers to those questions in a more thorough-going way. I regard this work as a contribution to philosophy.

What is my method? I hesitate to use tags. We do not have enough words to go around, and one of our severe shortages is in the terminology by which a manner of thought or a method might be designated. Without acknowledging any of the current classifications as applicable without considerable explanation, I simply describe the process of my thought in this work.

Since I am convinced that symbolizing and symbols can be understood only in the setting which I have indicated, I begin with a description of some personal experiences, and make some initial reflection on their structure, and on the variety of blends of elements. I am concerned with understanding symbolizing and symbols within the structure of human experience. Though I take note of the non-conscious factors in that experience, I am convinced that one can understand the structure of human experience best by reflecting on fully conscious experience. Consequently I discern and work out structures of individual conscious operations. This involves a personal re-working of accounts of perception, memory, imagination, insight, conception, judgment, emotion, volition, and motor action. Only after differentiation of these modes of operation, do I face the questions of their blends, their setting in their total field, and special roles of intellect.

Against the ground of that elaboration of the structure of human being and operation, I approach the question of symbolizing and symbols, work out my complete classification of symbols, consider their functions, and formulate my definition. Having concluded the basic treatment of my theme, I face some further questions, and indicate the opening to more than merely human symbolizing.

If one asks about the relationship between the two parts of this work, I should say that they are stages in a single movement of thought. The first part is a basic reflection upon structures of human operation. The second concentrates on symbolizing and symbols within that whole, and it continues the philosophical reflection on human being and operation. Symbolizing is itself symbolic of the human mode of being; and the elaboration of modes of symbolizing, kinds and functions of symbols, and the definition of symbol continues the movement of a thought which is directed throughout to a deeper understanding of the human way of being.

CHAPTER I

HUMAN EXPERIENCE

In all of the courses which I have taught in recent years I have sought to involve my students in the problems which I intended to treat, and in the gradual process of reflection and elaboration of thought. One of the exercises which I have assigned in courses on symbolism, or most recently on "Man the Symbolizer", was a short account of a vivid personal experience. I asked for a brief description and a reflection on the structure of the experience. The purpose was to prepare a setting for my reflections on the characteristics of human experience. Judging from student appraisals, I should say that the exercise was an effective preparation.

Approaching now the task of reflection upon structures and characteristics of human experience, I have decided to present brief sketches of four personal experiences. They are not sufficient to ground the ensuing reflection, but they should help to suggest a variety of structures and of prominence of certain elements. If my reader will pause and reflect on other personal experiences, he or she may consider more fruitfully the reflections which I shall make.

The first and third of the experiences which I shall sketch are relatively simple and easily isolated. The second and fourth are so deeply imbedded in my own personal and interpersonal experience through long periods of my life that they could neither be isolated nor be adequately presented. Nor, if they could, would it be fitting that they be. They are so deeply personal and interpersonal that they cannot be exhibited. My purpose here is to suggest four experiences of differing patterns, which may serve to suggest something of the ground for the following consideration.

Four Experiences

1. A New Day. Rome, May 9, 1977. This morning, when finally I resolved to get up, and sleep did not intervene again to prevent my carrying out that resolve, I moved for a few moments about my dimly lighted room. Then I went to the double window, opened it and the great outer shutters, and opened again on a new day's variation on a familiar scene. I did not, could not, take it in "whole", all at once and in all details. There were fleeting glimpses of the lovely Colonna garden, of a spottily clouded sky, of terraces below in the foreground; the feel of cool air on my face and the smell of its freshness; the sound of lively songs of many birds; the feeling of new life within me, of joy and eagerness; the urge to plunge into a full day; the grasp of the sense of my situation in my world. I closed the window, and as I turned again to the scene within the room from the window area, I knew how I would begin to write this section of my address on "Man the Symbolizer". A few steps and I had rounded my desk, snatched a sheet of old page proofs and a ball-point, and begun to scribble hasty rough notes, glancing up to check the hour: 5:52. This is enough for a start, for the account would never end, and I could never recapture all the explicit details, much less all the varying backgrounds.

2. Her Last Word. Genova, 12:20 to roughly 1:30 A.M., September 22, 1965. A loud knocking on my door stirred me and pulled me from a deep sleep. Jumping up, I opened the door. It was Father Superior: "Your mother—it's serious." Dressing hastily as he waited, I rushed out and down the stairs, into the street, along to the square and a taxi. From the cab I ran into the hospital and up to the room where I had spent most of the last ten days. In the eerie, glaringly lighted room four or five men and women, doctors and nurses, about the bed, and Mother, writhing in pain. As she saw me, she broke out with one word: "Bill!" It clutched me, crushed me, pulled me. I could only begin to surmise what she meant with that word, and begin to sense what it meant to me. It was her last. After cruelly long minutes of agony she suddenly relaxed, and smiled most beautifully as she died. Of all who had loved her most only I had heard that word and seen that smile, for she died far from home, and I was the only remaining member of the family.

3.   Eisenstein.   A mountain in lower Bavaria, July 1959. I was standing near the top of the eastern slope, my back to the late afternoon sun, looking down on Eisenstein, a village on the border between Germany and Czechoslovakia, poignantly beautiful in the sunlight.   On the way up to the mountain I had seen barbed wire and striped posts, marking the edge of the heavily-mined no-man's land along the border.   Now I stood and contemplated.   Eisenstein, they had told me, had been a lovely, lively little border village, a meetingpoint of two worlds. The railway station straddled the border.   The village had been a place of free passage for people from both sides, especially on Sunday and holiday excursions.   It was a beautiful village, set in the rolling, heavily wooded hills.   Now I was distracted from its beauty by the scars which marred the land: especially the wide strip of razed, seared earth, running ruthlessly over hills and through valleys along the border.   But persons count for more than places, and I thought of the men, women, and children, the people who were not there.   Eisenstein was empty. For miles back from the border no one was allowed to live. In the hour or so that I stood there I saw only one human being on the other side of the border, and he was symbolic: a soldier on a motorcycle, slowly making his way up a slope along a dusty road.

As I gazed, I thought of two contrasting symbolisms, one purely imaginary, the other the work of perception and imagination.   I imagined the village as it must have appeared in happier times, with signs everywhere of quiet village life, with smoke rising from every house, lights beginning to appear as the sun set, and the image of the gathering of families for rest, nourishment, and the shared joy of evening and the approaching night. Below me, on the contrary, lay a deserted, desolate village, with empty dark cold lifeless houses, a lonely land, and the seared menacing strip of mined borderland.   Where were they now? What did they feel now as evening drew on, wherever they were in their exile?   I felt a deep sadness, compassion, and longing to be with them, wild as the desire might seem: to share, to be somehow united in a redemptive suffering which seemed to offer the only hope of the eventual victory of a graced mankind.

4.   A Discernment.   For some days I had been engaged in a communal discernment, in search of a solution to a grave problem involving all of us, but in a special way involving me and others intimately concerned.   For days I had felt a steady

inexorable inclination to solution "A", and a heaviness and sadness which seldom left me. Weary, ready to end the whole
process and settle for "A", grim as it seemed to be, I went to
bed and quickly slept soundly. Shortly after midnight I awoke
from a dream in which the whole situation had been transformed.
Vivid, shifting dream symbolism, clearly associated with biblical
symbolism which had impressed me during those days, gave me
an insight and a total affective and volitional response which
were new. I lay for a while and reflected, sensing a new peace.
Again I slept, and the dream came back, picking up the themes,
shifting the symbolism, now involving variations upon the oval
shape of the rug on the floor of the room where we had spent
many hours seeking together to discern the right way. The
same basic insight was deepened and confirmed, and the total
affective and volitional and even motor response were strong.
I awoke and reflected and saw even more clearly what my way
must be. Again I slept and the dream resumed, with further
development of "reasons" and a continuing heightening of my
total response. I awoke, and continued to reflect and to pray
until after three o'clock. Then, completely at peace with my
decision, I slept until dawn. In a blend of experience of dream
and of lucid waking consciousness I had come to a firm decision
for solution "B". The next day, and through the days and weeks
that followed, I sensed a steady peace and joy in that project,
and for my part the decision was made. I am still convinced
that the decision was right.

An Initial Reflection

Regarding the preceding four sketches not as an adequate
body of data, but as sufficient to suggest to every person according to his own experience what characterizes that experience,
I should like to single out some features which strike me especially, and which will call for more careful and detailed consideration in the chapters which follow.

1. *Concrete unity.* Human experience, or any segment of
it which may be regarded somehow as a unit, is a whole in
which many elements may be discerned: cognitive, emotive,
volitive, motor.

In the first experience which I recorded, perception was
most prominent, but even the cognitive elements were many

and continually shifting. The perceptual field was multiple: visual, tactile, auditory, olfactory. At the same time there was a stream of memories and images, stirred by what I perceived, and in turn affecting my perception. Through them all ran a stream of feelings, and a vague pleasant sense of my situation in my world of that day, a determination to get about living it fully, and motor impulse and action.

In the account of "Her Last Word", a vivid peak experience involved many elements in varying degrees of intensity, and a special force of a flood of memories and feelings. "Eisenstein" had its own blend, with a prominence of imagination and the feelings evoked by the imaginings. "A Discernment" added another element: the continuity of experience in alternating dream and full waking consciousness.

First, then, concrete human experience is a marvelous blend of ever moving, ever shifting, interplaying operations, in unending process, in unity and continuity.

2. *Figure-ground structure.* In the whole of human experience one can discern a constant, analogous structure: in all elements of human experience, in a variety of modes proper to each. The most familiar instance is that of the figure-ground structure of the visual perceptual field. As I looked out the window, I was vaguely aware of the whole visual perceptual field, but I could not take it in whole. The eye is naturally a roving eye, flitting about continually, at times seeming hardly to settle its gaze upon any object. But it does settle momentarily and then rove again. Every time it settles, it fixes its gaze upon an object, a figure, a whole with its physiognomy. Every figure is set against a ground, and when the eye shifts, that figure slips into the background, as another figure is fixed front center.

As we shall see, this structure is characteristic of all modes of human experience: in all perception, of sight, sound, touch, taste, and smell; in our experience of time, of movement, of feeling, thought, and will. Moreover, the structure is discernible not only within every single mode of experience, but also in the whole of human experience. Every operation, of whatever type, may play the role of figure against the total personal ground. An act of visual perception stands out from the total conscious ground: cognitive in all its modes, affective, volitional, motor; and further, from the total personal human ground, from which conscious experience itself stands out.

Nor does the pervasiveness of this structure end in the person considered alone. It is characteristic of the experience of the person in his or her world and worlds: physical, socio-cultural, interpersonal.

Moreover, the figure-ground structure is an aspect of the mutual influence of all elements of human experience. Every act is somehow conditioned and qualified by its total ground. In turn every act modifies the total human ground.

Years ago, when I had my only opportunity to visit Sicily, I flew to Palermo, and then made almost the complete cycle of the island counterclockwise, as far as Messina. When I came to Siracusa and saw the sea, I felt that somehow, at last, the sea was in the right place! Through all the years of living in Rome and going down to the sea whenever possible something had been wrong, and now suddenly I knew what it was. I had spent my first nineteen years in Milwaukee, and for me Lake Michigan had been my sea, and it lay always to the east, and all my experience of it in all its moods was of a great body of water lying to the east, with all the consequences of land-sea-sky relationships at any time of day or night. I saw the sea from Siracusa in an act which stood out from my whole personal background, and that background affected my vision. In turn, the vision and the sudden insight into its rightness has affected all of my subsequent relationship to Lake Michigan as experienced by a boy who lived in a certain part of Milwaukee, at a certain distance from a certain part of the lake lying always to the east.

3. *Spatiality*. A certain analogous spatially marks all human experience, even the most intellectual. This is part of the mystery of our humanly bodily being. There is always an initial spatial situation, a factor in the perspectivism of perception and in insight into a concrete situation or image. There is always the unique point of view, from which a man may "move out" to engage in thought from "no point of view". Man is always probing a field, and however purely he refines his scientific or philosophic symbols, they leave a tell-tale wake which betrays their intuitive origins.

4. *Mobility*. We *are* by being in movement continually in all our modes of being. The roving eye and hands, the moving lips, the shifting head and body, the continual play of moving images, memories, feelings—all these are aspects of the continual

flow of our being in the world. In all our being we are mutable, plastic, in process.

5. *Temporality.* In all his modes of operation, in the very movement of reason, with its succession of steps of inquiry, discovery, formulation, and further question, man is temporal. By memory every man holds the pattern of his own temporality, the setting in which he understands his present reality and his prospects.

6. *Intersubjectivity.* As I looked out the window, in the early morning experience which I recounted above, much of what first caught my gaze was formed by man; and had a man appeared in the scene, he would have been figure against the background. Our first experience is that of the presence of another person, and happy the man or woman who began life with a sense of the loving presence of a mother, of a face and voice and embrace which as a whole expressed tender love.

Even when we are not focussing our attention on persons, the intersubjective world is the most important factor in the total setting of our life, in all our cognitive, affective, volitional, motor activity. Watch children at play in a treasure hunt. Competing individually or in teams, they count partly on their own hunches, partly on watching others for signs of their intentions. Men play similarly. Some great corporations spend part of their budget for research and development on industrial spying, a quicker and cheaper way to discovery. A colleague of mine told recently of the fruitfulness of a venture in deliberate, planned collaboration. Meeting weekends with his fellow workers, he teaches them Ugaritic, they teach him Accadian, and they work together sharing clues to foster insight into the mysteries of the Ebla tablets.

Persons are most precious in our world, and we live most fully, most richly, when we share most fully with persons. It is in the intersubjective world and worlds, purely human and transcendent, that all the higher ranges of human operation and the truly human dimensions of all human being are experienced and can be understood.

If, as I should hold, only man symbolizes, and there are no "natural symbols" independently of human experience, then our experience of the rest of the natural world differs radically from our experience of other persons. Encountering things, we situate them in a world, and they figure in the manifold symbolism which characterizes our operations. Encountering persons, we encounter other symbolizers, and we enter into a whole new intersubjective world or manifold of worlds.

Persons in the mode of their real being in the world defy both the intellectualist or idealist account of the "world" and the contrasting empiricist account. Persons are a gap in the perfectly objective world of the empiricist, and a blur in the perfectly transparent world of the intellectualist. One cannot live in the world, and account for the world in which one lives and of which one has direct experience, without taking account of "objects" which are not merely objects, but persons. Their being in the world, full of the mystery of interiority which we sense in ourselves, cannot be described without an account of their interiority. Moreover, it is not enough to describe other persons in the "third person": until one has encountered them in I-Thou relationships, one has not fully lived.

The appearance which we have for one another is not that of a pseudo-natural symbol, nor of things which figure as symbols only because they figure in the range of our symbolizing operations. Rather it is the appearance of another subject, a person, another autonomous symbolizer, creating or using symbols, and contributing to the meaning and value of the world.

7. *Continuity*. There is a continuity within every mode of human operation, and a continuity of all of the modes in the whole of human living. This is one of the keys to the understanding of man the symbolizer. It is a massive, all-embracing continuity, which extends beyond the range of a person's conscious experience, to include at least these: (a) the fully conscious and the subliminal; (b) the conscious, subconscious, and unconscious; (c) acts as intentional and as conscious; (d) focal and marginal awareness; (e) conscious acts and non-conscious vital acts which ground, condition, and qualify conscious acts; (f) conscious acts and their whole underpinning by all that makes the human body be what it is in the total higher organization of man's being; (g) the person and his worlds, physical, intersubjective, cultural.

8. *Perspectivism*. Every man lives his total experience from a unique point of view, ever shifting, always quite personal. He lives in a world which is unique, for all of his relationships have one term which is his alone. When he reflects on himself and others, he knows that his world in a sense is not theirs, that

the "world" which we share offers itself diversely to every person. This perspectivism is analogous, beyond the familiar aspect of perspectivism in the visual perceptual field. What is involved here is not merely one's position in physical space, but rather one's total personal "position", a function of all that he or she has been and is and hopes to be. All human experience is personal, and every event is set in a unique total personal constellation.

9. *The human a priori.* A manifold human a priori grounds the possibility of, and qualifies, all human experience. The basic human a priori is man's nature, grounding his proper mode of operating at all levels. Further, every man has a particular social and cultural a priori, a function of the society, the culture, the history in which he lives. Finally, every man has his own unique personal a priori, a function of all that he has ever been, conditioning all his experience, and in turn continually conditioned by all his experience.

10. *Infinite variety of relationships.* As a consequence of all the characteristics already noted, one may conceive of an infinite potential variety of relationships, grounded upon the interplay of all elements in a person's experience, and upon his involvement in his world. Many of these relationships are marginal, or "horizonal", passing unnoticed in conscious experience. Yet they feature in its total reality, and they may be fixed in dream or in the free play of imagination. Since every man has his personal point of view, his personal a priori, in a sense there is an infinite variety of ways of experiencing persons and things and worlds generally. We shall have to consider the consequences regarding the meaning of symbols.

11. *Potential constancy.* Notwithstanding all the rest, man can be constant, he can achieve steadiness of understanding and of will. The very laws of his human mode of being are constant, commanding as they do all manners of process; and all of his infinitely varying patterns are variations on a theme. A man can be steady in understanding, in truth, in love. He can grow in understanding and wisdom, in conviction, love, commitment. He is not the victim of his own mutability, his lability; for, though in all his being he is bodily, temporal, labile, he is also intelligent and willing. He can be both supple and firm, both solidly grounded and sublime.

12. *Primordial and explicit experience.* Another feature of human experience is the distinction between what can be called primordial or implicit experience, and all of the explicit operations of what some have called positing consciousness. What is primordial experience? It is the whole of our immediate experience of the world and of ourselves which has not yet become the explicit object of any act of knowledge or will, affectivity or motor activity. It is the whole of the background, the marginal, the "horizonal", which is never fixed as an object, never figures in explicit imagination or memory, but is part of our total experience, and can figure later, whether in dream or in unexpected images or memories whose origin seems so mysterious. Primordial experience is the great uncontained flow of our basic experience of the world and of ourselves, or rather the whirling, surging, blending flow of many streams which fuse into one. It is the stuff of all symbols. Its fulness explains the marvelous range and variety of symbols, and the variety of their adequacy and efficacy.

13. *Twofold basic intentionality.* Primordial experience is marked by a twofold basic intentionality, the matrix of all conscious acts. By conscious acts I mean acts in which the agent is aware of himself and of another: and indeed is aware of himself in the very acts in which he is aware of, and is referring to, the other. Conscious acts are *of something*: they refer to something. This something to which they refer is their object. Especially in philosophical thought influenced by Husserl, this characteristic of conscious acts is called *intentionality*. *Intentional* as an adjective is said first of the conscious act which intends (refers to) an object; and secondly, in a derived sense, of the object intended. Conscious acts will differ in intentionality as they refer differently to objects.

I should designate a twofold basic intentionality in primordial experience. Both are manifold, yet they differ radically through all their modes in the way in which they refer to objects. One is cognitional, the other is volitional-affective-motor.

The basic cognitional intentionality in all of its modes exhibits the general characteristic relationship of knower to known. The knower, remaining himself, somehow holds within himself the mode of being of the other. I should distinguish this basic cognitional intentionality as perceptual and intellectual. First, it embraces primordial perception: the vast, vague, implicit sensible awareness of the world and of ourselves. Man is present

to the world with all his sense powers. He is vaguely aware
of a field, a multiple field according to the diversity of his senses.
He has a vague grasp in the concrete of things-in-relationship.
Within that field, within that vast, vaguely grasped ground, a
succession of explicit perceptions will fix figure against ground,
hold things concretely in sensibly perceptible constellations or
configurations. Vague, implicit, primordial perception is a basic
cognitional intentionality, the matrix of all explicit perception.
Since perception is primary in sense experience, memory and
imagination in turn depend on radical, primordial perceptive
experience.

Basic cognitional intentionality involves secondly an intellectual element which pervades and transcends all primordial
perception, and which is itself twofold. First, there is a vague
grasp of relationships as intelligible, and a drive to grasp them
more firmly, and to define them. Second, there is a massive
existential affirmation of the world, which holds us to the task
of understanding and of explicit affirmation.

The basic volitional-affective-motor intentionality is a love
of all that is vaguely sensed to be good in the world, and a
tendency to union with that good. It is the love which makes
man cling to life, and makes him desire to understand the good
and embrace it and hold it more firmly. It is the radical response to the good as somehow known. It grounds hatred of
evil, and all consequent fear and shrinking from it. At its
highest levels love is the response to the good as understood.
In its permeation of all of man's bodily being this basic intentionality is the vague, implicit affective and motor response to
the good as vaguely sensed.

14. *The importance of primordial experience.* Our primordial experience holds us in contact with the whole of our world,
the one great world within which we move and experience in
this physical and interpersonal universe, embracing the many
little worlds in which we live in particular constellations. Its
twofold basic intentionality bears upon the whole of our world,
and grounds and contains all explicit intentional acts. It is the
ground of all symbolizing, as we shall see. The basis of symbolizing is not two or more "meanings", two or more relationships explicitly grasped; but rather the whole field of relationships, some grasped explicitly, but incomparably more only implicitly grasped in perception and vague understanding of the
world, affirmed in a massive existential affirmation, tended to

or from, shared in intersubjective experience. Within this whole field, an infinity of relationships may be discerned, and objects of all types of explicit intentional acts may be determined.

15. *The personal sphere.* Some phenomenologists speak of the world as the horizon of horizons, setting the limits of intra-mundane experience. "Beyond", in their acount, is the realm of the transcendent. With regard to the latter, I should prefer to say that we may penetrate the realm of the transcendent within this world, probing to find the deeper mystery of the world. Rather than the figure of horizon of horizons, I suggest that of the sphere of total possible experience. Every one of us is at the center of his sphere, from which lines of multiple intentionality may run out in all directions, in all the modes of human conscious operation, into the world of persons and things, within the universe of God and the whole of his creation. An infinity of potential objects can be constituted within the sphere. The figure suggests not the fanning out of different intention-alities, every one in its own direction, but rather a fanning out of clusters of intentionalities, every cluster bearing upon a given object. Our full act bearing upon any object has a multiple intentionality. I *am* in relation to this object in an operation which may have cognitive, affective, volitive, and motor dimensions.

16. *Some reflections on method.* Having set forth this first reflection on structures and characteristics of human experience, I should like to pause for a reflection on method. Let me take as a point of departure and of comparison Kurt Goldstein's account of Sherrington's notion of *synergy.*

Sherrington began with the simplest reflex, knowing that he was dealing with an abstraction. For him the actual reality of the organism was the sum total of reflexes. This sum is conceived of as the instrument of the order which governs the activity of the organism. "... The activity of the organism is guaranteed through the synergy of the reflexes which appears as a sum of numerous parts, which latter, regarded in isolation, do not exist at all, because they are mere abstractions ..." [1] In such a conception, *synergy* seems to be little more than linguistic glue, applied in vain to hold together a hopelessly atomized mental world, in which the whole organism as it really is has

---

[1] KURT GOLDSTEIN, *The Organism* (Boston: c. 1939, 1963) p. 89.

been disregarded systematically. If the *parts*, to begin with, are only abstractions in a method which disregards the concrete whole, then *synergy* is not as wonderful as it might seem at first sight to be. Small wonder that the effect of the operation of the whole organism exceeds the sum of the effects of the "parts", since the parts are only abstractions, the sum of which does not constitute a whole organism.

At the level of the organism, then, (1) the part cannot be regarded as having effects in isolation from the whole; (2) nor can the whole organism be regarded as having effects in isolation from its world and its environment. Further, at the human level, (1) no part can be considered adequately in isolation from the whole person; (2) no person can be considered adequately in isolation from his world, physical, social, cultural; (3) consequently one cannot add up parts to constitute a person, nor go on then to add up pseudo-persons regarded as thus constituted to make up an intersubjective world. A reasonably full consideration of man, of his full concrete reality, must be a reflection on man in the world or worlds in which alone he is, and in which alone he can be understood as standing in a full field. In that field many relationships can be discerned and defined. The relationships themselves are abstractions, relatively few of the potential infinity of relationships. Man is not the sum of all possible relationships. He *is* in such a way in his world and worlds as to ground all the relationships which may be discerned accurately. What we understand of man must be formulated in terms of a network of relationships, intelligible and understood. Such relationships are elements which figure in the constitution of our relatively inadequate intelligible or intellectual world. The whole of our consideration of man must be held constantly to a reflection on his whole concrete reality.

What, then, have I attempted to do thus far, and what shall I be attempting in the chapters which follow? Thus far, regarding the concrete reality of human experience, I have set forth what I consider some of the important discernible characteristics of such experience, some of the laws, if you will, which may be discerned in the dynamic structure of human experience. In what follows I shall consider a number of elements of human experience, a number of operations which exhibit proper structures and functions, and whose effects figure differently in the total personal and interpersonal experience. Such a reflection will be abstractive, discursive, linear in its course. It is not intended, however, to isolate elements or parts to be considered as being or functioning alone. All must be held in a thought which develops in a continuing consideration of the full concrete reality of man, and of the ever varying interplay of elements in the whole, a whole in which everything may be discerned to be related somehow to everything.

If one reflects on what I have just written about method, then he may be inclined to raise a difficulty—or perhaps this one among many. If there is an unbroken continuity of the whole of the reality of persons in their worlds, then how can one speak as I did at the outset of *an* experience, or of four experiences? There is a real difficulty here, but it may be reduced to the general difficulty of settling for human limitation. Our primordial experience is concrete, undifferentiated, massive, but it is limited. We *are* in a world and worlds which are in unbroken continuity. Our experience of our being in the world, however, is always limited. It is a personal participation. Further, our reflection upon our own personal experience, and our determination of structures in it which may be shared and checked and verified as intelligible by others, is also limited. Perforce we attend to certain segments of a concrete experience. But the segments need not be cut arbitrarily. There are clearly different modes of operations, and within them there are clearly discernible units, acts.[2] By reflection on significant portions of our personal experience, and on the clearly discernible modes of operation and their interplay, we may come to some understanding of the mystery of man, and of the particular mystery which I am considering in this work: man the symbolizer.

---

[2] See, for example, the treatment of *act* by SUSANNE K. LANGER, *Mind: An Essay on Human Feeling*, Volume I (Baltimore and London: c. 1967) chapters 8-11, pp. 257-444.

CHAPTER II

PERCEPTION, MEMORY, AND IMAGINATION

I shall begin my reflection on human operations with two orders of cognitive operations: in this chapter those pertaining to the realm of sense, at least in the conception of some thinkers; in the following chapter, those pertaining to intellect. I am not prejudging the matter of a "faculty psychology". Nor am I presupposing a systematic differentiation of sense and intellect. I begin with a reflection on some discernible differences of operations and their terms or effects. I admit that the differences which I find among the operations treated here are not clear in the works of many who have dealt with the same problems. Merleau-Ponty's *perception* includes much of what I think should be regarded as intellectual. Polanyi's *imagination* spreads widely over some of the same areas. Langer's *feeling* includes much which I think should be differentiated. The only basis for differentiation should be clearly discernible differences of structure and function. This is my immediate concern. Any further questions concerning the human a priori, such as those regarding powers or nature, are questions which I shall raise before concluding, but they could be answered only in the elaboration of a full philosophy of man. That is beyond my scope.

One question may be raised here, however, concerning order. In an attempt to understand man the symbolizer, why begin with a reflection on *cognitive* operations? Why not start with feelings, with the affective charge of symbols? One might be tempted to brush off a potentially annoying question by saying simply that it seems to be the obvious place to begin: everyone begins there. For a long time I began there largely because everyone else did, and I was concerned chiefly with the cognitive dimension of symbols. Now that I have faced the question of the multiple functions of symbols, I still begin with the cognitive. I think that there are good reasons. Clearly symbols are meaningful. They have a cognitive dimension. Most concern with symbols seems to be concern for their meaning. Moreover I should say that the cognitive dimension of symbols enjoys a certain priority of nature. Knowledge is prior to affective-voli-tional-motor responses, for those responses are given precisely to what is somehow known to be good or bad for the man who responds. Further, we are concerned with symbols and sym-bolizing as features of the whole conscious experience of man, and consciousness itself is part of the mystery of knowledge. I indicate these answers here. Their significance should appear as we move on.

So much for a transitional introduction to our present theme.

PERCEPTION

1. *Attempts at definition.* There is no generally accepted definition of perception. What may be formulated as a sort of least common denominator in philosophical and psychological usage will be understood differently by most who use the term. I shall propose a working definition and a differentiation of perception from memory and imagination.

Before that, however, it may be well to attempt some for-mulation of working definitions of three terms which I have been using thus far in reliance on a certain vague consensus concerning their meaning. By *experience* I mean an event or a complex of events occurring principally within human conscious life. I say "principally", for what I am dealing with as experi-ence most properly regards human conscious life; yet in a person there is a continuity of fully conscious and subliminal, of con-scious, subconscious, and unconscious. By *operation* I mean an event in which a person is somehow the agent, and in which and by which his manner of being in the world or worlds is modified. By *cognitive* I mean pertaining to knowledge, the whole order of operations and resulting modes of being in which a person, remaining himself, somehow embraces and holds within himself the mode of being of another. In intellectual knowledge there are two orders of operations. One regards answers to the questions "What?" or "What sort of?" The operation is *conception.* Its term is a *concept.* The second regards answers to the questions "*Is* it?" or "*Is* it such or such?" Both opera-tions terminate in a sort of union of knower and known, a sort of likeness, similarity of form. What is grasped and affirmed in intellectual knowledge is a relationship and a being in such or such a relationship, both of which are somehow proportioned to the manner of being of the thing known: it *is* in such a way as to ground all accurate determination of relationships and all affirmations concerning its mode of being. In another order of operations, perception, memory, and imagination, there is a different manner of holding the mode of being of another, and of being somehow one with the known. It is by an image in which the form of another is held as somehow incarnate in a sensibly perceptible likeness. It is the differentiation of this order of knowledge in perception, memory, and imagination which is our present concern.

Perception itself is understood in two senses generally: broadly it is taken as any act of cognitive experience; more strictly it is taken as an act which occurs under the stimulation of sensory receptors by a present reality. In this sense I am taking perception, and defining it at least tentatively thus: an act of sense knowledge, primitive and immediate, objective or subjective, global and unitary, resulting in an image which itself is a complex configuration.

It is cognitive, though in experience it is accompanied by a manifold complementary affective, volitive, motor experience. It is sense knowledge, though it is permeated by an intellectual experience which transcends it. It is primitive and immediate: an absolute beginning in cognitive experience, not a function of recall (in memory) or elaboration (in imagination), nor a function of intellectual reflection; it is an experience under the stimulus of a present reality, and it is possible only under such influence. Some understand perception as regarding only external reality: in that case it is objective only, not subjective. Others understand it as regarding also intraorganic reality: some then distinguish exteroception (in response to external stimuli, through sense organs or receptors near the surface of the body), interoception (in response to stimuli from within the body), and proprioception (regarding the position and movement of the body or its members). In any case, awareness and knowledge of changes within the body pose special questions, which I shall raise later in chapters V and VI.

Perception is global and unitary. It is not the result of the assembling of punctual excitations and sensations. It is usually a blend of many elements of sense knowledge, visual, auditory, tactile, olfactory, gustatory. It is accompanied by an awareness of feeling and movement.

The last element of the tentative definition may prove to be the stumbling block. Perhaps all of the elements of the definition preceding it can be understood in purely empirical, objective, third-personal terms: stimuli, receptors, excitations, reflexes. But *image* seems to introduce an element which separates the empiricist, analytical, objective account of experience from another which is phenomenological: a description of, and reflection upon the structures of, first-personal experience. I cannot rehearse the critique of empiricist, objective psychologies, which could be regarded as the great concern of Merleau-Ponty, and which figures prominently in the work of Ricoeur. I consider that critique effective. Consequently I am convinced that one must approach the treatment of perception, and then of memory and imagination, from within, so to speak: with an account of, and a reflection upon the structures of, personal experience. Beginning with an existential phenomenology, one can raise further questions and probe deeper the mystery of man. No other approach can even detect the kind of experience which is at issue, let alone give an intelligible account of man.

2. *Description and reflection.* There is an inherent difficulty and artificiality in existential phenomenology. Concerned with describing and determining structures of experience from within first-personal experience, without loss of a sense of full concrete reality, the phenomenologist himself assumes something of a laboratory attitude, and interferes with the normal flow and dynamic structure of his experience. He cannot attend to all aspects of his experience at once. If he begins by concentrating on perceptual experience, and in particular on visual perception, he alternates between a perception done with abnormally heightened attention and consciousness and a turning from actual perceiving to his reflection on perceiving.

This morning as I walked back and forth on the terrazza reflecting freely as I took the morning air, my visual field was wonderfully ample and rich in content, shifting as I changed directions in which I walked or looked. Since I was more intent on thinking than on gazing, the constantly shifting field and most of the potential focal objects in it went for the most part unattended, and visual perception served mostly the practical function of walking unimpeded. As I returned to my room, descending the stairs and going along the corridor, again my visual field was constantly shifting, shrinking, expanding, but I was not especially aware of it, intent upon getting to my room and setting about reflection on this portion of my treatment of perception. Within the room the potential visual field for the time was severely limited, and I deliberately held it to one direction, to perceive and to reflect on my perception of a needlework hanging about seven feet from me. My perception was as awkward as the operation of a skilled typist when he or she begins to look at the letters of the keyboard and to focus on them. Yet this is part of the structure of experience, and we may allow for it as we proceed.

I should make one more preliminary observation which is itself a reflection upon and a reminder of an aspect of our experience. I am beginning with perception, and first of all visual perception. Yet there can be no isolating of a visual perceptual world, or even a total perceptual world, except by an abstraction from the rest of a concrete experience in which it is embedded, and by which it is conditioned and continually qualified. We can only consider aspects of a total experience, considering every one in its relation to the rest, and attempting to determine what is proper to it as an aspect of the whole. In treating perception, memory, and imagination in this chapter, and insight, conception, and judgment in the next, and then other elements of experience, we are engaged in a consideration which is itself continuous, and which will come to some sort of term only at the end of chapter IV, with some conclusions regarding the total human world (in chapter V) and further reflections on the roles of intellect, which modify our initial conclusions regarding the other conscious operations, and make possible a more adequate consideration of their blend in total human experience (in chapter VI). The conception of the total human world then will serve as the ground, the setting, for the ensuing reflection on symbolizing and symbolizing man.

On the wall opposite me there are four needlework hangings, each portraying a tree, one for each of the four seasons. As I look now, on a February morning, the first faint sunlight is slanting down upon the nearest hanging, "Summer". The light will be different soon, and so too the tone and total feeling of the scene. As I see the scene, my perceptual experience is qualified by an important personal factor which affects all of my visual perceptive experience—and who knows how much more than that! I am red-green colorblind, and I have to recall what I have been told and can report, but not as part of my perception: the matting which provides the ground is for other perceivers a very beautiful blue-green. From here I cannot see the image sharply enough, much less appreciate details, and

I move to within three feet, directly facing the image. Movement, of the whole body to the right place, and of the head or
at least the eyes, is an important element of experience which
grounds, conditions, qualifies our visual perception.

What, then, is the structure of my visual experience? In
this case there is a special factor: within the "world" of physical
space which I embrace in my total visual field from this point,
there is the world which the artist has created in this image of
summer; and as I concentrate on it, I am directing my gaze
to an image contained physically in a space about sixteen by
twenty-two inches: the rest of my visual field is irrelevant for
the moment, the physical ground for an artistic experience.

I cannot take in the whole image, the whole scene, except
in a gaze which is not focussed, but directed to roughly the
center of the scene. To focus my gaze, to see and appreciate
the image at its best, I must gaze successively at minute elements of the image, each held in the whole image by the continuing marginal vision of the whole. I follow one of the
branches of the tree, or more sharply its lower or upper line,
return to a leaf, move along the edge of the leaf, back along
the branch to another leaf, shift up to the bluebird nesting in
a crotch of a high branch, and move on to fix and hold other
details of the whole scene. I follow—in normal, indeliberate
perception—whatever haphazard sequence may result from my
being drawn by one feature after another, and making every
one in turn figure against the ground of the whole scene.

I do not perceive by fixing my eyes on one focal point and
holding my gaze there indefinitely. I could not hold it indefinitely without discomfort, and without losing in fulness of the
perceptual experience. I perceive by scanning, flitting over the
whole, changing focus continually. Perception is not made up
of a multitude of fixed images, like photographic snapshots. Perceptual experience is continually shifting, flowing, with the gaze
seldom held fixed, and then not rigidly. If perception is halted,
fixed in a stare, one tampers with its normal pattern. Reflection on such a deliberate, contrived fixed gaze would reveal
only what perception in its normal functioning is *not*.

I mentioned the indispensable motor experience with which
perception is blended. Within perception itself there is an ever-
varying blend, for visual perception is in continuity with auditory, tactile, olfactory, and gustatory elements of total perceptual
experience of the here-and-now, in varying proportions, and
with varying degrees of influence on the visual perception itself.

It is in continuity too with other elements of my total experience which affect it. As I look, I remember other experiences associated with this scene. Though those experiences are past, not part of the present reality in my physical world, my remembering is present, and remembered reality itself can have a real bearing on my perception: what I see, what figures prominently, what stands out against the ground, may be determined or occasioned by remembered past experience.

So too, as I see this scene, I may be distracted intermittently by imagining other scenes. Again, the objects of my imagining are not physically present, yet my imagining is real, and the imagined reality too may affect my vision. I may have strong feelings, desires, acts of will, which similarly affect the visual element in my present experience. I may be affected variously by the presence of other persons, and my visual experience affected by my reaction to them. My visual experience, and my total perceptual experience, is continually permeated by understanding; and the structure of my visual experience, the choice of figure against ground, may be directed by my understanding and judgment of this scene. Finally, for purposes of present indication of other factors, my understanding of the transcendent, my sense of God's presence and of my relation to Him, may have a great influence on my perceptual experience.

The influence of these other factors is not a matter of their invading the perceptual field, and being themselves perceived in it. Rather, they condition my perceiving, direct it in ways of which I may not be conscious, so that of the many possible forms which could figure prominently in my perception, some do, others do not, for reasons grounded in all that I am and have been.

In dealing with perception thus far, I have been considering principally visual perception. It was fitting to treat it first. As there is a certain primacy of the cognitive over other modes of our conscious experience, so within the realm of perception as a mode of sense knowledge there is a primacy of the visual. Most of our knowing is through seeing, though visual perception has an all-important collaborator—and even challenger for primacy. Let us consider briefly these other modes of perception. Again, it is not a matter of isolating different perceptual realms: they blend in a single conscious life. Yet our perceptual experience has different modes, and it is not always the same mode which is most prominent in our conscious life. Every mode has its proper characteristics, and every one may stand out at

times as the dominant mode of our perception. It is enough
to recall the generally recognized different modes of perceiving:
by hearing, by touch, by taste, and by smell. Depending on the
keenness of the organs involved, a man or woman can be conscious chiefly of one or other of these modes, and dwell consciously for a time in the realm of experience proper to it.
One example may suffice: the gourmand at dinner.

Of all these other modes of perception, the most important
by far is that of hearing. It is auditory perception which complements most fully the role of vision in our cognitive life.
It offers too most possibilities of living in its realm as in the
dominant mode of consciousness. We can listen to the song
of birds and the general world of the sounds of nature, to
traffic and the competing sounds of the city, to music which
opens to us a wonder world of feeling, and above all to speech.
Hearing, in the living intersubjective world of speech, is the
great complement and rival of seeing.

In all of these modes, as in visual perception, one can detect
variations on the same characteristics found in vision. There
is no question of isolated sensations, but of a continuous flow
of perceptory experience, with a vast primordial, implicit perception serving as the ground from which explicit figures stand
out. There is a continual interplay and mutual influence, both
of perceptual modes among themselves, and of these modes
with other elements of total experience: intellectual, volitional,
affective, motor.

Further reflection brings out some variations on the basic
figure-ground structure. This structure may be observed not
only within every mode of perception, but in a far wider shifting
of figure and ground in the interplay of many modes of experience. At times, as I continue to see the scene, I am drawn from
sharp attention to it, to hearing and listening to sounds, which
now are a figure against the ground of the rest of my perceptual
experience. At times, continuing to see, I do not gaze attentively,
but wander in memory or imagination, or in affective acts, and
in those moments such acts fasten upon their own figure in the
total ground of conscious experience. At times, still continuing
to see, I am drawn to reflect on my act, and on myself, making
the act or myself now the object, the figure against the total
ground. Again, I interrupt my gaze continually to reflect on
the structures of my experience: I am doing a phenomenology
of perception, or rather a phenomenology of experience.

Summing up the results of this consideration, what pertains properly to perception?

3. *What is proper to perception.*

(a) First, to clear the ground, distinguish between perception and its conditioning and qualifying factors. Perception is conditioned and qualified by all of the other modes of experience which in the total flow of conscious life alternate as focal; by all the elements in my total experience which are or were marginally conscious; by many factors of my bodily existence which are not within consciousness; in short, by all that I have been and all that I am as I now perceive. These are conditioning and qualifying factors in the sense that they contribute in varying manners and degrees to channeling my perception in all of its modes, and thus to the selectivity of my perception of figure against ground. These conditioning factors, however, do not themselves enter the perceptual field as such: I do not perceive them.

Thus, I am not now perceiving Eisenstein, as I did in the experience which I recounted in chapter I. I did perceive it then. I remember it now. The memory of what I perceived and imagined and felt then may affect my perception the next time I view the countryside near Grottaferrata: what I saw and felt about elements of the scene at Eisenstein may occasion the direction of my gaze to selected elements of the scene near Grottaferrata, but they will not be part of what I actually see. Again, to take another example, I am not now perceiving a checkered Pierce Arrow. I once dreamed of one, as I remember vividly. It was a wondrous blend of an American luxury car which I loved as a boy, and a Checker Cab, which I also knew as a boy. That dream too may someday affect the course of my perceptive experience, but I will never see the dream car. Similarly, what I understand of a situation, and what I feel about it, may influence strongly the course of my perceiving; but I shall not see, hear, feel by touch, taste, or smell the relationships which I understand or the feelings of which I am aware.

(b) Positively, perception regards a unique object: present concrete reality in so far as it can be experienced by combinations of seeing, hearing, feeling by touch, tasting, smelling, and by whatever operations I sense excitations within me and the movements and the position of my body; a present reality held by the senses as a configuration of *this, here, now.* Perception has as its object a *whole,* which may be static or dynamic: static,

as in the instance of the filing case near me, which I perceive
as a still figure against the ground of the rest of my room which
falls in my visual field from where I now sit; dynamic, as in
the case of smoke seen belching forth from the chimney shortly
after the boiler has been fired, smoke caught by the fierce wind,
and whirling, twisting, dancing, scurrying as no frenzied band
could ever dance; or a single bird or pair of birds in flight;
or a flock of swallows careening against the glowing late afternoon sky. Whether static or moving, the object of perception
is a concrete whole, held in its unique configuration here and
now. The object of perception is not merely the figure, but also
the ground; not only the explicit, but also the implicit. The
difference between figure and ground, between explicit and implicit, is not a difference between real and unreal, or even actual
and potential. The ground, the implicitly perceived, is very much
a part of our total real experience. Within the ground or the
field of the implicit we attend to a succession of figures. In a
sense it is the ground, the horizon, which guarantees the unity
of the figure, held in a succession of glances as we rove over
the field. If it were not for the reality of the full perceptual
ground, the life of perception in its continual roving would be
impossible. In any hypothesis which reduces the perceptual
(or the "memorial", or the imaginary) to a manifold of explicit
images, modules, it is impossible to account for life and process:
one could conceive only of non-continuous, arbitrarily associated,
atomic "forms", which would never add up the whole concrete
reality, and never account for human experience.

(c) Returning now to the tentative definition which I proposed in section two of this chapter, I should say that the
definition could be held as a working definition, understood now
in the light of the description and reflection which followed.

4. *Further questions.* I wish merely to indicate here two
further questions, or sets of questions, regarding perception.
The first is this: how are our consciousness and our conceptions
of space, of movement, and of time developed? The second:
what is our guarantee of the "realism" or "objectivity" of perception.

Though either or both may be treated at times in the consideration of perception, I think that the questions cannot be
answered simply in terms of perception and its role in our knowledge. Other factors are involved, and I shall leave these questions for treatment in connection with intellectual knowledge
and in connection with the total conscious field, in chapter VI.

MEMORY

1. *Description and reflection.* We *are* in space, in continual movement in all our modes of being. We come to an awareness, and to a more or less adequate conception, of time: of the succession of phases of our living which we cannot hold together. If I trace a rough curve on a sheet of paper, I can reflect on the succession of phases, of conceivable sections of my action. I can attempt to designate a point at which I am *now*, and reflect on the portion of the curve which I have already traced, the present point where my pen rests now, and the anticipated continuation of the curve, which is not yet drawn. But by the time I have thought or said "now" I have already moved on, and that section or point which I designated—without really breaking the continuous flow—is already past: it is what I was doing when I said "now". The past is gone: I shall never again live that moment, that phase of my action. The future is not yet: I have "now" an image of my continuing movement, not yet accomplished: I anticipate it, look to it as another in the waves of "nows", which I live through, never to be lived through again.

Since we are continually in movement, in an unbroken flow of experience in all of our modes, our "now" is not really a point in the flow, but that short segment of what we are going through, together with what is nearest in our past. The immediate past is part of our "psychological now", along with the sense of anticipation of our immediately imminent future. It must be so, since we are in continual movement, not living a series of separate points. What I have just done a few seconds ago (releasing my typewriter as it jammed) is so close that I am aware of it, I know it, almost as vividly as I am aware of thinking and typing right now. But that recent past is slipping, and an hour from now it will be gone and forgotten, unless it involved an experience which stands out and which I somehow still retain. Yet I can hold the pattern of much of my past, with varying degrees of detail and of context. That holding of one's past personal experience is a unique kind of knowledge, and it is what I understand as memory.

Memory is a mode of knowing. Its unique object, by which it is differentiated from all other modes of knowing, is past personal experience. By memory I hold such knowledge of my personal past. I am not always aware of it, but I can recall it when I wish, and often I recall it without wishing, when by one of the infinite variations of association I am reminded of it.

Memory is not total: I cannot hold and recall all that I have lived through. For the most part I remember what has made a deep impression on me for any one reason or any combination of reasons, reasons which in turn may be purely personal. What strikes me and leaves a deep impression on me may pass unnoticed by another: we live in different personal worlds, and my experience is unique. Though memory is not total, it does extend to many modes of personal experience. In the case of a particularly vivid and rich experience or complex of experiences, I can remember what I saw and heard and felt by touch, what emotions I had, my inquiring, my understanding and what I understood, my judging and what I judged, what I desired and resolved to do, what I did. I can remember what I actually dreamed. I can remember what I imagined.

When I recounted my experience on the mountain overlooking Eisenstein, I chose it as an example of an experience in which perception, feeling, imagination, and further heightened feeling predominated. On that day I perceived Eisenstein. I did not imagine it, but imagined the lives of its scattered dwellers. Today I do not perceive Eisenstein, and perhaps I never shall perceive it again; but I do remember it. I do not imagine having been on that mountain overlooking it: I remember actually having been there. I hold many details of that total experience: the trip from Fürstenstein bei Passau with three companions in a Volkswagen; the driver—and how he drove!—the stop along the way to get out and see the striped posts warning of the Czech border and the mined strip; separating at the point of ascent, as two remained below and one went with me; the ascent in a sort of suspended seat drawn by cable with the passengers strung out in single file; leaving my companion, to go and stand alone at the top of the eastern slope; the hour's meditation which I have recounted in its essentials; rejoining my companion feeling somewhat embarrassed at having taken so long to stand there alone; rejoining the others at the end of the descent and feeling grateful at their joy that the experience had been so rich for me. ... That happened almost nineteen years ago, but don't tell me that I only imagine having been there!

As memory is fed continually by perception and all of our present experience, it is in continuity with present experience, and it extends and continues its functions. Perception is of *this, here, now.* Memory is of *this, then, there.* Like perception, memory is a mode of sense knowledge: it holds a particular configuration, static or dynamic. Perceiving and remembering, *I* grasp relationships by insight into the configuration: I understand. But I understand not by perceiving nor by remembering, but by the operation of intellect which permeates and transcends all of my perceiving and remembering. Memory is related to understanding and to affirmation, as we shall have to determine later.

Like perception, memory holds me to my full personal reality. It affords an extension of my perceptual horizon, a broader horizon within which I can locate individual events in my personal history, and which helps to guarantee my sense of the unity and continuity of my experience and of myself. By memory I hold many dimensions of my past experience: this event, this action in much of its total setting: what it looked and sounded like, in what visible, audible, tangible surroundings, what I felt, thought, willed, did ... Because that total configuration was uniquely mine, any event or symbol which now evokes a personal memory has for me a cluster of meanings which is unique. I know myself, in part, by being able to locate myself in the history, the personal history, which somehow defines me. This I have been, this I have done, this really bears on my present life: it is no mere imagining, no dream. Like perception, memory affords at least some horizon, some setting, some context which can be probed, both to reassure us of the reality of a detail, and to give us that configuration into which we can have insight, within which we may discern intelligible relationships. Memory does not hold a set of everfading snapshots: the images it holds may be static or dynamic, but it holds them in some context, diminishing though it be as the years pass. When I recalled my afternoon at Eisenstein, one of the details which was fuzzy was the manner of our ascent: we were conveyed, but was it in a cable-car? I could not remember, until I recalled another detail which stands out in memory: looking back and smiling and nodding to share our joy in this adventure: we were being drawn up by a cable, and were seated in individual seats, one behind the other.

2. *Memory, commemoration, appropriation.* By memory I hold the configuration of my past personal experience. What is unique in memory can be brought out more clearly, perhaps,

by a further reflection on the relation of such memory to history, to commemoration, and to the memory of a personal appropriation of a larger history.

History, as a record of the past, witnessed to by others, discerned in part by insight into the meaning of monuments, is a record of a real past, but not *mine*. Historical events in which I did not take part can never be set in the unique experiential, existential sequence which is mine. Yet there is something more to be recognized. Take "history" in two senses: (1) as past world process, especially past human experience; (2) as knowledge of that process. In both senses there is a history which is significant for me, which has its bearing on the meaning of my life. Moreover, at a certain point in the process I have become part of it; being born, I have entered into the process; and at a certain point in my life I have recognized its meaning for me, and I have made it my own.

As an example of commemoration and appropriation I should indicate a type of religious experience, and more particularly of Christian experience in its manner of continuity with Israelite experience in the Old Testament. If one could find an example of a purely natural experience of person in community, without any religious dimension at all, it might serve to illustrate what I am talking about. I do not think, though, that it could compare in depth and in complete transforming power.

Christian liturgical worship is performed in a ritual which is a symbolic celebration, commemoration, re-living of the great events of salvation history which for the Christian are all-important, reaching him personally, transforming him. As I take part in such an act of worship, principally in the Eucharist, with a knowledge of salvation history and the mystery of Christ, I re-live and make my own the momentous events of the past which affect me here and now. My participation in that symbolic action here and now is part of my life, part of my real experience. Thanks to it I sense a real participation in the larger history which is symbolized, in the long process which in fact preceded my very existence and possibility of sharing. Approaching this act with a sense of its meaning and its transforming power, responding in faith to the symbolic gesture in which God's saving action reaches me now, I am convinced of my encountering God, of being enriched by his gift of a fuller life as his saving action comes to term now in my own personal response. For me this is a real personal experience, a peak experience when I take part fully, a real appropriation of the mystery of a saving history which comes now to me. This for me is a real appropriation, not a sort of autosuggestion.

If one compares and contrasts memory with commemoration and appropriation, the likenesses and the differences may help to grasp better what is proper to each.

In a strict sense, memory is a mode of knowledge by which I hold the configuration of my personal past experience, conscious experience. In a broader sense commemoration and appropriation involve a knowledge of a larger history to which I somehow belong, even though I was not living to share in the events recorded, and now commemorated and appropriated. In an even broader sense, I am rooted in the process of the universe, going back to its remotest origins in the continuous process of which my present humanly bodily being is a term. I am rooted in the history of a nation, of a civilization, of a religious community. This too is my personal past in this sense: my participation in it is unique, by a unique line of descent.

There remain significant differences between this and memory. What I hold by a knowledge of history, and what I appropriate as my own in a larger sense, is not held in the concrete configuration which characterizes memory of what I have actually lived through. Memory is fed by actual experience in all its modes, and it holds as much as it can of the configuration of that experience. Commemoration holds the pattern not of what I have actually perceived and felt of the original events as it occurred, but rather the pattern of what I have been told. I have understood the word, imagined the scene of action, grasped my relationship to the momentous events; but I have not experienced them as they occurred, and I do not remember them. I do remember the acts by which I entered personally into that larger history: this I experienced; this I hold in memory.

Further questions arise, however, which reveal the inadequacy of what has been said thus far about memory. I have approached the consideration in a chapter devoted to sense knowledge: perception, memory, and imagination. I have defined memory as a mode of knowledge by which I hold the configuration of my personal past experience. In the context of a consideration of sense knowledge, such a definition would seem implicitly to limit memory to holding as much as possible of the configuration of what in the original experience was sensibly perceptible: visible, audible, and so forth. Yet I have said that memory is somehow total: holding as much as possible of all dimensions of the experience: not only sensibly perceptible, but also affective, intellectual, volitive, motor. This is only part of the perplexing problem. A number of further questions arise. They call for a suspension of the discourse on memory at this point, for their answers would presuppose other considerations which I have not yet proposed. At this point, therefore, I shall indicate some further questions which occur to me, and reserve for later my attempt to answer them.

3. *Further questions.* The questions which I raise, and perhaps all of the questions which others might raise at this point, bear in various ways upon the relation of memory to intellect. By memory I hold the pattern of my past experience: memory is clearly a mode of knowledge. Is it, however, purely a matter of sense knowledge? Here are the questions:

a) What is the role of memory in the larger mystery of consciousness and knowledge? The question may be occasioned by a contrast between memory and perception. Perception, as I have defined it, is a mode of knowledge whose unique object is present reality in so far as it can be experienced by combinations of seeing, hearing, feeling by touch, tasting, smelling, sensing the movements and the present position of one's own body: a present reality held by the senses as a configuration of *this, here, now.* Since perception is primitive and immediate, an absolute beginning of knowledge, it can be considered in itself and defined without a doubling of problems regarding any prior mode of knowledge. Not so with memory. Memory is derivative. Moreover, once one recognizes in memory a holding of a pattern of past experience in many dimensions, memory must be regarded as not just a sort of partial holding and recall of what has been perceived, but also a holding and recall of all the other dimensions of human experience. Those dimensions, I said, condition and qualify perception, but they do not enter its proper field. In the case of memory, however, we are faced with the problems of a mode of knowledge by which we know the pattern of former experience, not just in what remains of its originally sensibly perceptible configuration, but in structures which are not in themselves sensibly perceptible. Memory, as a mode of second order knowledge, if you will, poses the question concerning the manner in which we know the other modes of conscious operation in the first place. The question points to the problem of the relations of memory to intellect, and even more generally to the problem of con-sciousness and knowledge.

(b) How do we know our past experience as *past*, and indeed as our own *personal* past experience? Again, in a particular form, there is question of how in the first place we are conscious of, and know, our present experience. If memory held just images, what in the somewhat faded image would make it dis-tinguishable as an image of a past experience, to say nothing of it as an image of our own personal past experience as distinct from any mere imagining? The problem again bears on the whole question of consciousness and knowledge.

(c) If memory holds the patterns of my past experience, not only of what I saw and heard and understood and judged and willed and did, but also of what I really dreamed, and that I really imagined, then how do I distinguish the objects, the contents of memory? How do I distinguish the memory of what I actually did from the memory of what I actually dreamed that I did, or of what I actually imagined I had done? The critique of memory by which such distinctions may be drawn involves more than memory, and again we are driven to larger problems of consciousness and knowledge.

All of the questions call for answers which necessitate a prior treatment of intellectual operations and of the further questions of consciousness and knowledge. Having raised the questions here, and indicated that they cannot be answered at this point, I reserve the attempted answers to the considerations of chapters V and VI.

IMAGINATION

1. *Description and initial reflection.* Suppose that four men are winding their way up the streets of Rocca Priora, a few miles east of Frascati, perhaps fifteen to eighteen miles southeast of Rome. They have seen the peak as it can be viewed from the valley at the foot of Tuscolo, from the southwest. Now, from the northwest, they have approached by bus as far as the hill town, and on the way they have had an ever-varying view of valleys and lower hill towns roughly to the north, and some idea of the highlands off to the northeast. Now, as they near the belvedere in the little park on the peak, one asks: "What do you think we'll see? What will it be like?"

Four answers could be given by the four men, in terms of other peaks visible, valleys, rivers, lakes, trees, rocks, buildings, roads. , Those eight categories have meanings on which the four could agree fairly well. But as they speak in terms of the same categories, every one will have his own images accompanying his words and concepts, more or less vivid depending on the degree to which visual imagination is prominent in his conscious life. Every one can sharpen his images if he is asked to imagine what the rivers or peaks will look like, their shape, their height, the direction and angle of descent of the rivers, and so on. Agreeing as they do on the sense of the eight categories, every one will have his own images. No one can communicate fully to his companions exactly what he has imagined. He can attempt to describe, but again only with words which evoke concepts and accompanying images which for every hearer will be unique, particular. He can make a rough drawing of what he imagines, but even if he is skilled in drawing, what he portrays will be only a poor reproduction of the inner image.

When they reach the peak and gaze out at the panorama, they see the scene, and they can scan it as they try to take in details, setting a succession of figures against their grounds. Now they share a common view, though with a slight difference of physical perspective, and vast, incalculable differences of total personal perspective, a function of all that every one personally has been and is. They can probe the same field of vision, fix the same peaks as figures, compare their perceptual images as they could not share and compare their imaginings.

2. *Differentiation.* One can differentiate imagination and its operations and terms from several other operations and their objects and terms. In this comparison, for convenience and clarity, I shall use "image" only of the term of imagination, contrasting it with percepts, concepts, feelings.

Concepts, one of the terms of intellectual operation, holding and formulating definite relationships, can be common to many men, with a fairly high degree of common meaning, and they can be communicated especially through language. Images are individual unique, and they cannot be projected in such a way as to be fully communicable.

Images are free of all fixed relationships to time and place. Always individual, unique in physiognomy, they never refer definitely to the *here and now* of perception, nor to the *there and then* of memory. Consequently images have no "existential index" or existential import. Though I am aware of my images, and I can affirm that here and now I am imagining this or that, I cannot affirm that in my experience the imagined particular *is* or ever *was*. Though imagination draws on the configurations of perception and of memory, its own images are cut free from context, from the living, existential setting of personal experience.

I cannot imagine what I am now feeling, perceiving, thinking, feeling. The object of these operations, the reality to which they relate, is present. Though imagination may influence my present operations, directing and coloring them, my operations regarding a present reality are perception, thinking, feeling, etc., but not imagining. Similarly, with regard to what I have really experienced in the past: I can remember it; I cannot imagine it. Operations regarding a reality which is set in present or past personal experience are bound to that setting in a way in which no image is bound. The sense of this differentiation needs some clarification regarding feeling, emotion, or affect. My feeling may very well have been evoked by an image, but I am not imagining that I feel: I really feel anger, whatever may have occasioned my feeling. I am not imagining that I am angry.

Finally, another differentiation seems to be helpful. As I approached Gibraltar by ship the first time, I did not try to imagine what The Rock might look like: I had seen a well-known photograph of it, and I remembered it as I might have remembered if I had actually perceived it before. The image which I hold in memory after having seen a photograph is an image held as the result of a sort of second-order perception. Yet it differs. I had seen photographs of Michelangelo's *Moses* and of the *Pietà* before I saw them. The image which I held gave me a definite anticipation of what I would see later. I did not have to imagine them; indeed, having seen the photographs I could no longer imagine them as they could be seen from the same position. Yet the image held differed from what I could have retained in memory of an actual perception. Perception is not a matter of one or more snapshots: it regards figures and grounds in continuous shifting patterns, and one who perceives the *Moses* and the *Pietà* can vary his position, to take in the figure from different points of view, and form a much more complete impression of it. The image retained from having seen a photograph, on the contrary, is fixed and severely limited. It precludes imagining the same figure in the same ground, but it leaves one free to imagine what the *Moses*, or the *Pietà*, or Gibraltar would look like from another side, from another height.

   3. *Relationships.* To understand imagination better, having differentiated it from other operations, one must consider some of the relationships which cast further light on the proper function and the limitations of imagination.

   Imagination is intimately related to perception and to memory. From them it acquires its resources, the raw materials which it works upon. Though it is capable of wondrous variation and transformation in the elaboration of its images, it cannot produce images without some fund of likenesses, static and dynamic, drawn from perception and memory.

   Multiple, mutual relationships can be discerned between imagination and intellect, as we shall be able to determine more fully and more accurately when we consider the operations of intellect, in the next chapter. For now it may be sufficient to suggest some of these relationships. There is a basic mutual relationship in the development of knowledge. Intellectual insight is gained into images, as well as into the configurations held by perception or by memory. In turn, the process of thinking continually conjures up images, and may call up an image of a valley, for example, for the purpose of considering the concrete configuration and determining relationships in order to define "valley" more satisfactorily. It is a classic insight into human knowledge which led to the principle that there is no human knowledge unaccompanied by a phantasm or image. Correspondingly, there is no image in waking conscious life which is not permeated and transcended by intellectual operations, as we shall observe. With regard to this latter relationship of intellect's permeating and transcending imagination, a further important truth may be indicated here, to be established later: the secret of creative imagination can be detected only if one recognizes the intellectual factor in the grasp of analogy which underlies all play of imagination.

   Imagination not only draws upon perception and memory, and is continually permeated and transcended by intellect: it draws too upon actual experience of feeling emotion, of willing, of thinking, of moving. Though one may somehow imagine what it must be like to perform these acts, his imagining must be very inadequate if he has never really experienced them. It is hard to conceive of any but the faintest, most inadequate imagining of feeling the thrill of the applause of a great audience, or of working at a problem in metaphysics, or of making a firm decision in full clarity after full deliberation, or of experiencing full mutual love, in the case of a man or woman who has never had any such experience. Limits of personal experience may have, and I should say must have, consequences in the limitations of imagining and of dreaming. One who has never done ballet dancing, or never hit a golf ball with anything approaching deliberate good form, does not have the kinaesthetic images of such actions. He or she may imagine somehow what it is like to perform them, but it is by a kind of sheer hunch, and in such cases imagining or dreaming will be extremely poor, by the most remote analogy. Thus, in dreaming, one may dream of approaching and beginning the performance of such an action completely outside his actual experience, and awaken to recognize that his action was a poor caricature of an act which he has never performed. Memory of actual experience, on the contrary, would have supplied rich resources for the work of imagination, in waking consciousness or in dream; and the images or dreams would have been far more credible, far more lifelike.

4. *Resources.* To estimate the resources of imagination, and to understand its creativity, one must banish misconceptions similar to those which have at times muddled consideration of perception and of memory. If our basic cognitional experience were that of punctual sensations, to be combined into images of wholes, perception would be unintelligible—or rather, there would be no perception to be understood. If perceptions were simply a matter of explicit perception, as contrasted with implicit, primordial perception, we should have only a multitude of fixed images like snapshots, and there would be no living unity and continuity in our experience of the world and of ourselves, no experience of lived time, no memory, and no real creative imagination. Neither memory nor imagination is an image bank, a store of fixed images. Nor is creative imagination a matter of shuffling and combining such fixed images.

What, then, are the resources of imagination? All of the images of the sensibly perceptible aspects of our experience, grasped in perception and retained to varying degrees in memory: static and dynamic, of figure and ground, explicit and implicit, focal and marginal, fully conscious and subliminal, grasped in all our modes of sensing, objective and subjective. By the latter pair I refer to a distinction of images of externally perceived reality and images of the vague sensibly perceptible aspects of our own conscious operations, of looking, touching, thinking, willing and acting purposefully, and all sorts of motor

action. Our images of external reality are not just of static
forms, but also of the most wonderful variety of movements
and developments: of birds in flight, of the ever-shifting patterns
of a great flock of swallows, of a cat poised and then leaping
for its prey, of a waterfall, of a fountain with its falling drops
so many sparks in the light of the setting sun, of the water of
a volcanic lake four hundred feet below shimmering in the afternoon sun, a lake with a thousand moods and a million dancing
lights reflected by its waves, of trees swaying, groaning in the
wind, of leaves twisting, flickering, glistening in the play of
wind and sun.

5. *Creativity.* With all of the resources at its disposal, images drawn from all of our experience in its originaly sensibly
perceptible aspects, imagination works to create its own worlds,
beyond all perception, memory, and conception. Like perception
and thought, imagination is a living process, continuous, supple,
plastic; but it far surpasses them in scope, freedom, swiftness.
Unlike perception, imagination is not confined to the field of
present sensibly perceptible reality. Unlike thought, its movement is not linear, plodding, "logical". Imagination works with
images freed from their bond to time, place, and other circumstances, combining, transforming, evolving objects which we have
never seen or felt: forms of beauty or horror; movements of
swiftness and grace or incredible sluggishness.

In a broad sense one may speak of a certain "law" of the
process of imagination: analogy. One can recognize a certain
play of analogy, if one takes analogy in the widest sense, as
involving any similarity of relationships, or similarity of proportion of relationships. Thus its movement is not merely from
one image to another with a recognizable similarity of features.
It may work with any basic relationship: cause and effect, temporal simultaneity or succession, local proximity, affective charge,
personal relationships of any sort, pleasure or pain, and so forth.
In the images which it fashions—not merely of "forms" or objects, but of action and ever-shifting, developing situations and
sequences of actions—there may be a recognizable analogy of
proportion: similarity of the relationships between one pair or
set of factors and the relationships between another pair or set.
The only clue to the whole creation may be a relationship of
any kind between one element in the first pair or set and an
element in the second.

Are there any limits to the potential of creative imagination?

I should say that there are. Though imagination may have a relatively infinite range of potential transformation of the resources at its disposal, those resources are not unlimited. Though cut free from bonds to place, time, and situation, still the images are grounded in personal experience of the imaginer. I imagine with the resources of my imagination, grounded on the total fund of my own total personal experience in all its modes. Though the laws of imagining are the same for all men, grounded in the a priori of human being, the actual imagining of every man must be unique. There are no actual archetypes, for a "universal image" would be the image of nothing. A primitive man who has never encountered men of any race other than his own may well imagine an old man, in his waking reveries or in dream, but the old man will be like the old men of his own race whom he has actually seen. If he has never even seen a wheel, he will not imagine an automobile, to say nothing of a 1930 model black Pierce Arrow sedan.

6. *Further questions.* Most of the further questions which occur to me in reflection on imagination regard somehow its relations to intellect. Is imagination entirely a form of sense knowledge? It would seem that it is: it holds and works with images, configurations comparable with those held in memory and perception, limited to the originally sensibly perceptible aspects of external reality or our experience of ourselves. I can compare the house which I imagine with what I have perceived and with what I hold in memory: yes, the house which I have imagined is like this one which I now perceive, or the house which I remember from my childhood and of which I still have a few old photographs.

But can I imagine thinking and deliberating and deciding? I can in reverie or in dream, but it seems that it is a sort of shadow thinking and willing, and that the imagination can work up only the analogy of the sensibly perceptible dimensions of the whole experience in which one thinks and wills. Insight and judgment cannot be programmed, let alone imagined. Insight will come uncommanded as an intellectual grasp of an intelligible relationship in what is perceived, remembered, imagined: it transcends the concrete configuration of perception and imagination. Judgment is made only by an intellectual grasp and affirmation of actual existence. If there is a sort of shadow thought and willing in reverie and dream, there may be question of some minimal participation of intellect and will at a level far below full waking conscious thought, deliberation, and decision. The question, left open for now, regards the relation of imagination to intellect and will.

Other questions, too, regard the relationships of imagination to intellect especially. The first concerns the continual permeation of all imagining by intellect: *I* am imagining, and to the extent to which I am conscious I also grasp the imagined situation at least vaguely. The second concerns the critique of imagination: the discernment between real experience, present or past, and imaginary experience. None of these questions can be attended to here. The answers may be given, as far as possible, only after our consideration of intellectual operations.

COMPARISON AND CONTRAST

1. Perception, memory, and imagination, to the extent to which we have considered them, have this in common: all are modes of sense knowledge. Though penetrated by intellect and related to it and to other operations in many ways, perception, memory, and imagination are limited to a range of objects which have this in common: configuration of the originally sensibly perceptible aspects of our experience of the world and of ourselves.

2. In this whole order of sense knowledges, perception clearly is prime. Primordial and explicit, it is the original experience some of which is held by memory. It is the continuous source of all the images which constitute the resources of imagination. Imagination plays with the wealth stored up by perception: sometimes ineptly, like a little girl dressed up in her mother's clothes and shoes; sometimes like a valet more clever and more graceful than his master, displaying forms more perfect than ever grasped in explicit perception, movements more graceful than ever made in full sight of men.

3. Differing as they do, perception, memory, and imagination have their own worlds. The world of perception is all that is actually perceivable, by any sense or combination of senses, heightened and extended by the use of instruments, and including the realm of second-order perception of the variety of images by which men have added to the perceptible world. The actually perceivable is not necessarily the same as the actually

existing. When I hear the cannon shot from the Gianicolo, about a mile away, the cannon is no longer actually being fired. Some stars which we see in the heavens ceased long ago to radiate light. What is actually perceivable is not the existent as such, but the enduring modification of the physical universe. The world of perception is universal, shared by all living men. It is not a private world. Though perspectivism gives everyone his own point of view, and as a consequence there is an infinite variation of men's readings, still all are readings on one perceptible world. Personal probing and interpersonal verification make it possible to distinguish perception from hallucination, for which the "world" is a private spectable shared by no one. The limits of the world of perception are the maximum and minimum limits of human sense powers aided by instruments.

The world of memory is all that can be retained of one's personal past experience, and only what has actually been part of that experience. It includes, however, all modes of experience: what I have actually perceived, remembered, imagined, understood and affirmed, felt emotionally; all the movements which I have ever made; all that I have actually dreamed, for I remember *my* dreams: no one else can. Its limits are two: remote, somewhere this side of birth (or, if one will insist, this side of conception); proximate, ever shifting to embrace the ever-receding psychological "now". The world of memory is strictly personal, in no sense universal or shared by any other person.

The world of the imagination is the realm of all of the free images and all of their potential modifications and combinations, grounded upon actual experence of the world in which a person is and of his awareness and knowledge of himself. Even when I am stirred to imagine by the words or gestures or other symbols used by other men, I do so with the resources of *my* imagination, grounded always on the total fund of my own total experience. Hence, the world of imagination too is personal. Though it is similar in kind to that of other men, it is unique in every person. Though there is a relatively infinite potential play of creative imagination, its world is actually limited by its resources, which are personal.

4. All three are important in human life, every one in its own way. Perception holds us to the reality of our situation in the world, the present here and now, in which alone we can act. Memory holds us to the reality of our real personal his-

tory, as distinct from the dream world of imagination. The memory of that real personal past can be a powerful stimulus to present action, to present feeling, imagination, understanding, willing, and motor action. It can inhibit. It is always a factor in one's personal a priori. It is to be held always in the balance of an integrated personality.

Flimsy as imaginings may be, at times they catch elements of reality which were not held in the tongs of explicit perception, and there can be at times a fulness in the grasp and evaluation of a situation which was missed in prior explicit perception, reflection, conception, and reasoning: what was real but un-noticed in those explicit acts, passed over because it lay along the margins of perception, may be recovered in imagination, and may figure in a new, more adequate conception. Moreover, imagination opens us to the possibility of the new, the unrealized, the world to be carved out, the project. In this sense, imagina-tion and the insight into imagination open one to the possibility of what is most characteristic of man: the creating of new "worlds". Such creation calls for more than imagination: in-sight, a sense of the future, the will to create, to project, to venture; but imagination is an important element.

Chapter III

INSIGHT, CONCEPTION, AND JUDGMENT

We pass on now to consider man's intellectual operations. We could begin simply by reflecting on the nature of the reflection which we have made concerning perception, memory, and imagination. It was a sort of phenomenology, and it may be wise to reflect that a phenomenology of perception is not a perception of perception, much less a primordial perception of primordial perception. Concerned with man's immersion in his world, and with the beginnings of all of his knowledge, phenomenology itself is not an immersion in the very ambiguous situation which it is designed to describe and to understand. It is a philosophical reflection on perception and other elements of human experience.

Consequently, we could reflect on the relationships discerned: relationships which are neither perceived nor imagined, nor held in the memory as previously perceived or imagined. Reflection, discernment, and determination of relationships involve operations of a different sort, of an order which differs greatly from that of perception, memory, and imagination.

That would be one way to approach the present matter. By a sort of classic preterition I shall pass over that possible introduction. Let me begin instead with an account of, and a reflection upon, two experiences, one of which actually occurred, the other being an imaginary account, involving types of men whom I have known, and whose characters make their imagined actions quite plausible.

First, then, an actual experience involving three men. Shortly before five o'clock one morning I left my room to take a shower. As I reached the corner of the corridor, I noticed a pool of water, and looked up to see water dripping from a light fixture and from the meeting of ceiling and wall. What to do? Obviously, contain the dripping water and mop up what is already flowing. What do I need? Where can I get them? From three different places I hurriedly got two plastic washbowls of sufficient size and a heavy rag for mopping. Having set the bowls in place to catch most of the dripping water, I squatted and began to mop, wringing the rag out by hand into one of the bowls.

A second early riser came along. Seeing me mopping and wringing, he asked, "Did you call X [the man who normally would handle such a situation]?"

"No, I am busy doing this."

"Should we turn off the faucet up there (pointing up toward the terrazza, where there was a service sink)?"

"No, there is no way of knowing that the water is coming from it." It had been pouring rain all night. It was still pitch dark and pouring rain. The terrazza must have been covered with running or standing water. I was not about to go up and try to figure out where the leak was.

"Well, should I call Y [the man a rank higher, in general charge of such matters]?"

"Yes, if you like." He went and called Y by phone, and I saw neither of them for over an hour. As it happened, Y could not come for an hour or so.

When Y arrived, the rain had stopped, the bowls were fairly full, and the leaking had ceased. Then Y appraised the situation, followed a couple of hunches as to what had happened and what could be done, and did it. Later he explained to me what he had found and what he had done.

Three men faced successive phases of a developing situation, saw the problem differently, quickly figured out what to do, and did it, with a sense of the bearing of their action on the situation.

I saw the immediate need, was not concerned then and there about who ought to take care of it, or what the source of the trouble was and how it could be remedied. I stopped the flow of water which was spreading rapidly and threatened to damage the house. The second man had two rival appraisals of the situation and of what to do. The first was in terms of who ought to take care of such a mess. The second, a fleeting thought soon abandoned, regarded where the water was coming from and how it could be cut off at its source. The third man, leisurely assessing the situation when the emergency had passed, followed his hunches about the source of the water and the cause of the leak, and did what could be done at that time.

I was glad that I had come along first!

There are common elements in the three responses to this

situation, and they serve to introduce our consideration of intellectual operations All three men had insights into the concrete situation. What they saw, at various stages of the developing situation, was roughly the same: the sensibly perceptible
configuration of dripping water and flooding floor. Each seized
on relationships which could not be seen or imagined, but each
grasped a different set of relationships: (1) to the type of action
needed immediately, the suitable instruments, their location, and
the only person who was obviously indicated as the agent;
(2) to the structure of authority and responsibility, the means
of calling the matter to his attention, and who should do the
calling; (3) to the probable source of the water, the probable
defect, the possible temporary solutions, the instruments needed,
and the one to do the job.

Every one had insights: he grasped intelligible relationships.
At the moment every one could have described the situation as
he saw it, indicated the significant elements, and given an account which expressed fairly well his understanding of it. Later,
telling about it, he could perhaps improve on the sharpness of
the terms in which he expressed himself. In this he would be
conceptualizing and affirming the facts as he grasped them. In
this experience, the elements which transcend perception,
memory, and imagination are these: insights, concepts, judgments.

In another incident, this time imaginary, three men are
seated on the sloping lawn near a clump of apple trees. An
apple falls nearby.

The first man reflects upon the falling apple: a falling body,
such as that which occasioned a great physicist's insight into
the laws of gravitation. This man too is a scientist, and he
begins to talk of that discovery, and of the successive developments in science. He is not much interested in apples except
for eating. This apple for him is just a falling body.

The second picks up the apple and examines it. He is interested in apples, and he is preparing through university studies
to be able to cultivate fruit trees. He notices the size of the
apple, rather small, and the wormholes. Interested especially
in organic farming, he wonders about the condition of the soil,
fertilization, pest control. He notices too that the tree has
not been pruned.

The third is neither a physicist nor an aspiring scientific
farmer. He is interested in men, and here and now in the
sharp differences between these two men. Each of the first two

had perceived the same falling apple. One had had an insight
into the fall, situating it in a world of theory in which he dwelt
by preference. The other had had an insight into the apple
and the causes of its condition, grasped in the field of relationships which figure prominently in the world of one who hopes
to foster the growth of good trees and good fruit. The third
has an insight into the worlds of thought, worlds of meaning,
fields of relationships, modes of conceptualization, by which
these two men differ. Interested in them as men, he reflects
on the range of human thought and the problems of mutual
understanding.

Again, all three have the same basic perceptual experience.
Two set the event in different worlds of thought, grasping what
was not perceptible or imaginable, but intelligible. The third
reflects not on falling bodies or cultivation of fruit trees, but
on the wonderful variety of ways in which men think and find
intelligible structures of different orders. All three have insights,
concepts, judgments, every one in his own world of thought.

DIFFERENTIATION OF ACTS

A classic view of intellectual operations makes a twofold
division. One set of acts regards answers to the questions *What
is it?* Of *what sort* is it? and similar variations. The object
of such acts is what is called at times the "essences" of things,
or their attributes. The second set of acts regards the answers
to the questions *Is* it? or *Is* it such? In the latter type of
question the emphasis is on the *is*.

Watching a man working out on an athletic field, if I am
unacquainted with athletics I may ask about him: What is he?
The answer may be: a hammer-thrower, or hurdler, or running
broadjumper. I am apt to ask then: What is a hammer-thrower,
or hurdler, or running broad-jumper. Having received my
answer, and having watched for some days and come to a
fairly clear idea of what constitutes good form in any of these
sports, I may observe the same man again, and judge: yes,
he *is* a hammer-thrower!

One set of questions asked *what* he is, and sought further
clarification of the sense of the answer. If later a second
question is put to me, for a judgment of his actual prowess,
the question may be: *Is* he really a hammer-thrower? And my
answer may be: Yes, he *is* a hammer-thrower.

All through the experience or series of experiences I had the answer to an implicit initial question, so basic and so constant that it is seldom adverted to: *Is* he? We may become aware of the possibility of this more basic question in some special situations. When looking out into the distance, not sure whether we see an object on the horizon, we may first wonder whether there *is* anything there, and then as it approaches attend to the questions regarding what it may be. Or if we are looking out the window and someone asks from within the room, Is anything going on? we may answer no. If we answer yes, vaguely aware of something of interest going on, then we may have to look more closely, pick out details, get the general picture and their location in it, and answer the question fairly adequately.

We seldom put the basic question which could be explicit: *Is* it? *Are* they? *Is* there anything? Usually we are completely taken up with probing the field of what obviously is, to determine what it is, to sharpen our answers to the question What? and then to affirm not simply: It *is*, but It is a poodle. It takes a special effort to advert to and reflect upon the obvious, to ask *Is* it? or *Are* they? not so much looking for the answer, which is obvious from the outset, as wondering about the sense of *is* or *are* in seemingly stupid questions and obvious answers, and beyond that about the significance of the *is*, explicit or implicit, in all of our affirmations; and wondering too about the truly unique element in the experience of judging, as diverse from simply conceiving.

Yet the massive affirmations, It *is*, and They *are*, are basic to our intellectual life, and it is within the constant implicit affirmation of the existence of persons and things in our world that we continually search to discern their particular modes of being.

Considering these two types of questions, and the operations of intellect which regard their answers, one can reasonably hold that there are two basic acts of intellect: conception and judgment. Yet, further reflection on intellectual life may suggest a re-formulation of the classification, and also a consideration of the possibility of still another act of intellect or reason.

First, I suggest this re-formulation of the division of acts of intellect. I should say that there are two orders of acts of intellect. One pertains to the first act as described above, but embraces two acts which are distinguishable. The two acts are insight and conception. They are distinct, occurring in distinct phases of the intellectual operation looking to the answer to the first set of questions. I shall treat them distinctly, attempting to bring out what is proper to each. The second order is that of the second operation indicated above: judgment, in answer to the questions *Is* it? or *Is* it such?

Second, I should like to consider the suggestion of a third act, or order of acts, of intellect: reasoning. Man is not pure spirit, and even in his intellectual life he manifests his humanly bodily manner of being. His intellectual life is not a matter of instantaneous flashes, of simple acts of complete grasp and definitive affirmation. If he were purely intellectual, he would not have questions; and we can only conjecture what such a life might be. It is not the human mode. All of our life, in its highest intellectual operations, is marked by the mystery of movement, of process. It is the very *movement* of intellect which is reason.

Reason, then, is not a distinct act or set of acts of intellect. Rather it is a characteristic of all human intellectual life, in both orders of acts: in the movement from inquiry to insight and from insight to conception, and in the movement from judgment to further consequences, or from massive affirmation to explicit, determined, qualified affirmation of a mode of being

No logic of human reason can contain and adequately define the movement of human reason, for the manners of its movement are many and varied beyond possibility of complete classification. Certain patterns of coherent, valid reasoning can be established, with insight into why they are coherent and valid, and why certain deviations miscarry. Thus there can be a logic of reasoning, of discursive thought, in so far as it involves a movement from one proposition through another or others to a conclusion. Yet, in a larger sense, the movement of reason cannot be contained or prescribed, and there is a potentially infinite variety of the ways of movement of human reason.

Regarding the movement of reason as a characteristic of all human intellectual life, rather than as a distinct act or set of acts, I shall try to take account of it in dealing with the acts which I enumerate. Keeping in mind that the first division is a division into two orders, the first of which is subdivided, I shall deal successively with three acts. The first two, pertaining to the first order, are insight and conception. Judgment pertains to the second order.

First I shall consider all three as they stand out most clearly in explicit acts. Then, recognizing in all intellectual acts the mystery of process, I shall consider in a subsequent section the distinction of implicit and explicit which runs through all operations, and which has important consequences in our understanding of human intellectual operations, and human experience generally.

THREE INTELLECTUAL OPERATIONS

1. *Insight.* In those instances which are most memorable in our experience, insight stands out as a sort of flash of understanding, perhaps the act which is closest to what we might conjecture as purely intellectual, instantaneous. Like a flash, a sudden illumination, insight might seem to be more passive than active, something which we undergo rather than do. Yet, regarded more closely, it is recognizable as an act, or a moment in the continuing action of inquiring intellect: that moment in the continuing inquiry when, perhaps after a heightening of anticipation, there is a sudden breakthrough. What is the object of this act? It is a relationship or set of relationships grasped now clearly for the first time.

Insight comes unexpectedly, uncommanded, unprescribed, though long sought. There is no method for getting insights, though method may help us to approach the disposition in which we may come to understand.

Though the word *insight* is drawn from a metaphor inspired by affinity with seeing, and insight is a sort of seeing-in of a different order than visual seeing, it is important to recognize both its intimate relationships to perception, memory, and imagination, and its diversity from the sort of initial knowledge that is had by sense. Insight is an intellectual seeing-into what we hold by perception, memory, and imagination: a seeing-into the concrete configuration of a segment of the world in which we are. That configuration, because of the disposition of its elements, is potentially intelligible. In the concrete configuration relationships can be discerned. The discerning is an act of intellect: relationships are neither perceptible nor imaginable.

Insight is a moment in the movement of inquiring and understanding intellect, a moment prepared by the mysterious process of the preceding inquiry. It is a moment distinguishable in the process, a peak experience, often unforgettable, yet only a moment in a continuing process. For human insight is not complete understanding. It may be only a brilliant hunch which stirs us to continue to search, to make out the relationships more clearly, to fix and hold what we have grasped. A decisive moment in the process, insight is analogous to the commanding idea which monitors all elaboration of the complete work. We cannot rest in this moment. First, we are not made for an intellectual life which in its purely human mode can aspire to a completely satisfying understanding, in which all further stirring of a restless drive for understanding would cease. Although insight is an achievement, an unexpected but long sought-for fulfillment, it drives us beyond this momentary flash to consolidate and improve our understanding. There is a further, unending work to be done, as long as this life continues. What has been grasped in a flash must be worked out in further acts of intellect, developing the concept in which the achievement of one stage of intellectual effort may be held.

We shall turn in a moment to consider conception and its term, the concept. One more observation is in place here concerning the continuing role of insight through the process of conceptualization, a process involving a series of operations which terminate in the concept. As the insight of the painter or composer guides his continuing effort to work out and project in the art work what it is that he has grasped, so in the process of conceptualization insight functions as a sort of commanding idea: monitoring, censuring, guiding in the judgment of the aptness of the elements and their disposition in the concept.

This continuing guiding function of insight is part of the mystery of another aspect of intellectual life which we shall have to attend to more carefully later: the intellectual permeation of all sensuous elements of human experience. Conceptualization involves choice and elaboration of elements of a symbol which is always somehow sensuous. The commanding idea, the insight, guides in the running judgment of aptness of the symbolic elements and of the symbol which is the term of the process. In this I am anticipating what can be worked out fully only in the long discourse which lies ahead. Yet it is important to mark here a function of insight whose import will be more intelligible as our own conceptualization continues.

2. *Conception.* a. *Two lines of reflection.* My purpose here is to discern conception and its term, the concept: to determine what is proper to it, and how it is related to other operations. Perception, image, question, insight, conceptualization, and concept may be indicated as related moments in a particular thrust

of inquiring intellect, reaching the term of a limited effort to understand. The differentiation of operations and their terms may be revealed by pursuing two lines of reflection. Either of the lines alone would suffice, but their complementarity may help to indicate something of the variety and range of conception and concept.

Both lines begin with the same perception and at least some similar images. They diverge as different questions are put, and inquiry leads to different insights, conceptualization, and concepts. The two lines of divergent developments, illustrating what is proper to conception and the concept, suggest also the differentiation of realms which intellectual inquiry penetrates, worlds of meaning, of intelligible structure. The starting point of each reflection is the perception of the wheel.

Bernard Lonergan, in his classic treatment of insight, develops the first line of reflection.[1] Taking a cue from his treatment, I am developing this line without limiting myself to details of his thought. The object perceived is a cartwheel. The question, one of many possible questions, regards its roundness: why is it round? It is not enough to suggest that the spokes are of equal length: they might be set at different depths in the thick hub; or the wheel could be flat between the ends of the spokes. If the spokes were all equal and there were no possible flat interval between their extremities, the wheel would necessarily be round; if either condition were not fulfilled, the wheel could not be round.

Actually, no wheel is round, or ever could be. Nor is any image, the work of imagination, perfectly round. Hubs are thick, spokes cannot be exactly equal or exactly evenly set, nor can they be infinite: there is always the possibility of irregularity in the curve of the wheel. Nor can any image be perfectly round. Imagine a wheel as nearly perfect as you can. Draw it. Its center, at the position of the hub, is a dot. Its spokes are thin straight lines, as straight as you can imagine or draw them. Its circumference too is a thin line representing the curve of the rim. What would be necessary for perfect roundness? The hub would have to be a point, without any extension: not a dot, the best that you can imagine. The spokes would have to be lines, without thickness: not the thin strips which you imagine or draw. The spokes would have to be perfectly equal, and infinite, with no possible irregularity of the curve.

[1] B. LONERGAN, *Insight* (London-New York: 1957) 7-9.

Circles are round. They can be conceived, in terms of point, line, surface. A circle is a closed plane curve such that all of its points are equidistant from a point within, called the center. A circle can be conceived: it cannot be perceived or imagined. The concept or definition of the circle involves other concepts: point, line, and plane surface.

When one understands the relationships and fixes them in a definition of the circle, he has come to the term of a drive of intellectual inquiry. A number of steps may be involved: perception of the wheel, the question whether it is round, and then the further question: what would be required for it to be round; the play of images of wheels "nearly round", straining to approximate roundness; the insight into what relationships would be necessary for roundness; the conceptualization of point, line, plane surface; and the final term, the definition of the circle.

Beginning with the perception of the wheel, Lonergan chose one of several possible questions, omitting others not to his purpose: questions about carts, carting, transportation, and so on. His choice of question, and the type of insight and concept to which he comes, are especially appropriate to the type of intellectual operation and achievement which he regards as paradigmatic: mathematical and scientific thought, in which human intellectual progress has been outstanding, and whose characteristics may be so sharply delineated.

Concerning such a type of intellectual operation, beginning with the perception of the wheel and reaching the definition of the circle, one may claim that insight is gained into the concrete world of perception and imagination, and that what is grasped by insight finds its adequate expression only in the abstract formulations of mathematics and the sciences.

Clearly as this line of reflection establishes differences between perception and imagination in the order of sense, and insight and concept in the order of intellect, some aspects of this instance of human understanding may call for a complementary consideration. Although in a sense it may be said that insight is gained *into* the concrete world of sense and imagination, one might protest that really it is not so. Rather, from existing wheels and their representation in perception and imagination one moves to a realm of abstract thought in which alone circles "exist": the wheel is not a circle, and insight into the circle is not properly insight into the wheel.

There can be a complementary consideration of insight and

conception. It begins too with a perception of a wheel—as it might begin with a perception of a rose bush, a horse, or a man. It seeks understanding of existing things. It involves questioning, insight, grasp of relationships, and formulation of concepts which are never completely adequate, but which hold some of the intelligible relationships grasped in an always imperfect understanding of things in the world in which we are. It may illustrate equally well what conception is and how it differs from perception and imagination. In conjunction with the preceding consideration of the movement from wheel to circle, it suggests something of the variety and range of human understanding.

The second line of reflection begins with perception of a wheel or wheels and allows for the search for answers to several possible questions concerning wheels themselves. The concern here is with wheels, actually existing and functioning in the service of men who invented and produced them. Though the wheel is not a "thing" which has emerged as such in the physical world, it has a certain structure and intelligibility. Its intelligibility is multiple, for it may be considered in many relations to other elements in a variety of machines, to other factors in the variety of situations in which it is employed, and to a number of social and economic structures which are somehow connected with the wheel.

More than in the case of the intellectual process from perception of a wheel to the question about roundness and to answers in terms of the "truly round" circle existing in the mind of the geometer, here the characteristics of our perception of the wheel, and of our imagination, may favor both the raising of a number of questions and our success in experiencing insight and fixing relationships in concepts. It makes quite a difference whether I see a wheel by itself, leaning against a suburban barn as an ornament, or a wheel in place as part of a heavy wagon; whether I have just a fixed image of a wheel in either of those two situations, or a dynamic image of a wheel moving, groaning and squeaking under a heavy load, pressing into the earth or rolling smoothly on a paved road; rolling through mud or snow or stuck in either mud or snow.

From any one perception or image of a wheel, or any set of images static and dynamic, a number of questions may be raised concerning the purpose of the wheel, the factors involved in designing, making, and operating a wheel most successfully in a variety of circumstances.

Following up any one or more of my questions, I may come to an insight into the importance of such elements as the circumference of the wheel, the width of its rim or tire, the strength and distribution of weight of its hub, spokes, and rim, the kind of surface on which it may be moved best, the differences in structure and size depending on whether it is for a cart or an automotive truck, the size and design of its tires in relation to load, smoothness of ride, traction, and braking. Further questions may lead to insight into the importance of bearings, ball or roller, which by a strange twist of history may involve reverting to an insight which lay along the course of man's first discovery of the wheel. Moving heavy objects resting on fairly spherical boulders or sections of logs could have suggested the original insight into the wheel or pair of wheels. In turn, later problems of facilitating the rotation of a wheel on its axle under a heavy load could have suggested the ball bearing or roller bearing: thus giving to a hypothetical ancestor of the wheel a role in later success of the wheel itself.

The list of possible questions and lines of inquiry could be extended; for the wheel figures in such remote consequences as defining types of work, labor unions, and their jurisdictional quarrels.

But what is the point of all this? The point is that questions, insights, conceptualization, and concepts involve more than clear perception and vivid imagination. Insights are gained into relationships. Relationships are fixed and held in concepts, one or more. Relationships cannot be seen or imagined: they can be understood. The term of the movement toward understanding, whether of true roundness or of real wheels, is the concept, the definition.

As in the case of the artifact, the wheel, so too in the case of things which have emerged with their proper modes of being and operation in the physical world, some understanding can be reached. Natural things and men are far more complex than artifacts, instruments. Artifacts are products of human ingenuity. Whatever is proper to them is the work of the men who invented and produced them. Hence their intelligibility is relatively easily accessible. We never come to a full understanding of things existing about us, especially of living things, and most especially of man. We do come to some understanding. It is never a matter of adding up perceptions, but of discovering and fixing intelligible relationships.

b. *What is proper to conception and the concept*. At first

thought it may seem that it should be easy at this point to state clearly what is proper to the concept, and in so doing define the concept, have a relatively adequate concept of the concept. A little reflection suffices to make clear that the matter is by no means simple. It would be easy if we were concerned with one type of intellectual activity, one type of conceptualizing and concept. That, however, is not the case. We are trying to differentiate intellectual operations which occur in a variety of manners, and are embedded in a total human experience which is manifold and continuous in all its modes. Four difficulties occur to me.

First, insight, conceptualization, and concept are moments or stages in a process. Throughout the process there is question of acts which regard the grasp of intelligible relationships. The concept, as distinct from insight, must be considered as it is achieved in a full explicit act. Further reflection on degrees of conceptualization and concept in the course of the process, or in implicit knowledge, must be reserved for later consideration. What is proper to the concept should stand out clearly in its most clearly recognizable instance: the full, explicit act.

Second, human knowledge is always a blend of sense and intellect, and there may be a strong inclination to assign to perception and imagination some grasp of relationships. Against any such inclination I should hold that discerning and fixing relationships is the work of intellect. Perception and imagination present a concrete configuration in which relationships may be discerned. The relationships, however, are not perceptible or imaginable. The discerning is the work of intellect. Every image held in perception, memory, or imagination is concrete, with a relative wealth of particular details. Ten men may have images of a man, differing in height, shape, weight, complexion, color of hair, posture, and so on. Yet they may have a single concept of man which includes none of the varying details, and which fits all men, whatever may be their accidental details. Every one of the ten men will always have some image accompanying his actual conception of *man*, but image and concept differ. The concept holds a grasp of relationships which have been understood, which are common to all men regardless of their accidental variations.

Third, there are different modes of conceptualizing, and different kinds of concepts which correspond. Human understanding is not limited to the discursive mode, much less to the mathematical or scientific; and conceptualization does not always come to term in a verbal formula, or mathematical symbol. We shall have to face the question of divergent directions of human conceptualizing, of human symbolizing, and correspondingly different kinds of concepts, symbols. For the present I shall attempt to determine what is proper to the concept in any of its modes.

Fourth, because human understanding involves continual process, any given concept, representing a relative fixing of relationships which were first grasped in insight, is an achievement of intellect, but only a particular, limited achievement. It may occasion further questions, insights, conceptualization, and concepts. It is not, therefore, definitive, complete understanding. It must be defined somehow in such a way as to make clear its limitations. Anyone who has attempted to define may have had the experience of formulating a definition which for some time seems satisfactory, only to face further data or further questions regarding the same data, and to begin again, and again, and again. Every successive definition may be somehow an improvement upon the preceding, but there is no guarantee that it will be the last.

Setting forth what is proper to the concept, then, is not a matter of a swift stroke or two. I shall proceed in this order: (i) what immediately distinguishes the concept from insight; (ii) the limitations of the concept; (iii) its relations to percept and image. Since understanding the concept involves fixing it in its field of relationships, all of these steps are taken in the single movement toward a concept of the concept.

i. The concept is a work of intellect, a term of intellectual operation, which consists in a fixing of intelligible relationships by which an object is understood. All concepts, in whatever manner they are fixed, regard intelligible relationships. If one were to reflect on the sense of all of the categories elaborated by philosophers, he would recognize in every one some intelligible relationship or set of relationships, by which anything in the category is understood at least in part. Take any noun or adjective in an unabridged dictionary: the sense of every one ultimately involves some relationship or set of relationships. Every verb, transitive or intransitive, expressing a state or an action, involves reference to a mode of being or acting which is understood in terms of relationship. The two instances of conceptualization and concept with which we began, the circle and the wheel, are illustrations.

What is proper to the concept as differentiated from insight and from the process of conceptualization is that it is the term of a process begun in insight. Reaching that term is a decisive experience, as momentous and as thrilling at times as the first brilliant insight. Insight, on the analogy of visual perception, is like the experience of breaking through a forest into the open and catching the first glimpse of open country. Conceptualizing is like the careful attention to details of the scene, probing, observing relative position of particulars and composition of the whole. The concept is like the fixing of the perception of a figure against the ground, an image which best holds the impression of the whole. A description of the scene would involve conceptualizing, and the full description would be a sort of concept, setting lake, shore, trees, house, and sky in their multiple relationships. Every concept fixes and holds an intelligible relationship or set of relationships. Though definition is understood variously, according to various modes of thought, in every case what is called a definition is a relatively adequate concept of the object which is understood. Formulating a reasonably adequate definition at the term of a long process of probing and reflection can be a memorable experience.

ii. Every concept is limited. All human understanding, in the grasp of answers to the questions *What?* or *What sort of?* is partial, abstractive. By *abstractive* I do not mean abstract as opposed to concrete. Whether a concept is expressed abstractly or concretely (that is: indicating a formal intelligible relationship as distinct from the subject or as embodied in it) the concept is abstractive in this sense: its formal, intelligible content is only a portion of the total intelligibility of the thing which the concept signifies. The concept may be adequate to "hold" the thing, the object, in some intelligible relationships, but it never reaches complete understanding of the full reality of any existing thing. Intellect, in its process of conceptualizing, is like a pair of tongs, which firmly fixes and holds a block of ice, and enables one to lift and to maneuver it within limits, but which in no sense enables one to contain the full block.

Like perception, conception is characterized by an analogous perspectivism: as men see from different points of view, with subtle or great differences of perception, so too they conceive from different intellectual points of view, and they name the same thing differently, grasping different particular relationships which suffice to fix and hold the thing as it is grasped in a particular culture, in a particular language. What I call a "drawer" may be called the equivalent of "compartment" in another lan-

guage. I call it a "drawer" because it may be drawn from a
desk or chest. It could be called a "compartment" because it
divides the volume of storage space.

If we are intelligent in questioning and in probing for answers, we may reach some more or less adequate answers to
our questions. All are answers to particular questions. Sharper
questions seek more particular answers. The movement is ana-
lytic, but we never take the full reality of the thing apart, to
be able to reconstruct it and have complete understanding. Concepts are abstractive, and no sum of concepts will equal the
full reality of the thing which we seek to understand.

iii. Determining relationships between concept and perception and image is by no means easy. First of all, there is no
question of relationships among three *things*: *I* perceive in many
ways, *I* imagine, *I* remember what I have perceived and imagined, and in all and through all of these operations *I* have
some understandings of my situation, an understanding which
at times in some respects is increasing. Because I have at
least some vague understanding of relationships as I perceive
and imagine, it is not easy to distinguish, to the satisfaction
of everyone, what is proper to every one of the several operations, and in what relationships they stand. Only a pure cartesian would have illusions of perfect lucidity and complete
assurance in speaking of such matters. Only a pure empiricist
would have complete confidence in reducing all of the complicated experience to elements and combinations of elements
measurable according to his methods, disdaining all serious
concern with "imputed" inner acts and their differentiation.
Any attempt to come to an understanding of full human experience from within, by a careful attention to patterns of conscious operations and a reflection on their structures, involves
the difficulties and the frustrations of mapping a morass. Yet
something can be said.

First, if anything can be held as the result of our reflection on perception, memory, imagination, insight, and conception to this point, there is a relationship of opposition within
the order of cognitive operations and terms. All of these acts
somehow hold the mode of being of the known, yet they do
so differently. Perception, memory (in so far as it holds patterns
of former sense experience), and imagination hold only concrete
configurations, ensembles of segments of the world in which
we are. All such holding is limited to what can be held originally by sense perception. I can have a series of perceptions

of a tree, ranging over the whole and focussing successively on its parts, a series extended in time to allow for the perception of buds, flowers, fruit, and seed, differences of foliage according to season, and differences of size. I can perceive, in addition, photographic images, representing fixed images of the tree and its parts at various stages of growth. Every percept holds a certain configuration, static or dynamic. No percept or multitude of percepts of itself yields an insight into the living process of assimilation, growth, reproduction, the continuous organic process in which every discernible element is intimately related to all others in the mystery of the whole living organism. An understanding of the life process, imperfect as it always will remain, goes beyond what can be held by mere percepts and images. The difference is that of the intellectual grasp of relationships which are not perceptible or imaginable. The difficulty in recognizing this difference comes in part from the concrete unity and continuity of my human experience: I perform all of the operations, and it is as I perceive, imagine, and remember, that I come to understand. Dimensions of a total experience which are blended are easily blurred, and it is an arduous work of intellectual reflection to differentiate intellectual from sense elements in our cognitive life—to say nothing of the rest of our conscious life.

Second, in the complexity of human cognitive experience there is a mutual influence of perception, memory, and imagination on the one hand, and intellectual operations on the other. A given perception or series of perceptions, memories, and images can occasion questions and the subsequent progress toward understanding. Insight is gained into percepts and images. In turn, a man who is inquiring intellectually directs his perception, recalls what he has perceived, imagines variations: intellectual inquiry in many ways commands and directs sense operations, performed in the service of inquiring intellect. If I wish to analyze and characterize a city, I shall deliberately observe, for example, residential areas and types of houses and apartments, business, civic, industrial sections, streets and transport, parks, and so forth. What I perceive in great part will be the consequence of deliberately directed perception in observation.

Third, there is no understanding without percepts or images: in a classic formula, the phantasm is a permanent principle of human knowledge. Both sense and intellectual elements of human knowledge are present in all conscious life. A certain limited, particular priority in time may be recognized: a given percept or image is prior to the concept which results from insight into it. Absolutely, however, all perception and imagination is permeated by intellect. Sense and intellect are constant, inseparable factors of all human conscious life.

Fourth, there is a certain analogy, a kinship, of perception-image and concept. In different orders of knowledge each is related somehow to answers to questions of the first type which were indicated above in distinguishing operations of intellect: questions regarding *What?* or *What sort of?* If I am talking about something in words which someone does not understand, or if I am making something and he does not know what I am making, and he asks: What are you talking about? or What are you making? I can answer either by attempting to conceptualize and find words which he will understand, or by pointing to a thing standing on the shelf as an example of what I am talking about or what I am making. By the use of different words I attempt to communicate my concept directly. By pointing to a thing, I invite him to perceive it, and to understand as well as he can what I am talking about or making. His perception of the thing, and some vague insight into its nature and function, go hand in hand, and the latter permeates the former. At different levels, with different potential terminal results, both deal with answers to questions of *What?* or *What sort of?* The perception alone does not answer the question, but it occasions insight into the relationships which it exemplifies in the configuration which it holds. On the contrary, perception is not linked in this way with judgment. Experience of being, of the answer to the question *Is it?* is the exclusive realm of the operation of judgment. Judging is unique, the sole experience of its order. I can use an image, a drawing, a thing, to stand somehow for a concept; for the concrete thing or image embodies in its configuration the relationships which are intelligible and which are the answer to the question *What?* or *What sort of?* I cannot project in similar manner any image of affirming *that it is* except the utterance (or recognized equivalent, for example a gesture of assent) in which the judgment is actually made.

In another way there is a kinship of function of perception-image and of concept. As I can gain insight into perceptions or images, so too I can gain insight by regarding concepts and finding in them the occasion of further questions and subsequent insights and concepts. Both perception and image on the one hand, and concept on the other, hold the being of the known, and occasion questions, insights, and concepts.

3. *Judgment*. a. *Differentiation of acts in experience.* A man might have ten thousand concepts and yet, if he would never venture to join two of them, and to affirm: *X is m,* he would never come to what is regarded as the principal achievement of human knowledge: truth. Nor would he ever risk the principal failure: falsity.

Concepts, however complex they may be, however many terms may be used to express a sort of conjunction of many particular relationships which have been grasped, remain simple in the sense that they are simply the fixing of grasped intelligible relationships. I may know the meanings of all of the words and all of the simple concepts which go to make up a complex concept: "young, highly intelligent, well-informed philosopher". But until I recognize that someone really *is* such, and commit myself to affirming it, I do not reach truth.

Conceiving and judging are discernibly different acts, and the latter is far more momentous than the former. So much can be grasped in an initial reflection on personal experience of the two operations.

b. *The proper object of judgment.* Every judgment, explicitly or implicitly (with regard to the verb form used, or the equivalent of a verb form in a given intersubjective setting) regards the act *to be.* Affirmative or negative, the judgment may be expressed by using a form of the verb *to be,* or by another verb expressing a state or an action, or by a single word or gesture which in a given context is taken as expressing assent or denial. In any cae, the underlying sense of the judgment is that in one way or another, with or without indication of a particular manner of being, something *is* or *is not, is* walking or *is not, is* standing or *is not.*

It demands a certain reflection on this differentiation of acts of conceiving and judging, and of their objects, to reach what has been called "the philosophical experience of the act *to be*". That philosophical experience involves recognizing that *to be* is utterly unique. It is attained by human knowledge only in judgment, either the massive judgment, *This is,* or the limited judgment expressing a particular manner of being, *This is X.* We tend to take the copula *is* so much for granted that, unless we are challenged to reflect on its significance, we can pass our lives without noticing its uniqueness. As far as the verb *is* is concerned, without added predicate, most people perhaps could avoid ever using it to affirm simply that something *is*. That would be too obvious. Usually, if the verb *is* is used without the addition of a predicate, the predicate is understood as being implicit. Thus, "John *is*" would usually be the answer to our own question or someone else's as to whether John is such or such. It is just a way of saying *Yes*.

The very *is* of any thing which we encounter is not known by any mere perception, simple or complex. It is not grasped in a concept. What, then, is to be said of the *concept* of *being*? If *being* is taken in a substantive sense, it is a concept, but a concept of the second order, so to speak. It differs from concepts formed to fix relationships grasped by acts of the first order of knowledge: in answer to questions *What?* or *What sort of?* Being is that whose act is to be. The substantive *being* expresses a relationship, but only to the act of *being*: *to be*. That act is known first not in a concept, but in a judgment: It *is*.

Nor is the firm judgment *It is* reached only by a sort of syllogism, conditional or other, in which the conclusion can be affirmed only if the premise expressing the condition is affirmed. In any such paradigm of judgment, the question would return: how is the premise affirmed for sure? Unless one recognizes that human intellect is ordered by its very nature to two diverse acts, which regard, diverse objects; and that the second act of intellect, judgment, affirms directly that the very subject in question *is*, he can give no intelligible account of affirmation.

There is an existential factor in every judgment, whether the judgment regard the being of things existing in nature or truths in a given mathematical or scientific world of thought. Some critique of the sense of *is* is required, for not all true judgments regard being in the same order of reality. I shall return later (in chapter VI) to the general problem of the critique of human cognitive operations and the distinction of orders of reality, of what "counts" for man in various ways (in chapter V).

PRIMORDIAL KNOWLEDGE AND PROCESS

Considering insight, conception, and judgment thus far, I have concentrated on explicit acts. The reason is simply this: explicit acts of intellect, even in such modest achievements as I have

chosen as illustrations, reveal most clearly what is characteristic of the acts.   In such a reflection it is relatively easy to
discern and differentiate acts.   There remains, however, the
further mystery of the wide range of all three acts, and of the
continual process which is equally characteristic of all human
knowledge.   I propose now to reflect on that range and process,
and on variations of the basic figure-ground structure which
marks all human experience.

The ground is the vast primordial implicit awareness of
the presence of the world, and the vague sense of relationships.
We have insight not only in the flash of "getting the point",
but also in the vague running sense of our situation, in the
awareness of a field of relationships not clearly grasped, not
determined accurately, but sufficient for the present purpose.
For most of human living men rely on such insight.

As I move through my room, intent upon rounding my desk
and getting a folder from my filing case, I have a vague sense
of my position and movement at any stage.   That sense of position and direction which guides me is not made up of a thousand
explicit, ever-changing readings.   It is a general sense of the
whole situation and of my shifting relationships to familiar elements of my surroundings.   This is not just a matter of perception, at least as I have defined it.   There is an element of
knowledge of relationships, which I think must be attributed
to intellect.

Similarly, as I read the works of Merleau-Ponty, moving
through his thought, I am vaguely aware of many turns of his
underlying, relatively unexamined thought, which suggest a continuing cartesian influence, or husserlian, or other.   I have a
clear sense of my own purpose now, and of what I can gain
from assessing the personal achievements of Merleau-Ponty, and
I move with a sufficient sense of bearings.   I cannot turn aside
to follow up every hunch about such influences on his thought,
to take endless readings on his position in relation to Descartes,
and then on my position in relation to both Descartes and
Merleau-Ponty.   Life is too short, and the number of such
hunches concerning even one profound thinker is beyond all
reasonable demand for investigation.

Again, living with persons, I may have a vague sense of some
of the feelings, reactions, and attitudes of some to me or to
others: friendliness or hostility, apparent desires, hopes, fears,
joy, sadness.   I may sense personal problems, unrealized potential.   Yet I sense too the impossibility of sharing fully with

every one of these persons, in the hope of coming to some
mutual understanding of one another and of our personal mysteries. The more keenly I am aware of such feelings and problems, the more I am apt to feel sadness at my own limitations,
at the thought of the vast realms of personal mystery which
I cannot probe with a desire to reach a deeper mutual knowledge and love. In such cases—in most of our living with the
many persons who are prominent in our daily lives—we must
settle realistically for our limitations and go on living, guided
by a vague sense of interpersonal relations, seeking to find our
way with considerateness, tact, and kindness.

Reflection on such examples, or others which anyone could
propose, can lead to further insight into the range and function
of insight. Insight is not only the explicit, brilliant, momentous
flash, the extraordinary breakthrough in our life of knowledge;
but also the primordial, vague, implicit grasp of relationships
which is a dimension of all our conscious life. It is a vague
sense of our situation, of relationships which are intelligible,
and which could be determined more sharply, but which for
the moment are not our pressing concern. Such insight is sufficient for ordinary living. Indeed, unwillingness to settle for
it and get on with living could make life impossible.

Such a vague grasp of relationships is not held by mere
perception. Perception holds concrete configurations: it does
not grasp relationships, which are intelligible, not perceptible.
Perception too is primordial and explicit, with an ever shifting
pattern of figure and ground. All perception, however, is permeated and transcended by a constant intellectual grasp, which
ranges from the vaguest and most implicit to the clearest, explicit grasp of relationships. If it were not for primordial insight, the breakthroughs of explicit insight would be unintelligible. There would be no hunch, no "notion", no anticipatory
knowledge of what we are searching for when we do attend
to a situation and attempt to determine relationships more accurately. There would be no continuity in conscious life. Nor,
concerning explicit insight, could we affirm with any good reason: *here alone* insight begins; *here alone* intellect takes over
from sense.

Concerning conception and concept a similar conclusion can
be drawn. Conception and concept do not appear only at a
certain high level of intellectual performance, without any hum-
bler antecedents. Just as the flash of insight is preceded by a

vague sense of relationships, and by an initially vague probing
for clues in the perceptual world and images, so at any stage
of human life from early childhood there is some degree of
conceptualization, some fixing of relationships, however tentative
it may be. With a little patience and ingenuity we can draw
from almost any man, woman, or child some account of *what*
happened, what he or she feels, what he or she is trying to tell.
Poor as the result may be, it is an effort at conceptualization.
It is in continuity with previous experience. It will serve in
turn as the occasion for further questions, insight, and conception.

At every stage of human intellectual development conceptualization is possible in proportion to the degree of insight
which has been realized, but conceptualization lags behind insight, and requires some effort at elaboration. Further, there
is a certain symmetrical development of both insight and conceptualization. As we try to conceptualize, we focus more sharply
on the data, and our insight is sharpened even as we try to formulate what has been seized in earlier insights.

Two oversights would be possible regarding both insight
and conception. One would overlook all insight and conceptualization except that which is realized in scientific thought
or other higher realms. If one were to give an account of
insight and conceptualization only in terms of scientific thought,
he would be disregarding significant human achievements in
other modes of thought; and he might seem to be insinuating
that anyone who is not proficient in science has never had an
insight, much less a concept. We shall consider the range of
modes of conceptualizing when we take up the matter of the
range of symbols, in chapters VII and VIII. The other oversight
would be the disregard for the primordial, the implicit, the
vague conceptualization which precedes explicit conceptualization in any mode of human thought. Insight and concept do
not appear suddenly full-blown, to mark an absolute beginning
of intellectual life. In his intellectual experience, as in all other
dimensions of his life, man is in continual process. Development is slow, whether it be in science or in sagacity.

Finally, the same mystery enfolds judgment. In its explicit
act judgment regards the very *is* of a thing, or of the world
itself. The philosopher who is intelligent enough to ask about
what seems to be obvious, may affirm: The world *is*; things *are*,
and then set himself the task of understanding *why*. In its

primordial ground, existential affirmation is the massive implicit affirmation of the world present and existing, the world within which man begins all his probing.

Massive, primordial, implicit cognitive intentionality is the matrix of all subsequent intellectual acts: of all grasp of determinate relationships and all affirmation of being in all of its modes. The full reality of man and his world is more than he can ever hold in explicit perception and conception and affirmation. Facing a world which is, driven by an urge to understand, man lives more fully only by continuing to search and to find. As the world always exceeds his grasp, and any explicit act is only a relatively inadequate achievement, so too every explicit act is only a particular expression of a massive intentionality which is the ground from which it springs, the drive which it cannot contain. It is his primordial experience of the world and of himself which holds man to the task of transcending his present achievement.

As primordial perception of the horizon is a continual guarantor of the unity of the object perceived and of the perceiver, so at a deeper level, primordial intellectual experience gives a man a sense of the wholeness of his world and of himself. Beyond all the potential atomizing and fragmentation of a thought which can become ever more abstractive, and which can tend toward the disintegration of man and of his world, the massive primordial existential affirmation of the world and of himself in his world holds a man to his task of probing within a universe which holds together. It is one of the basic intentionalities which is a guarantor of wholeness and sanity. The other is a corresponding primordial love of all that is vaguely sensed as good in the world, beyond all conceptualization of particular goods, tending to the full reality of the good which is loved.

FURTHER QUESTIONS

Writing this sort of book, like guiding the visitor to Rome, presents some special problems of strategy and tactics. The writer, like the guide, may be tempted to keep his perplexities to himself, to preserve the semblance of calm and complete assurance, and to reply to any questions about his plan: "Just wait and see!" I prefer candor. There are certain perplexities here for me, and they are not unlike those of the guide.

The guide can lead his visitors out in a series of walks, starting from the Venetian Square and heading successively for eight or ten principal points of interest in various directions. His problem is like that of discursive reasoning. His movement is linear, with all of its advantages and disadvantages. He can give a clear running account of the principal sights along his route. He feels helpless to give an idea of what lies in the middle of the many jagged-edged slices into which his routes have cut the city. Moreover, he finds it frustrating to give a sort of synthesis of what lies along any one route: several monuments must be related to others which do not lie along this route, or any other single route.

My problem here is that several further questions could be raised at this point concerning intellectual acts, their mutual relationships, and their relationships with perception, memory, and imagination. My perplexity is this. On the one hand, the question of the blending and interrelationships of human conscious acts concerns not only cognitive acts, but also others: volitive, emotive, and motor. Only an unsatisfactory partial answer could be given now in terms of cognitive acts, and a second, more complete answer would be necessary after the consideration of volition, emotion, and motor action. On the other hand, some brief reflection on the unity and continuity of cognitive acts is necesary as a condition for the understanding of volition and emotion.

The only reasonable solution seems to be this: to note briefly now the blend of cognitive acts in the unity of human experience; then in the following chapter to consider volition, emotion, and motor action; and finally in a subsequent chapter to reflect on the unity and continuity of all modes of human conscious experience.

Perception, memory, imagination, insight, conception, and judgment are six modes of the operation of a single agent. They do not proceed from six different agents, nor six "things" within the single person who acts. I perceive, remember, imagine, understand, and judge. The mystery of the continuity of primordial and explicit experience pervades all the modes of my cognitive operation. Primordial perception is permeated by primordial insight and massive implicit existential judgment. Gradually I fix figure against ground, retain images of what I have perceived, recall my past personal experience, freely combine and create with the resources of imagination, and through the whole process simultaneously come gradually to a grasp of intelligible relations.   Classic problems of the genesis of understanding, and of the recognition of relationships as they are found again in *this* individual, find their solution only in the mystery of this blend of sense and intellect.   There is no inexplicable leap from the singular of sense to the "universal": *I* gradually come to discern and fix relationships which I understand, as I have repeated experience of the configurations which I hold in perception, memory, and imagination.   However far I progress in the refinement of concepts which hold universally of all members of a class, I never understand without an accompanying image, and I recognize *this* as a *man*.   The blend of sense and intellect alone makes intelligible the rise of all intellectual conception and the development of worlds of meaning.   That same blend alone makes human action intelligible.   For action takes place in the realm of singular existents, and the most refined and fully elaborated intellectual knowledge would leave me helpless to act if I could not recognize *this* as an instance of a singular existent which *is* in the mode of being which I have grasped and accurately defined in a concept.

It is this mystery which concerns us now, as we turn to consider other human operations in which man responds to the persons and things in the worlds in which he is.

CHAPTER IV

EMOTION, VOLITION, AND MOTOR ACTION

Man *is* in his world in a properly human manner. If "behavior" be understood in a broad sense, including a wide variety of modes of action and reaction, then human behavior is unique in this universe. Though it is obviously physico-chemical and physiological, it ranges beyond patterns which may be established according to the laws of physics or chemistry or biology.[1]

In the two preceding chapters we have considered the range of man's cognitive operations, by which in a variety of ways he registers the modes of being of the others with which he shares the world. All of these operations pertain to one basic order of intentionality: knowledge.[2] By all such operations man holds somehow the mystery of the being of others. Even such operations, however, do not terminate simply within the knower. All human knowledge has a dynamic thrust which tends to the projection and communication of knowledge, to sharing the known with other human persons. In a sense, then, even knowledge reveals a structure of action and response. Continually acted upon by things and persons whose influence is mediated by physical forces, man responds not only with the operations by which he understands and affirms the mode of being of others, but also in the expression of what he understands and affirms. No understanding or affirmation is possible except in operations which are symbolizing. Symbols, as we shall see, are at once the term of a process or set of processes within the knower and the means by which he shares his knowledge

---

[1] For a stimulating reflection on the variety of structures of behavior in the physical, vital, and human orders see MAURICE MERLEAU-PONTY, *The Structure of Behavior* (Boston: Beacon Press, 1967) esp. pp. 93-184. See also JOSEPH DE FINANCE, S.J., *Essai sur l'agir humain* (Rome: Gregorian University Press, 1962): in the introduction to his study of human action he reflects on action in the physical, vegetative, and animal worlds.

[2] See above, pp. 26-27.

with others. Knowledge itself, then, involves a human response
to the known world.

Yet this does not exhaust the mystery of the human way
of being in the world. Man acts upon the world not only by
sharing his knowledge with other persons, but also by reacting
to persons and things in the pursuit of his own fulness of being
and the enrichment of those whom he loves. He knows persons
and things as good or bad for him in a variety of ways, and
he reacts to them and acts upon them accordingly. This he does
with a variety of operations which pertain to the second basic
intentionality, appetitive: regarding persons and things basically
as good or bad for the knower. Reflection on the structure of
these operations is indispensable for understanding man the
symbolizer, for these operations too enter into the fulness of
human symbolizing.

EMOTION

As we began our consideration of knowledge with perception, so it may be most reasonable to begin this reflection with
a consideration of man's response to what he can perceive sensibly to be good or bad for him. In perception, by any form
or combination of forms of sense knowledge, man holds the
image of what is good or bad, pleasing or displeasing, attractive
or repulsive to him. Consequently he holds a similar image by
memory or by free imagination of what has been perceived.
To the sensibly perceptible good or bad for him he responds
spontaneously, positively or negatively, with more or less intense bodily resonance, and an impulse to the appropriate motor
action.

Even in his response to what is sensibly perceptible as good
or bad for him, however, man is not responding to what he
knows by sense perception alone. No perception, memory, or
imagination occurs in isolation from other cognitive factors in
a total human experience. All perception, even primordial, is
penetrated by intellectual factors: massive primordial existential
judgment and a vague intellectual grasp of relationships. I do
not merely sense what is pleasing to sight, touch, taste; nor
do I merely sense the general feeling of well-being or discomfort in my body. I also have from the outset some vague
grasp of the relationships involved, some understanding that

I am responding to what seems pleasing or displeasing to my senses.

As we approach the effort to disengage what is proper to emotion, two other aspects of its involvement with other factors of experience should be noted. First, beyond the fact that I understand that I am responding to what is sensibly perceptible, a further intellectual cognitive factor enters into the structure of some emotional experience. Though simple emotions may be immediate responses to what is perceived, remembered, or imagined, still there are more complex emotions whose differentiation can be made only in terms of relationships which are grasped as we come to an insight into patterns of experience. We shall see this in the case of hope and fear, for instance, in which there is an estimate of the relative difficulty in attaining the distant good or warding off or fleeing from the threatening evil. Here there is a question not merely of sense knowledge, but also of some intellectual grasp of relationships recognized in the concrete instance.

Second, as we shall see more clearly in treating volition, there is a voluntary element in emotion. As there is a developing intellectual grasp of what we are sensing as pleasant or unpleasant, attractive or repulsive, so too there is a corresponding volitional dimension of our response to the good or bad as known. The object is presented not only by sense for a response of sense appetite, but also by intellect for a voluntary response within the emotive experience. This voluntary dimension in emotive experience is one aspect of the blending of emotion and volition. The other, which we shall consider more fully later, is the emotive reverberation or resonance of our response to a good or evil grasped by the intellect, but always presented for action in a concrete instance. Here the good or evil as such can be grasped only by intellect, for it involves relationships which are not sensibly perceptible, good or evil which cannot be seen or felt. Yet, as our intellectual knowledge is never without images, so our volition of a good grasped intellectually and proposed concretely for action is accompanied by, and heightened by, emotion. Though in many instances we may be barely conscious of such an emotive response, the structure of human experience is such that one can reasonably affirm that some emotive factor is always involved. As there is no operation of human sense appetite which is purely animal, purely sensitive, with no degree of intellective or rational grasp of relationships, so on the other hand there is no purely spiritual human love, with no element of sense appetite. Granted this, one must admit degrees of the blend, from nearly pure sense appetite to nearly pure intellectual or rational love.

One final preliminary note regards the complexity of emotion and the diversity of formalities under which it is considered. Four aspects of total emotive experience may be discerned: (1) the relationship or cluster of relationships of the known good or evil to the agent; (2) conscious bodily resonance; (3) motor impulse and action; (4) physiological and neurological functions which may be verified or conjectured by objective study of emotive behavior. A phenomenological study of emotive experience regards the first three as aspects of the structure of conscious behavior. Different empirical psychologies study especially the second and third. Physiologists or physiological psychologists consider the fourth. A philosophical reflection should be concerned with all four, moving beyond phenomenological study of structures and objective studies of physiological and neurological underpinnings to reflect on the implications regarding the human *a priori*: a basic understanding of how man *is* in such a manner as to make *such* operations intelligible. My concern here is initially phenomenological, ultimately philosophical. I am interested immediately in discerning structures of human behavior. I am concerned too with implications regarding the human *a priori*, but in this work I am content with suggesting implications and asking further questions whose answers would involve elaborating a full philosophical understanding of man.

A few common types of emotive experience may suffice to recall its features. If, gazing upon a scene, we see a beautiful form (a lovely garden, a lake, harbor, flower, thoroughbred horse) we find it pleasant, and we are drawn to gaze more attentively, to feast on the sight, to rest in the pleasure of the good which is presented to our vision. Or it may be that a beautiful scene or form is not now present in perception, but remembered, or imagined. The image in memory or imagination can stir desire and stimulate us to return to where we can see it again, with an eagerness and heightened tone of our whole being as we go. The desire of a distant good stimulates our movement. But even as we dwell on the image we feel pleasure in the beauty imagined. On the contrary, if we look upon an ugly, repulsive thing (a filthy, disordered room; a ghastly decaying animal carcass) we shudder and turn from it with disgust, shivering and feeling a tension as we shrink from it. Again, even the presence of the ugly thing in memory or imagination is enough to cause a response of revulsion and the impulse of withdrawal. Similarly we respond to sounds and to touching and being touched: contrariwise, as the sense perception is pleasing or displeasing. Through most of the lives of men and women there is a keen experience of sexual attraction, stimulated by sight or sound or touch presenting any of the sensible aspects characteristic of a person of the opposite sex. At this level, at which we are considering solely the factor of sensible attraction and response, the emotive or passionate response is spontaneous, called forth entirely by the presence or image of a sexually attractive "object".

The response is emotion, called also by a number of other names: passion (especially in classic philosophical usage), affect, feeling. We may define it thus: *a conscious act responding to what is known by the senses to be good or bad, pleasing or displeasing, for the agent.* The response varies in structure according to the variety of objects presented, and according to the relationships of the objects to the agent. Part of this response is a felt change in the body, a resonance, varying according to the object and relationship. Simultaneously there is a felt motor impulse, and the beginnings of some motor action. All of this is part of the conscious experience. The non-conscious physiological and neurological functions underlying the conscious experience may be detected with a fair degree of probability by objective empirical techniques.[3]

Differentiation and classification of emotions can be attempted from various points of view, regarding diverse formal considerations. Some empirical psychologists, identifying emotion with sensation or with motor action, have sought to differentiate and classify in such terms.[4] Physiologists or neurologists or physiological psychologists have sought to give systematic accounts of what is called emotion in terms of its objectively observable underlying physiological and neurological func-

---

[3] For a remarkable sustained effort to identify the physiological and neurological functions corresponding to a variety of conscious emotive experiences see MAGDA ARNOLD, *Emotion and Personality* (London: Cassell, 1961) Vol. II.

[4] For a critique of such efforts, see MAGDA ARNOLD in the work cited, Vol. I, especially pp. 19-52, and 106-165. Insisting on the priority of a phenomenological study of emotion, she devotes much of her first volume to it: pp. 169-276.

tions. Without attention to first-personal witness to what is being consciously experienced, such efforts would be blind, meaningless probing. To take an illustration from another area of such observation, even a twenty-four-hour cardiogram is interpreted adequately only in the light of the first-personal account of what the patient was doing from hour to hour through the day. In short, the approach to any study of emotion must be by way of a phenomenological description of the structures of conscious behavior. As I have mentioned, phenomenological reflection regards three aspects of conscious emotive experience: the differentiation of object and of relationships of objects to subject; bodily resonance of the response; and motor action. Both bodily resonance and motor action vary according to the objects which evoke response, and they are appropriate to the response evoked. If we are looking for the most significant differentiation of emotions, therefore, we must consider the different objects and their relationships to the subject. This is a roundabout way of returning to a classic methodological principle: acts are specified and differentiated according to their formal objects.

How, then, are the objects and the relationships to the subject to be differentiated? I propose a personal formulation of a classic differentiation, of which elements can be traced to Aristotle, and a fairly consistent systematic account can be found in St. Thomas Aquinas, who has influenced a long succession of philosophers. Since the very mention of the name Thomas Aquinas may be enough to evoke an emotional response in some readers, I should like to indicate exactly what I am taking from him, what I am leaving unexamined, and why such a procedure can be not only innocuous but helpful. Distinguish three elements in Thomas Aquinas' treatment of emotions: (1) a reflection on structures of conscious experience, with a differentiation of objects and their relationships to the subject; (2) some account of physiology; (3) a philosophial theory of man, in terms of his composite nature and his powers. The second is primitive, even naïve, by modern standards: it is what an intelligent thirteenth-century thinker could gather from Aristotle and a long tradition of ancient and medieval thinkers, Greek, Jewish, and Arab, some of whom were medical doctors.[5] No one

---

[5] For a summary account of this tradition bearing on one element involved in the theory of emotion, see GEORGE P. KLUBERTANZ, S.J., *The Discursive Power. Sources and Doctrine of the *Vis Cogitativa* According to St. Thomas Aquinas (St. Louis, Missouri: The Modern Schoolman, 1952).

would take it seriously today. Magda Arnold has made a serious effort to provide at least a tentative account based on recent scientific research. It is beyond my competence to judge her work in this area. The third element is an impressive, not to say formidable, philosophical theory which is a challenge to thinkers capable of a long and difficult historical study and an independent critical evaluation. It would be ludicrous to repeat rejections which betray no signs of having taken the challenge. I have reservations about aspects of the theory, but for the present I neither take it nor leave it. The first element, though neither Aristotle nor St. Thomas knew enough to call it that, is a sort of phenomenology. In the process of serious thought about man it comes first. Embedded as it is in his theoretical elaboration, St. Thomas' phenomenological reflection might be scorned along with the theoretical elaboration. It merits consideration by anyone who can recognize it as an element of ancient and medieval thought which remains uncompromised by either of its complementary elements. In my consideration of emotion I draw only on this phenomenological reflection.

Considering the objects of emotive acts, and their relationship to the subject, I should distinguish two general classes of emotions: simple and complex. Simple emotions regard the sensibly known good or bad, pleasant or unpleasant, attractive or repulsive. These sets of contraries are relative to the subject: there is question of good or bad *for him*, in so far as the tendency of a particular sense appetite is concerned. Many persons or things do not fall into either category: they are simply neutral as far as the particular appetite is concerned. The hard or soft, and the hot or cold as such are neutral to my sense of smell. Complex emotions regard objects involving another factor beyond the sensibly good or bad, as we shall consider later.

Simple emotions, then, regard the sensibly known good or bad, and the two basic emotions are love (of a sort) and hate. As good is prior to bad, which cannot be understood except in terms of some negation of good, so love is the absolutely basic emotion, responding to the sensibly known good. A further differentiation is introduced in terms of the relationship of the presence or absence of the good or bad. Desire is the emotion responding to an absent good. Joy or pleasure is the emotional response to the present good. Love tends to union, and joy or pleasure are the emotions at the term of the process, if movement has been necessary to attain the good. Aversion, revulsion, and flight are emotional responses to an absent evil, presented only in image. Pain or sorrow are the emotional responses to the evil which is present. Hate tends to separation, and its term reached by flight is separation or liberation. Union with the good brings the highest pleasure. Union with the bad brings the greatest displeasure.

Complex emotions, presupposing the diversity of good and bad, are differentiated in terms of variables of another factor: relative difficulty in attaining the good or avoiding the evil. Hope is the emotion regarding an absent good which is judged to be attainable, though not without difficulty. Despair regards an absent good which is judged to be unattainable. Daring regards an absent but imminent evil which can be warded off. Fear regards an absent but imminent evil which seems unavoidable. Anger regards an evil which is present.[6]

Since I have mentioned Magda Arnold's treatment of emotion several times, I should say, to avoid any misunderstanding on the part of those who are familiar with her work, or who may be inclined to consult it, that I do not distinguish as she does between feeling and emotion. I do not wish to enter into detailed discussion of her conception, but I say simply that I consider her phenomenological account unsatisfactory in this regard. Feeling, pleasure or displeasure arising from the condition of the subject, or from the presence of a pleasing or displeasing object, fits into the scheme of emotions as I have elaborated it. Pleasure and displeasure regard the good or bad respectively, considered as present. The good or bad may be the very tone of the body. When I have had a fever and regain normal equilibrium, I feel good: I find the very balance and wellbeing of my body pleasant. When I have written for two hours, I am tired and tense, and thought is difficult. It is a bad condition, and I find it unpleasant. When I have rested and sought refreshment in a change of activities, and I return feeling fresh and able to think again, I rejoice in a present good.

Considering the emotions as I have distinguished them, I

---

[6] Elements of this classification of emotions, with some variations of scheme, can be found in St. Thomas, *Summa Theologiae*, Pars Primasecundae, question 23, article 4. The distinction of *concupiscibilis* and *irascibilis* is part of the theory in which his phenomenologically established relationships of act to object are set. Magda Arnold has a schematic presentation of the classification drawn largely from St. Thomas, in her work already cited, Vol. I, p. 195.

should like to point out the blend of cognitive elements involved. The simple emotions, regarding the sensibly known good or bad, pleasant or unpleasant, are responses to the good or bad as known immediately by sense. No intervention of another estimate is required. If a man says that this tea tastes bad, there is no sense in arguing with him. It may be that the tea is perfectly good and tastes good to me and to others, but there is no point in arguing about the personal fact: it tastes bad to him. There is no intellectual element required to pass judgment on this sort of good or bad. Yet, as I respond to the good or bad which I know as such by my senses, I *understand* what I am doing: I am enjoying what pleases my taste or hearing or sight. In the experience of complex emotions, on the other hand, not only do I understand that I am fearing an imminent, sensibly known evil, but also in the very estimate of the relative difficulty of avoiding or warding off the evil there is an intellectual factor, a judgment of a relationship based on previous experience. There may be a mistake in that judgment, and someone may reasonably seek to persuade me that I should not fear. Even here, though, the personal factor, my particular judgment of the relative difficulty for me here and now, is beyond censure by another.

Returning to the definition of emotion which I proposed, I should like to note a possible objection, which suggests some further reflection. I defined emotion as an *act*: a conscious act responding to what is known by the senses to be good or bad, pleasing or displeasing, for the agent. It may seem that emotion is not an act, but rather a sort of condition, or a vague, ill-defined process. Anger or sadness may be diffused through the whole of our being, suffusing our life, affecting its whole tone, conditioning our volitional action by a general inclination or disinclination, vaguely suggesting a succession of memories, images, and thoughts associated with the same feeling, which in turn deepen the general emotional condition.

All of this is true, and yet it suggests rather the breadth of the analogy of human action. Even cognitive acts at times are ill-defined, enduring through relatively long periods, continuous through fluctuations of degrees of awareness. Continued contemplation or a vague shapeless process of half-conscious reasoning are diffuse, and yet somehow they can be considered acts with a recognizable rhythmic structure. Emotion at times has a clearly recognizable structure when it breaks forth suddenly, intensely. After it reaches its peak it may subside slowly until it is barely discernible. At times there is no intense response, but only a mild emotion. In its suffused afterglow, and in its very mild responses, emotion shades off into what is more aptly called a sentiment, then a mood of longer duration, a continuing attitude, and even an habitual tone of life. Perhaps we could say that emotion as a fairly discernible act is part of a varying emotive element in our conscious life, a relative peak standing out from a general condition or tone. It is recognizable as a response to an object which is quite distinct. Where no such object is recognized, there may be question of residual emotion, sentiment, or mood.

A further reflection concerns the differentiation and classification of emotions. Any of the emotions indicated can take a great variety of forms, with a corresponding variety of bodily resonance and motor action. Thus desire differs greatly according to its object: food, drink, sexual gratification, or relief of great fatigue through a warm bath and rest in a comfortable bed.

There is a great variety of emotion too depending on the manner in which its object is presented. Desire or fear may be a response to any one of a variety of cognitional experiences, to an object held in focal awareness, or marginal, or subliminal. It may arise from the very condition of our bodies, from images associated with physiological conditions or changes.

Finally, emotions or sentiments or moods may be barely discernible because they are part of a complex experience in which two or more emotions may be blended and conflicting. Thus a feeling of heavy sadness may yield only after some time to joy evoked by a pleasant sight or melody, at first rejected, then gradually drawing attention and prevailing over the sadness.[7] Two emotions can be felt, one in its declining phase, the other rising.

Two other aspects of emotional experience reveal the intervention of volition, and may serve as a transition to our consideration of volitive action. In one typical instance, I may be drawn simultaneously to several pleasures of objects known by sense. Entering a garden, I may be attracted by beauty of sight, pleasure of touch (the freshness, coolness of the air), of sound (song of birds, rippling of a stream). Partly at times by simply

---

[7] For an instance of experimental data illustrating this blend and conflict see ARNOLD, in the work cited, vol. I, pp. 78-79, reporting an experiment by Koch.

following the whimsical play of perception, partly by deliberate choice, I fix my attention for a moment on one object among many. Even where there is hardly awareness of a deliberate choice, I go along with the attraction which beckons at the moment. In another type of experience I may be torn between two aspects of an action: pleasant and unpleasant. Seeing ripe blackberries in a thick, wild, overgrown clump, I am drawn by the desire of a better view and especially of the taste of the berries; but I am repelled by the prospect of being badly pricked by thorns. I must choose, in a situation where the very play of desires and dread stalls action for a moment. This play of multiple objects in our perception and imagination, contending for emotive response, is symbolic of a far greater, wider-reaching diversity of goods and evils which present themselves to us, and among which we must choose. With this reminder, we turn to consider the higher reaches of human action, in response to goods and evils which are not sensibly perceptible as such. This is the wider realm of volition.

VOLITION AND VALUES

Properly human action is a response to the good or bad known by intellect. It is a voluntary or volitive action, an act of rational or intellectual appetite. Without entering into the question of a theory of will as one of man's powers or faculties, I am concerned here simply with the objects of such acts, and of the relationships of the objects to the subject. They are diverse from the objects of sense, and they specify a diverse order of appetitive intentionality.

As we have seen, even in human response to a good or evil known and judged immediately and adequately by sense, intellectual knowledge permeates sense, and a volitional factor enters into the response of appetite to the sensibly presented good or evil: I know that I am indulging in a pleasure of sight or taste or touch, and I willingly do so. That intellectual and volitive participation in sense knowledge and appetite is, I have said, symbolic: it represents the far wider range of intellectual grasp of the good or evil, and appetitive response to the object thus known. A fresh ripe apple or a glass of scotch and water may appeal to my taste and evoke desire and then pleasure as I eat or drink. But I may, and usually should, take them or leave them for reasons which range beyond what my senses tell me about them as good. Either of them can be known to me as good or bad for me for many reasons, none of which can be grasped by sense. I understand the relationships between eating or drinking them and a number of consequences. Either or both of them may be judged good or bad, depending on a number of factors which I understand. They have their place, or several places according to circumstances, on my scale of values.

Volitive action regards values: objects known to be not merely good or bad in themselves according to their kind as sensibly perceptible, but good or bad for the person who is attracted to them, or repelled by them, for reasons which often are not sensibly perceptible. A man who is attracted sexually by a woman can respond immediately to her as a "sex object": he is simply responding to a good presented to his sex appetite, and doing so more or less aware of what he is doing, and more or less willingly. Making love with this woman may be desirable if he shuts out any other consideration of the act. But the thought that he is a married man, and that she is someone else's wife, shifts the estimate of good or bad to another level. Even regarding her as a person, not merely a sex object, changes his estimate of the act—if he is capable of rising to the level of understanding and respecting a person, and of a love more worthy of the name.

Classic philosophies of human action, moral philosophies, dealt with human acts as good or bad: properly human action is voluntary action whose object is a good presented by the intellect. More recent moral philosophy has recognized the importance of another notion, qualifying the good. It is the notion of value.[8]

What is value? It is a kind of good, and it can be understood only in the context of a basic sense of what we mean by *good*. *Good*, as an adjective, is so basic a concept that any effort to spell out its meaning involves using other concepts less immediately evident in their meaning. When we say that a thing is good, we mean that it has a relative fulness of perfection according to its kind, its own proper mode of being. From experience we come to know things according to their kind, and to recognize those which stand out as good. The *good* is said to be a transcendental attribute of being: everything is good to the extent that it *is*, to the extent that it has

---

[8] See, for example, JOSEPH DE FINANCE, *Essai sur l'agir humain* (Rome: Gregorian University Press, 1962) and *Éthique générale* (Rome: Gregorian University Press, 1967).

a relative fulness of the mode of being which is proper to it.
I say "relative fulness", because none of the persons or things
which we can know from experience is absolutely perfect. They
tend to their own perfection, and their success or failure in
attaining it is relative.

What is good is recognized as such, esteemed, and praised
for its perfection. To the extent, too, that it can contribute to
the perfection, the fulness of being, of another, it is desirable,
and is actually desired and sought.

Value is an attribute of a person or thing which is not
simply good in itself according to its mode of being, but good
for men, or for a particular person. Value does not necessarily
correspond to the degree of goodness which is said to be ontological, or transcendental: the goodness of the thing in itself,
proportioned to its fulness of being. Many things which are
good according to their kind have little value, or at least little
recognized value, for men generally or for a particular person.
On the other hand, a thing good in itself may have several different values for different persons. A beautiful apple is valuable
for the man who is hungry for it; for the boy who wishes to
offer it as a gift to please his teacher; for the artist who wishes
to paint it. Persons and things have value as they offer promise
of some sort of fulfillment of men in any of the many worlds
in which men live.

What is valued "counts" for something in the world of the
one who values it. It attracts him to act to attain it. Until
it is attained, it calls for action. When it has been attained,
it makes the action by which it was attained seem worth while.

Figuring in all the worlds into which a man can project
his action, at all levels at which he can act, values are of greatly
different sorts, and of different quality and degree of excellence
generally recognized by men. Moreover, values generally stand
out in opposition to their contraries, antivalues.

Considering the range of values which can attract men and
be the objects of their volitive action, philosophers have attempted to work out a scale or hierarchy of values. Here, somewhat freely adapted, is the hierarchy proposed by Joseph
de Finance.[5]

(1) *Infrahuman values,* so called because they are good not
only for men, but also for animals (though animals do not know

---

[9] *Essai sur l'agir humain,* pp. 372-379, and particularly for the notion
of moral value, *Éthique générale,* pp. 69-74 and 183-184.

them as such). Lowest on the scale are objects *pleasing to the senses*. Their contraries, or antivalues, are displeasing or painful. From the point of view of the subject, the value is pleasure; the antivalue is suffering or displeasure. Next in the rising order are *biological* or *vital* values: all that regards the maintenance, success, and expansion of animal life according to the perfection of the species. There is a paradox in the ranking of these two orders of infrahuman values. Sense pleasure, since it pertains to consciousness, in that respect would seem to be higher than non-conscious biological or vital values; yet the pleasure of sense is reasonably sacrificed to preserve a greater, more basic value, life and health itself.

(2) *Human*, but *inframoral* values, which are of various kinds: *economic*: prosperity, success, riches; *intellectual*: truth, depth, fecundity of knowledge; *aesthetic*: beauty, grace, elegance, sublimity; *social*: cohesion, prosperity, and power of society or nation or state, harmony of the classes, identity of ideal; and as perfections of the person in society: ease of relations, prestige, authority, charm, charisma; *perfection of will*: energy of character, constancy in undertakings, ability to rebound from failure, perseverance in solitude. These qualities of will, as De Finance points out, are often regarded as approaching moral values.

(3) *Moral value*, which is one, and which stands in a unique relationship to all lower values. De Finance first enumerates its characteristics, and then states what formally constitutes this value.

These, then, are some of the characteristics of moral value. First, it is a quality of a human *act*: a man is good or bad morally because he acts well or badly. Second, it is worthy of esteem, lovable, desirable for itself, not as conducive to some other value. Third, it differs from other "spiritual" values (intellectual, aesthetic, or pertaining to the will) in that it can never be surrendered for another value. In one's pursuit of moral value there can be no vacation, no strategic retreat. Fourth, it is the very reason for living: it gives sense to life. It is the proper value of a person, the personalizing value par excellence. Fifth, it is paradoxical in being absolutely individual and yet universal. It is individual in the sense that no one can provide it for me: I must realize it by my own action. Yet it is universal in two regards: acts which are morally good or bad are so for all men; and right moral judgment in any situation deserves to be approved by all who could understand the situation.

In what, then, does moral value consist? It is the agreement of both the volitional act and its object with right reason: reason faithful to itself and open to the ideal, the fulness of the good. The relation to the absolute good, the ideal, defines the rationality which is propter to moral value. The act which is morally good is not merely performed coherently, with grace. It is not merely in accord with universal norms. It is open to the absolute good.

(4) *Religious value.* Objectively it regards the sacred, the divine, and in its supreme degree God, the ultimate foundation of all values. Subjectively it is religion, respect, submission, confidence, piety, personal holiness. Religious value regards the subject's relation to the source of his being and of the whole order of values. In the moral value the ideal was regarded implicitly as the horizon of liberty. Here the ideal is regarded directly. There is no morality without religion; no religion without morality.

I should make three observations concerning this hierarchy. First, the last pair of statements about morality and religion holds at least in the so-called "high religions", and eminently in Christian religion. As one moves from a moral philosophy to a Christian moral theology, a moral act is right in relation to God. All good of objects and of acts, participates his goodness. All right reason conforms to his wisdom. Every morally good act is Godward: tending to him in every object which is good by sharing his goodness, and which promises to fulfill by drawing a man ultimately to the source of all good and the goal of all striving.

Second, the scale of values is not entirely coherent. The intention of philosophers in discerning a hierarchy is to arrange values in the order ranging from lowest to highest. Besides the paradox regarding the relative value of sense pleasure and biological values, there are other fluctuations in the judgment of relative excellence among the human, inframoral values. First, in the list given, no distinction is made between personal and common values and their relative rank. Moreover, the order of the personal "spiritual" values is not clearly established. Principally, however, the rationale of the hierarchy shifts with the introduction of moral value. This is not just one value to be compared with others of differing ranks. It is *the* value which

makes a man's act right in the pursuit of any value. It permeates and charges with incomparable value every act which is
right for a man who seeks to do what he should here and now
to be a man. As the moral value is recognized in a religious
setting, it is a matter of the right order of an act which tends
to God as the supreme good.

Third, I think that something is missing from the whole
consideration of values, from human inframoral to religious:
it is the distinction of personal, social, and interpersonal. The
distinction of personal and social is evident: it holds for values
of truth, beauty, and quality of will. The distinctive quality of
interpersonal value is not evident, and it deserves consideration.
Beyond the purely personal fulfillment by economic, intellectual,
aesthetic, and volitional values, and beyong commonly held values
in society, there is a unique fulfillment to be attained in truly
interpersonal sharing of any or all of these values. Truly interpersonal fulfillment in a mutual knowledge and love and sharing
of all human and religious goods is a value of a different order.
It is not just that two persons help each other to attain a greater
share than they could by unaided striving. Rather there is question of a kind of fulfillment which is possibly only in fellowship
as a distinct and supremely human mode of being. The distinction prevails through all human, moral, and religious values.
In the Christian view, we are all saved together: one can be
saved only by being in Christ, and one cannot be alone in Christ.
But beyond that sense of solidarity, there are differences in the
manners in which we may experience union and communion or
fellowship. Something is missing humanly when "we" does not
take on a new sense within lives fully shared in mutual interpersonal knowledge and love and full mutual gift. What is added
in such love is a uniquely human value, taken up into the mystery of our fulfillment in interpersonal relationship with Father,
Son, and Holy Spirit.[10] Apart from the uniquely beautiful Christian flowering of this fellowship, the distinctive human interpersonal value holds for all fulfillment in friendship and conjugal love.

Looking back upon this consideration of values, I should
distinguish two lines of thought. One regards objects or terms
of volitional acts. I say "objects or terms" to allow for the
distinction between acts which tend toward (or "intend" in the

---

[10] See WILLIAM A. VAN ROO, S.J., *The Mystery* (Rome: Gregorian University Press, 1971) pp. 269-284: "Love in Fellowship."

phenomenological sense) objects and those which tend toward persons, human or divine. Such objects or terms include sense pleasure, biological and vital values, intellectual, aesthetic, volitional, economic, social, and religious values. In this line of thought religious values too figure among the objects or terms of volitional acts. This range of terms includes what some distinguish as objective and subjective values. I can intend both the pleasant object and the desired feeling of pleasure. Furthermore, the distinction of personal, social, and interpersonal values expands the range of terminal values. The other line of thought regards moral value as the rightness of human acts themselves. Though the many objective or terminal values differ in rank, considered in themselves, still at any given moment a man must decide what is reasonable for him to do here and now. Without a change in my basic orientation to God, I must often ask what I am to do here and now, what is good for me in this situation: to go ahead working on this section, or to go for a cup of tea, or to listen to music; or, in another situation, to stop my work to help a friend or stranger in need. There is no absolute norm for such decisions. I must decide here and now, in view of my purpose in life and of the more particular goals within my personal vocation, what is really good for me to do. And hopefully I will do it.

As human intellect is open to an ever-challenging mystery, never to be held fully in understanding, so human striving for the good tends toward a bewildering manifold of values. The known good and evil embrace all that man knows by sense to be good or bad for him: for intellect and volition penetrate and subsume the whole range of sense knowledge and appetite. Far beyond the objects of sense knowledge—or beyond those dimensions of the objects which can be held somehow by sense— man can tend toward all the values which he can know, which he can imagine and conceive as possible, and to which he can aspire.

The basic act of will is love, universally regarding the good, ranging from the "love" which is pure sense craving or satisfaction to the noblest mutual love of two persons who crave and rest content in the wellbeing of the beloved. As a certain order may be discerned in the values which appeal to man, so too an order may be discerned in human volitional acts, or dimensions of volitional action. Philosophers and theologians have analyzed human volitional action, and have sought to work out a normative knowledge of the manner of acting which is worthy of men. It is beyond my concern to attempt to review here the results of their efforts. My only purpose now is to recall something of the vast array of values and volitional acts which make human life problematic. Man cannot act except for what seems to him to be good, even in the flight from evil. Faced with a bewildering manifold of values, he is often perplexed. Sadder than the perplexity of the person seeking to act as he ought is the disarray of the thought of the very moral philosophers who should offer him guidance. The complexity of man's life gives us some clue to the range of his symbolizing. Eventually, in the complementarity which characterizes reflection upon man, insight into his symbolizing and into the roles of his symbols can contribute in turn to some deeper understanding of man and his striving, of morality, and of religion.

Content with pointing to the general areas of the philosophy of man and of moral philosophy and theology for the investigation of human action, I should like to make a few reflections on the basic act of love and something of its mystery.

As love is the basic emotion or passion, and all other emotions are somehow intelligible in their relationship to love, so at the level of volitional response to good and evil love is the basic act, and it is somehow the source of all other volitional acts. Not only do intellect and will permeate and subsume emotions, but volitional acts parallel emotions, responding to aspects of the good and evil known only by intellect. So love, desire, joy, hate, aversion, sorrow, hope and daring, fear and despair, and anger have their counterparts at the level of will. In a sense they are not "counterparts", not another set of responses of "pure spirit" to a good or evil known by pure intellect. All of our intellectual and volitional acts are enfleshed. All intellectual grasp is conditioned by, and accompanied by, some image deriving from perception. All action, even in the pursuit of the loftiest ideal grasped by the most profound act of intellect, is in the concrete, in the world of existing persons and things. Our fully human response to good and evil is fully human: with the blend of all elements which together characterize the human mode of being. We are men, not angels with bodies.

There are some important implications of the priority of love in human life. Love, the response to what is known as good congenial, compatible, somehow fulfilling, is the source and the animating principle of desire and striving, and it flowers in the joy of union. Love tends to full union, but in its mystery it draws strength from an initial union: for the lover possesses the beloved in knowledge, holding the mystery of its being, and being impelled by the desire for the completion of a union which has already begun. Love gives meaning too to hate and aversion, fear and flight. In themselves these would be unintelligible: the liberation from fear and evil is itself a relative good, for the flight from evil is a flight from what menaces the good which is loved. Liberation is not an end in itself. Liberation and freedom are from something, but unless they are for something they are ultimately meaningless. Liberation without love, without a good which is cherished, would end in a shudder of relief, but with a sense of revulsion for a world which would hold no value, a world which would stir only a reaction of repugnance, and flight and liberation offering only freedom from evil in a meaningless void.

All love seeks some fulfillment, but there are varieties of loves, which vary greatly in their prospects of fulfillment. Any love may be frustrated by failure to attain the cherished good. Some loves can only frustrate even in the attainment. Consider, then, a diversity of loves and of their promise of fulfillment. Love is *of* something or someone, and *for* something or someone. A love which ultimately would be for some thing, for the benefit and fulfillment of that thing, would offer little hope of fulfillment of the lover himself. A man can save his money to provide for his pet dog, as some have done, but for all his good intent and generosity he is a sad spectacle.

All love is for the lover himself, even when he is seeking good for another person whom he loves. Though some have written of the beauty of disintersted love, selfless love, I think that completely selfless love is a mirage which vanishes when one draws near to examine it. Such alleged disinterested love is always regarded as an especially noble love, devoted to the beloved without regard for self. Yet, to love in this way is regarded as noble. Noble love, recognized as such, ennobles the lover himself: he is a better man for loving with complete devotion to his beloved. He knows that this is a noble love, that it is good for him to love in this way. He is enriched: such love is good for him too.

Yet noble love is not just for self, for the lover, but for one whom he loves, for whom he desires and seeks good. If love is considered from the point of view of the one for whom the good is loved, love culminates in a good which is for both lover and beloved.

If we consider the objects or terms of love, *of* which it is, the varying degrees of possible fulfillment are manifest. Whoever seeks sense pleasure or things faces ultimate frustration rather than fulfillment. His pleasures are fleeting, and he himself gradually wears out in their pursuit and enjoyment. External goods, riches, esteem, fame—all these leave him empty, for he cannot take them to himself: he loves a good with which intimate union is impossible. Of all possible terms of love, persons are the noblest, and persons cannot be had. They can love and be loved, they can be ennobled in the gift of themselves, and they can find the greatest human fulfillment in mutual knowledge and love, mutual gift of self, a blending of their lives in a fulness which is impossible except in mutual love.

Finally, I should like to say something about an ill-starred distinction between vertical and horizontal loves. As the notion goes, our love of God, or of the supreme Good, is a vertical love; our love of our fellow human persons and of things is horizontal. Such a conception distorts the human project, and rends the lives of those who take it seriously and seek to order their lives and their loves on the pattern of the twofold direction of love.

There is an element of truth in the notion of a horizontal love. A man whose sense of values is scant may grope and strike out in many directions toward particular values which are only relative in value, though he does not understand their limits. In a sense he tends horizontally toward some limited good or goods. He tends toward some goal, and all of his values are meaningful for him, they "count" in his world, in so far as they are related to attaining his goal. Various men, at times in their lives, may strive thus for the greatest possible pleasure, or for athletic prowess, or for intellectual achievement, or for political success. They simply have not faced a challenge concerning their supreme value. Yet they may live lives which are remarkably integrated, directed toward the achievement of what they desire most.

The problem, and the alleged distinction of vertical and horizontal loves, as some understand it, comes when a man or woman penetrates the mystery of his or her world, seeks the supreme Good, God, and tries to integrate his or her life. The distinction of vertical and horizontal loves is an illusion, and it tends to haunt and perplex, to rend the life of one who seeks to love both God and creatures as he or she should. One does not discover God, and affirm his existence and supreme goodness, by turning away from the mystery of the world and all that fills it. Rather, penetrating the mystery of its being and goodness, one finds that its goodness is a share in the goodness of God. For one who loves God and seeks to integrate his life in the pursuit of union with God, all noble love is Godward. He does not turn from God to love creatures, nor take away from God to give to creatures. Recognizing the source and ground of all their being and goodness, he loves God in them, and them in Him. Any love of a terminal good seeks that good in all else that is loved as somehow participating it. Any such love is single in its direction. When the Good which is the goal is God, then the single direction of all noble loves in an integrated life is Godward.

MOTOR ACTION

One element of human action remains to be considered: motor action. Since I *am* in space and time, I must *move* to attain a distant good. In fact I must move even to think about it or desire it, for I am in a humanly bodily way, and I am by being in movement continually in countless ways. Emotion involves a conscious motor impulse toward the attractive good, or away from the repugnant evil. Volition is not the act of an angel, not even of an angel inhabiting a body. It too has its bodily factor. Not only can I not will without expending energy, but also I cannot do anything about the good which is my goal without acting; and I act by moving somehow.

I do not move my body. *I* do not *have* a body. I am bodily, whatever else I also am. My "will" does not move my body. I respond humanly to a good which I know humanly. I act freely with a human freedom, not angelic, much less divine.

Human freedom and "movement of the body" is a scandal and an absurdity only to those who dogmatically limit reality to what can be established according to physical and chemical laws. But they are scandalized, and their scientific worlds are disturbed, before they face the problem of man. The living organism is a scandal and an absurdity to them, for they cannot approach it with a method which may hold its mystery and find in it some degree of understanding.

Acting freely in a human way, I do not violate the laws of the conservation of energy. The physical and chemical readings of my every action could be taken, if adequate instruments could be devised. What escapes such observation is the unique structure, the order, which characterizes human being in the world. That order can be observed, and it can be understood to some extent in the grasp of a field of relationships. But relationships, order, and structure are not palpable or measurable, nor do they function as added causes, rivalling—and at times seemingly frustrating—the "causes" which figure in the empirical scientific account of everything in the world. I am in a human way, and the "laws" of my being can be grasped. The laws are not elements which compose me, nor are any of the relationships which can be understood. I *am* in such a way as to operate in distinctive ways. I am not a set of relationships, nor a field of relationships, nor a structure. I *am* in such a way as to ground all of the relationships and structures which can be discerned and conceptualized in a reflection upon my mode of being. Any further eventual question about the human a priori, human nature and powers, pertains to a continuing thrust of inquiring intellect, and any eventual intelligible answers to such questions would neither rival nor seek to supplant what can be known of man by empirical science.

CHAPTER V

THE SPHERE

INTRODUCTION

Thus far we have considered some of the prominent features of human experience, and then reflected on the structures of man's principal conscious operations. Of all the characteristics of human experience, two are most important for us in our effort to understand more of the mystery of man, of his symbolizing, and of the wide range of his symbols. One is the unity and continuity of all human operations. The other is the ever-present, endlessly varying structure of figure and ground.

Having reserved some further questions along the way, we must turn to consider them now in a more profound reflection on the structures of human experience. With regard to continuity, against the background of our consideration of individual operations, we may reflect further on aspects of the blending of these operations in the full concrete human experience. Moreover, we must consider the mystery of continuity not only within every mode of conscious operation and among the many modes, but also between the realms of the conscious and the nonconscious, and in the larger mystery of man's links with others in the many worlds in which he lives. With regard to the figure-ground structure, we must consider it too in the larger mystery of the total setting of man's operation.

Since this will be a long chapter, crucial in the whole of this book, I wish to explain what I am doing and why. Symbolizing and symbols can be understood only in the setting of the mystery of man. When we begin to probe that mystery, we find a bewildering array of operations within the whole of human experience. The continuity of man's many levels of being and operating, his involvement in a manifold of worlds, and the suggested analogies ranging through the whole of his manner of being raise questions concerning the most suitable order in which to proceed. Where can we begin with the greatest hope of finding an intelligible structure which may help us to understand man and the range of his symbolizing activity? I am convinced that the best starting point is the reflection on the structures of fully conscious human operation. What we discover there can suggest an intelligible account of the whole range of human operations at all levels.

We can learn best about man and the structure of human experience not from the surd of sickness, fragmentation, or dissolution of human life, but from the mystery of health and fulness of life; not from the surd of the unconscious, through postulates and hypotheses concerning the unknown, but from the mystery of fully conscious life, with the richness and endless variations upon structures of the experience in which a man is most fully himself, revealing most properly what it is to be human.

We shall begin, therefore, with the mystery of fully conscious life. Considering the variations of focal and marginal consciousness, we may recognize the fulness of life in focal awareness, and the decline toward the marginal in the vague awareness of self in conscious action, and in the vague awareness of the marginal in the objective field. Again, we may find a relative fulness of conscious life in moments of keen attention, and a shading of structures in moments of relative inattention. Structures clearly grasped in fully conscious experience may help to understand barely intelligible structures of diminished consciousness, and even of subconscious and unconscious life. The phenomenon of thresholds of consciousness suggests a continuity of structure. What happens at the threshold is that I become conscious of an operation. What is new is not the structure of the operation, but its degree of intensity and my awareness of it at this degree. Only at a certain degree of intensity do I become conscious of an operation which has the same basic structure beneath or above the threshold. Beyond the reaches of conscious, subconscious, and unconscious, the seemingly vast realm of the nonconscious may be intelligible in terms of the analogy of structures grasped in full conscious life.

By "human operation" I mean much more than what moral philosophers and theologians have meant by the term "human act" and equivalents. For them a human act is one which is performed with full knowledge and consent: a fully moral act, good or bad, for which the subject is fully responsible. I am taking *human operation* or *human act* in a much broader sense,

including every act, every event in which the human subject
is somehow active, in the whole range of being and operation
which bears the mark of properly human organization. All
events which occur in the human person, from the fully deliberate act of knowledge and love to the firing of a neuron far
beneath the level of consciousness, bear the mark of properly
human organization. Every cell in my body is human, and is
uniquely mine. All of my experience is grounded in my total
personal human constitution. Moreover, all of my operations
stand out against the ground of my personal involvement in
the many worlds in which I am. They are somehow conditioned and qualified by all that has contributed to making me
what I am at the moment in which I act.

My working hypothesis is that there is a manifold continuity and analogy running through the whole of my being and
operation, and that I can come to understand my properly
human and personal being best of all by considering the structures which stand out most clearly in my fully conscious operations.

Although I do not intend to proceed through a dialectic of
opinions, it may be helpful to indicate briefly the relationships
of my reflection to aspects of the thought of others which may
be familiar to some of my readers. I should point to four
distinctions which bear somehow on the matter which we shall
be considering. First, Lonergan's distinction between acts as
conscious and as intentional[1] calls attenion to the sharp distinction between the subject's self-awareness, which is a feature
of all conscious operation, and his knowledge of the structure
of his operations, which, according to Lonergan, is reached only
by directing acts as intentional to the reflection upon the structure of conscious acts. In such a reflection one objectifies the
subject, working out the structures which are intelligible in
the data of consciousness. Second, Polanyi's distinction between
focal and subsidiary awareness[2] suggests an analogous structure
which ranges over awareness of both subject and object and
knowledge of the nonconscious. Fruitful as such an analogy
may be, it leaves unattended some basic distinctions between
awareness and knowledge, subjective and objective, and between
the knowledges which may be had from the data of conscious-

---

[1] B. LONERGAN, S.J., *Method in Theology* (London: 1972) 6-20.
[2] M. POLANYI, *Personal Knowledge* (New York: c. 1964) 55-65 and
passim: see Index under "focal vs. subsidiary awareness."

ness on the one hand and from the data of objective empirical observation on the other. Third, Merleau-Ponty's distinction between the phenomenal body and the body as object[3] marks the difference between a phenomenological reflection on structures of conscious experience and the knowledge of the human body to be gained by empirical science. Fourth, Ricoeur's distinction between the body as subject and the body as object again marks the difference between phenomenological and empirical knowledges of man; and Ricoeur's recognition of the role of diagnostic empirical knowledge brings out the fruitful complementarity of the two knowledges.[4] All of these distinctions bear meaningfully on aspects of the matter which we shall be considering. All of them call for further elaboration.

GROUND, FIELD, HORIZON, WORLD, AND SPHERE

To forestall as far as possible bewilderment at an apparently loose and fluctuating terminology in the reflections which will follow, I should like to indicate here the analogous senses and the relationships of five terms which I shall use: ground, field, horizon, world, and sphere. All of them are used in broadly analogous senses. They are related in their analogous senses, and I may use one rather than another as more apt in a particular context.

Lest this very effort at clarification of terminology be an occasion of misunderstanding rather than a help to understanding, I should like to indicate how the terminology in question stands in relation to rigorous scientific terminology on the one hand and fully philosophical terminology on the other. What I am using here is neither scientific terminology, particularly in what regards the notion of field or field definition, nor a full philosophical elaboration of analogy. The five terms which I am employing are metaphors from common sense thought and discourse, taken over to serve in a sort of phenomenological elaboration of intelligible structures. They are not a sort of poor man's pseudo-physics. They suggest from various points of view aspects of reality which escape the wonderfully sharp conceptualization of modern physics. They are, therefore, neither

---

[3] M. MERLEAU-PONTY, *Phenomenology of Perception* (London: c. 1962) 105-106.

[4] P. RICOEUR, *Le Volontaire et l'involontaire* (Paris: 1963) 12-16.

a surrogate for physics nor an impoverishment of thought. They are steps toward a kind of understanding which far surpasses so-called exact science, holding intelligible relationships which could not be discovered in the kinds of readings which physics takes as its data. Nor is the terminology strictly philosophical. I refer to analogy, but the five terms which I am using are rather metaphorical than analogical. When I shall have worked out the meanings which the terms have in my discourse, I shall indicate further what basic analogy underlies them. In that I shall be indicating how further philosophical thought would continue this phenomenological reflection.

I take *ground* broadly as the setting in which an act or an object stands out prominently. Though its sense is most obvious in discourse concerning visual perception, it may be understood in a far broader analogous sense which makes it an apt term in our wide-ranging consideration. In the context of discourse about visual perception, the ground is the setting of the figure which stands out as the prominent object perceived. Perception focusses at any moment on a figure. The ground, the surroundings, is perceived, but is not at the center, the focal point, of perception. Yet perception shifts continually, and what lay in the ground a moment before may now be the figure upon which perception focusses. In the continuing perceptual experience, the ground from which a succession of figures stand out may be said to assure the unity and continuity of the whole shifting perceptual experience, subjective and objective.

Extended beyond the realm of visual perception, *ground* may be understood analogously of any other mode of perception or of the total perceptual experience including all modes: visual, auditory, tactile, olfactory, gustatory. Against the ground, either an act or an object may be regarded as standing out as figure. Subjectively, the conscious act itself stands out prominently, as in the case of an explicit act made with full attention, standing out against a vague cognitive ground, or a mood or sentiment, or a half desire. Objectively, what the conscious act regards or intends stands out against the ground of the cognitive, emotive, volitional, or motor object.

In a series of further extensions of the notion, ground may be understood as the setting of any act or object. First, in the whole of conscious experience, any act of knowledge, emotion, volition, or motor action may stand out against the ground of total consciousness; and the object of such an act may stand out against its broader objective setting. Beyond the setting of the whole of conscious life, any conscious act or object can be understood as standing out against the full reality of the person, including the whole nonconscious underpinning of his humanly bodily being; and the full reality of the world in which man is involved beneath the level of consciousness. Finally, within the physical universe in which man's operations are set, every act or "object" may be regarded in its intersubjective setting, human or transcendent. As *ground* is extended far beyond its original usage, it becomes less apt as a metaphor or loose analogical term, and the wide-ranging conception may be expressed better in terms of field, horizon, or world.

From the outset, the common-sense notion of *field* is broader than that of *ground*. Whereas *ground* as applied to perceptual experience, is the immediate setting of a sharply perceived object, the *field* is the larger setting within which a succession of objects may be perceived in the continual shifting of perception. Applicable to both the subjective and the objective settings, *field* may be understood in the same series of extended usages as *ground*. It is more apt to suggest the "area" or setting within which persons, things, and operations may be understood in a network of many relationships.

Horizon may be taken in an original sense to designate the limit of the visual field, a limit which varies as one shifts position. Beyond this sense, the notion of horizon may be extended to the limit of any field of experience, subjective or objective. It is the present limit of a person's experience, a tentative limit, ever shifting as further experience broadens one's subjective and objective fields.

World, in phenomenological usage, is extremely vague, yet it has the advantage of suggesting important aspects of the mystery of man and of human experience. Merleau-Ponty took *world* as "the horizon of horizons".[5] Taking *horizon* as the present limit of visual perceptual experience, one would understand the world to be the all-containing reality setting the ultimate limits of perceptual experience. Even in this sense, pertaining to visual perceptual experience, the notion of the world can be held only in a uneasy relationship with that of the physical universe, which somehow sets the limits of all possible human perceptual experience. When one extends the notion of world to all orders of human experience, both the vagueness

---

[5] *Op. cit.*, 330.

and the suggestive power of the notion increase. Man lives in many worlds, and he can come to live in many more.

I suggest *sphere* as a metaphor more apt and more adequate that that of *world*. One cannot perceive a sphere, but one can conceive of it. Considering the sphere in relation to its center, one can suggest the most expressive comparison to bring out much of the mystery of man's way of being and operating. Whereas *field, horizon,* and *world* as "horizon of horizons" evoke the image of a plane surface, on which attention or action may be directed horizontally toward any point on the horizon, the sphere suggests an infinitely greater potential "direction" of man's multiple intentionality. Every person is at the center of a sphere. The enclosing surface is the total reality within which he is and operates. As an infinity of points may be designated on the surface of the sphere, an infinity of potential objects or terms of man's operation may be designated in the enfolding reality. Involved in continuous indefinitely varied interaction with other persons and things with whom he is, man reacts to them in special ways in the many modes of his conscious operation. Every conscious operation regards some one of the potential objects or terms, and with varying degrees of intensity and varying blends of modes of operation, man's act has a multiple intentionality: cognitive, affective, volitional, and motor.

All five terms, ground, field, horizon, world, and sphere, are metaphorical, somewhat vague and tentative. Without further attempt to sharpen instruments whose materials cannot be brought to a fine edge, I shall proceed in a manner which I hope will be intelligible. At the end of the chapter I shall attempt to indicate the basic analogy which underlies these metaphors.

The Conscious Field

We can approach the consideration of the conscious field by reflecting on what in a limited sense can be called the perceptual field, noting its limits, and extending our reflection to other elements which blend in the total conscious field.

A few days ago, early in the morning, I stood just south of what was once the site of the entrance to a residence hall in the 1100 block of West Michigan Street in Milwaukee. I had known the place long ago as a student of Marquette University, and then through the years of its decline before its recent

transformation. I was looking now south-southeast over a grassy
plot rising gently and then sloping down toward the new curving
streets, and beyond the lawn and streets to the sprawling expressway interchange, with its continual rush and roar of traffic.
What lay before my eyes was, in a limited sense, my visual
perceptual field, within which my gaze could wander and fix
in succession objects within that field. In a broader sense, my
perceptual field extended beyond what I saw as I looked south-
southeast from that point. I could turn, and take in other
stretches of a visual field in continuity with what I now beheld.
I could move and perceive other scenes and objects from other
points of view. In unbroken continuity my visual field lay far
beyond where I was, over the whole world through which I
could move. Rich as the notion of the perceptual field may
seem to be in this mystery of its seemingly endless unbroken
extent, it is a severely abstract, limited notion, only a first observation, a first reading taken upon a total experience which
is far richer.

The severe abstraction and limitation of that notion of the
perceptual field was brought home to me recently by a reflection on a hypothetical shift of positions which would show the
limits of the visual field in its isolation. Near where I stood
there is now a new office building, Coughlin Hall. I imagined
what the view might be from a window in an office of that
building. Later that day at lunch, by chance I talked with a
friend who occupies such an office, and I was able to compare
our two experiences of roughly the same scene. With slight
differences of perspective, the visual element of our experiences
was much the same. The abstractness of the visual experience
is brought out by partial further consideration of the two experiences in their fulness.

As my gaze wandered over that scene, I felt beneath my
feet the slope of the landscaped plot and the soft springiness
of the full turf, and felt on my face the soft warm humid south-
westerly breeze. I could hear only the steady roar of traffic,
from which repeatedly the louder roar of individual trucks stood
out. As I looked and felt and heard, I remembered, and imagined, and felt joy at the simple beauty of the sloping lawn,
sadness at the thought of the life which had once enriched this
place and which was no more, and awe, revulsion, and wonder
at the monstrous expressway, symbol of our age. Against the
ground of all that I had been and all that I was, I lived that
fleeting moment in one man's life, and from where I was I

prayed. My experience was not merely perceptual, much less merely visual. I grasped my situation in that world, and something of the mystery of the many worlds which were symbolized in all that I saw and felt and understood. I felt and willed and moved, musing as I went.

From where he sits daily in his office in Coughlin Hall, my friend looks out at times upon the same scene. He hears, and feels, and remembers, and imagines, and understands, and prays, but how differently! In his soundproofed room he hears no roar of traffic, but the music from his radio, which he uses to cover distracting noises and to provide a gentle soothing auditory background for his work. He does not feel sloping springy turf and soft summer breeze, but carpeting and swivel chair and conditioned air. His memories are not of this scene as it was years ago, for he came only recently from a distance, and never knew here what was once a neighborhood. And so on through all the modes of his conscious experience he looks on that scene from another man's unique point of view, in another unique total conscious experience.

Our total conscious experience is rich and complex. Without pretense of cataloguing elements of which it is composed as if of parts, we may discern aspects of a whole which is visual, auditory, tactile, olfactory, gustatory, "memorial", imaginative, intellectual, emotive, volitional, motor. We are aware of space and time, and of our total situation. We are aware of others, persons and things, and respond to them in the endless interplay of all the persons and things with which we share our world. Our total conscious experience itself is a ground against which a succession of varied figures stand out, as one mode of experience and one object or term takes its turn at front center of our lives.

Our conscious life is manifold, a blend of many elements in continuity. All of its elements are "conscious": they figure in our consciousness, in our awareness. What is it that makes them "conscious"? What permeates all of them? Is it a form of knowledge? What is the relationship of consciousness and knowledge? These are the questions to which we must turn.

1. *Consciousness, intentionality,* and *knowledge.* I understand consciousness as a state or condition of a subject which is capable of knowing. Below the human level one can consider the consciousness of animals, of varying modes and degrees of perfection. My concern is human consciousness. Conscious-

ness is awareness. The notion is simple and irreducible. One can grasp it in the experience of that clear awareness which stands out as one wakes from sleep, or regains one's senses after a fainting spell or a period of anesthesia. We know from experience the contrast between awareness and unawareness— or. more properly, we are vividly "aware of awareness" in our return to it after it has been interrupted. Besides the contrast between awareness and nonawareness, we come to reflect upon the distinctions between two diverse orders of awareness: in waking consciousness and in dream.

One can distinguish three senses in which *conscious* is used. First, and most properly, a person who is aware is conscious: *I* am conscious: aware of others, and of myself in the very acts in which I am aware of others. Secondly, in a derived sense, the acts of which I am aware are conscious acts. Strictly speaking, they are not conscious: they are terms or objects of my consciousness. In a third sense, by further extension of usage, one can speak of one's conscious field: the whole range of subjective acts and their objective terms, of which one is conscious.

Taking *conscious* in the second sense, as applied to acts of which a person is conscious, one can speak of such acts as being both conscious and intentional. Conscious acts are *of* someone or something. Their being *of* some object or term is the relationship which in phenomenological terminology is called *intentionality*. Intentionality is the relationship of acts to objects or terms, and it is multiple. Cognitive, emotive, volitional, and motor acts are all related to terms or objects: they are *of* someone or something; they *intend* (in this technical sense) or *tend to* some object or some other subject. Their intentionality differs according to the difference of their structure as acts and their relationship to their terms.

Whereas intentionality is multiple, and cognition is only one of the modes of intentionality, consciousness is always cognitive. I am conscious of my cognitive, emotive, volitional, and motor acts, but my consciousness is always a matter of some sort of knowledge. I am not conscious *by* an emotive or volitional or motor act. I am aware of myself in my cognitive, emotive, volitional, and motor acts. I am aware of the acts, and in a derived sense I am aware of their terms or objects. Awareness is a state in which I somehow hold the mystery of the being and presence of others, and of myself in the very acts in which I tend variously to them. It is an aspect of cognitive intentionality, and we shall have to consider further its place in the full mystery of human knowledge.

Earlier in this chapter I mentioned Lonergan's distinction between acts as conscious and as intentional. He is concerned with the distinction between awareness of self and knowledge of self, and with a sense of what is involved methodologically in "intentionality analysis", which is the reflection upon the structure of one's intentional acts. In such analysis, according to Lonergan, one turns acts as intentional upon acts as conscious, to reflect on the structure of the conscious acts and acquire a knowledge of them. Subsequently, for Lonergan, one appropriates this knowledge of the structure of one's conscious acts: acting now consciously with a knowledge of the structure of conscious acts.

As I understand the matter, there are two obscurities in Lonergan's thought here. One regards the distinction between conscious and intentional, and the prescription of turning acts as intentional upon acts as conscious, to observe their structure. The other obscurity clouds the important "appropriation" of the knowledge of structure. I shall say something here of the first obscurity, and return later to discuss the second.

Lonergan's obscurity in the first matter results from an apparent momentary disregard of what I have distinguished as the first and second meanings of *conscious*. He slips from conscious subject to conscious acts, and deals with acts which are both conscious and intentional. In the strict and most proper sense, *I* am conscious. I am conscious of others, of the intentional acts by which I regard others in various modes (cognitive, emotive, volitional, and motor), and of myself "caught in the act" of intending. If I slip from the consideration of the conscious subject to that of conscious intentional acts, I slip into an equivocation of *conscious*, which blurs the problem and the solution.

How, then, can the problem be brought into sharper focus, and the solution be given clearly and unequivocally? I should put the matter in this way. I am conscious of my intentional acts, and of some differences of the structure of my experience in acts of cognition, emotion, volition, and movement. To know the structure of my intentional acts, I reflect by cognitional acts bearing upon all four types of intentional acts. The knowledge which I acquire in such intentionality analysis is gained not by turning acts as "intentional" upon acts as "conscious", but by deliberate, explicit cognitive acts focussed successively

on the different types of intentional acts. The analysis should
be attributed not vaguely to "intentional acts", but sharply and
properly to cognitive acts.

So much for the first obscurity. I shall deal later with
the second: "appropriation".

What is overlooked in Lonergan's whole treatment of consciousness and knowledge is this: consciousness itself is a kind
of knowledge. It is somehow part of the mystery of my knowing. My consciousness of others, of my intentional acts, and
of myself, is itself intelligible only as an aspect of the mystery
of knowledge. The distinction between my consciousness of
myself and my explicit knowledge of myself, gained by a reflection on structures, is due to the limitations, the imperfections,
of my human knowledge. I shall be dealing at length in this
chapter with consciousness as knowledge.

2. *Threefold consciousness.* I am conscious, or aware,
(1) of the other persons or things which are the terms of all
of my intentional acts; (2) of all of my acts by which I intend
them (cognitive, emotive, volitional, and motor); (3) of myself
intending them. Consciousness of others could be called *objective* consciousness: awareness of objects and of other subjects in one's field of action. Consciousness of one's own intentional acts and of oneself could be called *subjective.* Returning to the three senses in which *conscious* is used, I recognize that I am conscious of both the acts which are called
conscious in the second sense, and of the objects which are
conscious in the third sense. I am conscious in the first sense,
as the conscious subject. Yet I am conscious of myself only
as I am aware of myself in the acts by which I am consciously
intending others: only in these acts do I "catch myself".

In all three instances, in the consciousness of others, of
one's own intentional acts, and of onself, there is a mystery
of distinction and multiplicity which are rooted in human limitation. I *am* in a very limited mode, to a limited degree. I act
continually to transcend my present limitations. I act with
respect to a manifold objective field, for I am in a world in
which being is diffused and limited. I seek the true and the
good in which I can come to the realization of my own potential
fulness of being. As the true and the good in the world of
persons and things is diffused and multiple, so the acts by
which I intend them are multiple. These acts are the radiation,
the fanning out, of my intentionality, my multiple relationships

to the true and the good. I am related to the true by the many cognitive acts of all modes, in which and through which in different degrees I come gradually to a greater knowledge, to the truth by which I am more fully. The multiplicity of the modes of my cognitive acts (perception, memory, imagination, insight, understanding, judgment) and the succession of acts in every mode, are part of the mystery of limitation and diffusion of my humanly bodily being. So too I am related to the good and the bad by acts whose variety (emotive, volitional, and motor) and number reflect my human manner of being. By all the acts through which I am united with the good, principally through the love of the good, I grow in the goodness which in the most proper sense brings me to my relative fulness of being.

The mystery of division and multiplicity runs to the heart of the conscious subject, aware of himself. Because I am not perfect, but seek to transcend my limitations in acts by which I tend to the true and the good, I am obviously distinct from both the others which I intend and the acts by which I intend them. I am neither the others nor the acts by which I transcend myself in tending to others. But there is a further mysterious division. Since it is only in my conscious intentional acts, distinct from me, that I can become conscious of myself, there is a strange division between me, the conscious subject, and the self of which I am conscious. So my "self" is a strange, unique sort of "other", of which I am aware only as I catch myself "dwelling in" my intentional acts. By another series of cognitive acts I can reflect upon my conscious acts and upon myself, "objectifying" them and myself, coming to a knowledge of the multiple relationships by which both the conscious acts and the self are intelligible. The self, then, is a unique sort of "other", revealing and concealing itself in its acts, to be detected and known explicitly by a process of reflection upon intelligible structures, but never to be laid open completely, since it is part of the mystery of the very act of laying open. In every successive act by which I reflect upon the structure of my intentional acts and upon myself, I am conscious of myself reflecting, and it would take another act of reflection to know the self detected in that act, and so to infinity.

3. *The peak of consciousness.* Following the general strategy which I have indicated, we shall seek to discover the structure of human experience by reflecting on what can be called the peak of consciousness: full awareness of object, act, and self.

a. *Four variables.* In the reflection on the peak of consciousness as contrasted with lesser degrees of awareness, four variables must be kept in mind. First, we must distinguish *focal* and *marginal* consciousness, a distinction bearing on the terms of consciousness: what we are conscious of. Focal and marginal is a variation on the distinction of figure and ground. Second, distinguish *objective* and *subjective* among the terms of consciousness. The objective includes all that is other than the conscious subject and his acts: the term *objective* is somewhat loose, since it applies both to objects (things or "elements" in a field) and to other subjects, persons. *Subjective* covers both the intentional acts and the self of which the subject is conscious. Third, again among the terms of consciousness, distinguish the kinds of intentional acts of which one is conscious: cognitive, emotive, volitional, and motor, with all of their variations. Finally, regarding what could be called qualities of intentional acts, mark variations of attention, intensity, or concentration.

Regarding these sets of variables, I should call attention to the relationship of the first two sets. The distinction between focal and marginal can be applied to both the subjective and the objective fields. Its application to the objective field is obvious in the normal consideration of figure and ground. It is important to note its application to the subjective field as well. Human experience is complex, and we experience a varying blend of operations, any one of which may stand out as figure against the ground of our general conscious subjective field. As I sit here composing at the typewriter, I am aware of many aspects of my total present experience: posture, bodily tone, relative freshness of mind, multiple perceptive experience, understanding of my situation, a varying play of emotion and will and motor impulses and action. I am aware principally of my efforts to continue this reflection and to elaborate my thought, and when I succeed in holding to that task with attention and concentration, that effort stands out as focal in my subjective conscious field. Yet I am not a machine which can be turned on and trusted to continue running regularly. Weariness, flagging attention, the intervention of any number of possible distractions setting off acts of memory, imagination, emotion—any of these can occasion or cause a shift in my focal awareness of my own subjective field.

b. *The peak.* Since any of the modes of intentional acts may be dominant at any moment, and none occurs in isolation

in total human experience, let us suppose first a situation in
which one is at the peak of consciousness in a dominantly cognitive mode of operation. I am fully conscious when, with full
attention and deliberate marshalling of my cognitive powers,
I perform a series of cognitive operations, all directed to knowing the object upon which I am concentrating. Knowing is not
a matter of a flash, occurring in one of the modes of cognition.
It involves deploying a series of operations of perception, memory, imagination, insight, conception, judgment, reasoning. It is
a process of probing, grasping, reasoning, judging, and reflecting
critically upon the fruit of one's effort. It occurs in no fixed
pattern. It cannot be programmed rigidly, without danger of
impeding the occurrence of an insight which could come only
in the course of the free play of all of the cognitive powers,
applied as they are necessary to follow the developing cognitive
experience.

At any moment of such predominantly cognitive experience
I am fully conscious in an act which regards some object as
focal in the total cognitive field. Full consciousness at the focal
point is continually shifting, and involves a succession and variety of focal-marginal relationships. First, as long as my operation continues in a predominantly cognitive mode, a cognitive
act and object stand out as focal: all other modes of operation
blended in the total concrete experience are marginal: emotion,
will, motor action. Second, within the cognitive experience as
it proceeds, a succession of different acts and objects are focal,
depending on whether at the moment I am probing the perceptual field, or memory, or imagination, or relationships which
I have grasped and which I am now trying to hold in a single
intelligible structure as I conceptualize.

The distinction of focal and marginal, then, regards the
objective and subjective fields. Within the latter it applies
to cognitive as opposed to other modes of intentional operation.
Within the continuing, varying cognitive process the distinction
applies to the act and object which stand out at any moment,
in relation to the total subjective and objective cognitive field.

Analogously, any other mode of intentional operation may
stand out as dominant in my awareness at any moment: emotive, volitional, or motor. Within the dominant mode, at any
given moment one act and object are focal in relation to the
rest of the subjective and objective intentional field of that
mode.

c. *The slopes.* If consciousness is full at the focal point, the peak, then one can contrast such full, peak consciousness with a variety of modes and degrees of diminished awareness. We may say that consciousness diminishes as it descends two slopes, objective and subjective. In both the objective and the subjective fields, what is marginal figures less prominently in our consciousness, less and less as it is farther from the focus. We are only dimly aware of the extremely marginal, the horizonal, in both objective and subjective fields. Again, the descent or diminution can regard the relationships of acts and objects within one mode of intentionality, or the relationships of acts and objects of one mode to those of all other modes at a given moment.

With regard to cognitive experience in particular, we are at the peak of consciousness in an act which either focusses upon an object which we are probing in the objective field, or objectifies the subject in an act of reflection in which we probe the structure of our intentional acts or advance further to consider our self. We have a lesser consciousness down the objective slope, regarding all that is marginal in the objective field, or down the subjective slope, regarding our intentional acts or our selves as we are aware of them in acts which directly intend the other.

d. *The continuity of consciousness.* One could reflect upon the continuity of consciousness in at least two different senses. First, continuity of consciousness could be considered as the unbroken oneness, the unity in diffusion and duration, of the conscious subject. Second, one could understand continuity of consciousness as referring to the unbroken unity of the conscious field, subjective and objective. In this second consideration, *conscious* would be taken in the second and third senses which I indicated above: [6] the acts and objects of which I am aware are conscious: it is of them that I am conscious. For the moment I am concerned with the second sense of continuity of consciousness.

Looking back upon the reflections which have preceded, we may note various aspects of a certain continuity of our conscious field, subjective and objective. First, there is a continuity of focal and marginal: within the marginal field we shift focus continually. Within any period of waking consciousness (in the sense of the subject's awareness) we experience a continual succession of conscious acts, regarding a succession of objects dif-

---

[6] See p. 114.

fused in our unbroken experience of space and time. Second, there is a simultaneity and varying blend of all of our modes of intentional acts, cognitive, emotive, volitional, and motor. In an unbroken experience we shift modes of dominant intentionality. Third, there is a continuity of our awareness of ourselves in all of our intentional acts and our knowledge of our acts and of ourselves which we attain as we focus cognitive acts upon them to discern the intelligible structures of our modes of operation and of being. The self of which I am aware in all of my conscious acts lies somehow within my cognitive field. As I can shift from one figure to another in my objective field, so analogously I can direct cognitive acts to my act or to myself, objectifying what lay in my subjective field, making a previous conscious act, or the self detected in such an act, now the object of cognitive acts, held in focus. Though these modes of shifting differ, they are all aspects of a basic analogous continuity of our conscious field.

4. *Consciousness and knowledge.* Consciousness is part of the mystery of knowledge; yet certain distinctions must be made, and we turn to consider them now. The most important distinction is that of objective and subjective consciousness: awareness of objects, terms of our intentional acts, on the one hand; and awareness of our acts and of ourselves acting, on the other hand. Within the realms of objective and subjective consciousness we may determine differently how consciousness pertains to knowledge.

In objective consciousness let us consider first certain differences regarding cognitive acts. In full focal awareness in a cognitive act, there is a perfect coincidence of consciousness and knowledge. It is in such focal acts that we attain explicit knowledge of an object: not in a flash, not in a single isolated act, but in a continuing process of probing, understanding, and affirming, as I have described it above. In our marginal awareness of the objective ground or field, on the other hand, we have a vague, implicit, primordial knowledge. Focal and marginal objective consciousness, therefore, correspond to explicit knowledge and implicit or primordial knowledge. They are in continuity. Within the objective field there is a continual shifting of focus, of figure against ground. The shift from implicit knowledge to explicit knowledge occurs, however, within the objective field, in a movement from one object or figure to another.

In other kinds of intentional acts, or rather in conscious

experience in which other modes of intentionality are dominant (emotive, volitional, motor) there is full focal awareness, and obviously there is a cognitive element, since we know the term of our emotive, volitional, or motor act. Moreover, in that knowledge there is a difference of focal and marginal: we are tending to this known object as it stands out against the ground. Yet cognition is not dominant: in an emotive or volitional or motor act we are not concerned primarily with probing the object to know it more explicitly. I should say, therefore, that in spite of the focal-marginal distinction within our knowledge in such an experience, knowledge itself as a whole element of the experience is marginal. To shift to explicit focal knowledge, we should have to shift the pattern of our experience, concerning ourselves now with knowing more clearly and adequately the object of the preceding intentional acts.

In subjective consciousness the matter is different. Here, within any act in which we intend an object or term, we are aware of our act and of ourselves. Such awareness too is part of the mystery of knowledge. It is marginal, not focal. It is marginal in another sense, however, from that which we noted in the objective field. In the objective field, in any explicit intentional act, there is always a figure standing out against the ground, and in a dominantly cognitive act we have explicit knowledge of the object held in focus. The shift from one figure to another, from one focal point to another, is always within the objective field. It always involves acts which regard data of sense, or data external to the subject. In subjective consciousness, on the other hand, we are aware of acts and of ourselves with a marginal knowledge; but we cannot shift to an explicit focal knowledge of our acts or ourselves by a simple shift from one figure to another, from one focal point to another, as we do in the objective field. Awareness of our intentional acts and of ourselves is always a marginal knowledge. We can come to an explicit focal knowledge only by a more radical shift from data of sense to data of consciouness. In such a shift we make a previous intentional act the object of an explicit reflection, and to the extent to which we discern the structure of that act we come to an explicit knowledge of it. By a further continuation of reflection on the implications of such acts we come to an explicit knowledge of ourselves. Awareness of acts and of ourselves as we experience it within all of our conscious operations is, therefore, always a marginal, implicit knowledge. We come to explicit knowledge only in the process of objectifying our acts and ourselves. Such objectification always lags a step behind full conscious life. In the very act by which we objectify our previous act, or ourselves as we were detected in the previous act, we are again aware of our act of objectifying, and of ourselves caught in the act of objectifying; and that element of subjective awareness would have to be objectified in turn if we desired to know it explicitly and enhance our knowledge of ourselves. Reflection on subjective consciousness, therefore, can never be complete: it would run to infinity.

A number of further questions could be raised concerning consciousness and knowledge, but they would swell this chapter excessively. I reserve them now for treatment in the next chapter, in which I shall make some further reflections on the role of intellect.

One thing remains to be observed concerning the conscious field. It is the relationship of full waking consciousness to dream. In one of the examples of concrete human experience which I described in the opening chapter (pp. 19-20) the most striking feature was the continuity of dream and waking consciousness. My dreams are mine. In dreams I am not fully aware as I am in waking consciousness; my dream does not have the consistency and coherence of waking experience; I do not have the full knowledge and deliberation and volition which would make me "responsible" for my apparent action in dream; yet when I awake I know that *I* was dreaming, and often I can recognize the links between remembered experience and dream. Consideration of the structure of figure and ground which runs through all human experience can help in the further interpretation of dreams. As every act of waking consciousness stands out against the total ground of my conscious field, and indeed against the total ground which we have not yet considered fully, so analogously my dream situations and actions stand out against my total ground, and can be interpreted only in their total setting as *my* dreams. We have begun with a reflection on the structure of full waking consciousness. What we discover there has its bearing on the interpretation of dreams.

THE NONCONSCIOUS PERSONAL GROUND

The two major themes of our reflection thus far are these: the continuity of human experience in all of its modes, and the pervading, analogous structure of figure and ground. Every human act stands out as figure against ground. Our reflection to this point would suffice to trace the total personal ground of human operations if man were a spirit, or mind, or "consciousness", as he is regarded at times by thinkers influenced by cartesian and postcartesian thought. Man is not a spirit, or mind, or consciousness, not even an incarnate spirit, mind, or consciousness. He is and he operates in a humanly bodily way. His acts stand out against a total personal ground which is more than his conscious ground. Every cell in his body is specifically human and uniquely his personally, bearing the traces of all of the physical, chemical, and biological factors conditioning his humanly bodily being and operation. Further elements of the total personal ground of human operations, therefore, are all the nonconscious underpinning of those operations. We must take note of these elements here, for they too are important for understanding man.

I am more than the sum of all of the data of my conscious life. Some aspects of the mystery of my human and personal being cannot be probed by reflection on the data of consciousness: such reflection does yield explicit knowledge of my conscious acts and of myself, but the knowledge is inadequate. Although I shall never come to a complete comprehension of myself, I can complement the knowledge which can be gained by reflection on the data of consciousness. The complementary knowledge is to be gained by the methods of empirical science. Physiology, anatomy, biochemistry, physics: many objective, empirical sciences can take readings upon me and contribute to a total knowledge, which holds in complementarity what is known from reflection upon the data of consciousness and from objective, empirical study of the human "body".

My conscious acts, therefore, stand out against not only my full conscious ground, but also what can be called my full personal ground, which includes all of the nonconscious basis of my conscious life. Only in that larger setting, and in the even larger setting which extends beyond my merely personal being, can my conscious act be somehow understood.

The Physical Universe

Continuing to broaden our consideration of the total setting of human action, we may consider next the total physical setting, the physical universe. Man is in the world, in many worlds of different orders. Like any thing which is bodily, in space and time, every human person lives in a continual manifold interplay of physical forces in the universe. Conditioned by the universe and the particular physical setting in which he lives, man more than any other living thing is selective in his responses to physical nature enveloping him, and he modifies more and more radically the physical setting of his life. Obviously his action can be understood only in its total physical setting and in the continuing drama of man's influence upon his physical environment.

THE HUMAN INTERSUBJECTIVE WORLD

Vaster and richer than the physical universe as the setting of man's action is the total human intersubjective world. The uniquely human character of this world, and of the relationships which are proper to it, can be suggested by a further reflection on differences of structure within human experience.

What is involved in this reflection is a further refinement and elaboration of the conception of conscious, intentional acts. In our earlier consideration I proposed the basic notion of conscious, intentional acts (pp. 113-116). Conscious acts are *of* someone or something. Their being *of* some object or term is the relationship which in phenomenological terminology is called intentionality. Moreover, I differentiated intentional acts according to the structures of their relationships to their objects or terms. Thus they are classed as cognitive, emotive, volitional, or motor. What remains to be considered is the significance of the distinction indicated in two ways in that previous account of such acts: they are of *someone* or *something*; they are of some *object* or *term*. That twofold indication of a distinction implicitly marked my reservation of a further question regarding intentionality. Usually intentional acts are said to be of an *object*. Even when cognitive acts are directed to the explicit knowledge of the subject's acts or of the subject himself, the process is called *objectification* of the subject. In such usage *object* is used loosely or broadly of both objects (things or aspects of things) and persons, subjects. I meant to suggest my own uneasiness with that usage by distinguishing *someone* and *something*, *objects* and *terms*. *Term* is to be understood in a broad sense as applicable to both objects and subjects, things and persons. *Term*, in the sense of what the act regards, and what somehow terminates the act, is more apt to express the broader sense than *object*. The radical opposition of object and subject makes the broad use of *object* at least awkward, if not ambiguous.

Beyond such concern with usage, there is the further, more important matter of the significant differences of structure of intentional acts as they regard persons or things. I turn now to that differentiation. Subsequently I shall reflect upon its significance for the total setting of human acts.

I shall be considering acts which in different ways are personal, and it may be good to note first two senses in which an act can be called personal. First, more obviously, an act is personal in so far as it is the act of a person. In this sense one may speak simply of personal acts, and one may discern degrees of the personal quality of acts, in proportion to the degree of involvement or commitment of the person who acts. In a second sense an act may be called personal because it regards a person, or is directed to a person. It is in this second sense that I shall take *personal* here, and differentiate personal acts as first-, second-, or third-personal.

(1) *Differentiation of acts.* (a) All conscious acts are first-personal, in so far as they involve the subject's awareness of his act and of himself. We may speak of first-personal acts, therefore, not as of a separate class of acts, but as an aspect of all conscious acts: only in acts by which we consciously intend others are we aware of ourselves as intending.

Since awareness or consciousness is part of the mystery of knowledge, and self-awareness is unique, the first-personal aspect of our conscious acts plays a unique and very important role in our awareness and knowledge of others. We are aware of other persons in all of our conscious acts which regard them. We come to know others in explicit probing of them by cognitive acts. We are aware of ourselves in all of our awareness and explicit knowledge of others. We know ourselves by a radical reflection, directing cognitive acts upon previous conscious acts and upon ourselves detected in them. The two sets of awareness and knowledge, of others and of ourselves, are complementary. Each is indispensable for the other. Each contributes in its own way to the relative fulness of the other.

In a sense, self-awareness, the first-personal dimension of our conscious acts, is primordial: I should never experience the unique awareness of another person if I were not aware of myself. I should never come to a more explicit knowledge of another person if I did not have some primordial, marginal, implicit knowledge of myself in my very self-awareness.

On the other hand, I should never come to a relatively full awareness of myself if I did not have the unique experience of direct awareness and knowledge and love of another person. I become more fully aware of myself as a person only as I come to experience more fully, more richly, the mysterious blending of lives which occurs only in direct mutual knowledge and love of two persons in an I-thou relationship. Consequently I can come to a more adequate explicit knowledge of myself and of my potential fulness of being only if I can reflect upon my awareness of my acts and myself in such interpersonal encounter.

Within the mystery of the first-personal dimension of conscious acts, I should differentiate three stages. First, there is the awareness of self in all conscious acts. Second, there is explicit knowledge of self attained by a unique reflection. Third, there is an appropriation of self-knowledge: having come to some understanding of the structure of my conscious acts and of the manner of my being, I act consciously with an understanding of these structures in my concrete acts. Appropriation is a mystery which we have not probed as yet. I shall deal with it more fully in the following chapter on the role of intellect. I mention it here because it should be mentioned as a distinct element in our experience, and for the present I shall merely indicate what is involved, without further explanation.

Appropriation is a step beyond explicit knowledge of structure. In explicit knowledge consciousness is focussed in a cognitive act or a series of acts bearing upon the object which is being probed. In the case of explicit knowledge of self, the subject's acts or the subject himself is the term of explicit cognitive acts. The subject's acts or the subject himself is "objectified". Within the conscious act in which such objectification is achieved, there remains a dimension of subjective focal awareness: a keen awareness of self in the very acts by which the self is being probed. The explicit knowledge attained is a conceptualized grasp of intelligible relationships. Like all conceptions, such knowledge is universal: it grasps and expresses a structure which may be discovered in any similar human act.

How, then, does appropriation go beyond explicit conceptualization? It involves a recognition of structure in a concrete, individual act. Retaining the knowledge of structure, I now act consciously, focussing upon an object or term in an act which

may be predominantly cognitive or emotive or volitional or
motor. I am no longer focussing upon the structure of my act,
but I am acting with a knowledge of the structure. Knowledge
of structure, like awareness of act and of self, is now marginal
in my consciousness. Appropriation, then, involves a special
instance of knowledge of universally prevailing structures recognized in the singular. In this case, the singular is not an individual object, but an individual subjective act.

Appropriation, therefore, is a distinct element of experience.
It differs from explicit knowledge, in the manner in which I have
just indicated. It differs too from mere awareness of self, the
first of the three stages which I enumerated. Mere awareness
of self, prior to explicit knowledge of the structures of one's
acts, involves only the vaguest, most implicit, primordial, marginal knowledge of self. Appropriation holds the intervening
achievement of explicit knowledge, attained in the second stage.
The mystery here, still to be probed, is this special mode of
knowledge of the individual. It is this further mystery which
I reserve for consideration in the following chapter.

(b) Second-personal acts regard another person or persons
in an interpersonal encounter. I should distinguish these acts
as *full* or *diminished* in what concerns their second-personal
character. Full acts regard one other person in an I-thou relationship. Such acts can occur only when I relate directly to
another person, another subject, another "I", now involved in
an interpersonal relationship with me. In this situation two
persons are involved directly in an interplay, a mutual influence,
which affects their awareness and knowledge and full conscious
behavior. We are aware of each other as persons. We affect
each other. Involved in a mutual second-personal relationship,
aware of the unique presence of the other person, I act differently than I would if I regarded one or more persons as
him, *her*, or *them*, more remote, not directly involved in an
interplay of two persons face to face. Far more does my
action differ from that in which I regard things, not persons.

Full second-personal acts occur originally in an encounter
by the meeting of eyes, by voice, by touch. By any one of these
actions, or by a blend of two or more, we have a unique, original experience. What is involved can be known only by experience. Any man or woman who would ask what an I-thou relationship is, without having had experience of what the words
designate, could never understand any answer or explanation.

Only by such acts can two persons relate fully to each other, come to a mutual understanding or a frustrating mutual mis-understanding, to a mutual love or hatred, which profoundly affects the lives of both. In mutual, interpersonal knowledge and love, in the blending of two lives in a unique union, two persons come to a fulness of human being which cannot be achieved in any other way, and which, as long as it is not ex-perienced, is simply not known in its full reality. It is one thing to "know about" love, to have a "theory" about it. Unless one has loved, such "theory" is not grounded in experience, and it has a hollow ring.

Originating in immediate encounter, the mutual interper-sonal I-thou relationship can be fostered and enriched by other acts of love directed to the distant beloved. Even in physical separation, lovers remain united consciously and are enriched by continuing acts of love which affect the quality of their lives. Even such acts are full second-personal acts, for they are part of the mystery of a union which can blend only two persons. Every person is unique, and every blend of two per-sons is unique. Varying as it must in every instance, the union of two persons is a mode of human being which is unique.

Although there is a sense in which the first-personal aspect of our conscious acts is primordial, indispensable for our aware-ness and understanding of other persons, there is also a sense in which full second-personal acts are the most important for our awareness and knowledge both of ourselves and of other persons. Only in full second-personal acts do I reach a unique fulness of human being, and an awareness of myself in acts which realize my personal potential. Only by the experience of myself and *another* in such acts can I come to an awareness and knowledge and appreciation of *others*. The mutual revela-tion of personal being in mutual full second-personal acts is the only way to a deep sense of the mystery of the human person, and consequently to an abiding sense of the mystery, the value, and the inalienable dignity of all other men and women.

As every person is unique, and every blend of two persons in mutual knowledge and love is unique, so the endless variety of persons makes possible an endless variety of relationships which somehow are second-personal, within the framework of the meeting of two persons, yet fall short of the ideal of a mutual interpersonal relationship. In some cases there may be an unrequited love: one person meets another, seeks under-standing, offers love; yet there is no return, or only a partial return. It is a one-way, blighted second-personal action and

relationship, painful to one or both. In other cases there is
mutual half-hearted, inhibited search for understanding, and mutual half-hearted, controlled effort to "do good". There is a
certain mutual love here, but it is hardly interpersonal. Too
many inhibitions prevent its being truly personal in the first
sense of *personal*: involving a sufficient commitment and self-
gift on the part of one or both. So the world is full of unrequited loves, and of half-hearted matching one-way "loves" which
are rather a mutual doing good at a safe distance. In some
cultures or social circles, and too often in some sorts of in-
stitutionalized lives of "charity", such loves are all that can
sprout when poor seed is cast upon infertile soil.

As the experience of mutual knowledge and love enriches
Full second-personal acts, and full mutual interpersonal
knowledge and love are of different kinds, and a number of
such loves can contribute to enriching human life. The loves
of mother and child, father and child, brother and sister, friends,
and in a unique way husband and wife, are complementary.
Though conjugal love may foster a sharing and blending of
lives beyond any other purely human love, it is always limited,
for in its ideal it is the mutual exclusive love of one man and
one woman. Each reveals to the other the mystery of his or
her being, with its severe limitations. Inconceivably more of
the human mystery exceeds any such revelation. The other
kinds of loves, compatible with that unique, exclusive conjugal
love, make possible a deeper insight into more persons, and
a richer sharing of varying personal mysteries; and thus they
complement and enrich even ideal conjugal love.

As the experience of mutual knowledge and love enriches
both persons, so the privation of love leaves men and women
stunted and unfulfilled. The tragedy does not begin normally
with failure in friendship or courtship or broken marriage in
full adult life. A child who has never known true love of mother
and father, who has never witnessed and come to understand
the beauty of conjugal love in the lives of his or her parents,
and never felt love and trust of a brother or a sister, will hardly
have an inkling of the human potential for love. The tragedy
of men and women who seem unable to love, inhibited, fearful
of the gift of self, may have begun in a loveless infancy and
childhood.

As in the case of first-personal acts, so in second-personal
acts we may distinguish three stages: (1) initial awareness of
you, face to face with me; (2) explicit knowledge of the structure of your acts and of your personal style; (3) appropriation:

recognition in your individual acts both of the general structure of human acts, and of variations upon what I have come to know as your personal style. My knowledge of you is both of the general human character of your acts and mode of being, and of your style. Knowing you, I know better and better the pattern of your behavior, and I read your moods and sense your feelings more surely.

Thus far I have been considering what I called full second-personal acts, regarding you, one person with whom I deal face to face—or in some other manner of direct communication, person to person: by telephone, or by voice in another situation in which we cannot see each other. There are also diminished second-personal acts. By *diminished* I do not mean acts which are inhibited, half-hearted, lacking in intensity, as in the many instances of imperfect acts regarding one person in direct interpersonal relationship. Rather I mean acts which essentially, by their very structure, in all instances, have less potential for full union and mutual influence of persons in direct contact. These are the acts by which I regard you, two or more of you. I cannot meet the gaze of two or more persons simultaneously, and in the presence of a group or crowd I can have only a fleeting meeting of the eyes with relatively few. I do not come under the steady influence of one person, but under the influence of many who in some respect are one in mind and spirit. The situation is essentially different. The pattern of behavior is different. The mutual relationships are different.

Here too one can distinguish (1) initial awareness; (2) deepening of explicit knowledge both of what characterizes persons generally and of the character, style, and mood of this group; (3) appropriation of that knowledge in recognition of the pattern of a particular action of the group.

There is a certain blending of full and diminished second-personal acts in my dealing with a community or group or crowd. As I address all of you, one of you or a few of you may stand out, and in continued meetings with the same group I may be acting more and more directly in relation to the one or the few, with a growing sense of mutual interpersonal contact within the contact with the group as a whole. This occurs at times when I have no previous personal acquaintance with the one or the few. It occurs also where I have had previous acquaintance or established friendship, and the one or the few now stand out in the community or group. They affect my impression of the community. My previous impression of them too may be conditioned now by my experiencing them in the setting of the community.

(c) Third-personal acts regard him or her or them: persons, not things. I am aware of him, her, and them as utterly diverse from things. More and more by observation I come to know their manner of acting and of being. More and more surely I recognize patterns in particular actions. He, she, and they are not involved with me now in direct mutual interpersonal action. He, she, or they may be acting in relation to me, but not in direct contact affecting my awareness of them in a second-personal way. I may be thinking or willing or feeling or acting with regard to them, in ways affected by previous interpersonal contact, but now I am dealing with them without such contact.

All that I have come to know of one person in full second-personal relationship, and of myself as I have experienced such interpersonal relationship, affects my conception of the human person, and my esteem of, and action regarding, him, her, and them. They too are human persons. They can never be things for me.

(2) *The human intersubjective world.* Reflecting on our personal acts brings out strikingly the variety of personal relatoins, and invites us to probe the mystery of the human inter-subjective world. I say "human", to limit our consideration to human intersubjective action, and to the reality of an order established by human interaction. This limitation leaves open the further question of a possible or actual transcendent inter-subjective order, in which men deal with and are affected by a transcendent subject, God.

First, then, persons are not things. Reflecting on this com-monplace affirmation, and trying to bring out the significance of the distinction between persons and things, one might be tempted to approach the matter in the following manner. En-countering things, I am aware of them and of myself. I seek to understand them, to situate them in a field of intelligible relationships. I evaluate them and react to them as good or bad for me. I use or avoid them. When I encounter a person, I am challenged, alerted to the presence of another who is aware of me as I am of him. He reads the mystery of things from where he is. He evaluates, reacts, tends to use or avoid them. We may try to deal with each other as things, and we shall be brought up short and challenged to face a mystery deeper than that of things.

This, I say, might be a way of trying to bring out the distinction between persons and things. A bit of critical reflection, however, should make one realize that this approach is quite unrealistic, in no way describing the course of our experience. None of us began life as a solitary explorer of the world of things, probing, evaluating, and using or avoiding them until one day he met another explorer, and had to confront the mystery of a person like himself. We are born into a world in which from the outset persons figure most prominently, especially our own mothers. It is in the matrix of a world of persons that we do our probing, and even in that probing we are prodded, guided, confirmed continually by language, the unique means by which men influence one another. We enter into a shared understanding of the world, and within that world come to distinguish persons and things, and to value most of all what can have meaning and value only for persons.

Differentiating personal acts, I indicated especially the role of mutual knowledge and love. That is not the whole of the network of actions and relationships which can be discerned within what can be called the human intersubjective world. What, then, is this "world", and how does it enlarge our concept of the total setting of human action?

The human intersubjective world is an intelligible order of operations, effects, and relationships which are proper to men. It is not "within" the physical world, nor is it "supported" by the physical world. Both the "physical world" and the "human intersubjective world" are human conceptions, abstractions, grounded upon the full reality of the universe of being. We cannot grasp and hold in a single concept or a single intelligible order the totality of being. The "physical world" is a conception of the intelligible order discovered in the data of physics and chemistry. All that is in the universe of bodily being can be embraced within that intelligible order, for the physicist and the chemist can take readings upon you and me and all else that is bodily. Not a single human operation evades such inquiry, for all of our being and operation is physical: it can be observed, classified, measured by methods of the physical sciences. That does not, however, establish the existence of a "physical" universe which is "real" as opposed to any other intelligible order which transcends physics and chemistry. *We* are real, and so are all the persons and things which *are*. Aspects of our mode of being and operating fall within the range of the methods of the physical sciences. Other aspects are simply beyond observation by those methods. Properly human operations, such as we have discerned and differentiated in the earlier chapters of this book, can be observed and differentiated only by a method which somehow begins with a reflection upon structures of conscious operations. The human intersubjective world is the intelligible order discerned in the interplay of men, acting upon things and upon one another by properly human operations, and the effects and relationships which result from such human operations.

We share a universe in ways in which only men can share. We share insights which we have gained in great part by mutual stimulation and suggestion. We share feelings, will, effort to transform the resources of the world as known by the natural sciences. We fashion properly human works. Science itself is our work, a properly human creation. All of our culture, our social and political structures, our laws, our formulations of rights and of duties—all are part of a properly human organization, an intelligible order discerned, elaborated, and effected by men sharing a universe, organizing their own efforts and the operations of the resources of the universe whose laws have been grasped and whose activities have been managed.

Properly human action can be understood only as it is situated in the whole of this intelligible order of human operations, effects, and relationships. Man is intelligible to man alone in the universe of bodily being. Human interpersonal relationships, and all of the works of man, have meaning for man alone in the totality of bodily being. Every human act stands out as figure against ground. It can be understood only as it is located in the total human field.

THE TRANSCENDENT GROUND

Through the study of monuments of former peoples and cultures, and from a knowledge of our contemporaries of varying cultures, we have come to a knowledge of a broader field in which human action occurs, or a deeper ground of human action—though "ground" here takes on different senses: it is that which is the ultimate foundation of all human action, its ultimate source, and its final goal. The field or ground is the transcendent, God. Men of varying cultures have witnessed to their awareness and inadequate knowledge of this source of their very being, and their actions are set ultimately in relation to this transcendent. Thus the transcendent field or ground is the last in our series of larger settings within which human action is to be understood.

Men who have had intimations or convictions of the transcendent have expressed their thought and feeling and will in its regard in a series of accounts ranging from earliest myth through a variety of religions and theologies. Though some of their fellow men, especially today, may dismiss such conceptions and actions as illusory, much of human action is unintelligible if it is not understood in relation to the transcendent, and in the broadest sense of the word to god or God.

It is beyond my scope here to establish the grounds for the affirmation that God *is*, and that human life can be understood ultimately only in relation to him. For the present it is enough to acknowledge what can hardly be denied: many men have been convinced that God is; they have lived lives consciously related to him; their lives and their actions are intelligible only in the total setting of their relation to God. This is very much to the point in our present reflection on the total setting of human operation.

REALITY

Earlier in this chapter (pp. 108-111) I suggested the conception of the person at the center of a sphere. The enclosing surface of the sphere is the limit of the total reality of the universe within which he is and operates. Every human operation may be somehow understood as it is set in the total enfolding reality. In successive stages through this chapter I have gradually developed the conception of that total setting of human operation, the total ground or field, the manifold worlds in which man lives and acts.

One question remains to be answered, regarding especially the human intersubjective world: the realm of properly human oprations, their effects, and the relationships which are said to be based on those operations and effects. In what sense is this intersubjective world *real*? The question can come hesitantly from a man or woman with a common-sense view of the realities of the world in which we live. It can be pressed relentlessly, with something like a crusader's zeal, by a contemporary empiricist thinker, for whom persons and things are dissolved, and all that is "really real" is readings upon points in a four-dimensional manifold. The man or woman of common sense may be impressed with the obvious reality of the geographical or physical world, of the persons and things visible and palpable in their physical being and operation. The empiricist thinker, reducing all reality to what can be accounted for in terms of physics, will have banished persons and things as illusions of common sense, and will have progressed beyond all representations of particles or forces to pure relational concepts.

(1) *What is reality?* What is *real*? The real is what *is*, in any mode whatever. Both the common-sense prejudice in favor of the geographical or physical world, and the empiricist reduction of reality to readings on points in a four-dimensional manifold, are abstractions. Each is a kind of flattening out of reality and existence. Each is one of many readings which can be taken upon the whole of reality.

What *is*, in any mode whatever, is real. Whatever *is* in the universe *operates*. It makes its presence significant. It *counts*. Its operations are real, for they are part of the mystery of its manner of being. Its effects are real, and so are the relationships which are grounded upon the continual operations and interplay of all that is in the universe. All that *is* counts for something: it has its value, it makes a difference in the universe of being. Every man or woman who is makes a difference, in all the ways in which he or she is and operates. *Knowing* is a mode of being. So is *loving*. So are all other human operations, their effects, and the relationships grounded upon them.

In short, the real is the existing universe in all of its concrete fulness. There are countless possible readings which may be taken on that total concrete reality. Every such reading involves the grasp of some relationships, for all understanding is a grasp of relationships. The relationships are real, grounded on the modes of being and operation. Yet they are not what basically constitute the universe of being. They are abstract, partial. They are not principles of the basic being of things, but principles or elements of our human knowledge of things. Since knowing is a mode of being, the principles or elements of our knowledge are real, and pertain to the total being of the universe, as part of the mystery of the way in which men *are*.

The relationships which we can read and fix in concepts are real in their own way, and they are significant, but only for man. They pertain to human knowing, an aspect of human being. Based on the infinitely varied interplay of all that is in the universe, the readings on reality are many and varied, taken

from countless different points of view, spontaneously or with
a great variety of methods. Empirical "facts" or "events", and
the whole of empirical science, are only one order of knowledges,
one set of types of readings, grounding particular kinds of interpretations or explanations of the universe. They are real, and
they are human achievements of great value. Yet they are not
the only type of readings which are taken, nor do they rank
as the supreme human achievement. Other modes of knowledge,
in the vast range of human culture, may be esteemed more
highly by some men. Beyond all knowledge, if one looks to
the excellence by which men do most to enhance the perfection
of the universe, men make their greatest achievement and contribute most to the fulness of being of the universe by the
quality of their love: by their union of love with what they
know to be supremely good, and by their living together in
mutual understanding and love.

(2) *Thought, emotion, and will.* Thinking is a way of being;
and thought is an achievement, a relative fulfillment, a heightening of the thinker's being. A man who has made a single true
judgment has bettered himself and the world in which he lives,
though the reality of his achievement and betterment escapes the
net of the empiricist of any brand who would reduce reality
to what is measurable in terms of physical energy. To grow
in knowledge and truth is not to increase the total physical
energy of the thinker or of the universe. On the contrary,
every act of thinking, like any other distinctly human operation,
involves bodily factors, the "firing" of nerves, the "consumption"
of energy. Measured in such terms, any act leaves the human
body and the universe in a worse condition rather than a better
one: it is another step in the grim process of entropy. Yet a
perfection of a higher order is achieved, beyond the merely
physical, beyond the merely vital.

When living things are studied with any sense of the unique
mode of being of the whole organism, the biologist comes to
know order and organization which cannot be reduced to merely
physical and chemical terms.[7] Beyond the mystery of man's
vital organization, the most marvelous vital structure which we
know, there is the higher mystery of modes of being which
transcend the merely vital. Beyond his unique ways of shaping
his physical environment to support his physical life, man can

---

[7] Cf. K. GOLDSTEIN, *The Organism* (Boston: c. 1963); and M. POLANYI,
op. cit.

grow in distinctly human ways : by knowing and loving he can grow in truth and goodness.   By understanding and judging truly he grasps and affirms relationships among the many persons and things with which he shares the universe.   He somehow holds the mystery of their being.   Beyond the actual physical reality which he faces, beyond even the human reality of the lives of the men and women whom he knows, he can conceive of other potential orders, other worlds, and he can project his action to realize them.   Knowledge and truth are an enrichment, a sort of union of knower and known, a partial remedy for the divisions and the dispersion of the universe, an opening upon horizons and worlds of which man alone can conceive.

Man's operation is not confined to a role in the interplay of physical forces in the universe, nor to the efforts of an organism to modify its environment and develop and prolong its existence and that of its species.   Any estimate of man and of human being and operation which is limited to the measurement of physical and chemical factors misses the mystery entirely. A sculptor is not a mere stonecutter, and his work of art cannot be reduced to physical terms.   The figure which he carves has meaning for man alone, a meaning which pertains to a uniquely human realm of thought and feeling.   Not confined to his immediate physical, geographical setting, man ranges in his thought and his action to the realization of orders and structures within the power of only human thought, imagination, will, and action. Human thinking is real, and human thought and human projects are real: they *count*; they make a difference.

Carried to its extreme, a purely empiricist thought not only misses the meaning of man, but negates the empiricist.   Pure empiricist thought first reduces all reality to what is observable by the methods of exact physical and chemical analysis.   Having flattened out all reality and pulverized it, empiricism goes on to remind us that the specks are not real, but phenomenal. In the "real" world of pure science there are not "things". In this world it seems at first that men of science are studying what seem to be things but are not, reading marks on gauges and machines, though the marks, gauges, and machines themselves are not.   Nor really are the men who seem to be reading, nor the marks which they make, nor the collections of marks which they call books, nor the gullible men for whom the books are written to communicate science.

Empirical sciences are great achievements, but they are

abstractive, partial. Pure empiricists are a menace when they disregard the abstractness of their thought, arrogate to themselves total reality, and take on the style of other totalitarians.

The mystery of man and of his total reality is that of human transcendence. Man *is* such that by his properly human operations he tends somehow to transcend "himself", and yet only by going beyond "himself" to become fully what he can be. He *is* in such a way that all of his properly human operations are the unfolding of a basic twofold tendency of his nature, a basic twofold intentionality, cognitive and emotive-volitional-motor. We have reflected on the characteristic structures of his intentional operations. Our present reflection on the "reality" of human thought, emotion, and will go to the heart of the mystery of intentionality.

In the preceding paragraph I have enclosed the word *himself* in quotation marks, to suggest the need of a further reflection on the self which is transcended and the self which is actualized only in so-called self-transcendence. Let me approach the matter by recalling a distinction from some classic thought concerning man and human thought. Some have held that when one speaks of an act of human thought, a cognitive act, one should distinguish two aspects: entitative and intentional. By *entitative* one would designate the act as a modification of the being of the person who thinks. In terms of a philosophy of Aristotelian origins, such a modification would be a mode of accidental being, classed in one of the categories or supreme genera of being. It pertains to the being which persons and things have "in nature", as they are and operate in the interplay of persons and things in the universe. By *intentional* one would designate not the being which persons and things have "in nature", in their basic being and interplay in the universe, but rather a sort of diminished being which the known has in the knower, and the loved in the lover.

This classic distinction of *being in nature* and *intentional being* is well founded and highly suggestive, but in my judgment it has not been thought out sufficiently. Intentional being, vaguely designated as a sort of diminshed being, tends to be disregarded as real being, pertaining to the total consideration of any philosopher concerned with the whole mystery of being. Both natural and intentional being pertain to the consideration of the metaphysician—if metaphysics is a basic philosophy of being. Moreover, both modes pertain to a basic philosophy of man. The mystery of man and of human self-transcendence is that of persons who come to their fulness of being in knowledge and love. Men and women *are* more fully, they come to realize more of their potential, as they advance in knowledge and in the love of what they know to be truly good. In the fullest sense they realize their human potential as persons in fellowship, in mutual interpersonal knowledge and love.

The human person, then, "transcends himself" only by going beyond the initial stages of his human being, realizing his ideal "self" in richer life in knowledge and love, coming to a relative fulness of truth and goodness, in personal and interpersonal life.

In the realization of the fulness to which he tends by his very nature, in his continuing growth by operations within the scope of his twofold basic intentionality, man *is* more fully. His knowledge and love, truth and goodness, are *real*. They truly *count* in the universe. He *counts* for more by achieving them.

Moreover, knowing and loving and all intentional acts are intentional in their very being: they are entirely intentional. This is their "nature". It is only in acts which are *of* someone or something, in the various modes of intentionality, that persons come to *be* more fully. The original distinction of being in nature and intentional being should have been only an invitation to reflection on what is unique in the fulness of being to which men tend by their very nature. Speaking properly, I should say not that a man's intentional operations *are*, and are in the unique mode which is intentional; but that in his very intentional operations of all types *man is* more fully, with a heightening of his being in modes which are uniquely human.

There is another aspect of the matter, and it points to the object which will be our concern in much of the reflection which remains to be done. We must recognize the *reality* not only of man operating intentionally in various modes, but also of his properly human works: the thought uttered or written, the emotion felt, the decision made, the agreement reached between two or more persons, the marriage union established, the statue carved, the symphony played, all of the works of man in arts and crafts, mathematics, science, and philosophy, religion and theology. All of these *are* and *count* in the various worlds in which men are. All are real, every one in its own way. Symbolizing man is real in his very symbolizing. His symbols, too, in their own ways are real. They count.

The Metaphors and the Basic Analogy

Briefly concluding a long chapter, I should like to note the relative advantages and limitations of the metaphors which I have used, and to indicate the underlying analogy.

As I have pointed out, the notion of the sphere has advantages over those of ground, field, horizon, and world. What we are seeking to express as adequately as possible is the total setting of any human act, especially of an intentional operation. Regarding man as situated at the center of his personal sphere suggests best of all perhaps the infinite range of possible directions of his multiple intentional operations, and the total enfolding reality which is the setting of his operations.

Recognizing this relative advantage of the metaphor of the sphere, one can note too its inadequacy for the expression of some aspects of the total setting of a human operation. It is adequate to suggest the total objective setting. It cannot suggest, at the center of the sphere, the total subjective setting of the act.

What is the basic analogy underlying all of these metaphors? I should hold that analogy in the strict sense pertains to the realm of an existential metaphsics, and it concerns the ever varying modes of being, unity, truth, and goodness The modes vary, and they vary proportionately. As anything *is*, so it is one, true, and good. As man *is* in his specific mode of humanly bodily being, so too he is one, and true, and good. Being bodily, he is diffused in space and time. Being humanly bodily, he has a potential for truth and goodness which must be achieved in a succession of acts, all of them realized according to the basic tendency of his nature, within the matrix of his basic twofold intentionality. Being in a world of persons and things diffused as he is in space and time, and acting successively with varying blends of a multiple intentionality, he is characterized by modes of unity, truth, and goodness which are proportionate to his mode of being, Human experience is marked by unity and continuity in all of its modes: a unity in diffusion and multiplicity. The other most striking characteristic of human experience is the ever varying structure of figure and ground. Within the unity and continuity of his being, man comes to his relative fulness of perfection only by a succession of acts by which he grows in truth and goodness.

In man there is a proportion between the subjective and

the objective, and by reason of both he is and operates in his distinctly human way. Objectively, he faces a world, an objective setting, in which the potential terms of his multiple intentional acts are infinite, and he must act always regarding one term after another, concentrating on one among many. The multiplicity and succession of his potential terms impose upon him a mode of acting marked by unity in continuity, and by a concentration upon figure against ground. He is multiple and complex in his modes of operation, and he can come to his relative fulness of being only by a succession of operations of different modes in varying blends. Subjectively, he is in such a way that his acts must be successive and varied, and every act must stand out in its turn against the total subjective ground.

The unity and continuity of human experience, and the constant, ever-varying structure of figure and ground, are based on the unique way in which man is in his world. As he *is*, so he is one, and true, and good.

Saying "man is" or "he is", we must not forget one of the most important phases of our whole consideration: *we* are, in a setting which most importantly is intersubjective, and *we* come together to the fulness of our perfection, to our unique union of truth and goodness.

Chapter VI

FURTHER REFLECTIONS ON THE ROLES OF INTELLECT

It may seem strange to propose here a chapter entitled as this is. In a sense the preceding chapter may seem to have contained the elements necessary to conclude a basic treatment of man, in preparation for our consideration of symbols. Yet some further reflections are necessary, and they had to be reserved until this point.

My treatment of individual intentional operations in chapters II to IV was necessarily abstractive and tentative. I was concerned with discerning and differentiating operations. Further questions concerning the blend of operations, and especially concerning the roles of intellect, had to be put off for the moment. Now, after the consideration of intellectual operations and of the conscious field, it is possible to face the further questions and to attempt some further reflection.

Two elements of our preceding reflection are most significant here: (1) the concept of the broad range of intellectual intentionality; (2) the realization that consciousness is an aspect of the mystery of knowledge.

It is the wide range of intellectual intentionality which grounds the notion of the permeation of all conscious operations by intellect. All of our conscious, intentional operations are permeated by a twofold intellectual factor: massive existential affirmation holding us to the total reality of the world and of ourselves, and a massive initial grasp of relationships and tendency to discern and differentiate, which drives us continually to understand the world and ourselves, and to affirm explicitly what we have understood. The permeation of all conscious, intentional operations by intellect necessitates a re-assessment of every intentional operation, and some modification of our understanding of how it occurs in concrete human experience.

Since consciousness is part of the mystery of knowledge, all conscious operations fall somehow within the realm of knowledge. Not only are they blended with intellectual operations, as they are with other intentional operations, but they pertain to intellect in a special way precisely because they are conscious: all pertain to our awareness, to our marginal knowledge of the operations, of their objects or terms, and of ourselves.

I shall proceed first by re-examining individual intentional operations, to consider particular roles of intellect in their regard; and then by reflecting on some further aspects of the all-important role of intellect in human experience.

PERCEPTION

As I have remarked before, Merleau-Ponty's *perception* includes much of what I think should be attributed to intellect. The reasons are historical in great part, and it would take a careful historical investigation to trace influences. As I see the matter, for Merleau-Ponty the terms *intellect* and *intellectual* had been flattened out in thought influenced by Descartes, Kant, and transcendental phenomenology. In that tradition of thought, intellect was a power for which all is transparent, and by which all is constituted. Such an intellect was in no way mired in the flesh. Concerned as he was with the "ambiguous"[1] situation of an enfleshed human consciousness, part of the mystery of man who is in the world, and who comes gradually to a knowledge of the world in which he is involved, and which he has in no sense constituted, Merleau-Ponty sets his perception over against any idealist or rationalist type of intellect.

No one can command the use of words. I have used *intellect* and *intellectual* in a different way; and, consistently with my discernment and differentiation of operations, I should say that perceptual experience is permeated by intellect.

Perceptive consciousness, in all of its modes, is consciousness; and human perception involves at least a vague intellectual awareness and grasp of self and of relationships in the perceptual field.

The perceptual field itself cannot be understood in terms of perception alone. The perceptual field is not what I hold now in perception, but what I know from the experience of

---

[1] See ALPHONSE DE WAELHENS, "A Philosophy of the Ambiguous," foreword to the second French edition of M. MERLEAU-PONTY, *The Structure of Behavior*, translated by ALDEN L. FISHER (Boston: c. 1963) xviii-xxvii.

perceiving to be the situation in which I perceive, and what I know to be the potential extensions of my perceptive experience. I know that if I turn around I can see the wall behind me; that if I leave my room I can see the corridor; that outside this building I can see the Piazza della Pilotta, and that I can move on to see much of the wide world. This I *know* from experience, by an understanding of my situation in the world. My *perceptual field* is a concept which I have of an aspect of my human way of being.

My perceptual field, and the selectivity of my actual perception, are affected by many factors in my total conscious experience: memory, imagination, feeling, will, motor impulse, and action; and by much of the nonconscious underpinning which conditions and qualifies my bodily existence. Most of all, my perceptual field is affected by what I know of my situation, by an ever deepening and broadening insight into the world in which I perceive.

My perception generally occurs in patterns which have been formed gradually by experience. I take in a familiar scene with a certain habitual style and method, and I scan a new scene in ways which are similar to my scanning of previously perceived scenes. From the outset I am vaguely aware of the patterns. I have a vague, marginal, implicit knowledge of the patterns of my perceptual experience. In special situations I exploit this knowledge of patterns, and I direct my perceptual experience in the interest of inquiry, of intellectual probing and verifying, or of some other sort of satisfaction.

Moreover, what I perceive is not merely an object of perception. Within my perceptive experience I come to some grasp of relationships in this object, some intellectual knowledge of this individual person or thing or situation or event.

AWARENESS AND KNOWLEDGE OF SPACE AND TIME

From the whole course of my reflection it should be obvious that I am not proposing a theory of "constituting consciousness", according to which space and time and the world of external things are constituted by consciousness, as in all idealistic tradition. Yet one must recognize that our consciousness does develop. We develop our "sense" of space and time. Though we do not constitute the world, which *is* prior to us and independently of us, still we do develop in our conscious involvement in the world, and in the many worlds of meaning which are constituted by men.

In that total process, what is involved in the development of our awareness and knowledge of space and time? Certainly that development involves our experience of perceiving both the external world and our own internal processes. But more is involved.

Our sense of space is developed by experience of both seeing and touching and moving to grasp or probe an object. In visual perception we have the experience of scanning a visual ground or field, shifting from one focal point to another, holding all points in a total ground or field, in a configuration or constellation in which their mutual relationships can be determined. Yet the purely visual element is only part of the experience. Permeating, penetrating, and finding the sense or pattern of the scanning operations, grasping the relationships of points in a notion of space as a whole which is present simultaneously: all this is the work of intellect. Within our visual perception we progress from a first vague awareness to a gradual insight and explicit grasp of relationship and of a simultaneous whole, held in the configuration of visual perception. Similarly we penetrate the operations by which we move our hands, reach and grasp and probe. Gradually we form at least a vague notion of space, enough to enable us to follow a reflection upon the structure of our experience and understand an explicit account of space.

The intellectual factor in the development of the notion of time is more evident, for time is a more difficult concept, to be achieved after a more complex reflection on experience. Within our observation of moving things, and our experience of our own movement, gradually we come to a sense of the pattern of successive experience, of elements or moments in a whole which are not simultaneous and yet somehow are in continuity. Our sense of time is no matter of mere perception, but comes only with gradual insight into patterns of movement in external objects and in our own flowing experience. Full awareness and grasp of space and time are the work of intellect, penetrating and finding the meaning of our perceptual experience, and aspects of the world which we perceive.

MEMORY

In Chapter II we considered memory as a kind of sense knowledge, in which we retain and can recall elements of original perceptual experience. That was a tentative, partial, abstractive treatment of memory as it pertains to the realm of sense knowledge. If memory were limited to this realm, it would hold and recall only aspects of configurations or constellations which originally were sensibly perceptible.

Is that all that we remember? Clearly not. I remember many other aspects of a total experience: not only what I perceived, but also what I remembered at the time, what I imagined or day-dreamed, what I felt, what I understood, what I willed, what I did, and the pattern and style of my action. By memory I retain and can recall many dimensions of my total past conscious experience, and many features of the objects or terms of my multiple intentionality. In particular I vividly remember peak experiences, whatever their dominant mode or blend of modes of intentionality.

Memory pertains to the realm of knowledge, and it has many intimate relationships to intellect. First, it is a kind of conscious operation, and thus falls within the realm of our operations of which we are aware, of which we thus have at least a vague, marginal knowledge. We are aware of, and can come to an explicit knowledge of, the patterns of our remembering. We are aware, and can come to an explicit knowledge also, of ourselves in this aspect of the mystery of our human being. Second, by memory we retain and can recall what we have understood and affirmed in the past. Third, holding much of a concrete past experience of many dimensions, memory holds an object or a sequence of events which we now understand. As we penetrate and find the meaning of what we perceive, so too we can come to grasp relationships in what we remember, and recognize patterns or structures in a particular, concrete instance which is recalled. Memory is part of the mystery of our knowledge of the particular, both subjective and objective.

Our first question regarded the total object of retention and recall. There is a further question, more difficult, running more deeply into the mystery of memory. What is unique and proper to memory is the retention and recall of past personal experience precisely *as past personal experience*. How do we hold and recognize past personal experience precisely as such?

How does memory differ from what can be retained or conjured up by imagination? What is held and recalled by memory is not just any collection of images, or succession of images. Nor does memory hold and recall images to which some mysterious mark were added, identifying them as "pertaining to my personal past", and hence distinguishable from what I merely imagine. How, then, is past personal experience recognizable as such?

Knowledge of past personal experience is a matter of recognizing the structures, the patterns, of which we were vaguely aware as we lived through the original experience. It is a matter of some degree of insight into the structure of the whole flow of our conscious experience. Because we retain and recall at least some aspects of a whole experience, there is not a question of a multitude of atomic, unrelated images, like a lot of snapshots. What we remember, somewhat like what we perceive—though to a far lesser degree—has a certain fulness, a certain solidity. Like the perceptual field, so to a lesser degree the whole course of a remembered experience can be probed. It can be tested and submitted to a critique, as it is in the cross-examination of witnesses.

All memory involves some such critique, at least implicit, and it is open to further probing, to the recall of further details which confirm or conflict with some element of what was first recalled. That critique, as we shall have to consider more fully later, pertains to the role of intellect.

Memory is part of the mystery of the human mode of knowing, a consequence of our humanly bodily being. We are bodily, in space and time. We are aware of the flow of our experience and of its concrete patterns. We can be only by acting, and all of our action is singular, in our concrete personal human existence. Every action is set in its living context. What we are aware of, and can come to know explicitly by reflection, is not some universal, abstract pattern, nor some multitude of unrelated images, but the concrete pattern of our personal experience, unique in many ways, recognizable as such because of the particular blend of details and circumstances which can be singled out in it. As we live, we are aware of the pattern of our experience. In memory we recognize that pattern, and the recognition involves a blend of the functions of interior sense and intellect. Interior sense is involved, for we are dealing now not with data of immediate external perception, but with images retained, holding something of the configurations held in the original perception. Intellect is involved, for we grasp relationships, at least implicitly, and we probe and judge critically details of what may be either memory or fancy.

One final reflection remains: the play of memory and intellect in our total sense of time, our grasp of the mystery of past, present, and future. It is a commonplace to speak of our conscious experience as a flow or stream. The metaphors are suggestive, and the underlying analogy is part of the mystery of the human mode of being. The "flow" or "stream" of consciousness is unique. It is not like a stream of running water which can be scanned. The whole moving body of water is there, spread out for us to behold. We can look upstream and see the water which is not yet here, and downstream to see the water which is no longer here, but is there. All of the water *is*: up there, here, or down there. The "flow" of consciousness is not such. We cannot look "upstream" and see the future, as if it were already "there" and approaching. Only the present is. The future is not yet. The past is no longer. I cannot see the future. I hold an image of the past and sense that I am somehow still clinging to it, for I have lived through "it" and "it" has become part of me.

What is unique in our total experience of time is the element of expectation, of "protention", matching our retention of the past. Here we find another indispensable role of intellect. Only by my understanding of the patterns of past experience can I have a grasp of the imminent future. The future is not, and cannot be held in perception, much less in memory. Our sense of the imminent future comes only with insight into the structure of our experience in time. By memory we hold patterns of lived sequences of events, in which every moment is a former present and future. We have lived continually the pattern of succession, and have come to distinguish the relationships of events in their sequence. With insight into the pattern of lived sequences, I understand the passing of the present. The past is a former present. The present will be, is becoming, another past. With insight into the pattern of "flowing" human experience, I have foresight, protention of the future, and this is an insight into the mystery of fleeting human existence, a precious bit of human wisdom which we share with Job. I relish his words in the old Douay version: "For behold short years pass away, and I am walking in a path by which I shall not return" (Job 16.23).

IMAGINATION

Since I am conscious when I imagine, I have some intellectual awareness of my operation. I am aware that I am imagining, not actually perceiving or recalling a previous experience. I am aware of what I am imagining, and of my operation, and of myself operating. I am more or less aware of patterns in my experience of imagining, and I can recall and reflect on those patterns. The awareness and the knowledge of the patterns is intellectual.

Like perception, imagining can be directed by the inquirer, who deliberately imagines objects of a certain type, to promote understanding by probing them. Similarly, imagining can be enlisted in the interest of some other type of conscious operation: emotive, volitional, or motor. As an example of the last, if I am trying to improve my swing as a batter or a driver, I can imagine myself in the batter's box, or on the tee addressing the ball, to focus upon some of the principles of athletic form in baseball or golf, and get the feel of the proper swing.

In the free play of imagination, in its creativity, it is not confined to re-working configurations similar to those previously held in perception. It can work freely with all the dimensions of an imagined experience: cognitive, emotive, volitional, and motor. In all of its modes, imagining is part of a larger experience in which I am either vaguely aware of patterns and relationships, or recognizing patterns which I know from reflection, and which I find now in an individual instance.

As memory in its own way pertains to the properly human way of knowing and of being, so too does imagination. Memory is a mark of man's being involved in the process of being in space and in time. Imagination witnesses to a certain liberation and transcendence which are equally characteristic of man. Never freed fully from the conditions of his bodily being, constrained in all his flights of thought to hold images which are part of his total experience of thinking, still man achieves a certain freedom from some of the conditions of bodily being when he imagines. In thought accompanied by free imagining—and in free imagining always penetrated by some intellectual awareness and sense of relationships—man is freed somehow from the conditions of space and time.

I say that he is freed "somehow". He is not entirely freed, for every image is of someone or something somehow extended in imaginary space; and continued imaginary experience necessarily represents successive stages or actions or events, and implies a certain imaginary time. Yet free images and the free creative play of imagination are not bound like perception to the here and now, nor like memory to the then and there, of present or past personal experience.

Freed from the constraints of the here and now, or the then and there, of actual experience, man can range in imagination through whole realms of possible experience, in patterns which he has never known. It is in this free-ranging creativity of new patterns that thinking-and-imagining mark man's freedom from the shackling conditions of bodily being in the here and now, and his transcendence of a way of being entirely bound to matter. Not bound to the here and now, man can imagine and conceive of the possible, and project his action beyond the present physical setting of his life, to transform the physical world and create the many worlds of culture in which he lives most fully.

Man transcends mere bodily modes of being. but he transcends them always in a human manner: the image is always there to remind him that he is a man, not an angel, much less a god. He cannot think the sublimest thought except with an image accompanying his thought. He cannot think except in an act which is itself singular, and of which he is aware with a sense of the pattern of his action. He cannot create or venture into new worlds except as he stands upon or is launched from the earth. He fashions all of his works by actions which are somehow bodily.

EMOTION, VOLITION, AND MOTOR ACTION

As I treated emotion, volition, and motor action together in Chapter IV, so I shall here with regard to special roles of intellect in them. In part that common treatment seems reasonable because all three pertain to my total human response to what I know as good or bad for me: they are distinct but intimately related modes of intentionality. In part it is suggested because of a parallelism of what must be said concerning all three.

(1) *Emotion.* I should like to reflect upon two aspects of the role of intellect in emotional experience: in the discernment

and judgment of what is good or bad for me; and in my awareness and knowledge of emotion.

If I speak of a role of intellect in the discernment of what
is good or bad for me, obviously I am not concerned with the
judgment of good or bad, pleasing or displeasing, in what is
grasped immediately by the senses within the range of their
objects, and in the experience of what I have called simple
emotions.[2] Such experience surely is penetrated by intellect,
but there is no question of a special role of intellect in the
judgment of the sweet or bitter as such, or of anything else
which falls within the range of the immediate sense reaction
to the pleasant or unpleasant.

Quite apart from such simple emotional experience, there
are areas of emotive experience in which discernment and judgment seem to pertain to the intellect.

First, I should indicate a role of intellect in the complex
emotions generally, in which the good or bad for me is not
immediately perceptible sensibly. In fear of the harmful, or
in desire of the useful, the harmful or the useful as such is not
sensibly perceptible. If in such experience one distinguishes
perception, appraisal, and emotion,[3] how can one explain the
appraisal? One element of a classic philosophy, developed from
Aristotle, culminating in St. Thomas, and still retained by some
recently, is the attribution of such appraisal to a special power.
In animals it is called the estimative power. In men it is given
the name *cogitative sense* or *discursive power*.[4] In my judgment
the notion of such a power is ungrounded. The "data" which
are cited in the earliest speculations and repeated through the
centuries are pure conjectures about what a lamb perceives,
for example, in a wolf, and how it knows that the wolf is dangerous and to be fled from. Without any knowledge of animal
perception, it was supposed that a lamb sees what a man would
see in a wolf, and any knowledge that the wolf is dangerous
must be attributed to a special inner sense, detecting aspects

---

[2] Cf. above, pp. 89-90.

[3] See, for example, MAGDA ARNOLD, *Emotion and Personality* (London
and New York: c. 1960) Vol. I, p. 226; and Index, "appraisal," p. 290.

[4] For a thorough historical account of the development of the doctrine
and a systematic presentation of St. Thomas' theory, see GEORGE P. KLUBER-
TANZ, S.J., *The Discursive Power* (St. Louis, 1952). For an account of the
roles of the estimative or cogitative or discursive power in a recent
philosophy of man, see the same author's *The Philosophy of Human
Nature* (New York, 1953): see the Index, "Discursive (estimative) power."

not perceptible by external sensation. What was postulated as an estimative power or sense in the animal suggested a corresponding power which would participate reason in man.

With regard to what perception and response to values may be like in animals, one can get a good idea of the range of modern studies, and of the difficulties of the matter, by consulting Susanne Langer's treatment.[5]

As for human emotion in response to what is known as good or bad, useful or harmful, it seems to me that the element of appraisal can be accounted for adequately by the permeation of all conscious operations by intellect, and the knowledge of relationships gradually acquired through experience and held in memory.

Beyond this role of intellect in the complex emotions generally, the function of intellect is even clearer in types of complex emotions in which the object of fear or other emotion is in no way sensibly perceptible, but is grasped only in an understanding of a complex situation. Strong fear can be aroused when one knows, or imagines with an understanding of the imagined situation, all sorts of consequences of the dreaded evil. The student approaching an examination and dreading failure with all its consequences in his world, fears an evil which is not sensibly perceptible, but intelligible or imaginable. In the imagined consequences he understands the situation which he fears will result, and he is panic stricken at the thought. A patient approaching a formidable surgical operation, or even a diagnosis such as a cardiac catheterization, with a knowledge of the possible results, may be filled with fear of what is not perceived, nor merely imagined, but understood. Even if he does not feel much emotion, his reaction to his understanding of the situation and of his prospects may be revealed by an etxraordinarily high blood pressure.

Besides the role of intellect in the discernment of what is good or bad for me, we may recognize another role in our awareness and knowledge of emotion. How am I aware of an emotion, for example fear? And beyond that, how do I know the emotion fear? There is a question here of a special instance of awareness and knowledge, and it takes some close attention even to discern the problem, let alone work out its solution.

Let us begin with an example, and attempt to locate the

---

[5] SUSANNE K. LANGER, *Mind: An Essay on Human Feeling*, Vol. II (Baltimore and London, 1972) chapters 12-15, pp. 3-214.

question. Suppose that I am starting out in the evening on
a long trip, with plans for a series of engagements in several
distant places. I am carrying some money, my ticket, travelers
cheques, personal possessions, documents, and most important
to me: my personal notes, which represent months or years of
work, and which are necessary for the engagements of the coming months and for the book which I am engaged in writing.
Walking alone with my baggage, on a dark street with no one
in sight, suddenly I see two men approaching me. From their
appearance and manner I suspect their intentions: robbery, and
very probably—whether I resist or not—mugging. With a quick
estimate of the situation I feel a surge of fear.

What am I fearing? Not merely the men before me, sensibly perceptible, but what I understand of the situation: what
they could and probably would do to me, what I would lose,
what effect this would have on my plans and on all of the
persons involved in my engagements for the next few months.

How do I experience fear? Of what am I aware? And what
is my knowledge of fear? This is not a question of what I
perceive and understand in the object of fear. Rather it is a
question of how I am aware of fear, and how I know fear, its
structure, its intelligible pattern.

Some elements of the experience are perceptible, in part
by external perception of effects upon my body, but chiefly by
internal perception of physiological changes: perspiration, rising
temperature, pressure, pounding of the heart, shivering, goose
flesh, weakness and seeming hollowness of legs and knees, impulse to flight. Only some aspects of the total emotive experience are perceived and known in such cognitive acts. Hence,
if one considers only such physiological aspects, and identifies
them with emotion, emotional experience seems to be ambiguous, polyvalent; and the behaviorist is apt to dismiss it as
fictional. For him, such data can be observed in other patterns
of behavior, and emotion has no identifiable character. If emotion were simply the cluster of physiological changes, the behaviorist would have a strong argument. But emotional experience cannot be reduced to the sum of physiological changes,
nor can it be the object of direct perception.

We are facing a special instance of consciousness and knowledge. We can attempt to show how it is special by comparing
and contrasting it with perceptive experience. In perception
I see, hear, feel by touch in a multiple experience. I see, hear,
feel the objects of my various senses. I am also aware of my

acts of seeing, hearing, and feeling; but it is not by seeing, hearing, and touching that I am aware of my acts, discern them, and unite them in a total experience.

At this point in some classic philosophical reflection on man and human behavior, philosophers call for an internal sense, the common sense, by which one knows his external sensory acts, discerns them, and unifies them.[6] Whether or not a philosopher may hold the theory of common sense, other aspects of the problem which we are concerned with call for a special role of intellect in this instance of conscious operation, and in others.

There is a twofold function of intellect in the experience of fear. One regards the object feared: *what* I fear is not merely what I see or hear or otherwise perceive by my senses, but what I grasp of the total situation; the multiple relationships, the intelligible consequences of a number of possible elements in a developing situation. This first function of intellect pertains to the consideration which I have made in the preceding section, regarding the discernment of the good or bad for me.

The second function of intellect regards our conscious experience, our awareness, of fear, or of any other emotion. Awareness of fear, conscious experience of fear, involves not merely awareness of the phyiological factors in the experience, but also of the total situation: the field of relationships in which those physiological events take on special meaning and are recognized as elements of a total experience. I do not *perceive* emotion by perceiving its physiological factors. I am conscious of emotion by a vague intellectual awareness which embraces objects, acts, and self at different levels and in different modes of a single consciousness.

In this vague awareness all that pertains to the first function of intellect is included. In that first function I grasped the object and the situation in an experience which was predominantly cognitive. Now, in the actual emotional response, my conscious experience is predominantly emotive, not cognitive. Yet all that I have grasped in the object of fear remains. The cognitive element is marginal in consciousness now, but

---

[6] For an accurate account of the role of common sense in the theory of St. Thomas Aquinas, see BERNARD J. MULLER-THYM, "The Common Sense, Perfection of the Order of Pure Sensibility," *The Thomist* 2 (1940) 315-343. Not concerned here with elaboration or critique of a theory of powers or faculties, I abstain from evaluating the theory of common sense.

it is essential for the total structure of the emotive experience.
I *feel* in response to the known object.

Since awareness, or consciousness, is a part of the mystery
of knowledge, we may ask what sort of knowledge is involved
in emotive experience. Recalling the distinction between focal
and marginal awareness and knowledge, and supposing that in
the moment of keen emotion it is the emotive mode of experience which is dominant, we may give some account of the sort
of knowledge which is involved.

First, the dominant intentionality at this moment is emotive, not cognitive: I am *feeling* strongly, and at the moment
I am not concerned predominantly with cognitional probing of
an object to advance my understanding of it. I am reacting
to an object or a situation known as bad for me. Cognitive
intentionality, therefore, is not focal now in my consciousness:
it is marginal. In that marginal consciousness I have a vague
understanding of the total experience: an understanding of the
pattern of the experience itself, as distinct from the objective
situation which I face. I have a sense of the "shape" of the
feeling of fear, a vague sense of the structure of the experience
of fearing.

Tomorrow, when I can recall and reflect upon this experience, I may be able to come to an explicit formulation of my
knowledge of the structure of the fear which I felt. It will
not be comprehensive, but it will fix and hold some of the
relationships which I can determine in the experience, relationships of which I was only vaguely aware during the moments
of fearing.

What am I attempting to say about the role of intellect in
the awareness and knowledge of emotion? I am indicating two
moments, two functions. The first moment is that of the actual
emotive experience, and in that moment the role of intellect
is to hold a vague grasp of the total structure of the experience,
the shape of the experience of fearing. The second moment
is that of reflection, in which the role of intellect is to determine
explicitly some of the relationships which can be recognized
in the full concrete experience which is now recalled.

The two moments are extremely important, and the two
functions are quite different. If there were no vague, implicit,
primordial grasp of structure at the moment of experience,
there would be no consciousness at all, and nothing at all on
which to reflect. If there were no vague sense of the shape
of the whole experience of fearing—as much more than a

mere succession and blending of physiological factors—then two kinds of human symbolizing, and two kinds of symbols, would be unintelligible. As we shall see, there are two diverse modes of symbolizing, one terminating in the art work projecting the form of human feeling, the other (in this instance) terminating in a philosophy of man, elaborating the structure of human emotion as part of a theory of man. Neither the artist nor the philosopher could do his work if he did not have some experience of the shape of feeling. The artist elaborates his art work, his symbol of human feeling, not by working out an account of explicit relationships, but by fashioning a work in which he projects the form of feeling in a striking and unmistakable way. The philosopher elaborates a theory which is the result of patient reflection and determination of relationships, and of a coherent intelligible structure. We shall have to consider at length both modes of symbolizing, and the vast range of symbols which they yield. For the moment it is important to fix one point: the role of intellect in conscious experience in the emotive mode. It grasps vaguely and holds the shape of the whole experience: the vaguely sensed structure of the subjective response, and the vaguely held structure of the objective field evoking the response.

In human experience the conscious is part of the intelligible field. Consciousness is part of the mystery of knowledge, of the fanning out of intellect over the whole range of the intentional operations of a man who is composite and complex in his relationships to both the true and the good. Consciousness is not an agent, but a condition or state of the human agent. I am conscious, aware of all of the objects which I intend with a variety of intentional operations; aware of all of my intentional operations and of their vaguely grasped structures; aware of myself operating. I am aware of emotion not as of a thing, but as of a kind of experience: an event of a particular structure in which I am somehow active in a unique manner. I am aware of fearing, of the general structure of the objective field in which the feared object is known, and of the general structure or shape of my feeling of fear. My knowledge of these structures in the moment of keen feeling is marginal; but if it were not at least marginal, I could not focus upon it to reflect and know explicitly the shape of my conscious experience.

One aspect of experience of emotion remains to be considered: degrees of participation in emotion. Consider a series of events involving several persons. A little girl riding her bicycle is struck by a passing car, thrown to the pavement, and lies writhing, crying, bleeding. Her mother, who had been standing nearby, rushes to her side, and holds her tenderly, full of love and compassion and the flood of emotions of a mother sharing her child's pain. Other bystanders or passersby, sensing the child's pain and the mother's anguish, stand by in respect. They share the feeling of compassion for the child, and for the mother in her grief; but they do not rush to the child's side, as they might have if the mother had not been present. One dear friend of the mother, coming along a few minutes later, comes up to comfort her. An artist among the bystanders, witnessing the scene, feeling compassion for child and mother, later recalls the scene, senses the structure of the feeling, and begins to work to express the feeling of child, mother, and comforting friend in an art work, whether it be a painting, or statue, or poem, or drama. Long after, other men and women behold the artist's work, and sense the emotion which he has portrayed.

All of these men and women, in different ways and to different degrees, share somehow in the child's pain and the mother's compassion. All of them experience emotion, real emotion, at different levels or in different registers. In different total human situations, they experience different blends of insight, emotion, will, and motor impulse. Even in the last instance, the aesthetic emotion of men and women who behold the art work is real emotion, one of the modes of participating in the original experience. In Aristotle's theory of drama, the pity and fear felt by spectators of a tragedy was real emotion, though it did not call for the response of a real-life situation. In some religious rituals among primitive peoples, dramatizing in ritual afforded an outlet for emotions which normally were suppressed in accordance with the structure and custom of society.

In all of these various participations in emotional experience, the participant is conscious of the emotion, and has at least a vague awareness of the shape of the experience. As we shall see later, this vague awareness or marginal knowledge of the shape of emotion plays an important part in the life of man the symbolizer.

(2) *Volition.* As in the case of emotion, so in that of volition, one can recognize a twofold role of intellect. The first and more obvious is in the discernment of the good or bad. Since the act of the will is a response to a good or evil known

intellectually, and since the voluntary action may involve a series of distinct phases in deliberation, decision, and action, philosophers have recognized a complicated interplay of intellect and will. The analysis of acts of intellect and will, and the elaboration of sequences in which they alternate, are commonplaces in the philosophy of man or of human will, and I shall not attempt to compress here the results of such reflection.[7]

The second role of intellect regards awareness and knowledge of the act of willing, and of the subject who acts. Having dwelt sufficiently on the general theme of the role of intellect in conscious action, I shall indicate here only one feature of awareness and knowledge of the act of the will. I am aware of *this* act as I perform it: an individual act, embedded in the total process of my conscious life, set in my personally lived time. Beyond this feature of my initial awareness of my individual personal act, there is a corresponding knowledge of the individual act in the appropriation which follows upon reflection and knowledge of the structure of voluntary acts. By reflection upon the voluntary act of which I have been aware, I can come to a knowledge of the structure of voluntary action, in its relations to both intellectual action and the manifold involuntary factors in human action. Such knowledge is universal, philosophical. Having come to such knowledge, I can act with full awareness of my will and with a knowledge of the structure of voluntary action, recognized now in my individual experience.

This distinct role of intellect in awareness and knowledge of the individual voluntary act is extremely important in human life. I cannot live a fully personal life without this element of human experience. I must decide here and now. I must determine the course of my life, in so far as it depends upon my free action. I must commit myself and know that I am committing myself, if I am to play a personal part in the world. Corresponding to such awareness and knowledge of my present

---

[7] For examples of such reflection, one could consult one in a tradition of philosophy developing largely from St. Thomas Aquinas: GEORGE P. KLUBERTANZ, S.J., *The Philosophy of Human Nature* (New York, 1953), Chapter X, "The Will," pp. 227-259, with diagrams of the relationships of acts, pp. 249-251; the other in the independent study of PAUL RICOEUR, *Philosophie de la Volonté*, vol. I, *Le Volontaire et l'involontaire* (Paris: 1963), in which the interplay of intellect and will runs through the whole of his profound reflections on the complementarity of voluntary and involuntary factors in human action.

action, there is memory of my past action. What I decide and will today I must keep in mind and remember tomorrow: I did decide, resolve, agree, commit myself; and much of the meaning of my own life and of the lives of other men and women depend on both memory of such voluntary action and fidelity and constancy in holding to a course of action consistent with my pledge.

(3) *Motor action.* Again, two roles of intellect can be indicated. One is obvious, and needs no elaboration. It is the role of intellect in proposing the goal of motor action. I move to or from a good or evil which I know not merely by sense perception but also by intellectual grasp.

The second role again regards my awareness and knowledge and appropriation of my motor action. Aware of this motor act, as I am of all of my conscious acts, I can reflect upon its structure and come to a knowledge of it, whether it be a common action such as walking or running, or a special action such as a particular artistic or athletic performance. Knowing the form, the "shape", of the action generally, I can act with a knowledge of the shape of my action: a knowledge of the general form which I have come to know, and which I have recognized now in my individual performance, with some sense of my own personal style.

DISCERNMENT, CRITIQUE, AND HOLDING IN UNION

I have made passing reference to the alleged role of a power called the common sense. Having abstained from evaluating such a theory of a power, I do not intend to attempt an evaluation here. It may be helpful, however, to consider the problems which the theory of common sense was intended to solve, to move beyond to further problems, and to consider other aspects of the role of intellect in conscious life.

I see, and hear, and taste. In every instance my sense act has an object which I know by sensing it in the appropriate mode. I am also aware of my seeing and hearing and tasting, and I somehow know my acts. But it is not by seeing that I know my act of seeing. Nor is it by seeing or hearing or tasting that I am aware of and know the distinction of my acts of seeing, hearing, and tasting. Nor does any one of my external senses enable me to hold all of the objects and acts, discern them, and unify them in a single conscious experience of the object of perception.

To explain how we are aware of our acts of sensing, know them, discern and unify them in consciousness, St. Thomas and those who followed him proposed the theory of the common sense, in which all external sensation was discerned and unified. Common sense was like the center of a circle, a point common to all the lines running out as radii representing the different external senses.[8]

The problem concerns the awareness and knowledge, discernment and unification of external sensation in a single sense consciousness. Without pausing to evaluate common sense as a solution to the problem thus proposed, I should indicate that the problem of awareness, knowledge, discernment, and unity of consciousness is far greater, and that a solution can be found only in recognition of further roles of intellect.

First, the problem is vaster than that which was proposed concerning external sensation. It regards the whole conscious field, and all of our intentional acts of all modes. Gathering all of the problems of external sensation into one complex problem, I have the problem of perception. I do not perceive my perception, nor is it by perceiving that I am aware of perception, or differentiate the modes of perception. Beyond the problems of external sensation, thus gathered into one problem of perception, I must ask similar questions about all acts of all modes of intentional operation.

I not only perceive, but also remember and recall, imagine, understand, judge, reason, respond to the known good or bad for me in all the bewildering variety of acts of emotion, will, and motor action. I am aware of all of these conscious acts, and in that awareness I have a certain marginal knowledge of them. I discern them, implicitly and explicitly. I am conscious of all the objects of my acts, and I am conscious of my acts and of myself acting. All are unified in my one personal consciousness: *I* am conscious. All of this awareness, both objective and subjective, all ultimate discernment of my many modes of intentional acts, and my holding all in a single consciousness must be attributed to intellect.

The conscious field is part of the intelligible field, and all

---

[8] See the article of Bernard J. Muller-Thym cited above. I am not suggesting that St. Thomas first proposed the theory.

of the aspects of experience which I have been proposing can be understood only in terms of functions of intellect. I shall distinguish three functions: discernment, critique, and holding in union.

Discernment. Consciousness is part of the mystery of knowledge, and it is by intellect, primordial and explicit, that I am aware of my whole conscious field, objective and subjective, and that I can discern the different intelligible structures of my various acts. Consistently with our preceding reflections, we can differentiate stages in this intellectual discernment: (1) a vague, implicit, primordial grasp of relationships and structures in our awareness of our conscious acts of various kinds; (2) determination of proper structures by reflection upon the patterns of our experience; (3) appropriation of this knowledge in the recognition of structures in the acts which we perform.

Critique. Either in a general reflection upon experience and its structures, or in a reflection upon a particular instance of one or more intentional acts, one may raise questions about the reliability of our cognitive acts, or the quality of our emotion or act of will. In general, how is perception different from hallucination or imagination? What guarantees the truth of our judgment? What is the possibility of differences in love: authentic or inauthentic, illusory? What is the criterion of a full act of decision or commitment? In particular, here and now am I seeing or experiencing an hallucination? Am I recalling what I actually experienced, or what I dreamed, or what I imagined? Or am I not recalling, but imagining a past personal experience? How do I test my judgment here and now? Is this love authentic or inauthentic?

(a) *Of perception.* Do we need a critique of perception? In ordinary living we trust our perception implicitly, confident that we are in the world, open to it, holding it somehow in our manifold perceptual experience. Yet we know from experience or report that there is a difference between the "real" world and the figments of dream, imagination, hallucination. On the one hand our experience or acceptance of that distinction makes us certain that there is a difference: that there is real, authentic, reliable perception as contrasted with hallucination. On the other hand, in a given instance, we may be challenged to probe our experience, to make sure that what we seem to have perceived is "real", not imaginary or dreamwork or hallucinatory. The acknowledgment of the difference, therefore, entails a willingness to face that challenge in rare instances.

How do we effect a critique of perception? How do we guarantee that we have perceived, that we were not dreaming, imagining, or suffering hallucination?

There can be no question of a sort of self-authentication of perception, either implicit in direct experience, or explicit in a sort of reflective discernment and judgment. We do not perceive our perception: we are aware of it. Much less do we perceive the difference between perception and imagination or dream or hallucination. We do not perceive something in the object which distinguishes it from any mere figment. When critique is called for, we perform it by probing the object and the act in their total fields, objective and subjective. As the representative function of the perceived object depends on our insight into the concrete whole of which it is a part, and into the many relationships which we can establish, so the reality, the authenticity, the dependability of perception is grasped only by insight into its setting in the whole of our experience. We can probe our perception and its object in their total objective and subjective fields, and in their setting in an intersubjective field of experience which we share with others.

The conscious field is part of the intelligible field, and the probing and critique of any conscious act and its object is the work of intellect. "Dwelling in" our action, aware of it by intellect, we probe and discern and judge our actions and their objects by intellect. Our perceptual field, and our perceptive experience, have a certain solidity. They can be probed. When it is necessary to face the challenge of illusion, we can probe both the objective and subjective fields, and determine relationships, and judge that this is "real": it *is*, beyond any need for further appeal for authentication. All of this probing is directed by intellect, because only by intellect can we understand the possible difference of acts and objects; only by intellect can we understand the relation between figure and ground, check the ground, contrast the full ground of perception with the groundlessness of dream and hallucination, and contrast the perceptual world shared with others and the private spectacle of the victim of hallucination.

Such probing and critique does not involve us in an infinite series of probings, every one of which would involve perceiving again, and would in turn raise the doubt about this last perceiving. It is not done by multiplying instances of perception, but by the probing and judging of inquiring intellect which pervades all of our conscious life. Within the matrix of our basic cognitive intentionality, in which primordial perception, primordial existential affirmation, and primordial grasp of relationships are the ground of all explicit acts, we come to an explicit understanding and judgment of the reality of our perception and our perceived world. There is no court of further appeal.

In a sense our perceptual experience is self-authenticating, or rather it involves a continuous implicit running critique. We "dwell in" our perceiving. We are conscious of it, and have a certain vague sense of its structure. Furthermore, perception is of present reality: the perceived world is present to us, to be probed. Probing is of the very nature of perceiving; for perception is not a single fixed gaze, yielding an image once for all. We perceive by roving continually over the field, probing, fixing details, locating them in the whole, returning to impress details more sharply. By reason of the full presence of the reality which is its object, and by reason of the very self-reassuring pattern of its operation, perception involves a continual spontaneous critique. Ultimately, however, this running critique is characteristic of human perception, in human consciousness, within the mystery of an all-pervading intellectual awareness, understanding, and judgment.

(b) *Of memory.* Earlier in this chapter, dealing with the roles of intellect in memory, I reflected upon a certain degree of critique involved in memory. Memory is the form of knowledge by which I hold the pattern of my real past personal experience. It may embrace all the modes of my experience: what I have actually perceived, felt, understood, judged, willed, done by motor atcion, or merely imagined, or dreamed. I mention dreaming, because what I have actually dreamed is part of my real past personal experience, set not in waking consciousness, but in the succession of periods of dream consciousness which are part of my total experience.

In my earlier reflection on the role of intellect in memory, I considered the element of critique involved in knowing my personal past precisely as my personal past, as distinguishable from what I may merely have imagined doing. In the latter case, the imagining is real: I really imagined. The action imagined is not real: I did not do it. Some aspects of the critique of memory call for further consideration. Since I can hold and recall elements of all modes of former experience, I may wonder at times whether some elements which I hold and recall belong to the whole of an actual past full waking experience, or are

objects or actions of which I dreamed, or which I freely imagined doing. The question concerns the whole texture of what
we seem to remember: does it contain now a blend of elements
from actual full waking experience, full conscious action, with
other elements which are figments of imagination or dream
or hallucination, or some other kind of diminished consciousness? In memories of a long active life of a person who has
also a vivid imagination and a lively dream activity, such chal-
lenges of memory can demand a critique. How is the critique
to be effected?

As remembered experience is somewhat like actual present
experience, though increasingly fragmentary, its critique must
be somewhat like that of perception or other actual experience,
but it becomes less and less adequate and decisive. Memory
does not hold the full present reality of the original experience.
The object or event held in memory is no longer held in its
total setting. Hence probing memory is more difficult, and remembered dreams and imaginings are more formidable rivals
of memory than present dreams and imaginings are of perception. In the case of the critique of perception, I can "pinch
myself" and know for sure that I am awake, not dreaming.
In memory I am removed from the original experience, and
the discernment of modes of past experience becomes more
and more difficult. Did I actually do this, or did I imagine
or dream that I did it?

To the extent that memory holds the pattern of my lived
experience, a pattern of which I was aware and which I can
recognize, memory can be probed somewhat as perception is
probed. It has some ground, some context, some setting which
can be probed. As in the case of perception, so here the probing
and critique is the work of intellect. Here the critique is incomparably more difficult. What is marginal in the perceptual
field can be probed: it is "there" to be scanned and focussed
upon. What was marginal in the past experience often has
left no recognizable trace within the range of waking conscious
recall.

(c) *Of imagination.* Beyond the discernment of imagination
in the critique of perception and of memory, can one speak
properly of a critique of the imagination? Surely not with
regard to its free-running, spontaneous, infinitely resourceful
creativity. Essentially free of all bonds to actual existence and
experience past or present, imagination is not subject to the
sort of critique which we have considered in the cases of per-

ception and memory. Yet there is a certain critique of what may be called the aptness or adequacy of images. If one looks at a series of photographs of racing cars, winners over a period of fifty years, he will notice striking evolution of design, and he can easily conjecture the corresponding differences of design and engineering of motors, transmissions, and other features not exhibited in photographs showing mostly body design. Reflecting on these examples of evolution, he may speculate on the directed play of imagination which entered into every phase of the development of racing cars. Much of the play of imagination in such a process is directed. The creative designer, like the artist working at a painting, has a guiding idea, a goal, regarding some aspect of automotive engineering. If he is concerned with increasing traction, he may imagine a series of variations of wheel sizes and proportions of tires. If he is working at a particular problem of air resistance, he will imagine various designs of body. In all such play of images, there is a critical function of the artist or the creative engineer, who judges the adequacy of the imagined—and then drawn—forms for the accomplishment of the desired increase in traction or decrease in air resistance. In all such critique, insight, the guiding idea, is the criterion by which one monitors and judges the aptness of the successive images which come in the directed flow of creative imagination. As we shall see, such monitoring and critique of images plays an important role in much of human symbolizing.

(d) *Of conception.* Is there a critique of conception? Not in the sense that there is a critique of the truth of judgment, for concepts are not true or false. Yet they are relatively adequate or inadequate, and there is a critique and a sort of verification of concepts, of intelligible structures. It consists in the testing and judgment of the adequacy of a given conceptualization to hold all of the pertinent data, all of the relationships which have been determined and which have been recognized as significant. When I propose a definition of symbol, it may be subjected to a critique and be judged to be relatively adequate or inadequate to hold all that pertains essentially to the wide range of symbols and their functions. Concepts are more or less adequate. Without illusion of the possibility of coming to perfect definition which grasps and formulates the "essence", one can recognize relative adequacy, and probe and judge concepts and definitions in terms of such adequacy. This critique plays an important role in the development of discursive or conceptual types of symbols. Insight, or rather a succession of insights, provides the criterion. At any stage of conceptualization, concepts may be probed for their adequacy or inadequacy in formulating the relationships grasped in an insight or a series of insights.

(e) *Of judgment.* The classic problem of critique regards the truth of our judgments. Judgment, in the first instance, is not a conclusion of a reasoning process. Basically, in its own right, judgment is an act of intellect whose object is the very *to be* of the thing known. It may be affirmative or negative; simple and unrestricted or limited to some mode of being indicated by the predicate. Strictly speaking, one can make a simple, unrestricted judgment only in the affirmative: "This *is.*" What is affirmed is simply the existence of the subject. No predicate is added to indicate a particular manner of being, and thus to limit the affirmation: "This is *alive.*" There can be no simple negative existential judgment except in the form "XY is not," in which X and Y are incompatible, and it is impossible that there be any instance of an existing XY. Judgment is true when one affirms or denies in conformity with the actual being of things.

How, then, does one judge the truth of judgment, so as to say: this judgment conforms to the actual being of things: what is affirmed to be, or to be thus, actually is, or is thus; what is denied to be thus actually is not thus. The truth of judgment in the simple, basic instance is reduced to the evidence of the sensibly perceptible existing world: not in the sense that judging is a matter of seeing, or of any other mode or combination of modes of sense perception; but in the sense that the man who sees also affirms at least implicitly that this *is,* and understands relationships which may be grasped in what is sensibly perceptible, but not by an act of sense perception. Intellect permeates, penetrates all perception, all conscious experience. The irreducibly simple intellectual judgment is made within perceptive experience, and is grounded in irreducibly simple evidence known only by intellect within such perceptive experience.

In appealing to an irreducibly simple existential judgment, based on irreducibly simple evidence of what is sensibly perceptible, I should call for some reflection on the human manner of knowing. There is a certain similarity in the human manners of perceiving, conceiving, and judging. First of all, negatively, they are not instantaneous, atomic acts, performed in a flash,

like photographic snapshots. Snap perceptions, snap conceptions, and snap judgments are similar in their defects. Perception occurs normally in a process, and the roving eye is symbolic of the mode of all of our perceiving. Conception occurs
at the term of a process, and yields to further questions, inquiry, reflection, and perhaps more adequate conception. Judgment, even simple existential judgment, occurs not in an instantaneous act, but in an assent which is given as we dwell
in the total process of our probing of the world.

"Mistaken" judgment is due to a neglect of the evidence,
or a hasty leap beyond the evidence, a leap which involves an
inference, usually latent. Take a simple example. John returns
home, and as he enters his yard he sees a man prying open a
window in John's house. He judges: he is breaking into my
house! And he leaps into action. John happens to have been
wrong, and eventually he learns what was really happening,
which may be one of several possible events. The man at the
window, Paul, was answering a call for help from within the
locked house, trying to get in to rescue whoever was calling
for help. Or he was trying to repair the window, having been
called by Mary, John's wife. Go back and reflect on John's
judgment: he is breaking into my house. John went beyond
the evidence, and his pronouncement was the conclusion of an
implicit, hasty, erroneous inference. The unexamined, deceptive
premise of the latent reasoning was roughly this: Anyone prying
open a window is breaking into the house (where "breaking
into" means burglaring).

What is involved in the critique of an erroneous judgment?
It is simply a reflection, a return to consider the actual evidence.
What did you actually see? What actually is happening? What
is clearly perceptible and intelligible in this event? How much
are you inferring? Is your statement a simple judgment based
on the evidence, or is it the conclusion of a hasty, implicit,
barely conscious reasoning from a general "principle" which is
not true? Separate the evidence from the hasty interpretation
and reasoning. What can you affirm on the basis of the evidence?

What, then, grounds a true, certain existential judgment?
Not another judgment, or series of judgments, for every one
in turn would call for similar grounding, and the process would
go to infinity. Not a reasoning process of any kind, for the
steps of the reasoning themselves involve judgment, and again
the search for a foundation of certitude is unending. Unless
one recognizes the unchallengeable truth and certitude of a

simple existential judgment based on what is perceptibly and intelligibly evident in fully conscious human operation in the cognitive mode, he is incapable of any affirmation, let alone a critique of knowledge.

One final note. This account of the critique of judgment does not mean limiting human knowledge to what is sensibly perceptible. Science and philosophy go far beyond what is perceptible in determining the intelligible structure of the world. Yet the beginnings of human knowledge are in the judgment concerning the sensibly perceptible existent. Moreover, verification of any hypothesis can occur only by some series of particular judgments based on the sensible observation of things and events, at least in the reading of instruments.

(f) *Of emotion, will, and motor action.* As we are conscious of our response to the known good or bad in emotion, will, and motor action, so we discern and judge the quality of our emotion, will, and motor action. I indicate these vast realms simply to acknowledge the full range of the critical role of intellect. I shall give only a few examples. With regard to emotion, two instances may suffice.

First, there is a critique of the authenticity or "reality" of emotion. Merleau-Ponty developed the distinction between true and illusory love. True love calls upon all of the lover's resources. It concerns him in his entire being. Misguided, illusory, inauthentic love touches him only in some role. True love ends when the lover changes, or when the beloved changes. Misguided love is revealed as such when the lover returns to himself. Illusory or imaginary feelings are really experienced, but only on the outer fringes of ourselves[9] .

Second, in the realm of religious experience, what is called technically the discernment of spirits involves a critique of emotions, understood in their dynamic setting. The purpose of the discernment is to determine whether or not a proposed course of action is truly inspired by God or not: whether it is a real personal vocation coming from God, or some sort of illusion. The technique is largely one of reading signs: judging the emotions experienced in their full setting.[10]

With regard to the will, the role of critique is highly im-

---

[9] M. MERLEAU-PONTY, *Phenomenology of Perception* (London, 1962) pp. 378-380.
[10] See WILLIAM A. VAN ROO, S.J., "Law of the Spirit and Written Law in the Spirituality of St. Ignatius," *Gregorianum* 37 (1956) pp. 417-443.

portant. Moral decisions are often difficult, involving a discernment of motives, of values. They demand a discernment of
a number of subjective factors which affect the quality of the
decisive act of the will. Awareness of the dynamic pattern of
decision-making and full consciousness of the decision taken here
and now involves the implicit concrete judgment: I am deciding.
Tomorrow I must be able to recall and hold to that decision,
with a full knowledge that I made it. Without a critique of
decision, I could not know now or later whether or not, in
the play of motives and of various factors in my total experience,
I really decided or not.

   With regard to motor action, I should indicate a role of
critique somewhat similar to that concerning imagination, without suggesting that this is all that may be involved. As images
may be judged for their aptness or inadequacy, so too our
motor action may be discerned and judged for similar qualities.
With a consciousness of the form of my action and of my personal style, I may be able to judge its relative aptness or inept-
ness. My guiding idea, my goal in this action or performance,
may monitor my effort, and enable me to judge and try again
for a more adequate realization.

   Holding in union. I say "holding in union", rather than
"unification". I need not be unified: I am one. My consciousness need not be unified: consciousness is not a subject. I am
conscious, aware that I am and that I am one. As the conscious
field is part of the intelligible field, it is by intellect that I am
aware that I am one, and that all of my conscious acts are mine.
I am one in a manner proportioned to the way in which I *am*:
in a humanly bodily way, with a unique personal mode of being
human. Aware of all the objects and terms of all of my intentional acts, I am aware of the complexity of my being. Yet
I am not a compound of all of the elements or factors which
I can discern in my operation and being. It is within the
unity of my personal human being that I discern my many
modes of operating. I establish many relationships in my
objective and subjective fields. These relationships do not constitute me: they are grounded in my very being. It is because
I *am* in my uniquely personal human way that all of these
relationships can be discerned and conceptualized.

   Perhaps I should not even say that the role of intellect in
this regard is to *hold* my conscious life in union. Rather: it
is by intellect, by an intellectual awareness and marginal or
explicit knowledge that pervades my conscious field, that I am

aware that I am one, and that I can determine fairly well some aspects of the unique way in which I am and am one.

I am aware of my whole conscious field, objective and subjective, and aware of its unity in complexity and diversity. I am not a "mind" or a "consciousness" for which all is transparent. I am in the world in a distinctively human way, in my own personal mode. My whole conscious life in the world develops within the matrix of my twofold basic intentionality: cognitive and affective-volitional-motor. From the outset of my conscious life the world is present to me, and my actions and my self are present to me in the vague primordial twofold cognitive factor of my being: massive existential affirmation, and vague, primordial, implicit grasp of relationships. I am aware of the world, and of my action in the world, and of myself. Within that massive awareness all discernment, differentiation, elaboration of relationships, conceptualization, and explicit particular affirmation occur. I am, and am one. My world is, and somehow is one. It is within the mystery of the life of intellect that I have this awareness and knowledge of my unique being and being one.

By intellect I have the awareness and the knowledge that I am one and that my objective conscious field is one. The mystery goes beyond the limits of waking consciousness. By intellectual awareness I know too that I am one in a unity that enfolds both waking and dream consciousness. My dreams are *mine*. I dream, and in dream I function intellectually, and I am aware of operating intellectually, sadly reduced though the mode of operation be. I recall my dream, and on waking I discern clearly between waking and dream consciousness, but I am aware, I *know* that *I* was dreaming. In dream, as I can recall, I lived through hectic, ever-shifting patterns of experience. I understood, reasoned, decided, resisted, desired, struggled to move to or from the good or evil present to me. Though it was all in a shadow world, with no consistency and no constancy except at times the awful recurrence of patterns and situations, still it was I who was dreaming. I am the one, now awake, who dreamed. By intellect, in a properly human and uniquely personal way, I am aware of and know that I am and am one, through all the sequences of waking and dream consciousness. Within the unity of my human being, the discernment of my waking and dream consciousness is too a function of my intellectual life.

Grasp of Analogy

All understanding consists in the grasp of relationships, from the vague initial intimations in primordial knowledge to the most refined concepts of mathematics, science, and metaphysics. Relationships are grounded in the way in which persons and things are, and the way in which we are in the world of persons and things. Persons and things are together, interact in many ways, and are involved in a manifold interplay. Because they are together and interact, all sorts of relationships may be discerned: spatial, temporal, quantitative, qualitative, causal. All are intelligible, grounded in the being and operations of things, amenable to determination and formulation in concepts and systems. The range of such relationships is the whole of the objective and subjective fields of men who can understand and formulate their understanding. The discernment and determination of relationships is obviously the function of intellect.

Among all such relationships, one vast realm may be designated as that of analogy, which I should take in the sense of a certain likeness prevailing in spite of difference or diversity. It may be a similarity of sensibly perceptible form or configuration; or a similarity of intelligible relationships, of logical structure.

As we shall have occasion to note repeatedly in following chapters, the grasp of analogy pervades all symbolizing, from myth to mathematics and metaphysics. By another name it may be called isomorphism; likeness of form, where *form* is understood in the broadest sense, ranging from sensibly perceptible configurations to intelligible structure. We shall note a multiple isomorphism: within the objective field, or within the subjective field in the structure of the operations of the subject, or ranging widely over both objective and subjective.

Such analogy or isomorphism is one of the grounds of the play of association of all kinds: perception, memory, emotion, thought, will, motor impulse. It helps to understand the kinship of all forms of human symbolizing, which enables us to discern and differentiate symbolizing and symbols ranging over the whole gamut of human operations.

The grasp of analogy is based on the way man is in this world, for he is proportioned to his world. In all of his being in this world he is bodily, yet all of his conscious operations are permeated by intellect. From the first vague sense of the shape of his experience and of the world which he is experiencing to the deepest insight and understanding and expression of thought and full response to his world, he is and knows and loves and moves in a human way. He symbolizes in many ways, as we shall see; and the intellectual grasp of analogy runs through all his symbolizing.

OBJECTIFICATION

Another important role of intellect, an aspect of all its functioning, is objectification. Some reflection is necessary to bring out the universality of this function and the analogy of its modes.

Object, objective, and *objectify* correspond somehow to *subject, subjective,* and *subjectify.* When something is called an object, it is named not simply as it is in itself, but as it somehow stands over against a subject. Things are objects in so far as they are regarded by a subject, or can be regarded by a subject, and can be the terms of one or more acts of the subject. Thus we return to the notion of intentionality, the relationship of a subject's acts to some object or term. It seems, therefore, that from the outset the two sets of terms regarding object and subject stand for opposites, and that they are somehow correlative. *Object, objective,* and *objectify* (to constitute or regard as an object) clearly are the secondary and dependent series. Things in themselves may be independently of a subject. But things are objects only for a subject.

There may be, then, some neglect of this basic relationships in some discourse about *objective* as contrasted with *subjective.* *Objective* at times seems intended to suggest being not only external to, but also independent of, a subject. Correspondingly, *subjective* may suggest being confined to the realm of the purely subjective, and hence being somehow a figment of the subject, to which nothing corresponds in the "real", objective world. In such discourse all virtue lies in being objective: *subjective* is a pejorative term. But philosophical discourse varies, and there is another type, postcartesian, in which all virtue and fulness are in the subject: objects, the objective, and "being" are products of "constituting consciousness". In such a philosophical atmosphere one may speak disparagingly of certain types of earlier thought as *objective*, antedating the "turn to the subject".[11]

What can be said of the matter consistently with the reflections which we have made? I should say that the objective is so called always in relation to a subject: the objective is somehow the work of a subject, or is called thus in view of such a work. It is not simply the fulness of reality of things in themselves, as contrasted with an alleged limited or figmented subjective world "within" the subject. The objective as such is the term of a human act which regards it in one of the four basic structures which we have considered: cognitive, emotive, volitional, and motor. Within the cognitive order, one can say, and must say, that all thought is objective. It is the work, of a subject, who in all of his cognitional operations seeks understanding and truth concerning the world in which he is, and concerning himself. If he probes the world in which he is, that world is his objective field: the broad term of his probing. Within that world he fixes on particulars in their setting, and every such particular is for him an object, the term of an explicit cognitive act. Discerning relationships, he gathers data concerning objects in that total field, and in the data thus gathered, "external" data, or "sense" data, he comes to some understanding of the objects in his field. In every act by which he probes his field or fixes an object, he is objectifying: constituting an object, not constituting the thing in its being. The world in which he is, into which he came, is independently of him, as it was before him, in its own relative fulness of being. It becomes his objective field, and particulars within it become his objects, as they terminate his cognitive acts, or his intentional acts of other types.

Conscious of his acts and of himself, he may direct his probing to his own acts and to himself. Then his acts, and he himself, are the terms of his cognitive operation, and he objectifies them. He is probing the data of consciousness, to find in them their own intelligible structure.

Objectification, therefore, ranges through all of human cognitive action, and all other intentional operations. It is always the work of a subject, regarding particulars in his total conscious field, objective or subjective.

---

[11] For an example, see Ricoeur's judgment of the thought of St. Thomas Aquinas, in his treatment of determination and indetermination: *Le Volontaire et l'involontaire* (Paris: 1963) pp. 172-186.

Objectification is always somehow abstractive, partial in its grasp of persons and things. What is true of the perspectivism of perception is true analogously of all thought: from person to person points of view differ, and what is perceived and grasped intellectually is somewhat different in every instance.

The objective is the work of a subject, regarding an object which he himself forms as he probes the world in which he is. Physics and chemistry and all empirical sciences are objective, but they are the work of men who objectify, who abstract as they consider their world from a particular point of view, with a proper method. Every symbolic form is the work of a subject: it objectifies, yet it is a "subjective" creation, which is not the simple raw reality of the world and particulars within it as they are in themselves, independently of man's intentional operations regarding them.

Some recent and contemporary thought is characterized by what has been called the "turn to the subject" or the "turn to subjectivity". It is so called because it is directed to understanding the intelligible structure of conscious, intentional operations, and of the conscious subject. Such thought differs from the "purely objective" thought of empiricism in that it probes a diverse field and reflects upon diverse data. The field and the data are those of consciousness, of one's own operations and of one's self. Yet even such thought "objectifies" the subject: not reducing oneself to a thing, but making oneself and one's own conscious acts the term, the "object", of intelligent inquiry. Only by standing back from immediate first-personal experience can I probe and determine the structure of that experience. When I objectify my conscious acts and myself, I am proceeding in the only way possible to arrive at some understanding of the experience of which I am aware. Such reflection is first-personal, since it can be directed only to first-personal experience: conscious acts and awareness of self are inaccessible to anyone but the conscious subject. Only because of the limits and imperfection of human being must we come to a knowledge of ourselves by standing back and regarding a unique sort of "other", the very self of whom we are aware, but whom we can know only by reflection, by a turning back to discover the structure of a previous conscious act.

In all of my knowledge, of things, of other persons, of myself, and even of God, I objectify: not flattening all out into things in an "objective" world of cartesianism or empiricism, but making them terms of my cognitive acts, grasping and affirming what I can of them, with a full awareness that I can never hold the full mystery of their being.

There is a universal objectifying which characterizes all human thought. There is also a discourse which can range over all being, and speak of things, persons, and God, without reducing them to the flattened-out "being" of postcartesian thought. But here the road divides, and one would have to enter upon another long reflection to set out what has eluded even very subtle postcartesian thinkers. Before I end my discourse in this book, I shall say something of what lies beyond it in the direction of a full understanding of man, of a metaphysics understood in a very particular way, and of a natural knowledge of God.

INTEGRATION OF KNOWLEDGE

In a preceding section I reflected on the role of intellect in holding the unity of my total conscious field.[12] There is a further function of unification or integration of knowledge. Its necessity appears when we recall and reflect upon the implications of the total sphere of human operation, as we considered it in Chaper V.

Though my total conscious field is extremely important as the setting or field or ground of every one of my intentional operations, it is not the total setting. Nor do I acquire knowledge even of myself solely from the data of consciousness. If I seek to understand my operations and myself, I must take into account what can be learned from empirical study of the nonconscious personal ground of my conscious acts. For a knowledge of self, and for a basic knowledge of man, we must integrate the knowledges which can be acquired by reflection on the data gathered both from conscious life and from objective, empirical study of man and human behavior.

The importance of such integration may strike one when he experiences modern scientific health care. In the meeting of patient and doctor, and in the course of diagnosis and treatment, two complementary factors are important. The patient not only entrusts himself to the doctor as a "body" to be examined and treated, but tells as fully as possible what trouble he has experienced. The doctor, with his knowledge of both

---

12 Above, pp. 170-171.

the human body and its workings, and the interplay of psychic and somatic factors, may be fairly sure of his initial hypothesis of what is wrong. Yet normally he will have the patient undergo a complicated examination, a series of tests, to gather the empirical data by which he may not only confirm his original hunch, but also complete his diagnosis. If the doctor himself is not too narrowly specialized, and is able to recognize the significance of his patient's description of conscious experience, he may not be content with one series of tests which yields negative results. The patient, for example, may have reported a cluster of experiences which suggest some heart ailment. The cardiogram shows nothing serious. Yet the doctor, taking seriously the patient's account of what he felt, orders a stress test, and finds vague indications of abnormality. Still unable to diagnose accurately, the doctor sends his patient to a cardiologist, who recommends diagnosis by cardiac catheterization. The results enable the cardiologist to locate and measure the disease, and to prescribe the necessary treatment. If the cardiologist and the general practitioner deal understandingly with the patient as a person, they share with him as much as they consider necessary, to enable him to understand his disease, and the condition of his body underlying the symptoms which he felt. He does not thereby master medical science, but he comes to know enough to understand his condition, to live prudently and with tranquility, and to interpret eventual signs of danger. Whatever he can understand through scientific, empirical tests of his body complements what he knows from conscious experience.

Analogously, one can come to a deeper knowledge of the mystery of man, and of oneself as a human person, by study of, and reflection on, the physical universe, the human intersubjective world, and the transcendent ground of his being and operation. A simple example concerning the physical universe is the knowledge of various kinds of pollution, which have a serious effect on our health. Such knowledge too complements what we experience consciously, and helps us to understand our experience—especially how we feel at times—in its setting in our physical environment. With regard to the human intersubjective world in which we live, we can integrate two sorts of knowledge which are complementary: what we can learn from sharing our lives with other persons in truly mutual, interpersonal knowledge and love; and what we can learn from the many sciences which study human behavior empirically. With

regard to the transcendent ground of our being, again two complementary knowledges can be integrated : a philosophical knowledge which can ground the certain affirmation of the existence
of God, and discourse coherently about him in a purely human
rational manner; and an experiential knowledge from an interpersonal union by faith and love in response to the initiative
of the revealing God.

In all of these instances, one can progress in the understanding of the mystery of man, and of one's own personal
mystery, by the integration of many knowledges.

KNOWLEDGE OF THE SINGULAR

Some readers who are familiar with classic thomistic philosophy, in particular its theory of knowledge, and some rare
readers who were familiar with some of my own earlier work
in philosophy, may wonder about the relationship of my present
thought to such philosophy. In particular, with regard to the
role of intellect, some may wonder what is to be said of the
knowledge of the singular.

The classic problem of the knowledge of the singular arose
within a particular natural philosophy and metaphysics. We
should have to make a long side trip to survey that philosophy,
and it would be a difficult task to evaluate it and work out
the relationships between my account of human knowledge and
such a philosophy. I shall not attempt it here, nor, perhaps,
elsewhere. Long ago I did my apprenticeship in such philosophy,[13] and I retain a deep respect for it. I do not think that
my present account involves the same problem regarding man's
knowledge of the singular. I mention the classic problem merely
to register the fact that I am aware of it, and to state candidly
that I abstain from the attempt to deal with it.

In the context of the reflection which we have made, however, something remains to be said concerning the role of intellect in the knowledge of the singular. We have approached
a theory of knowledge by reflecting upon structures of human
cognitive operations within the whole of human experience. In
that account of knowledge, one notes the process from primor-

---

[13] Cf. WILLIAM A. VAN ROO, S.J., "A Study of Genus in the Philosophy
of St. Thomas Aquinas," *The Modern Schoolman* 20 (1943) pp. 89-104;
165-181; 230-244.

dial, implicit, massive awareness and knowledge to explicit acts in which we understand by fixing and formulating relationships, and we affirm that things are or are not in such relationships. In such an account of knowledge, there is no illusion of coming to the complete knowledge of the essences of things. In what I indicated as the first kind of intellectual operation, we seek answers to the questions *what is it*? or *of what sort is it*? In the knowledge which we acquire in answer to such questions, we gradually fix relationships which we have grasped. In a sense one could say that the ideal term of our process in such knowledge would be the grasp of the essences of the things which we understand. It is, however, an ideal term of a process which in human life is unending. The process could terminate, and hopefully will terminate, in the vision of God, of the divine ideas.

What we grasp in understanding is relationships, and we recognize a universality or generality of such relationships. If we say that we grasp the forms of things, what do we mean? The form which we hold in knowledge is the relationship or set of relationhips which we have grasped. Is it the form of the thing which we know? Is it *in* the thing? It is only in the sense that the thing *is* in such a way as to ground the relationships which we have grasped. The form is a principle of knowledge, an element of knowledge. It is not a principle of the thing in its being independently of our knowing it. This is not to deny that there are principles of things, that there is an a priori in the thing, a nature or essence according to which it is. Quite the contrary: I should suggest that a full philosophy of man involves the recognition of such an a priori, essence, nature, principle of bieng. Our knowledge of man, however, is not acquired by somehow grasping fully that essence or nature. We advance in our knowledge of man, without expectation of reaching complete knowledge in this life by matching the fulness of human being.

Human knowledge, like human being, is *human*: somehow bodily in all of its operations, and intellectual through the whole realm of conscious life. All of our intellectual operations, of which we are conscious, are singular, performed with the expenditure of the only kind of energy which we have: bodily energy. All understanding begins in the grasp of relationships in the being and operations of individual existing persons and things. Though we come to a grasp of relationships which have a certain generality or universality, we recognize them in individual instances, in both our objective and our subjective fields. What we have come to know of human nature we recognize in the case of John or Mary. What we have come to know of the structure of human conceptualization we recognize in an individual act in which we conceptualize.

Because we know in a human way, our knowledge always involves a certain blend of sense and intellect. Because this blend is universal, our knowledge of the singular ranges over the whole of our objective and subjective fields.

CONCLUSION

With this chapter on the roles of intellect we come to the end of our basic reflection on the structure of human experience. We have prepared the necessary setting for a consideration of human symbolizing. It is not that we have finished our philosophical reflection on man. Rather we have completed one phase of a process which in a way is dialectical. The mystery of man's symbolizing is part of the mystery of man, and whatever we can learn of the manifold process of symbolizing and of the range of its works will contribute to a deeper understanding of man himself. At the end of our reflection on symbolizing and symbols we shall be able to make some further reflections on man, and indicate further questions whose answers could come only in a complete philosophy of man.

Our special consideration of intellect has been necessary, for, as we shall see, all of man's symbolizing and all of his symbols are aspects of the expression of a human experience which in all its modes, in all its dimensions, is "haunted" by insight, penetrated and permeated by intellect. In the universe of being, and true, and good, man *is* in a unique way. He is bodily, and yet all of his vital organization is in the service of a conscious life which rises to operations beyond comparison with those of all other living bodily things. So his mystery is that of a blend of the bodily and of what has been called spiritual. So it is that in his response to the true and the good, he understands and wills. But there is a bodily radiation of all aspects of his response to the world. In the cognitive order, his operations include the many modes of the intuitive factor in human knowledge: what we have considered and discerned in so-called sense knowledge, in perception, memory (in some of its elements), and imagination. Corresponding to his volitive response to what he knows as good or bad for him, there is the radiation of the whole range of emotive and motor response.

All human conscious acts are "haunted" by insight, not, as the figurative language might suggest, by some occupying spirit, but in the sense that man in all of his being is intellectual. The intellectual dimension is not added somehow to the bodily, in all of its cognitive, affective, and motor aspects. Man is not an animal plus a spirit. Rather he is human, with a higher organization which characterizes man in all his being, and which is radically intellectual, rational. The true and the good or evil are present to him as he grasps them, in an experience of his world which always has some intellectual, rational core. The human mode of being, with its unique blend of elements, exhibits always the consequences of being intelligent and willing in a human body: of being man.

All of man's experience is human experience, qualified by the higher organization which is properly human, and geared to a total experience and development which is that of the human person in community. All of man's symbolizing involves some blend of all of the elements of the human way of being and operating, since it is always a human person who is symbolizing.

Since all elements of human experience, all modes of human operation, are properly human, and function in the unique way which is human, our initial treatment of perception, memory, and imagination as sense knowledge was abstractive and tentative. We had to return to consider other dimensions of human perception, memory, and imagination, which could be understood only after we had reflected on intellectual operations. Moreover we had to reflect on the blend of all, and on the roles of intellect in the discernment, critique, and unity of conscious operations and of the conscious field; and on all of the other functions which we have just considered.

We may turn now to consider human symbolizing and its works.

Chapter VII

SYMBOLIZING

A glance at the table of contents of this book would suffice to give some knowledge of the order in which I shall treat matters in this second part. Yet it seems good to give a word of explanation of the basic strategy. I am approaching symbolizing as a distinctively human operation, and symbols as human works. Symbols are made by man, and any discourse about natural symbols is intelligible ultimately only in the context of the natural process of man's symbolizing. Hence I begin with that process. I say "process" in the singular, though the modes of symbolizing and the symbols produced are many and varied. There is a basic analogy running through all symbolizing and symbols, and we can understand any one mode of symbolizing or any one kind of symbol best if we can locate it in the wide range of a wondrously varied human work.

Though symbolizing is done in the setting of a human community, and the community has an indispensable role in the development and continuing life of symbols, still any given symbol is the work of one person, a contribution to the life of his community. It is reasonable, then, to concentrate first on the process of symbolizing, of the creation of symbols in various manners. In the chapters which follow immediately, therefore, I do just that. Some other questions, consequently, must be held in abeyance, and I merely mention them now and wait to take them up later.

Among the matters which I shall treat later on, these may seem to deserve earlier treatment, and delay in considering them calls for a word of explanation: (1) the role of the community in the creation of symbols; (2) the continued use of symbols, as distinguished from their creation; (3) non-cognitive functions of symbols; (4) so-called natural or essential symbols, which seemingly are not products of human symbolizing.

With regard to the role of the community in the creation of symbols, I shall try to bring it out clearly later, and I put it off now only because one cannot do everything at once, and it seems reasonable to reflect first on the process by which any man or woman in the community symbolizes, and their symbols enter into the life of the community. There are, of course, symbolizing actions in which a whole community acts in unison, and the symbol is the work of many, not of one. Yet in every person who participates in such action, the personal process is realized, with a unique personal manner and degree of participation. Even in the case of such symbolizing, therefore, the action of the group can be understood only if one understands what is involved in the personal action of every participant.

Continued use, adaptation, and vitalizing of symbols in the life of a community obviously presupposes the original creation. I shall mention non-cognitive factors in the first section of this chapter, and indicate why I delay the treatment of these factors in symbolizing. It will be clear in the chapter on functions of the symbol that I lay great importance on the non-cognitive functions. This is one of the distinctive features of my whole treatment of symbols. I shall take up the question of "natural" symbols after working out my definition of symbol, since some notions of natural or essential symbol may occasion difficulties with my definition. I believe that the matter can be treated best at that point.

With regard to this chapter, I divide it into three very unequal sections. The first is brief, because I have done the basic reflection in chapter III, and chapters IV, V and VI supplement that reflection. Yet insight marks the absolute beginning of all symbolizing, and it must be mentioned here briefly in the first place. The other two sections mark distinctions which lay out the whole realm of symbolizing and the rich variety of symbols.

INSIGHT AND TOTAL RESPONSE

All symbolizing begins with insight, the grasp of intelligible relationships. As we have seen, there is a primordial, vague, implicit grasp of relationships at the beginnings of all human experience. It ranges over the whole of man's conscious field, objective and subjective. With continuing inquiry by the person, driven by his very nature to understand more clearly, insights are sharper, explicit grasps of relationships. Among the many kinds of relationships which can be grasped, and which can be part of our understanding of the world and of ourselves, I indicated the importance of the vast realm of analogy.[1] When symbolizing begins with a grasp of analogy, the whole process of symbolizing is marked in a special way by analogy.

One might suppose as a general principle that the sharper the insight, the better will be the symbol. Ironically, however, that is not the case universally. For some types of symbols, sharply conceptual, the principle would hold. But there are other types of symbols, different in the basic tendency which governs their creation, which may proceed from very vague insights, mere intimations. They are different from sharply conceptual symbols, but they are not necessarily inferior. Who is to determine the relative excellence of the symbols of Shakespeare and of Einstein?

Insight is always partial, and in that sense it is always abstractive. It catches some aspect of the being and operation and interrelationships present to man in the world in which he lives. It may grasp any relationship in the objective field, among persons and things present to the one who begins to understand. It may grasp some aspect of the relationship of the subject to his world. It may grasp vaguely the shape of the subject's own experience.

Insight is the beginning of a process of a man's response both to his world and to the beginnings of an understanding of himself in his world. The total response is manifold: it embraces all modes of intentional operation. Initial grasp of some intelligible relationship may spur a man to seek to formulate what he has begun to understand, and his understanding comes to a relative fulfillment in conception, or in some other manner of fixing and projecting the relationship which he has grasped. Insight into the good or bad for him initiates his emotive, voluntary, and motor response. It is in man's manifold response to insight that symbolizing occurs. Symbolizing may be predominantly cognitive, or emotive, or volitional, or motor. In every case, the symbol is the immediate term of the process. I say "immediate term", because symbolizing tends beyond the production of the symbol. Symbols themselves function in the continuing life and operation of the person symbolizing and of the interpersonal world in which his or her symbols have meaning for others.

---

[1] Above, pp. 172-173.

Whatever may be the dominant intentional mode in any given conscious operation, in any symbolizing and in the symbol which is its term, there is always a cognitive factor. In emotive, volitional, and motor action, which take their full shape in some sort of symbol, I know the object which is good or bad for me, and I have some knowledge of the shape of my action.

Since the cognitive factor ranges through all symbolizing and symbols, we may begin our consideration reasonably with a discernment and differentiation of symbols in terms of that cognitive factor, and then face the question of the varying degrees and blends of other intentional factors in different kinds of symbols. Only after having considered all of the functions of symbols shall I attempt to formulate a definition which may be relatively adequate to hold all the essential elements in an intelligible structure.

Two Modes, Tendencies, and Elements

I propose here a triple consideration of symbolizing: three pairs of modes, tendencies, and elements. The two modes of symbolizing are two ways of forming a symbol, of coming to the term of intentional operation in one or more types of intentionality. The modes are contraries, like two poles in a field. Corresponding to them, there are two tendencies. All symbolizing tends toward either of the two poles. The poles are pure positions, toward one of which any kind of symbolizing may tend, as toward an ideal. The positions are never reached in their purity, with a complete exclusion of the contrary mode. Consequently, there are two elements in all symbolizing and in all symbols. Both modes are present in all symbolizing, to varying degrees. Any type of symbolizing, and every symbol which is produced, is marked by a tendency toward a pure position, but is held in tension between the two poles. Elements of both kinds of symbolizing enter into the process and into the symbols which result. The triple division of contraries is not a criterion for the classification of symbols, but an insight into the complementarity of two factors which are found in varying blends in all symbolizing and all symbols.

(1) *Conceptual.* I deal first with the conceptual, since the other ternary is understood best by contrast with the conceptual. The conceptual mode is the way of proceeding from initial in-

sight to sharper, more accurate determination of relationships grasped, and their formulation in concepts, which eventually constitute a system or a world of meaning. Concepts are elaborated by the shaping of a sensuous medium. For the most part, the medium is articulate vocal sound in speech, and its derivative written signs in written language. In more specialized thought, such as mathematics, another system of written symbols is developed, forming a system which bypasses speech and the polyvalence of the spoken word in a multitude of languages. In cases of special need, not without sacrifice of wealth and suppleness, the sensuous medium may be, for example, visible gesture in sign language.

The tendency in conceptual symbolizing is to move from the vagueness and polyvalence of primitive common-sense language toward an ever sharper, more univocal set of symbols. One tends not only to separate the formulation of the conception of the relationship from all non-cognitive elements of an original experience, but also to isolate the grasp of a particular relationship, and to differentiate it from all other vaguely associated intelligible relationships. In common sense language one tends to cut through figurative expressions to the plain, unadorned, simple literal expression of relationships. Even in this realm of common sense one strives for relatively adequate definition of terms, and distinction of meaning according to context. The process continues and is accelerated in the development of technical, scientific, and philosophical language, or in a substitute symbol system, as in mathematics. One goal, attainable with considerable effort at definition and distinction, is that in any given discourse a term will be understood to have only one meaning, one relationship which has been grasped. The unattainable goal of the pure position would be a purely relational language, with no trace of its origins in primordial, intuitive experience. It is unattainable because it would be freed from all links with the human mode of being and operating. All human speech, however technical or scientific, has its sensuous base, its moorings and launching ramps in the world of perception, and it is "vulnerable": the purity of its abstract, univocal meaning is constantly threatened. Even mathematical symbols can be read in the common languages of those who use them, and must be read or spoken to be introduced and explained. When a purely univocal mathematical symbol, bypassing the babel of spoken language, is read as "function" or "funzione", its antiseptic mathematical sheath is penetrated, and it is vulnerable to infection by the polyvalence of "function" and "funzione" in spoken English or Italian.

The conceptual element is the dominant factor in conceptual symbols. It is never the sole constituent, for there is always some measure of the contrary element, which is intuitive. In his remarkable study of the development of mathematical and scientific symbols, Cassirer makes it clear that the ideal of a purely relational symbolism, with no trace of its intuitive origins, is beyond human striving.[2]

Conceptual symbolizing has a number of characteristics. First, it has its distinct way of being abstractive. To begin with, it is abstractive in its concentration on the cognitive factor in experience, excluding as far as possible other modes of intentionality which would distract from the effort to discern and formulate relationships. Then, in its progress toward understanding, it fixes one type of relationship, moving into one world of meaning, with its limited interest and its own method. Intent on the grasp and formulation of intelligible relationships, it tends to disregard intuitive factors in the process of symbol formation, though it never completely eliminates them. Conceptual symbolizing is characterized by what Langer called isolating, generalizing abstraction.[3]

Conceptual symbolizing is linear, successive. It cannot hold and exhibit its whole object simultaneously, as one beholds in perceiving, or as the plastic artist projects a whole work, a painting or statue or building, which can be contemplated as a whole, present to the beholder. Michelangelo could set forth his conception of Moses, and it remains in its entirety, to be contemplated. I can set forth my conception of man the symbolizer only gradually, moving slowly along a single line of thought, then following another, in the execution of a strategy which calls for many distinctions and divisions, and the slow movement of syllable after syllable, word after word, proposition after proposition, in the fixing and formulation of many relationships, and the elaboration of a whole work which must be read with a similar linear, discursive operation.

Effective by its technique of dividing and multiplying its linear movements to explore and discern and fix successively every significant relationship, such symbolizing is rigid, and

---

[2] Cf. ERNST CASSIRER, *The Philosophy of Symbolic Forms*, III (New Haven: 1957) 385; and concerning physics, 479.

[3] SUSANNE K. LANGER, *Mind*, I (Baltimore: c. 1967) 153.

limited in its achievements. As it relies more and more on written or printed symbols, linguistic or other, it tends to reduce the intuitive element to the visual in perception, memory, and imagination. Unable to exhibit a whole simultaneously, it cannot match the representative power of the plastic arts, nor can it hold and express human experience with the fulness of drama or music. They too are successive, but they are not limited to the cognitive dimension of experience, and they are more capable of exhibiting the full dynamic pattern of human experience.

Conceptual symbolizing, by its very nature, is capable of progressing toward the ideals of understanding in mathematics, science, and some kinds of philosophical reflection. Even in philosophy, however, such symbolizing cannot suffice for the elaboration of an adequate metaphysics without being submitted to a process of purification and transformation. I shall say something of this later, when we turn to consider worlds of meaning.

(2) *Intuitive.* The contrary mode, tendency, and element is the intuitive. Although *intuitive* has a wide range of meanings, I take it here in a sense which it often has, as pertaining somehow to the order of sense knowledge. The intuitive mode of symbolizing involves the formation of an image, a form, similar to the configuration or constellation which is held in perception, memory (of what was once perceived), and imagination. Like the image or form in perception, the intuitive symbol may embody a form which is static or dynamic. Intuitive symbolizing does not grasp and formulate a relationship, holding it in isolation from its setting in the concrete world of existing things. Rather, exploiting the resources of perception, memory, and imagination, it shapes a sensuous medium to form an image in which relationships which have been grasped perhaps only vaguely are set forth embodied in a sensibly perceptible or imaginable whole. Instead of proceeding from insight to an isolation and refinement of the relationship which has been grasped, this sort of symbolizing turns back to the realm of the sensuous, and presents the relationship concretely, incarnate, somewhat as it is beheld in the full reality of persons and things and scenes and events as they are perceived, remembered, or imagined. Not merely copying sensibly perceptible reality, intuitive symbolizing proceeds from insight into sensuous analogy to form a sensuous medium into some sort of image, likeness, semblance of reality. We shall consider many of these

kinds of images in detail in the next chapter, when we consider the range of symbols.

Corresponding to this mode of symbolizing, the intuitive tendency is toward a more and more vivid, adequate representation of reality, in which significant features of a total experience are presented in such a way as to be recognized unmistakably.

The intuitive element is sensuous form, similar to the forms held in perception, memory, and imagination. It is an element of all symbolizing, even the most refined conceptual symbolizing, which can never be disembodied. Even in the most adequate, vivid intuitive type of symbol, however, the intuitive is still an element: dominant, but not the sole constituent. All intuitive symbolizing too has its conceptual element, for it is penetrated and permeated by insight, and it has its origins too in some grasp of relationships, some vague knowledge which could serve as the beginning of a process toward conception.

What, then, are the characteristics of intuitive symbolizing? First, it too is abstractive, but in a manner different from that of conceptualizing. Intuitive symbolizing abstracts significant sensuous form. From the whole of concrete reality as perceived or remembered or imagined, intuitive symbolizing eliminates the irrelevant, to hold only that sensuous form which sets forth vividly the aspects of reality which have been grasped. Hence, in its greatest achievements in works of art, such symbolizing sets forth an image which is more vivid, more impressive, than everyday reality in its fulness. It abstracts not by isolating a relationship which is understood to be general or universal, but by fashioning a concrete, sensuous whole which exhibits a form more strikingly by freeing from distracting, irrelevant features of its setting in real life or in the world of nature.

Intuitive symbolizing presents a concrete whole. Whether its symbol exhibits a whole which is simultaneous, as in the plastic arts, or a whole which is somehow successive, as in music or drama, it has a fulness which cannot be held in conceptual symbols. An art critic may have a keen sensibility, and may experience much of the meaning of a statue or painting or symphony, but if he tries to spell out that meaning in a discursive account, he fails miserably. Any great work of art, in any mode of artistic creation, is untranslatable. No discourse can hold and present the full meaning of the sensuous form. The intuitive symbol is a whole in which everything is related to everything, and any attempt to spell out all of the relationships, to give accounts of all the elements and of all their inter-relationships, is a waste of time and effort.

Springing from an insight into sensuous analogy, intuitive symbols at their best suggest a multiple sensuous analogy, with a suppleness and inexhaustible richness of the full meaning of human experience. Their elaboration involves a return to the fulness of experience, and the concrete image which results suggests the emotive, volitional, and motor charges of real experience.

In its humble origins, intuitive symbolizing is characteristic of the beginnings of all human experience. All primordial experience, in any period of human history, in any culture or world of meaning, is intuitive. Though mythical thinking is intuitive, not conceptual,[4] it would be a mistake to confine intuitive symbolizing to mythic experience. Rather, it is what gives livingness to human knowledge of persons and things at any period of history, in any culture. It holds the full concrete reality of the world perceived, with its physiognomic characteristics. Within the matrix of such primordial experience, in any culture, all differentiation and elaboration of relationships occurs. One need not revert to mythic consciousness, therefore, to hold the mystery of persons and things in their concrete reality. Even in primitive society, not all intuitive consciousness is mythic. As I shall point out in the next section on worlds of meaning, the evidence seems to call for a certain differentiation of consciousness even in primitive society, and the recognition of modes of thought and of language which are primitive but not mythic.

In its supreme achievements, in great works of art and in rich acts of worship, intuitive symbolizing reaches a perfection of realization and expression of human insight and feeling which is unique. Diverse from the great works of mathematical, scientific, or philosophical thought, such symbols are in no sense inferior to them. Their excellence, their adequacy as expression of thought and feeling, and their efficacy in communication are of a different order. We shall consider some of the qualities of these intuitive symbols in the next chapter, dealing with the range of symbols.

For those who recognize a basic complementarity in human sexuality, some further reflection will be meaningful. First,

---

[4] Cf. CASSIRER, op. cit., II, 62.

there is an analogy between the complementarity of conceptual and intuitive symbolizing and the complementarity of masculine and feminine. In each case, one finds varying degrees of participation of contrasting characteristics. In neither case does one find the "pure position": the absolute and exclusive realization of one of the sets of characteristics. As there is no conceptual symbol free from all intuitive elements, so there is no man in whom there is not some degree of the feminine, and no woman who has nothing of the masculine. Second, and more impressive than the merely formal consideration of the complementarity involved, the conceptual and the intuitive are themselves generally regarded as characteristic of the masculine and of the feminine respectively. This interplay of two complementarities should not surprise us: they are perfectly coherent aspects of the mystery of human being.

(3) *Blending.* Beyond the simple fact that every symbol has something of both the conceptual and the intuitive, one can note various aspects of the blending of the complementary modes, tendencies, and elements.

First, there is a certain likeness of structure of intellectual and emotional experience, and a similar manifold function of great works in both the conceptual and the intuitive mode. Insight which comes suddenly in the course of a long inquiry usually brings a thrill of emotion. So too a masterful presentation of a profound insight and conception in philosophy can not only communicate understanding to the reader who comes to share the insight as he reads, but also stir great emotion at the grasp of the beauty of the truth expressed. Profound philosophical discourse, then, can have a beauty, a splendor of form, which stirs emotion no less than a work of art. I have in mind works of Plato and of St. Thomas. On the other hand, a lyric, or a statue, or a drama can occasion deep insight into the structure of human feeling. Within the total experience of the perceiver, there is a rich conceptual dimension which is communicated by the work of art. The discursive element of that conceptual element does not express the full meaning of the art work, but catches some aspects of a total experience. A very human symptom of this complexity of experience and blend of symbolic modes is the oral presentation of a deep philosophical or theological thought: often, with styles and degrees which vary according to temperament and culture, such discourse is inseparable from the most vivid gesticulation.

As there is a certain isomorphism of feeling and motor

impulse, so too there is an isomorphism, a sensuous analogy, of intuitive symbolic forms. The impulse to dance, or to fly if one could, is inseparable from some feelings. So too a lyric can move one to sing, and song can move one to dance. A statue portraying a woman seemingly springing into flight is akin to the wondrous leaping movement of ballet, and any powerful art form may stir some beholder to a cry of emotion, to the jubilation which expresses the ineffable.

Little wonder, then, that symbols often are complex, and one form assimilates another, or even several intuitive forms. It is this blending of conceptual and intuitive, and of different intuitive forms, which alone can account for the unique character of some art forms. One cannot say, with full concern for the problems involved, that a lyric poem or a novel seems to be discursive but is not; or that the words of a song are now merely musical elements. It is only the blend of conceptual and intuitive that can suggest an account of the unique character of every one of the arts which use language. It is the mystery of isomorphism and blend of intuitive forms which account for the assimilation of the words of a lyric in song, or the assimilation of many intuitive forms in the commanding form of drama or ballet. Words of lyric poetry are taken up into music, but they make a difference. There is an assimilation of one form by another, but what is assimilated contributes in its unique way to the total form. One of the most complex instances of such assimilation and continuing qualification by the assimilated elements is medieval Latin hymnology, in which music is affected not only by the sense of the words taken up, but also by the character of the Latin language and the complex play of a double metric system, in which both quantity and accent are significant.

(4) *A universal function.* Through all variations and blends of symbolizing a single function is being performed analogously: a particular is integrated into a whole, in which alone it has its full meaning. In predominantly conceptual symbolizing, every concept is set in a whole intelligible field, and it has a definite meaning in that field, that context of thought. Cassirer has illustrated this in mathematical and scientific thought.[5] If one desires a humble example, it can be drawn from a rather intellectual type of leisure activity: contract bridge. There are many systems for playing bridge. In any given system, a single high-

[5] *Op. cit.,* III, 279-479.

ranking card (the ace of spades, for example), a single bid
(opening two no trump), a lead, or a discard, has meaning for
a partner or opponent or onlooker who knows the system. For
one who does not know the system, its meaning in this context
is unknown. In intuitive symbolizing, a simple symbol (a gesture
or an exclamation) is grasped in its setting in a whole human
experience. Every element of a complex symbol has its meaning
only as it is set in the whole, and it contributes to the communication of the full meaning of the symbol: cognitive, emotive,
volitional, and motor. In Old Testament worship, the sense
of a given act of sacrifice was grasped as it was set in a whole
act of worship which included a recitation of salvation history
(Dt 26.1-11). In Christian worship, any portion of the baptismal
ceremony must be understood in its setting in the whole, and
the whole ritual and prayer can be understood only in its setting
in the whole of salvation history, of God's saving action reaching
this person here and now.

WORLDS

What is the *whole* into which a particular is integrated in
every act of symbolizing, and in every symbol? It is one of
the many worlds of meaning. We must consider now the range
of such worlds.

Yesterday, after working for a while at this problem, I
paused, turned on my radio, and tuned in the BBC, to get the
news at ten o'clock. It was about seven minutes before the
hour, and I listened to the last part of the program "The Farming
World." An expert was being interviewed on the sort of advice
which he and his colleagues give to developing countries: what
sort of machinery to invest in with a view to modernizing and
developing agriculture on a large scale. Then, in the closing
minutes of the program, another expert was introduced, having
been introduced as one who represented an entirely different
approach. She told of the sort of advice which she and her
colleagues give to farmers in countries which have no realistic
prospect of big development perhaps for the next half-century.
All of her advice regarded not investment in big modern
machinery, which they could never have afforded, and which
was out of proportion to their situation. What they needed was
advice concerning small farming, sufficient employment, and
small systems of power for local use in a country which for

a long time would not be able to supply electrical energy from big central power plants.

What struck me was that "the farming world" is not one world, but several. The two experts lived in different mental worlds, corresponding to the realities of two completely different situations. Their programs of action made sense for the types of situations which they envisioned, and only for those types. Every element in each program had meaning in relation to the whole, and to all other elements in the program.

So it is with the wholes into which symbols are integrated, and within which alone they have their intended meaning. Symbols have meaning. They are the terms of processes which begin with insight. They are the works of men, the results of human operations which are set in the total fields or worlds which we have considered: objective and subjective. Since the symbols may be predominantly cognitive, emotive, volitional, or motor, their meaning can be correspondingly chiefly cognitive, emotive, volitional, or motor. That is to say that they are understood by being fixed in fields of intelligible relationships which vary according to the prevailing type of intentionality. A given word or movement may be understood as a formulation and expression of knowledge, or as the final stage of an act of emotion, or as an externally manifested decision, or as part of a total motor effort: a single stride in the whole of a sprint. But in every case the symbol has meaning: it fits into an intelligible whole. The intelligible whole into which every symbol fits is the world of meaning in which it is intelligible.

How many such worlds can be designated? If one considers several rather general divisions of such worlds of meaning, and the infinite variability of persons, one could say that the worlds of meaning are simply infinite. Every person is unique. His every operation is set in a unique total personal context. Even his way of doing mathematics, or rather of operating in any one of the many worlds of mathematics, is unique. Considered in this way, the worlds of meaning are beyond classification, and "world of meaning" becomes meaningless except in terms of every person's private world or set of worlds.

Yet some reasonable and recognizable distinctions and divisions can be made. Allowing for inevitable personal differences, there are clearly differentiated general settings in which persons operate, and in which they communicate. Their symbols are meaningful for other persons who have some familiarity with the world in which they are set. Some range of different worlds of meaning can be indicated, therefore, but in doing so one must allow for both variations in style and the emergence of new worlds as human creativity continues.

Perhaps the best order in which to present such worlds is that of a recognizable progress in the development of persons, societies, and cultures. Where should one begin? Cassirer seems to have changed his mind in this matter. In the first volume of his *Philosophy of Symbolic Forms* he dealt with language and linguistic thought, as he called it. He traced the development of worlds of meaning as witnessed by the development of language from its intuitive, imitative beginnings. In his second volume he dealt with the mythic thought world. There he traced the development of an intelligible world in terms of the distinction between sacred and profane, and in doing so he set forth another history of patterns of development of relationships of space, time, subject-attribute, and cause. By the time he came to write his third volume he held that all thought begins with myth.

If one compares Cassirer's accounts of development of the thought of primitive man, he may ask a question which Cassirer himself, to my knowledge, did not raise: how is it that the same primitive men had two different lines of development in their concepts of space, time, subject-attribute, and cause? It seems to me that one can answer only by recognizing some differentiation of thought worlds in primitive society. There were two primitive realms of thought: that of intuitive knowledge in everyday life, and that of a particular kind of intuitive knowledge in terms of the sacred and profane, a distinction made with some insight into the mystery of the world and of human life.

I shall begin with what we can surmise of primitive, intuitive knowledge in everyday experience. Cassirer's evidence from the studies of language development suggests such a world of thought, and it seems reasonable to regard it as most basic and universal. Myth, on the contrary, depends on a particular set of insights into the mystery of the world and of human life. Eventually the distinction of sacred and profane pervades all of the world as it is viewed by primitive man. Yet this universality of mythic thought in primitive society seems to be a special development. Moreover, apart from the hypothetical priority in primitive societies, one could say that the primitive stage of an intuitive world view prevails through all human history, in all cultures. Personal development begins from this stage. Within the matrix of primordial, intuitive knowledge all relationships are fixed gradually, and all progress begins from this initial phase.

On the contrary, although wonder at the mystery of the world and of human life is a constant experience throughout human history, mythic thought is found only in primitive cultures. Myth is a particular, primitive response to questions concerning the transcendent, the sacred. It does not survive the development of a culture in which deeper insights prevail, and in which a religion is based on belief in a historical divine intervention.

In the following account of worlds of meaning I attempt some differentiation, beginning with what may be regarded as first in time, but continuing without regard to a single line of chronological development. I am not proposing a conjectural history of the development of worlds of thought, but some effort at discernment and differentiation. This is true especially with regard to the place in which I treat Christian religion and theology. I consider them last, as I considered the transcendent world last in my reflection on the total setting of human operations in chapter V.

(1) *The primitive, intuitive world.* This is a phase of human development which one would expect to find, consistently with a reflection on the structure of human experience, in which there is a gradual progression from primordial knowledge to explicit conceptualization. There is evidence of such a stage in the record of development of language, from almost purely sensuous, mimetic language to increasingly sharp conceptualization.[6] Two features characterize such a world of meaning: (1) the dominance of the sensuous: what is experienced in perception, memory of what has been perceived, imagination, and dream; (2) the prominent awareness of the distinction between self and non-self. In the paragraphs which follow, I shall treat some aspects of the manners in which basic relationships are grasped and expressed in primitive language.

---

[6] I give here some of the elements from Cassirer's first volume. For a more complete presentation of the material, see my article, "Symbol According to Cassirer and Langer," *Gregorianum* 53 (1972) 517-526, with detailed references to Cassirer's work. Cassirer's interpretation of language and linguistic thought is not representative of more recent and contemporary linguistic studies and linguistic philosophy; but it is based on earlier historical studies, and it is an intelligent reflection which is worthy of consideration.

Space and spatial relationships are expressed with great precision and almost imitative immediacy. There are ten ways of standing, and twenty ways of sitting. In the expression of *here* and *there*, *near* and *distant* a basic sensuous metaphor runs through several languages: similar sounds are used. In various languages too there are similar sounds to indicate *I*, *thou*, and *that*. The first opposition which is expressed is that of *I* and *not-I*. Subsequently such sounds express proximity and distance. There is a basic differentiation and determination of relationships in reference to the speaker's own body. Progress in conception is noted: from relations of together, side by side, and separate, to various other qualitative relations, dependencies, and oppositions. Similarly, from spatial *whence* there is the development of the causal *whereby*; and from spatial *whither*, to aim or purpose.

Time and temporal relationships are conceived with greater difficulty, since temporal factors are not given to consciousness simultaneously. Gradually spatial terms are adapted to signify temporal relationships: *here* expresses both *here* and *now*; *there*, both *there* and *earlier* or *later*. First there is an awareness of distinction and distance, or of now and not-now. Gradually temporal modes in action are distinguished: completed and incomplete, continued and momentary. Only slowly does one come to a sense of the unique and irreversible direction of time, and later to the pure concept of time as an abstract concept of order.

Differentiation of number starts from the human body and its members. "... the first 'counting' consists merely in designating certain differences found in external objects, by transferring them, as it were, to the body of the counter and so making them visible. All numerical concepts, accordingly, are purely mimetic hand concepts or other body concepts before they become verbal concepts ..."[7] Since a definite order of the parts of the body is observed, such primitive intuitive beginnings contain in embryo the relationship which later will be made explicit: a system of positions with an order in progression. In primitive numbering there is no notion of factors necessary for later explicit conception of number: homogeneity of strictly similar units, distinguished only by position in counting, and by no other material attribute. For primitive man counted objects must be present in all their tangible concretion, and touched

---

[7] CASSIRER, *op. cit.*, I, 229.

and felt; and the counting units are differentiated by concrete sensuous characteristics. Primitive arithmetical systems are distinguished by the natural material group on which they are based: quinary (one hand); decimal (both hands); vigesimal (both hands and both feet).

For primitive man number is a quality of things, and he has different sets of numbers for different kinds of things. Instead of contrasting unity and plurality sharply, he marks gradations between them: dual, trial, and in some languages a double plural to designate few or many.

In general, primitive languages express every detail, but come only gradually to general terms. Thus, American Indian languages have no general verb *to eat*, but many verbs expressing variations of the action. The often-cited example of abundance of concrete detail is a list of 5,744 Arabic words expressing details concerning the camel.

Returning now to our general problem regarding worlds of meaning, one can understand how any particular is integrated into a whole by primitive linguistic symbolizing. The whole is the world of perception, memory, imagination, and of the immediate sensuous presence of a world somehow opposed to the self. All vaguely grasped relationships are expressed in linguistic symbols which have their meanings in terms of relationships prevailing in such a world of thought.

Though the intuitive factor is dominant in the very beginnings of the life of every person, one could not say that every child now born into any culture goes through the experience of primitive man, and re-lives the whole process of evolution of thought and worlds of meaning. We are not left to our own devices, nor are we born into a primitive society—at least most of us. We are born into a society and a culture of a certain degree of development, in an intersubjective world, and our probing of the world is stimulated, channeled, guided by the ever-present influence of persons, who by various blends of pointing and naming and complex speech introduce us into that particular world of meaning, that variation on the world of common sense, which is our own.

(2) *Mythical worlds.* I say "worlds" in the plural, to allow for the numberless variations in particular mythical conceptions and representations. One can recognize certain general characteristics of the mythical mode of thought. I mention here only some of those cited by Cassirer in his second volume; others

seem to me to be somewhat conjectural. I shall conclude with
a brief critical reflection.

Mythical thought, and the variety of mythical worlds, are
concerned with what we can call the transcendent. The basic
insight is of the sacred, and the basic opposition is that of the
sacred and profane. The sacred is the extraordinary, unusual,
mysterious, which is vaguely grasped as the power which lies
behind the world and the wonders of human life. The profane
is the ordinary, the commonplace. Yet somehow the sacred
permeates all. The opposition between sacred and profane characterizes the basic categories of mythical thought: space, time,
and number.

Cassirer gives two accounts of mythical space, without
noting their radical difference. One is built up in reference to
the human body. Since the world is thought to have been
formed from parts of a human or superhuman being, it retains
the character of organic unity: the parts of the world in mythical geography of this kind are organs of the human body. The
other principle of organizing mythical space is based on the
opposition of day and night, light and darkness. East, west,
north, and south have their specific reality and significance, a
definite divine or demonic, friendly or hostile, holy or unholy
character. The east as the origin of light is the source of life.
The west as the place of the setting sun is full of the terrors
of death. The sacral ordering of the heavens in turn became
the principle for marking zones of the earth, for the limitation
of property, the structure of the city, camp, and home.

Mythical time is the time of origins. Specifically human
existence, usages, customs, social norms and ties are hallowed
by being derived from beginnings in the primordial mythical
past. That mythical past is the explanation of all. It is an
absolute past which is somehow permanent in its influence,
somehow timeless. Mythical thought does, however, have a sense
of sequence and temporal relations, and time is articulated in
terms of the interchange of light and darkness, day and night.
Consequently a special holiness is attributed to time and to particular phases of time. Specific sacral acts are assigned to definite sacred times and seasons, outside of which they would lose
their sacral power. With a subtle sensitivity to the proper
rhythms of human life, mythic thought marks birth and death,
pregnancy and motherhood, puberty and marriage, with specific
sacred rites.

Number too is concrete, with an affective tonality. Every

number has its own essence and power, and the basic opposition is worked out in a system of sacred, mystical numbers.

This is an extremely jejune account of some features of mythic thought, but it may suffice to differentiate it from what I called more generally the primitive intuitive world. I am aware of some of the vast modern and contemporary literature devoted to myth, and I consider that many such studies have rectified an age-old misconception of myth as a disease of the primitive and ancient mind. Without attempting to survey and evaluate some recent thought, I simply register here some reservations.

First, I regard as questionable the attribution of the beginnings of all human thought to mythical thought. If one contrasts the two sets of basic concepts of space, time, and number which I have recalled, and if one considers that supposedly it was the same primitive man who had both kinds of concepts, then it seems necessary to recognize some differentiation of worlds of thought even in primitive man. One develops simply from primordial experience, with vividly mimetic concrete representations. The other develops from a basic insight into origins of the world and of human life, institutions, and usages. It is equally vivid and concrete in its highly intuitive mode of thought, but it seems necessary to regard it as special, not as the sole, universal matrix of human thought.

Second, there is a certain irony in some exaltations of mythic experience by scholars who piece together bits of evidence from widely scattered places and different times, and try to give some notion of the concrete mythic experience. Moreover, some find in mythic thought a fulness and profundity which allegedly would be a salutary complement to the thought worlds of "western" man. I should observe that not all immediacy and fulness is proper to mythic thought: it is characteristic of primordial human experience in any epoch, any culture. Moreover, as I shall note a bit farther on in this treatment of worlds of thought, immediacy, fulness, and wholeness can be conserved in some modes of highly advanced philosophical and religious thought worlds, and in some rich contemporary experience of human interpersonal relationship.

As for the profundity of the insights of mythical man into the mystery of the universe and of human life, a further critical reflection seems to be in order. Myth expresses intimations of the sacred, the mysterious power which is at the source of the world and of human life; but intimations are beginnings, and a considerable world of religious and philosophical thought has enriched some later human experience. Myth is concerned with endless variations on aspects of the mystery of human life, and in particular of human sexuality. Yet the concern hovers over basic mysteries of genitality and generation. Certainly some recent insights into human sexuality, into the full range of the complementarity of masculine and feminine, man and woman, and the mystery of full conjugal love surpass what could be gained by a nostalgic effort to return to the alleged fulness of mythic experience.

(3) *Worlds of common sense.* Again I say "worlds": they are beyond number. To move from one to another, it is enough to move from one neighborhood to another within the same city. One who has lived abroad for many years comes to feel that he is always in a strange world of others' common sense; and when he returns to what was his own, he finds that it is no longer the one he knew.

The world of common sense may be designated roughly as the whole range of worlds of thought which characterize varieties of human living from the first progress beyond primitive life and pure myth to the approaches of science and philosophy. It is not limited to a period prior to the development of science or philosophy, but rather to a state of human development which stops short of science or philosophy in any age. When science and philosophy may have had a considerable achievement, the world of common sense is studded with bits of popularized science or philosophy, and scientific or philosophic or psychologic language is affected by some who do not really know its meaning. Common sense is said cynically to be the kind of knowledge with which the world muddles through. Yet it is the kind of knowledge which must suffice for most men and women to live, to cope, and in many beautiful instances to achieve true human greatness. It is the world of advancing insight into relationships, of vaguely conjectured intelligible structures. Men and women of common sense use symbols of many kinds, without notable achievement in any, except for the precious persons who succeed in expressing beautifully in life a goodness and loving kindness which they could not begin to define. Their symbols too integrate a particular into a whole, and one must have a fairly adequate sense of the whole pattern of thought and custom to be able to understand—and dare to use—some words or gestures. Common sense can be the world of great human living, and it is despised too often by those who lack it.

(4) *The worlds of art.* I do not refer here to the range of art symbols, the works of art; but to the worlds of thought and feeling in which artists live, and within which they seek to create their symbols. There are many such worlds, for there are many kinds of artistic sensibility, though some men and women have been gifted with more than one. The artist whom I knew best, and whose experience I shared most intimately, was a painter. His worlds of special sensibility and insight into sensuous analogy were those of color and form. After a day's excursion he was weary, but not as any ordinary traveler would have been worn out by the physical stress of hours spent on a bus. He was weary from over-stimulation and exhilaration of hours in which he reacted keenly to the colors of the landscape. His awareness of form, and his grasp of sensuous analogy, inspired one painting from two details which he glimpsed along the way: the angle of the back of an old woman sitting along the roadside, and an infant's foot. Each suggested the shape of a whole figure and feeling, and eventually both were elements of a painting of the Madonna and Child.

I shall say more about some forms of art and art symbols in the next chapter, but it is enough here to note that the artist too integrates a particular into his world of human feeling, with his sense of analogy, and of the shape of human feeling. His world too is one of predominantly intuitive experience. His special gifts are perhaps three: keen sensibility, rare grasp of sensuous analogy or metaphor, and above all the creative gift of fashioning some sort of likeness of what he has grasped.

(5) *Mathematics, science, and technology.* Again, there are many worlds, with a certain kinship. Mathematics alone is a whole order of knowledges, with wide-ranging influence on the sciences and technologies within which it is applied. These orders of knowledge progress by reducing intuitive, representative elements, and striving to elaborate a system of concepts and symbols which express pure relationships. According to Cassirer, these are the requirements of the scientific concept: (1) the postulate of identity: the same sign must always be chosen for the same concept; (2) every new concept that is set up in scientific thought is related from the outset to the totality of this thought, to the totality of possible concept formations; (3) it follows that concept signs must form a self-contained system; (4) the sign must disengage itself from intuitive existence far more energetically than was the case in the sphere

of language; (5) no intuitive secondary meaning adheres to concepts: they are pure vehicles of meaning.[8]

Mathematical symbols and scientific and technological concepts have meaning only for the initiate, for whom they fit into a whole intelligible structure.

In a sense, my distinction between worlds of meaning, which I am treating here, and kinds of symbols, which I shall treat in the next chapter, seems to lose its significance in the case of mathematics, science, and technology. In these realms one can hardly treat the worlds of thought without mentioning the very special symbols by which those worlds themselves are elaborated. Understanding is reached in these areas only as one perfects the concepts in which it can be formulated. It is true that every single concept then is integrated into a whole, and has its meaning in a given world of thought. Yet the world of thought is a work of intellect which is effected only by the elaboration of a highly abstract, almost purely conceptual set of symbols, approaching the ideal of expressing nothing but the relationships which have been grasped.

Given the highly abstract nature of the symbols and of the world of thought, it may be worth while to reflect here in particular on the reality of these works. The question does not concern the reality of the works done by the application of these knowledges: they are palpable and observable and increasingly wondrous. But are the worlds of thought themselves *real*, despite their abstractness? Of course they are. They are works of human intellect. Thinking is a mode of being, and is real. Thought, taken in the sense of a body of knowledge, or that which has been understood, is real. For all its abstractness, the highest mathematics is real and has its existential aspect, though that is not the concern of the mathematician, and it cannot be considered with the methods of mathematics. In what sense are mathematical propositions existential, and who is concerned with them as such?

I should suggest that in two senses mathematical propositions are existential. First, at least in their remote beginnings mathematics involved insights into intuitive, empirical foundations and reflections on experience. More to the point, at any stage in the development of the most abstract mathematics, the insight and the formulation of concepts, axioms, postulates, from which a whole system is generated, is the work of a man,

---

[8] *Op. cit.*, III, 337-340.

who acts at a given place and time in human history. Mathematical concepts and propositions are not just "there" to be beheld, nor do mathematical systems and mathematical truth exist from all eternity. They are grounded in the properly human events in which men conceive and create an ideal world.

Who is concerned with the existential aspect of such thought? Not the mathematician, but the kind of philosopher who is concerned with being, the very act of being, and all of the modes and limitations upon it. Human thinking is a way of being, and though it be called "intentional being," still it is a mode of being, and it pertains to the total concern of the kind of philosophy which I call metaphysics. I shall have occasion to say something about it in its proper place.

One further reflection is necessary in the interest of what could be called intellectual sobriety. At times excessive claims are made for mathematics and for physics by those who are impressed by their magnificent achievements and unaware of their limitations. What I say here refers not to what mathematicians or physicists or other scientists think, but to the claims made at times by theoreticians or philosophers of mathematics and science.

In his treatment of "cognition" or "knowledge"—taken in the sense of the supreme developments of conceptual, relational type knowledge, Cassirer exalts the achievements of mathematics and of physics. First, in the realm of mathematics, Cassirer notes the unique excellence of the scientific concept of number. "...All exact concept formation starts from the realm of number... Once thought thus differentiates the pure form of the numerical relation from everything that can enter into it, it can make unlimited use of this form ... 'There is nothing that evades number' (Leibniz) ... The root of this ontological universality of number is that it provides an absolutely universal and ideal standard. This standard is applicable wherever any multiplicity of contents, however constituted in other respects, meets one condition, namely that it fixates elements which may be ordered and articulated according to a determinate viewpoint ... It is through the universal system of signs provided by number that thought is first enabled to apprehend all being toward which it turns as a thoroughly determinate being, and to understand it under the category of the universal and necessary." [9]

Second, regarding physics, Cassirer notes two achievements.

---

[9] *Ibid.,* 341-342.

One is a new concept of substance,[10] and of the permanence and invariance which characterize it. The other is a world view which transcends all points of view of particular observers, unifies them, and makes them understandable. The new concept of substance transforms the category of thing-attribute which is found in mythical thought, and the common-sense notion of substance, in which things have a certain permanence and invariability as they undergo change. As science moves away from the realm of intuitive representations, away from the here and now, it goes beyond the whole of space and time, and beyond the limits of intuitive representation and all representability. Physics has left the realm of representation and representability for a more abstract realm, in which the schematism of things has given way to the symbolism of principles. "... The world is defined with systematic unity as a $(3+1)$ dimensional metric manifold; all physical field phenomena are expressions of world metrics." [11] The ultimate physical reality is no longer a thing, or matter. "... the substantial is completely transformed into the functional: true and definitive permanence is no longer imputed to an existence propagated in space and time but rather to those magnitudes and relations between magnitudes which provide the universal constants for all description of physical process. It is the invariance of such relations and not the existence of any particular entities which forms the ultimate stratum of objectivity." [12]

The world view of physics unites the "... totality of aspects resulting for different observers, so as to explain them and make them understandable; but in precisely this totality the particularity of the viewpoint is not extinguished but preserved and transcended. In this whole movement scientific knowledge confirms and fulfills, in its own sphere, a universal structural law of the human spirit. The more it concentrates in itself, the more clearly it grasps its own nature and strivings. the more evident becomes the factor in which it differs from all other forms of world understanding, and the meaning which links it with them all." [13]

In these achievements mathematics and physics are hailed

---

[10] Here in particular I should note that this new concept of substance is to be found not in the thought of physicists, but in Cassirer's interpretation of their work.

[11] *Ibid.*, 472.

[12] *Ibid.*, 472-473.

[13] *Ibid.*, 479.

implicitly as the modern wisdom, transcending and unifying all particular knowledges, holding all in a vision from a higher point of view.

What is to be said by way of reservation? First, regarding the universality of the concept of number, and of the world view of modern physics, it is achieved by a powerful abstraction, a partial view of reality, which leaves much beyond the range and methods of mathematics and physics. This wisdom is an extremely limited universal, higher understanding. It leaves simply unaccounted for all that is unique in the mystery of man, and the full reflection on being and all its modes, which is the realm of metaphysics: a metaphysics of a different kind than Cassirer seems to have known.

As for the new concept of substance, leaving behind the notion of "things" which is proper to myth and intuitive types of thought, it would seem to follow that for Cassirer and others who would think similarly, persons and things in their concrete reality can be recovered and known only by having recourse to myth or other modes of intuitive, representative thought. Here too there is a realm in which metaphysics of the type which I have been hinting at has an important role. It is possible to hold persons and things in an understanding which is of a different type, but no less an achievement of human intellect than modern mathematics and physics.

(6) *Philosophy.* What can one say of the worlds of philosophy? Here one finds a different kind of pluralism, which can seem bewildering. The pluralism of mathematics, of the sciences, and of technologies corresponds to clear degrees of abstraction, and is realized by a methodical division and expansion. The pluralism of philosophies, on the contrary, may seem to progress in a disintegration and dispersion of thought, and to result in an ever-increasing alienation of individuals and movements. Yet the situation is not quite as desperate as it may seem.

Granted that there are differences of quality in philosophical thinking as in all other, and that serious philosophers diverge widely—or, to resume my figure of the sphere, move out, every one from the center of his own sphere in the direction of his own interest, with his own personal variation on a method—one can still read philosophers profitably, and advance toward some deeper knowledge. The difference in quality of philosophical thought will soon be apparent to anyone who has the intelligence and the temperament which make him apt for philosophy. The wide divergence of serious philosophers will not dismay him.

One can learn from any serious philosopher, and one can go on to make personal progress and some contribution to men's understanding of themselves and of their worlds, if he will persevere in his effort to understand.

What does this mean? When one has had the good fortune to find a philosopher whom he recognizes as worth studying, he must enter into that philosopher's world, come to grasp his problems and his answers, evaluate them both critically, ask further questions, recognize this man's position in relation to others which he has determined and evaluated, pay attention to his own hunches and gathering insights, and when the time comes strike out in the effort to formulate his own insights and advance toward his own further understanding. One does not enter another's world to lose one's self in it. Nor does one gather bits of philosophy from several thinkers, and try to put together a mosaic from pieces which will never make sense together. If one is to be more than subservient to the thought of another, and more than a maker of philosophical patchquilts, he must work out his own insights and elaborate his own thought, in the hope of understanding and helping others to understand.

Let me say something of three orders of philosophical thought: philosophy of man, metaphysics, and a natural knowledge of God. In making this threefold division I am not judging the question of whether the second and third can be really separated. In all three orders any serious philosopher will elaborate a world of thought in which every concept, every proposition, has meaning as it is integrated into the whole of his world of thought.

First, then, regarding the philosophy of man, I should say that one can tend toward a basic understanding of man, unifying one's knowledge of man, not by piecing together bits made by others, but by coming to a vision of the whole from a higher point of view. Particular positions, and particular elaborations, make sense as they are held in a single intelligible structure which is itself a personal achievement. It is my intention to contribute to such an understanding of man by the elaboration of this book. What that means concretely is laid out on the pages of this book. Whatever my achievement may be, it can be judged only by one who enters into this world, considers terms, concepts, propositions, as they have their meaning in the whole thought which is being worked out, and tests the whole by the only process of verification which is relevant to such works. Does it constitute an intelligible whole which truly accounts for and holds all of the pertinent data? Can further questions be answered satisfactorily with the result that the further answers themselves fit harmoniously and continue the inner movement of the thought itself? Before I conclude my work in this book I shall indicate some further questions and point out the direction in which I think the thought must continue. The object of philosophical reflection in this order of knowledge is the fulness of *human being*.

Second, I should say what I mean by metaphysics, why it is needed, and how it can be elaborated, to complement other kinds of philosophical thought which have been called metaphysics. It is fruitless to abandon the name "metaphysics." It would be vain and arrogant to attempt to dictate how the word should be used. It is reasonable to state clearly what I mean by the word, so that anything which I may say about it may hopefully be understood in its proper context. Given the wide use of the word "metaphysics" and my limited concern to state what I mean by metaphysics, two complementary conclusions are evident: what I say about metaphysics may not fit in someone else's metaphysical world of thought; and what someone else says about metaphysics may be irrelevant to what I am talking about. There is no question of defect, only of difference. Obviously this is not the place to elaborate a metaphysics. I shall say briefly what may suffice to indicate it as a distinctive world of thought.

By metaphysics I mean a basic, absolutely universal knowledge which is concerned with all that is. What distinguishes it is that it regards not some relationship which can be discerned directly and fixed in a concept, but the very act by which a person or thing *is*. Language breaks down here, for it was elaborated not for the expression of metaphysical thought, but for common-sense thought and scientific and technical thought, all of which are concerned with particular relationships, particular modes of being. Taking for granted the fact that things are, men tend generally to understand those things by fixing their relationships and holding them in intelligible patterns. All such relationships are only particular aspects of the full concrete reality, grounded on that full reality, but not constituting it as so many parts or elements. All concepts grasp relationships. All are partial, abstractive, regarding some aspect of the whole. What is accomplished in a hit-or-miss manner by

common-sense inquiry and insight and conception is done meth-
odically and far more effectively by technical and scientific
thought.

Metaphysics, on the contrary, looks to the meaning of the
judgment: It *is*. Reflecting on the act expressed in that judgment, it finds its unique object. That object is not held in any
concept. It is not a relationship, a particular mode of being
which has been grasped. The very *is* of the thing is not grasped
in a concept. It is affirmed in a judgment, and only by reflection on what is unique in the act of judging can one approach
the unique data and problems of metaphysics understood in
this way. Recovering the mystery of being in its relative fulness
in everything that is, such a metaphysics is concerned with reflecting upon all the modes of being. It too establishes relationships and fits them into an intelligible structure, its own
world of thought. But it does so by concepts which are, so to
speak, second-order concepts: concepts working out aspects of
the mystery of what cannot be grasped in a concept in the first
place.

Since the metaphysician uses words which were developed
in ordinary thought and speech, and uses them to hold in
second-order concepts what cannot be held in concepts in the
first place, one might be tempted to say that metaphysics does
violence to human thought and speech alike. Not quite. The
metaphysician is not doing violence to human thought, but
carrying the effort of inquiring intellect into the most difficult
realm. He is adapting terminology consciously to a sense which
it could never have had in the first instance. In doing so he
is not doing violence to language, but illustrating one of the
universal characteristics of speech and language: men do not
make absolute beginnings in fashioning concepts. There is no
elaboration of thought without some symbol. Linguistic symbols are adapted gradually to the expression of newly discovered
meanings. At first the adaptation is done with a sense of sensuous metaphor or analogy. In the instance which we are considering, the analogy is not sensuous but intellectual, and the
adaptation is done with a deliberate effort to give words new
meaning as they become the sensuous medium for the elaboration of concepts of another order. In this world of thought,
as in all others, the particular is integrated into the whole in
which alone it has its proper meaning. The integration is deliberate and difficult, for this is the realm in which human intellect
is champing at the bit.

Some of the modes of being are those which run through the whole range of being, and are aspects of the deepest mystery of being in all that is: being *one*, and *true*, and *good*. They are the transcendental modes of being: aspects of all being, varying as the degree of being itself varies. They are proportionate to being: as a thing *is*, so it is one, and true, and good. Other modes are limitations on being, determining it to be such or such, or of such a degree. They are discerned and diversified by attending to the various ways in which *is* is said. Diverse modes of being are expressed as one affirms different predicates, for example, of John, who is: a man, six feet tall, a farmer, the father of Tom. In every case subject and predicate are linked by *is*. If one attends to the sense of the statements, one can discern and diversify modes in which *is* is being said in a series of judgments. Basic categories are determined by such a reflection.

Having said this, I have given some answer to the first and the third of the questions. One can say what one means by metaphysics only by giving some introductory demonstration of doing metaphysics.

The second question remains to be answered: what is the need of metaphysics? Metaphysics is necessary for a fully intellectual knowledge of all that is, in the fulness of its being, understood by being situated in the whole range of the many modes of being in this universe, and grounded in the transcendent ground of all being. Metaphysics is the intellectual remedy for the fragmentation and dispersion of thought which follows upon the process of abstraction in increasing specialization. Contemporary man, sharply abstractive in his intellectual life, living in severely limited intellectual worlds, or living a dehumanized unintellectual life in the performance of his role, entirely devoted to some minute portion of the work of a technological society, tends to lose his sense of the fulness of reality. He suffers from the disease of man fragmented in a world dominated by mathematics, natural science, empirical sciences of aspects of human behavior, and technology, all of which are abstractive, and all of which leave a man with a loss of the fulness and wholeness of being by which he could be fully human.

I say that metaphysics is the intellectual remedy. It is not the sole remedy. A number of predominantly intuitive worlds of experience are recognized more commonly as remedies. It is too late for modern man to have recourse to myth: though some speak of a second naïveté, by which modern man could somehow experience the intuitive fulness of mythic conscious-ness, I suggest that for modern man such experience is intuitive, but not really mythic. He cannot enter into an experience which would involve limiting himself to a world view which for him is simply not satisfying. He may be deeply moved by symbols which express intimations of the mystery of the world and of human life, but he cannot quite become a man with a mythic consciousness. The symbols may be affecting him powerfully, yet he is experiencing them and responding to them within his own personal modern artistic, philosophical, religious, and theological worlds.

There are other full intuitive types of experience accessible to modern man: a return to an open wonder in the intuitive experience of the world about him; experience of the arts; rich ritual experience in a religion which is credible, and which does not call upon one to play a role as a pseudo-mythic man; and a full, rich life in the human intersubjective world. In all of these worlds of experience man can recover a kind of knowl-edge which holds the fulness of concrete reality, and which is only part of a total experience which is also emotive, volitional, and motor: it is fully human.

Though these other intuitive remedies are available, and are often prescribed for the maladies of contemporary man, I should say that there is still a unique role for a knowledge of metaphysics. Man need not return to mythic consciousness to recover the fulness and the livingness of persons and things; nor need he have recourse only to other predominantly intuitive types of cognitive experience. He can develop intellectually, strive for deeper and more satisfying understanding, transcend and unify all of his other most highly refined knowledge in a metaphysics which holds him to the task of understanding as far as he can the full concrete being of the universe.

Finally I should indicate the need of such a metaphysics for the understanding of a cluster of problems variously referred to as those of intercultural relations, a transcultural point of view, and inculturation. Metaphysics rises to the point of view from which all such problems can be surveyed and held in a single intelligible framework. All cultural differentiation de-velops within the realms of the intuitive and the conceptual. The resources of intuitive representation, and the modes of con-ceptual grasp, are numberless. Rising above the order of all intuitive and conceptual grasp, to consider the full act of being

and to reflect upon all the modes of being, all its possible variations and limitations, metaphysics reaches a point of view from
which the differentiation of cultures is intelligible. One can
reach that point of view from any culture: whether or not a
given language has a verb equivalent to *to be*, in any language,
in any culture, men judge and affirm and deny. They can reflect
on what is unique in that experience, however it be expressed
linguistically. Attainable from any cultural base, and rising
above the level of cultural differentiation in the order of concepts, metaphysics of this type is a transcultural knowledge.
In that knowledge, all variations of modes of being can be held
in the intelligible framework of the analogy of being. Without
reaching such a point of view, and such an understanding of
what is at stake in cultural differences, hermeneutic or interpretation of one culture to men of another moves about in
dark lowlands.

   I mentioned three orders of philosophical knowledge. Let
me say something briefly about the third, the natural knowledge
of God. Some do not divide it from metaphysics, since the
movement toward understanding of being continues until one
reaches the transcendent ground of all the being which man
first encounters. If metaphysics is difficult, and calls for a continual adaptation of human modes of conception and speech,
the natural knowledge of God is the most arduous of all works
of human intellect within the range of its natural powers. In
my judgment, it cannot be achieved without the kind of metaphysics which I have sketched. Though men commonly have
intimations of God, and arguments for the existence of God,
it is only by way of a metaphysical reflection on the implications of existing things that one can come to a rigorously intellectual, certain affirmation that God is. Only consistently with
that affirmation and all that it implies can one go on to talk
about God, with a constant attention to the adaptation of thought
and speech. I can do no more than indicate here what I think
is involved in such a world of philosophical thought. As for
its excellence and its need, I hold that it is indispensable for
reaching that kind of understanding of God which is possible
wthin a life of faith. It would take a long book to establish
that position. Having worked in this realm for many years,
I hope eventually to write that book.

   (7) *Religion and theology.* There are many worlds of religion, and within any of them there may be many theologies.
As in the case of all other worlds of thought, every religious

or theological symbol or concept can be understood only as it is integrated in a whole. Without any attempt to survey world religions and compare them, I shall illustrate what I have to say in the present context with examples from Christian religion and theology. A further modest limitation of my scope is necessary: I speak from within a Roman Catholic's experience of both the Christian religion and the varieties of theology.

Within these limits, then, what do I mean by a religious world, and a theological world? Such a Christian religious world is the total setting of the life of men and women for whom the universe and especially all human history has been affected and is being affected by God's self-revelation and gracious saving and sanctifying action in and through Jesus Christ. The Christian world view is transformed by faith. The Christian, believing and trusting and entrusting himself to the revealing God, has a unique interpretation of the universe, of human history, of the meaning and value of his life, of his ultimate goal. He believes in the transforming power of God's action in human history, in himself, in his fellow men and women, and in the universe. He believes that he lives in a process, continuing a long history of saving action, and tending toward a fulfillment in everlasting life.

This Christian world view in its essential features is one. The essential beliefs are affirmed in the great professions of faith in the Christian community, the "symbols" of faith: formulae which are compendia, standing for the whole of Christian revealed truth. Religious experience in this world is as varied as are men and women personally.

In a sense, theology is as varied too. As an activity, it is a continuing effort to understand within a life of faith. As a work, it is the fruit of such effort at any stage. There are many theologies, with varying degrees of intuitive and conceptual symbols. In every theology one attains some understanding, whether in the framework of salvation history, or in the reflection upon what can be understood of the God who saves, of man and his enrichment by grace.

These, then, are some of the worlds of thought, worlds of meaning, into which a given symbol may be integrated. Now the time has come to consider some kinds of symbols.

CHAPTER VIII

SYMBOLS

Symbolizing, as I understand it, is a properly human operation, and symbols are human works. Moreover, as I have indicated from the outset of this work, I take *symbol* in a very broad sense. As a nominal definition of symbol at this stage of our inquiry, I should be content with some such formula as this: *a human work in which the sensuous is somehow meaningful.*

To what sorts of works, then, would such a nominal definition be applicable? What is the range of symbols? How can one classify them, group them according to kinds? The answer is not easy. The nominal definition is broad enough to include the images of perception, memory, imagination, and dreamwork; and all of the works by which man attempts in full waking consciousness to fix and express his insight and his response in any mode of intentionality, or in any combination of modes. What are the difficulties of classifying this broad range of symbols?

First, I have a difficulty of my own making. Early in the preceding chapter I stated that all symbolizing begins with insight.[1] How is that statement compatible with acceptance of a nominal definition of symbol which extends to the works of perception, memory, and imagination, which seemingly precede insight; and to dreamwork, which involves insight only in a complex of operations which are like shadows of fully conscious operations? There is a real difficulty here, and I shall attempt to handle it by providing for such symbols in my effort to classify. But how can I affirm that all symbolizing begins with insight, and still recognize the images of perception, memory, and imagination as symbols?

I should reply that such images are *meaningful* in so far as they are set in human conscious operation which is per-

---

[1] Above, p. 184.

meated by intellect. In particular, in this case, it is the all-pervading primordial grasp of relationship which gives any image its representative value and function. The relationship of figure and ground, the integration of any particular sensuous datum in the whole of human experience in space and time, and its "meaning" or "meaningfulness" or representative value must be attributed to primordial insight and understanding, primordial grasp of relationships. Meaning is intelligible relationship. The sensuous which is meaningful is a sensuous in which some degree of intelligible relationship has been grasped. From the outset this is the work of intellect. Having said this, I leave the remaining difficulty to be treated in its proper place, where I shall deal with some special characteristics of the whole class of symbols involved in perception, memory, imagination, and dreamwork.

Other difficulties in the classification of symbols occur when one either reflects on the efforts of others or attempts his own classification. Cassirer's project for a complete philosophy of symbolic forms is an illustration. He takes *symbol* in the broad sense of all phenomena in which the sensuous is filled with meaning.[2] Two ambiguities cloud his vision of the range of symbolic forms. First, he does not seem to have reflected on a basic ambiguity of *sensuous*. For Cassirer, as a philosopher in a kantian tradition, the formation of the sensuous does not seem to extend beyond the process within the symbolizer—or rather, within "consciousness", which is quite another matter—a process which begins, according to Cassirer, when the flux of sensation is given form by perception.[3] Unconcerned with things in themselves or with the subject in itself, Cassirer does not seem to have reflected on the diversity of the problem involved in the artist's formation of an external sensuous medium, or even in the formation of articulate sound in ordinary speech. In both cases the sensuous is some medium external to the subject. On the contrary, in Cassirer's treatment the outer limit of the reality considered is the flux of sensation within consciousness. Something must be said about the apparent diversity of the sensuous.

The second ambiguity in Cassirer's treatment of the range of symbols is that *symbolic form* has two different senses: (1) a mode of thought, or a world of meaning; (2) a kind of

---

[2] *Philosophy of Symbolic Forms*, III, 93.
[3] Cf. *op. cit.*, III, 232; II, 35; III, 155.

symbol. In the first sense he deals with myth as the mythical mode of thought, and with language as the common-sense type of thought. In the second sense a given myth or linguistic expression may be a kind of symbol.

If, with Langer, one were to make a basic division of discursive and non-discursive (or presentational, or metaphorical) symbols, one would have trouble carrying out the division through the art symbols and symbols of worship, in which language figures in various ways. It does little good to say that in poetry one seems to have discourse but really doesn't, or that in song the words have become merely musical elements. I am not suggesting that Langer attempted such a general classification: on the contrary, her best work in my judgment is her treatment of individual art symbols, without any attempt at a general theory.

If one were to propose a classification according to differences of sensuous medium, one would end in bewilderment. Articulate sound would have to be divided somehow to include all sorts of language from myth to mathematics, and all sorts of music. Solid material would be somehow common to sculpture, architecture, and sign-making. Where would one place written conventional signs? How would mathematics as spoken differ from mathematics as written or printed? What would be the sensuous medium of the images of perception, memory, imagination, and dream?

Differentiation of symbols according to worlds of thought would not succeed, since it is impossible to establish differences which clearly divide formative processes and corresponding symbols. How would one differentiate sharply the symbols of commonplace thought and action, myth, religion, and art? What are the essential differences of gestures, language, and shaping of solid materials as they occur in ordinary life, myth, and arts and crafts? How does one sort out the conceptual and linguistic resources which would be proper to myth, religion, and art?

Finally, as I noted in the preceding chapter, my distinction of two sets of modes of symbolizing, tendencies, and elements does not provide the basis for an adequate classification of symbols. Both sets pertain in varying degrees to all kinds of symbols. Any symbol can be judged to be more or less conceptual or intuitive, but other factors must be considered if one is to sort out kinds of symbols.

I should say that no single criterion suffices for a satisfactory classification of symbols. Symbols vary endlessly, for symbolizing is as complex and varied as human operation. Indeed, as we shall have reason to affirm, all human conscious, intentional operation is somehow symbolizing, and the unity and continuity and endless variety which characterize human operation are characteristic of symbolizing and symbols. One can establish an analogous notion common to all. One can define symbol in such a way as to hold all symbols in a single concept, if one considers the wide range of symbols, and all of their significant factors. Without rigid divisions and classifications, one can recognize different modes within the analogy, and thus mark some factors which afford bases of differentiation.

REFLECTIONS ON THE NOMINAL DEFINITION

One may sense a certain perplexity concerning the nominal definition. On the one hand, one cannot define symbol unless he has some adequate notion of the range of symbols which he is trying to hold in a single concept. On the other hand, if he tries to sketch the range of kinds of symbols, he may seem to be begging the question: how do you know that *these* are symbols: if you cannot as yet define symbol, what is your criterion for placing X, Y, and Z among the kinds of symbols?

The matter is not quite as hopeless as that. What is involved is a gradual, continuing reflection on patterns of human experience, of the sort in which we have been engaged throughout this study. A great variety of human operations and of human works have been discerned and compared and interrelated. By a deliberate choice I have taken *symbol* in a very broad sense, as somehow naming many phenomena in human experience. Gradually I shall try to formulate an adequate definition of symbol. But first, in the early stages of this process of conceptualization, we may be content with a loose, tentative, "nominal" definition. One could formulate it somewhat as Cassirer did, to embrace all phenomena in which the sensuous is filled with meaning. I suggested another formula: a human work in which the sensuous is somehow meaningful. My insertion of "a human work" may seem to narrow the notion, but in fact Cassirer too is concerned with the range of the products of the formative operations of "consciousness".

Even our nominal definition calls for some clarification, however, and I propose some initial reflection on two elements: the *sensuous*, and *meaning* or the *meaningful*.

Mentioning a difficulty with Cassirer's broad notion of symbol a few paragraphs above, I indicated what seemed to me to be an ambiguity in the *sensuous*. It seems at first that one must distinguish a twofold sensuous. One is the sensuous within human experience. It is the sensuous flux of impressions which, according to Cassirer, is fixed and formed in explicit perception. Moreover, in all of the works of "consciousness", in all worlds of thought, there is a sensuous factor, an intuitive element, from which not even the most abstract mathematical or scientific thought can escape entirely. Criticizing this notion of the sensuous, I said that Cassirer did not seem to have reflected on the difference between such a sensuous element and the sensuous medium which man forms in shaping external matter, whether it be in ordinary speech or in the variety of works of art.

Taking this critical observation as an occasion for further reflection, I should say that the two realms of the sensuous are intimately united. The whole of the sensuous, whether it be discernible as an element of conscious experience, or be regarded as belonging to the external world, pertains to an irreducibly human reality.

First, the sensuous image in perception, memory, imagination, and dreams cannot be reduced to physical elements, to the physicist's light or sound. It cannot be reduced to the data of biochemistry or of physiology. Quite simply, it cannot be *reduced* without eluding consideration. The sensuous image is an original, irreducible reality, an element of humanly bodily being, of the properly human response to the world.

Moreover, when we speak of forming or shaping or giving meaning to an external sensuous medium, the external sensuous medium as such cannot be reduced to physical, or chemical elements. It is the visible, the tangible, the audible. Furthermore, the "form" or "shape" which we give it, by which it has "meaning" for us, is sensuous form, form for us, form as it appears to us through the mediation of any sense or combination of senses. The external sensuous is the phenomenal: it is the world which we encounter as it appears to us.

Moreover, the phenomenal is real. The phenomenal is the world as it appears to man, and it figures in real human behavior, real human experience. It is real: part of the mystery of the uniquely human mode of being in the world. The world which we encounter is the world as it appears to us, in which we grasp intelligible relationships.

As the world has a sensibly perceptible face for man, and an intelligible structure, so in the human response to the world in all forms of symbolizing man fixes and expresses meaning: shaping the sensuous and communicating the intelligible structures which he has found and elaborated. More properly, it is only as he succeeds in forming the sensuous that he elaborates and communicates meaning. Man's world, as it appears and is intelligible for him and for his fellow man, is real, but with a mode of reality which can be perceived and understood and evaluated and responded to only by human persons.

What, then, do we mean by *meaning* and or *meaningful*. The very reduplication involved in asking what we *mean* by *meaning* hints at the sort of answer which we can expect. When I ask what something means, I seek to understand it. When I find the answer, it is in the form of some intelligible relationship: I understand somehow what it is by fixing it in relation to some other or others, which in turn are similarly fixed. All are understood to some extent as they figure in a field of intelligible relationships.

The verb *mean* and the verbal noun *meaning* have clusters of meanings which seem to bear ultimately upon the sense of a sort of intransitive verb and its corresponding verbal noun. When I say that X means YZ, or that the meaning of X is YZ, I am saying that the answer to the question "What is X?" is is "YZ." X is intelligible in this way: it *is* in this way.

Once removed from this basic sense of *mean* and *meaning*, there is the transitive verb and its corresponding verbal noun which is involved in statements about what I mean by my words or gestures: what I am trying to express and communicate. When I say X, my word means YZ. I mean YZ, and my word X means YZ: YZ is the object of my act, a transitive act bearing upon its object. Yet my act in this case is purely cognitive: I act, and I act in relation to an object, but my only purpose is to express and communicate my understanding of the object.

Another sense of *mean* and *meaning* presupposes knowledge, but expresses directly a sort of act of will: intention. By the act of intending I *mean* to accomplish something beyond what I am doing immediately: my meaning or intention in doing X is to accomplish Y. Here too, obviously, there is a question of a sort of intelligible relationship. The action X is intelligible as it is understood to be performed in order to accomplish Y. But to mean Y in performing X is not a cognitive act, but an act of will. The act of will itself is intelligible in terms of its relationship to its object.

Any other intentional act, of emotion or of motor action, also has a meaning: it is understood as bearing upon its object. The act of emotion or motor action presupposes knowledge of its object, but it is not cognitive: its object is not intelligible relationship or truth. Yet it too is intelligible: within conscious life it has its structure, of which I am vaguely aware, and which I can probe and determine. If now we consider a cognitive act as having its own structure, of which I am aware, and which I can probe, then it has a meaning also in this derived sense of *meaning*: it is intelligible, it can be understood in relation to its object. So we come full cycle. The first meaning of *meaning* is the intelligible relationship which is the object of inquiring intellect: when I understand what a thing is, I grasp its intelligible relationship, its meaning. So the first sense of meaning is the very object of the act of understanding. But in a derived sense, the act of understanding, analogously with other intentional acts, is intelligible: it has a meaning which is grasped when its intelligible relationships are grasped.

Consideration of *meaning* and of *meaningful*, then, brings us back to the familiar terrain of the intentional. All intentional acts are meaningful, analogously, every one according to its own structure, its own type of relationship to its object or term. When we define symbol tentatively as a human work in which the sensuous is somehow meaningful, we are attempting to fix our object, with the hope of defining it more satisfactorily after further reflection. Symbolizing is properly human, and symbols are human works. They are the immediate terms of human intentional acts: immediate, not ultimate, since they are intended somehow to affect the worlds in which men and women operate. They are sensuous, for they are a part of the mystery of humanly bodily being.

Symbols, then, are meaningful sensuous terms of intentional acts. Like the conscious, intentional acts which they terminate, symbols are within the realm of human knowledge. Symbolizing man is aware of his symbolizing in all its modes, and of the meaningful sensuous terms of his symbolizing. He knows what he knows; he is aware of his knowing, and he has a vague sense of its structure in his very consciousnss of knowing; he is aware too of his feeling, willing, and moving, and in his very awareness of them he has at least a vague, marginal knowledge of their structure. He himself senses the meaning of his symbols, manifold as it may be in some cases.

Moreover, men mean something to one another. Men and women share an intersubjective world, and their experience of one another is an original, irreducible human experience. They have a meaningful appearance for one another, and they come gradually to read fairly surely the meaning of each other's symbols. The better they come to know one another, the more surely and more completely do they come to sense the multiple meanings of each other's symbols, and respond appropriately.

What, then, is the range of symbols, and how can they be somehow classified? I should propose this as a feasible working division: two general classes: internal and external symbols; and a subdivision of the latter into elementary and complex symbols. The reason for the first division is the radical diversity of sensuous medium and the corresponding "situation" and functioning of symbols.

Internal symbols are within subjective conscious experience. The subject is aware of them as "within" himself, occurring in the flow of conscious experience which characterizes humanly bodily being. Though empirical science, with delicate instruments, can detect bodily factors of such experiences, the experiences themselves, and the symbols in which they terminate can be said to be internal. They are not expressed or projected. They do not have an existence and a consistency outside the subject. They do not serve to communicate meaning in an intersubjective world.

On the contrary, external symbols are manifest to others. They have at least some fleeting existence outside the symbolizer, even if it be only the visible appearance of a grimace, or the ringing of a cry. They function, or are capable of functioning, to communicate meaning to others in an intersubjective world. The subdivision into elementary and complex external symbols seems reasonable. There are symbols which are simple and elementary, and which may be found as elements in many different kinds of complex symbols. Both elementary and complex symbols are general classes which may be further divided.

INTERNAL SYMBOLS

1. *Images in perception, memory, imagination, and dream.*
Having treated the first three rather fully in earlier chapters,

I shall not repeat what differentiates them. Nor shall I attempt an adequate treatment of dreams. All four, every one in its own way, are sensuous, meaningful, occurring entirely within subjective consciousness, functioning in countless ways in the complex interplay of events within that consciousness. Every such image, of any kind, has meaning as it is grasped at least vaguely in its setting, as it is integrated into a unique personal world of perceptual, memorial, imaginative, or dream experience. All such images may function in the endlessly complicated interplay of all modes of intentional operations.

With regard to dreams, one would have had to devote a full intellectual lifetime to dream analysis and to theories of analysis and interpretation in order to speak with any authority. As a matter of fact, several full lifetimes of intellectual activity would have been necessary to enable anyone to become an expert in the many matters which I have had to treat in the course of this study. Without any pretense of special competence, I suggest some reflections on dreams as they may be situated in the whole field of human experience.

First, it is obvious that they involve a type of symbolism which is entirely internal; and that fact has important consequences for any scientific study of dreams. Dreams occur only within the dreamer. They are beneath full human control. They are also beneath direct observation and verification. Consequently they are beneath the field of the analyst, who can study not the dream (not even his own) but only the account given later by the ex-dreamer in his waking consciousness. Dream analysis and interpretation may be regarded as an empirical science, but it involves a larger measure of the non-empirical than most empirical sciences. There is a considerable amount of non-empirical operation involved in any science. Though the empiricist may say of himself that he works only in his field of observation, that is not entirely true. He does his observation in the field, but he may do his thinking elsewhere, and return to his field for verification. For the dream analyst even this is impossible. He cannot even investigate or verify in the field, if the "field" is actual dream experience. Between him and his object there is always an impenetrable screen. He gets his data not from the dream, but from the verbal account given in post-dream waking consciousness of his subject, or from his own memory and subsequent verbal account of his own dream.

Second, the dream world is a uniquely personal world, somehow to be understood on the basis of what one can know of the dreamer's total past conscious experience and the larger total personal and interpersonal setting of his past. No theory of dreams should avoid further questions concerning the origin of the images with which the dreamer operates: they are grounded somehow in personal past experience in all its dimensions, focal and marginal. No analyst has access except to his own dreams. Freud, then, had more than one reason for analizing his own dreams. He was his own best, most reliable witness. More basically, he was his only witness, and his own dreams were the only ones to which he had access. Any analyst who had not dreamed personally would be incapable of knowing his object. Any analyst who did not analyze his own dreams would overlook the only data which could be called somehow firsthand. At best, dream analysis bears upon the subsequent account of the dream given in waking consciousness; but in the case of one's own dreams one has the relatively "solid evidence" of personal memory of his dream, to which he can return for verification and further probing.

Third, though there is a further work of interpretation done by the analyst on the basis of the dream account, there is a real meaning within the dream itself. Within the dream experience, as one recalls later, one grasps intelligible relationships, and one senses the meaning of his dream actions. Within the dream, at the level of the fleeting, shifting shadow world in which one is aware of moving, there is a multiple meaning: cognitive, emotive, volitional, and motor.

Fourth, there is a kind of thinking—and willing—which goes on within the dream experience. Often the dreamer is inquiring, understanding, and judging—within the limits, and with the tormenting fleetingness, of the shifting dream situation. Often the dream thinking is recognizably in continuity with inquiry, problem solving, and deliberation which has been going on recently in full waking consciousness. Moreover, the thinking is not to be attributed to some other "operator"—except in a very technical sense of the word. No other subject is involved: it is I who think in both waking and dream consciousness; and often I can recognize the continuity of the two modes of operation. What is true generally, perhaps, is that the type of thought involved in dream tends almost exclusively to intuitive symbolizing. I have had the experience of dreaming of a metaphysical problem at which I had been working intensely for days, and of having a vivid sense of insight in dream, only to recognize on awaking that the insight had been caught in a vivid visual and emotive imagery which could not be conceptualized. In other types of dream insight, what is grasped in dream is amenable to conceptualization, but prior to the dream experience it has remained marginal and unconceptualized. I gave an example of such an experience in the opening chapter.[4] In the experience which I recounted there I understood in dream factors of a total situation which I had not focussed on in my waking deliberation. Reflecting on the dream experience, I recognized the relevance of those factors, and the course of my deliberation changed. What had remained marginal in waking conscious deliberation came into focus and was recognized as significant in dream.

What do I consider to be the significance of these reflections on dreams? They are not a contribution to any new technique of dream analysis and interpretation. They may help to locate dreams within the total human field, and help to understand further the human mystery. To the extent to which such a deeper understanding of man could help any analyst do his work more intelligently, so much the better. In reflection on dream experience we find further evidence of the significance of the figure-ground structure, of the continuity of all modes of human experience, of the role of the marginal in conscious experience. Such reflection may suggest at least something concerning the origins of the symbols with which the dreamer operates: from previous focal conscious experience, from the whole of the marginal, and from his total human field, personal and intersubjective.

2. *Conceptions, reasonings, judgments.* I include here all conceptions, reasonings, and judgments which are unexpressed. They may be fully elaborated in silent thought. They may be inchoate, half-formed. In either case, and whatever the degree of formation which has been achieved, they are not "imageless thought". To the extent to which they have been elaborated, they involve the elaboration of the sensuous: there is no thought without symbolization, the formation of a meaningful sensuous element. Half-formed conceptions may be still relatively shapeless, and may be held in mind together with vague, half-formed intuitive images of one sort or other. From that state the artist would tend toward the elaboration of a sharp, significant intuitive form; the scientist or philosopher would tend toward

---

[4] Above, pp. 19-20.

a relatively adequate concept. Neither would finish his work
until he had elaborated his type of symbol. When one says,
"I know what I mean, but I cannot find words to express it,"
he has illusions of having thought the matter out. Until he
has worked out the adequate symbol, linguistic or equivalent
in the case of conceptualizing, he has not thought it out. What
concerns us here is the fact that there can be even fully elaborated conceptions and firm judgments which remain internal:
they involve a formed sensuous element, and they are ready
for expression, but at the moment they are unexpressed. They
are important, however. Though they do not figure in the interplay of persons in an intersubjective world, they may be affecting the thinker's emotional and volitional life now, and
they are a highly significant element in his or her personal
experience.

3. *Emotions, acts of will, and motor impulse.* Similarly,
feelings, acts of the will, and motor impulses must be numbered
among internal symbols, in so far as they remain incomplete,
unexpressed, unexecuted. They figure prominently in one's conscious experience, and often they are powerful influences on
one's eventual action. They clearly involve a sensuous factor
which is meaningful in one or other mode of intentionality.
They stand out in personal consciousness as figure against
ground, highly significant, representative. Some of the bodily
factors which they involve may be detected by instruments of
empirical investigators. But as long as they remain unexpressed,
incomplete, unexecuted, they do not figure in the interplay of
the intersubjective world. They too are symbols, but confined
to the personal experience of the one who experiences them
within himself.

4. *Body image.* Under this term I should include all that
pertains to our awareness of our body in our situation in the
world. Our sense of position, of bodily tone, of needs, of our
physical and intersubjective surroundings as they affect our
personal bodily being—all this and more can involve internal
symbolism: highly meaningful sensuous factors in our personal
condition. They are part of the total personal, physical, and
intersubjective setting from which our full external symbols
stand out. Are they symbols in the sense in which I have insisted: human works, the effects of human symbolizing? Yes:
they are the result of our grasping somehow aspects of our

total bodily condition in the world. They fix aspects of our total sensuous bodily being and setting which are figure against ground, significant, representative, meaningful in a field of relationships of which we are at least vaguely aware. Every throb of pain from an injured or ailing part of our body is representative of a whole; and if it is the throb from an ingrown toenail, it may strike us as an ironic symbol of human fragility: how little it takes to hobble a man!

EXTERNAL SYMBOLS

By external symbols I mean those works in which the shaping of the sensuous is completed by a human action which takes external form, perceptible in the body of the symbolizer or in some formed sensuous medium outside him. By such symbols one manifests or projects the term of his intentional operations, making possible the communication of his meaning to others in his intersubjective world. External symbols have a twofold function: immediately, in the personal life of the symbolizer, they terminate his operation. Mediately, in other persons in his world, they communicate—or are capable of communicating— his meaning, and may function in many ways in the interplay of human persons. In the intersubjective world symbols have an efficacy, a mode of causality, an influence, which eludes the observation and reflection of empirically minded thinkers who recognize the reality only of those causes and effects which can be measured physically.

Without attempting to consider all possible types of symbols, I shall differentiate first some elementary symbols, which may be recognized in their relatively simple forms, and which figure in varying ways in more complex symbols. This second class, complex symbols, I shall call developed symbols. I shall attempt to differentiate a sufficient variety of such symbols to set the problem of formulating a fairly adequate definition of symbol.

1. *Elementary Symbols.* a. *Facial expression and gesture.* The most immediate external symbolization is that which is achieved by sensibly perceptible modifications of the symbolizer's own body. Recently the expression "body language" has been fashionable. I should prefer to hold to old common terminology and speak of facial expression and gesture. Both are bodily

movement which has meaning. They involve countless ways
of moving the face and the rest of the body, shaping it as one
completes a meaningful act which is perceptible in the very shape
of the body: its position and movement. Because we are in
the world in a humanly bodily manner of being, we are involved
in the physical and intersubjective worlds by our bodily action,
and we manifest to other persons our multiple response to the
world of persons and things in which we are involved.

From the first wriggling of the child in the womb, bodily
movement is expressive, or, perhaps more properly: sensibly
perceptible bodily movement is the external, manifest aspect of
a total human operation. Gradually such operation takes on
greater complexity, and our bodily movement and facial expression are the external, sensibly perceptible completion of acts of
multiple intentionality. When we speak of gesture or facial
expression as meaningful or significant, it is fitting to recognize
that from the outset "meaning" and "significance" have their
full sense of intelligible relationship, in any mode of intentionality.

In a limited sense gesture and facial expression may be said
to be meaningful or significant as expressions of knowledge.
Where men do not have a common language in which to communicate, or more often where their common language is inadequate to express their thought adequately, gesture has a cognitive function: it expresses meaning in the cognitive sense. For
the most part, such cognitive function is performed by a sort
of intuitive symbolization. Gesture and facial expression are
imitative, vividly presenting aspects of familiar sensibly perceptible reality. They supply for or complement an inadequate
conceptualization, and they contribute at times to total expression of thought in a complex symbolizing involving linguistic
symbols and gestures. Rarely, however, do they do so without
carrying also other intentional charges, emotive, volitional, and
motor.

The extreme case of sign language brings out the limitations
of gesture as a means of expressing and communicating thought.
Less supple than vocal sound, bodily movements simply do not
afford the resources for subtle differentiation of relationships
and communication of thought. In comparison with oral language, any conventional sign language must always be awkward
and inadequate.

Yet the polyvalence, and the proper suppleness of bodily
posture, movement, gesture, and especially facial expression force

one to recognize in them important complementary symbolisms. Every man or woman has a personal style, and "body language" has a power of revealing the person, and nuances of his or her thought and feeling, which words and tone of voice do not reveal—which at times they veil.

Ironically it is the suppleness, polyvalence, and subtlety of body language which should warn against any pseudo-scientific effort to classify significant expressive positions or movements, and to afford a key to the interpretation of personal actions. When one has classified a given number of degrees of opening of the eyes, or any other aspect of facial expression, how does one capture tenderness? How does one capture personal style, which only gradually becomes known to intimate friends, and which is revealed in the least movement?

b. *Vocal sound.* One of the important actions of the new-born babe is to cry out, and that sound is the beginning of another personal history of signifying by vocal sound. The initial potential variety of that sound is beyond conception. If developmental psychologists were multiplied a thousandfold and deployed around the world to classify human vocal sound and its developments in speech, song, and sheer inarticulate out-bursts, all of their work together would be beyond comprehension, and would point beyond itself to a variety beyond reckoning. In every personal history actual patterns of sound are developed within the limits of a mother tongue and many factors of physical and social environment. Language itself is a developed symbolism which exploits some of the resources of articulate human vocal sound. Song is a form of symbolism in which vocal sound can break the bonds of language, and words can be given meaning which hints at the expressive power of the human voice beyond all developed language and speech. Even the inarticulate cry of uncontained feeling and will—St. Augustine's *jubilum* in response to the presence of the ineffable, and I should say also genuine speaking in tongues in charismatic experience—is limited by the patterns of vocal development in a given physical and cultural setting. Vocal sound, inarticulate and articulate, is the most supple of all sensuous media which men can shape, and it is the most important of all elementary symbols. Its inexhaustible wealth makes possible the development of many types of complex symbols which exploit it.

c. *Instrumental sound.* I take *instrumental* here in a broad sense, including sound produced and shaped in various ways by use of either bodily organs or instruments in the strict sense.

Sound produced bodily, for example by the clapping of hands, is a distinct elementary symbol, beneath all comparison with the richness and suppleness of vocal sound, yet not without its functions in human life. Instrumental sound has a far wider range and potential, from mere signals to the whole of music.

d. *Formed external material.* By *external material* I mean any material external to the body of the symbolizer—beyond vocal sound, which we have considered as a case apart. By *formed* I mean modified in any way in its sensibly perceptible form or condition. Men symbolize in countless ways by shaping external matter, and this class of meaningful sensuous includes a wide range of symbols, from the almost entirely intuitive to the almost entirely conceptual. Statues, paintings, and all of the works of the plastic arts symbolize by the significant sensibly perceptible form given to matter. Written or printed words or mathematical signs approach the limits of conceptual symbolizing, holding and communicating intelligible relationships with the least intuitive residue. Formed external material, then, clearly is a distinct elementary external symbol, which enters into the constitution of a wide variety of complex, developed symbols.

2. *Developed symbols.* Without attempting a complete classification, I shall treat what I consider to be the principal kinds of symbols which are elaborated by the use of one type of elementary symbol, or of two or more types in composite symbols. Since speech and language figure prominently in many of these symbols, and yet are not a general class which can be divided in an orderly way to yield a classification, I shall make a preliminary reflection on speech and language. They are a realm of symbolizing, in which men develope all sorts of symbols by the shaping of vocal sound in speech, and by some shaping of external materials in writing and printing. Speech and language, then, are not one kind of symbol, but rather a complex mode of symbolizing which is involved in the elaboration of many kinds of symbols, some purely linguistic, some composed of linguistic and other elements.

After this preliminary reflection on speech and language, I shall treat the principal kinds of symbols in this order: conceptual symbols in science, mathematics, philosophy, and theology; intuitive symbols in works of art; symbols in ordinary life; symbols in religion. Following this order, I hope to bring

out what is distinctive of both conceptual and intuitive symbols
in the works which are the greatest achievements of man the
symbolizer. Then it will be easier to recognize the blends of
elements involved in the symbols of the third and fourth classes.

a. *Preliminary reflection on speech and language.* What
shall I say about speech and language? This is not the place
for a capsule holding a compressed history of human speech
and language, and an account of comparative linguistics, linguistic analysis and philosophy, and other related disciplines.
For our present purposes we can reflect on some aspects of
speech and language, man's most common and most important
mode of symbolizing, and his richest, ever-increasing store of
symbols.

First, speech is the manner of symbolizing by the use of
articulate vocal sound to hold and express man's thought, feeling,
and will. We have discerned a number of intentional operations.
Speech is intimately linked with them. Why does man speak?
It is not because he must release his pent up thought and feeling.
Rather, he cannot think without some symbols in which his
meaning is incarnate. He can think only by symbolizing, and
speech is at once the easiest and the most effective way of
symbolizing in most human experience. It is the easiest: it
needs only vocal sound as its sensuous medium, and any normal
man or woman has an endless supply of it. It is the most
effective for most purposes, since it is the supplest of sensuous
media, susceptible of endlessly varying formation. A single
syllable can carry an incredible variety of cognitive and emotive
charges. There are enough ways of saying "Beh!" in Italian
to convey worlds of thought and feeling. How many characters,
in how many different situations, with what varying thought and
feeling, can be imagined uttering the English "Well!"

We cannot reconstruct a satisfactory history of the origin
and evolution of speech and languages. We can understand
something of the function of both, and of the laws of their
development, by reflection on experience. Observe intelligent,
articulate parents teaching their child, whether it be how to
stand, or to walk, or to eat, or to set a spoon in place. With
a combination of gestures and words, a variation of facial expressions and tones indicating approval or disapproval, they
lead the child to learn things and actions together with the
words which signify them. Relations are learned together with
the prepositions which express them: on, under, in, into, to,

from. They are learned as they are involved in the blend of action, facial expression, gesticulation, and words, with a variety of emotional and volitional charge.

We can conjecture something of the ways in which men came to shape vocal sound to hold meaning. Cassirer and Langer have gathered much of the evidence of historical studies, and have reflected intelligently on some aspects of this vast development.[5] There is evidence to support the opinion that certain sounds in many languages are naturally associated with elementary thought and feeling. It is fairly clear that the history of language traces a development from vivid imitative beginnings, with a great variety of words expressing concretely the many different ways of standing, walking, eating, to a stage in which such vivid meanings are lost, and words come to be used in a general sense, loosely fitting all the varieties of the things or actions in question.

Whatever be the historical pattern in a given people or culture, words are shaped articulate sounds or combinations of sounds which express an intelligible relationship which has been grasped, and which is fixed and held only by means of the word. We shall have occasion later to reflect on the relationships of community and meaning. Suffice it here to say that men and women develop speech and language in collaboration. What one man hits upon and holds by coining a word is understood by those near him in the same situation, for they have a vague sense of the same relationship, and they sense what he has hit off well with a word, uttered perhaps with a gesture, and given a tone charged with emotion. The word is understood, and it has become part of their language.

There is a similarity of structure, an isomorphism, of understanding and of speech. What is involved in understanding was indicated in the Greek word for the process: συνίημι — *I put together*, grasp, catch the meaning of. We understand by putting together, noting a relationship. We go through this experience only by putting together sensuous elements and forming a symbol which registers and holds and expresses what we have put together in our intellectual grasp of relationship. A syllable, or a group of syllables joined, put together, are the sensuous factor of our total experience of understanding. We put together other relationships, for we recognize several relationships in

---

[5] CASSIRER, *op. cit.*, I, 115-277; SUSANNE K. LANGER, *Philosophy in a New Key*, 94-127; *Mind*, I, 62-63, 186-197.

the thing or action or event which we are experiencing; and as we put together the relationships, we put together the words of the phrase which holds the set of relationships. Words are put together in a certain order, to form a phrase which is the sensuous factor of our thought, our grasp of this thing with some of its characteristics. Words, speech, then, are involved in our process of understanding. It is not that we are full of understanding and consequently burst into words. Rather we understand only as we fashion a symbol which is the meaningful sensuous factor of our thought; and words are the most apt meaningful sensuous factor for most thought and for much feeling.

The isomorphism of thought and speech does not end with the word and phrase. We not only grasp relationships, giving them sensuous form in words, but also we affirm or deny that things are in such or such a way: we judge. Our judgment too is performed only as we symbolize, most aptly by a further putting together of words. As the experience of judging is distinct from that of understanding, so the arrangement of words is different. We reach truth and commit ourselves to it only as we judge correctly, and the sensuous factor of our judgment is the sentence, which we *construct*, arranging words together in a meaningful way which alone expresses our judgment. The significant verbal element may be the copula *is*, or the verb which has an implicit existential sense, or in some cases a syllable or a nod which is understood as the equivalent of "It is" or "It is so". Languages differ in their resources. Chinese, for example, has not the equivalent of the verb *to be*. Whatever linguistic form it be given, the experience of judging and affirming, as distinct from simply getting an idea, is common to all peoples. The Greeks had a word for it, and so in English do we, the verb *to be*. The copula is not any link whatever of words: there is a great difference between the joining of words in a phrase and the joining in a sentence.

Speech is primitive and original and living. Language is its product, its store, and the fund of elements ready for use in new combinations, new joinings of words. Language too is the record of the laws of arrangement: grammar and syntax and the sense of style affecting meaning become part of the treasure of a language. The sentence is uniquely important, for without it or its equivalent nothing really is said, affirmed or denied, and truth is not attained. Style and sentence structure are important. Word order makes a subtle difference in sense. It is an important device for emphasis of the characteristic expressed in the first or last word. It is an important device for holding attention, to guarantee that the listener will pay attention to the very end, and get all of the details of the sentence. If I say, "You cannot get my meaning until you hear me say the last word and indicate by the tone of my voice that it is the last word," you may not be interested in getting my meaning, and your attention may end when you have heard the word "meaning". All that I added concerning aspects of sentence structure will have been lost. If I say, "Until you hear the twenty-eighth word of this sentence and recognize by my tone that it is the end of the sentence, you will not know my meaning," I have a better chance of holding attention to the last word, and communicating all that I wish to state about sentence structure.

If speech were just a matter of being the indispensable sensuous factor of thought, and thought were entirely taken up in the advance of science, then the ideal of both would be scientific thought and language, severely abstract, rigorously univocal, as far as possible freed from intuitive residue. It is not so. Vocal sound can be beautiful or ugly, alluring or repulsive. As human experience is not solely the pursuit of exact science, but is enriched by other forms of knowledge, and by a full emotional, volitional, and motor response to the world in which we are, men have sensed and exploited other riches of vocal sound, and have shaped it to realize and express a far richer, more varied experience. Besides its aptitude for the expression of relationships which have been grasped, vocal sound serves wonderfully in the elaboration of intuitive symbols. With its variety of vowel and consonant sounds, of tone, inflection, and rhythm, speech is an element of many arts. The mystery and power of poetry and song and all of the arts which are at least partly linguistic lies in the varying blend of conceptual and intuitive symbolizing which is possible with a medium which can be shaped to image both intelligible relationship and intuitive form.

Speech and language, then, are not one kind of symbol among many. Rather they are a vast realm of symbolizing, in which a great variety of symbols may be discerned.

Speech is the vocal symbolizing of living, active men. Language is its stock, and to some extent its norm. Language has its laws, its principles, established by the men who spoke and wrote, and daily stretched or bent by some who speak and write. Standing on the laws of language is like standing on a barrelful of eels, for a living language is continually shifting, and not even a national regulatory academy can succeed in mortifying by absolute regularity the language of a living people. Part of the beauty and fascination of English is the variety of ways in which it is spoken. It would be a dull world if one could not be surprised by variations such as this: "Do loo a me li tha!" which is written everywhere as "Don't look at me like that!" One who is familiar with the law of the Lord is not surprised to hear in Boston of the lore of the Lawd.

Daily teased into new adventures in meaning, a living language is continually undergoing both impoverishment and enrichment. One of the ways in which it is gradually impoverished is the shift from a multiplicity of vivid, concrete words to a paucity of general words. In this passage from twenty vivid ways of expressing different manners of walking to a regular use of "walk" there is the illusion of progress from a primitive, intuitive culture to a more advanced one, with sharper conceptualization. Yet how many men or women who regularly say "walk" could define walking satisfactorily? What has happened is not the development of sharper conceptualization, but the gradual dulling of perception and smudging of thought and speech. When we read in some of our translations of the New Testament:

> And Jesus increased in wisdom and in stature, and in favor with God and man (Revised Standard Version)
> As Jesus grew older he gained in wisdom and won the approval of God and men (Goodspeed in the "Chicago" Bible)
> And Jesus grew up, both in body and in wisdom, gaining favor with God and men (Good News for Modern Man)

we may be tempted to check these variations and compare them with the original. In the Greek there is a single verb, προέκοπτεν. There lies the clue to a long development. A verb which originally meant something like "cut/strike/smite/beat one's way forward" was gradually tamed to mean "progress, advance, increase, improve". It is good to come to have words of general meaning, and to understand their meaning. It is bad to lose the sharp representative image and the flavor of προκόπτω.

A sad type of impoverishment is the shrinking of language in reaction to the success of a subculture in attaching one distasteful meaning to a word or phrase. Many words which have

a rich variety of meanings and an honored place in works of
literature are no longer used because they have been laid under
a sort of taboo: they have come to be associated most prominently with their use, for example, in a subculture which ironically is called "gay".

There is a daily enrichment of language, usually shortlived,
in the continual creative speech of men and women struggling
in the catch-as-catch-can of many worlds. They brighten language kaleidoscopically with words and phrases, completely new
or newly used, which flash and delight and fade. Most such
words and phrases suffer the effects of their sudden success:
they are so over-used by so many men and women who have
only three or four live words in their vocabularies, that they
soon mean everything and nothing. When almost everything
is "cool" or "super", nothing is.

Some of the characteristics of linguistic symbols can be
determined by a reflection on the words which are the units
of all such symbols, and which are themselves simple linguistic
symbols. Since every word has a meaning or meanings, and
sentences as complex linguistic symbols are constructed by
putting words together, one might venture this formulation of
characteristics of such symbols: (1) Words are the units, which
correspond on a one-to-one basis to aspects of the total meaning which is achieved and expressed in the complex symbol.
(2) Since words can be defined in terms of other words, dictionaries can be composed, setting forth the meanings of the
units. (3) Since there are various languages, which have similar
stores of words, one can translate from one language to another.
These might be suggested as characteristics of ordinary speech
and language, whose purpose is to serve in the elaboration of
thought.

Some reservations or modifications are called for. First,
words have *a* meaning or *meanings*: the latter is almost always
the case in ordinary language. We do not have enough words
to go around. Most words have many meanings, and their meaning in a given linguistic symbol may be grasped only as they
are set in context. Consequently, dictionaries offer only limited
help, and often one is driven from one term to another, from
one definition to the definitions of the words used in the definition; or none of the meanings seems to fit the present context.
Finally, languages differ as perspectives and possible ways of
understanding differ. What is called a *drawer* in one language,
because one fixes the relationship to the action of drawing or

pulling, may be called the equivalent of *compartment* in another language, because in another culture men have fixed this thing by the relationship of part to the whole of a storage space. Clusters of meanings of individual words differ, clusters of objects signified by apparently equivalent words differ, and translation is never more than a rough approximation. It is not just a work of literary art which cannot be translated: nothing quite corresponds to anything in another language. And so the traveler must know the many meanings of one word, and the many words for one thing, if he is to make his way smoothly.

In short, words, as elements of linguistic symbols, have the characteristics of the elements of all complex symbols. The element has its meaning only as it is integrated into the whole. No words, of any language in any period of a relatively highly developed culture, escape this law. One of the great myths often repeated concerning the Latin of scholastic philosophy and theology is that of the exactness and uniformity of meaning of its terminology. No important statement of any scholastic philosopher or theologian can be understood apart from the context of his thought, and his words have nuances of meaning which can be known only from painstaking intelligent study of his works and the works of many others from whom he differs.

Speech and writing are the processes in which linguistic symbols are created, used, and gradually adapted to kindred meanings. Language is the store of elementary linguistic symbols and the set of rules for putting them together to form complex symbols. Literature is the treasure of great complex symbols, unique creations in one language. From any linguistic base and fund of symbolic elements men can fashion linguistic symbols as they think and as they succeed in somehow expressing what they feel. They fashion their symbols by a subtle shift of meaning of the elements, discernible only from the intelligible structure of the whole.

Linguistic symbolism is a vast realm, within which one finds a great variety of symbols. Some are the products of men who have elaborated their thought and achieved an ever sharper and more adequate conceptualization. These are the symbols of science, of mathematics (as spoken, not as written or printed in non-linguistic symbols) of philosophy. Such symbols are more and more conceptual. Other symbols are prevalently intuitive. Most of them are the symbols found in everyday thought and speech and writing: roughly hitting off the meaning vaguely grasped, or expressing the feeling barely understood. Relatively few are works of art, either purely linguistic or partly linguistic.

Linguistic symbolizing is not co-extensive with human experience: much of human thought is inchoate, and has not yet come to term in a symbol; much of human feeling and insight into feeling is ineffable, or can be captured and projected better in non-linguistic symbols. Yet linguistic symbolizing ranges most widely of all, and it enters into the creation and use of many different kinds of symbols. We shall have occasion to note the manner and the degree to which it is employed as we examine some of the principal kinds of developed symbols.

b. *Conceptual symbols in science, mathematics, philosophy, and theology.* Allowing for reservations which I shall make concerning theology, symbols developed in all of these forms of knowledge are prevalently cognitive, and tend toward the ideal of accurate formulation and communication of intelligible relationships which have been grasped. Every word or phrase, or non-linguistic symbol in mathematics, is fashioned to be the sensuous factor in the term of a human act of understanding. It is a symbol which is integrated into a whole intelligible structure, which is elaborated in a whole work. In its sensuous form it has a likeness of structure, an isomorphism, with the intelligible relationship which is part of the whole intelligible field. It serves both as the term of the cognitive act of the knower and the means of communication to others who understand the sense of the symbols, and who can follow the development of the thought, the elaboration of the whole intelligible structure, as they listen to or read the symbols.

Such symbols are prevalently cognitive. Though the symbolizer may be developing and communicating his knowledge with great emotion and strong will, with the passion of which Polanyi wrote with such conviction,[6] still in the elaboration of his symbols and of his whole work—which may be one great complex symbol—his operation is predominantly cognitive. Though the hearer or reader too may receive the symbols and respond with enthusiasm and desire in a total human experience, still his experience in hearing or reading symbols of these kinds is normally predominantly cognitive. He grasps the succession of intelligible relationships and the whole intelligible structure which is communicated to him.

Except for the written or printed symbols of mathematics,

---

[6] Cf. MICHAEL POLANYI, *Personal Knowledge* (New York, c. 1964) 132-202, 299-324.

and auxiliary illustrative symbols such as diagrams, pictures, or any other type used to present concrete examples from which to foster an insight and develop a concept, these developed symbols are linguistic.

Furthermore, they tend toward the perfection of speech and writing in their role as conceptual symbols. In these realms of knowledge, the speaker or writer would be defeating himself if he reveled in vivid intuitive symbols which would delight his listener or reader, but turn him from the task of sustained thought. The movement of thought is resumed when the intuitive symbol has performed its function: insight is gained, and the process of conceptualization goes on.

What kinds of symbols have I elaborated in the writing of this book thus far? Since I have begun with description of concrete human experience, I have often elaborated intuitive linguistic symbols to foster the insights and initiate the conceptualization which are essential for the movement of thought. Since I am writing for anyone interested in the mystery of man the symbolizer, and not merely for a few who would follow a discourse unrelieved and unrelieving in its tendency toward the purely conceptual, I have used a considerable amount of figurative language. Yet all is ordered to the scope of a discourse which is philosophical in its aim. The essential movement of thought is resumed and sustained in those portions of the book in which I seek to conceptualize and to define with relative adequacy. The gradual discernment and differentiation of intentional operations, the movement from helpful metaphors (ground, field, horizon, world, and sphere) to the basic mode of humanly bodily being, the further determination of roles of intellect and of the intelligible structure of man, the discernment and differentiation of modes, tendencies, and elements of symbolizing, and my present effort to differentiate kinds of symbols: all of these are essential elements, stages in a continuing process of thought which tends toward a more adequate understanding of human being. Every word or phrase in which elements of that understanding are formulated is a symbol which is prevalently conceptual. Every such symbol is itself an element, which has meaning as it is set in a discourse which elaborates an intelligible structure. My words and phrases and sentences have their meaning in the whole thought which is being elaborated in the book, and they take on added meaning as the elaboration continues. The whole book tends toward the elaboration of an understanding of man the symbolizer, and it is part of a larger movement of thought tending toward a more adequate understanding of man, of human being.

It is not without some reservations or distinctions that I should include theology among the knowledges in which men elaborate highly conceptual symbols. First, I am speaking only of theology as it has been developed within the Christian world of thought, and within a Roman Catholic's experience of that world. I am considering such theology not as the only one, but as an example. Its symbols have characteristics which should be reckoned with, if one seeks to work out a reasonably satisfactory concept of symbol.

I take theology, as an activity, to be the continuing effort to understand within a life of faith; as a work, it is the result of that effort at any stage in the process. Two distinctions are necessary. First, theology must be distinguished from other activities and works which are elements of full Christian experience. Second there are many theologies, many ways of "doing" theology even within a Roman Catholic Christian world.

Theology is not just any way whatsoever of formulating and affirming truths of Christian faith. It is not a profession of faith, though I should hold that only a believer can be a theologian in the full sense: striving to understand within a life of faith. Theology is not a form of prayer, nor another act of religion, though the theologian fittingly prays for the grace which may enlighten him, and his theological work fittingly is motivated by love and the desire to honor God. In itself, as an activity with its proper character, theology is distinct from the act of religion which motivates it. It is not mere catechesis, though catechesis and all teaching of religion should be enriched by theology. Theology in itself is a cognitive activity, an effort to understand, to formulate intelligible relationships in a total intelligible structure which is discovered and elaborated within the Christian mystery affirmed by faith.

Beginning with the men inspired by God to write the books of the Bible, there is a long history and a great variety of Christian theologies. From our present point of view, they differ in the degree to which their symbols are more or less intuitive or conceptual. Even intuitive theology, employing highly figurative language, differs from prayer, from emotional exclamation, from exhortation. It too is a cognitive activity, elaborating an understanding which is formulated in figurative language. It is cognitive, but it could hardly be classed with science, matheamtics, and philosophy as a mode of knowledge which elaborates highly conceptual symbols. The theology which I include in this class is characterized by a strong tendency to conceptualization, an accurate sense of analogy, an accurate determination of intelligible relationships, a proper mode of highly developed thought, with its own highly conceptual symbols.

c. *Intuitive symbols*: *works of art*. I shall approach the task of defining and differentiating art symbols by reflecting upon the structure of an experience of a work of art. Then I shall propose a definition of the art symbol or work of art, reflect upon the process of artistic creation, propose a differentiation of the arts, and add some reflections.

Especially if it is a rare treat, attending a concert stands out from ordinary experience. From the moments of preparation, leaving home, and travelling to the theatre, to the last moment of suspense as the lights are dimmed and the orchestra poised, one feels a mounting excitement in anticipation of a unique sort of peak experience. With the sweep of the baton and the swell of the opening chord, one enters a different world, a mysterious world, whose meaning is communicated only by the music. Listening to a great symphony is a uniquely human experience, and uniquely personal. Only a human person can enter into that world, and every man or woman enters alone: for the world in which the marvelously complex shaped sound has its meaning is the world of imagination, and that world is unique for every person.

Similarly, in any other experience of a work of art, one senses the significance of the experience itself, its difference from the rest of living. While one listens to a story, or contemplates a painting or work of sculpture or architecture, or watches a play, one is struck by something which does not belong to the here and now, to the visible, palpable reality of one's everyday world and life, or to the conversation which preceded and which will follow the experience of the art work. A great work of art strikes the beholder, fixes his attention, impresses a meaning, and stirs feelings: but the meaning and the feeling somehow belong to another world.

What is it that has this effect on the beholder or listener? What is a work of art?

(1) *The work of art*. A work of art is an intuitive symbol in which highly meaningful form is set in an imaginary world. First, the art symbol is clearly intuitive. The artist begins with an insight, but he moves not toward sharper and sharper abstraction and conceptualization, but toward a vividly formed

sensuous medium which strikes the beholder or listener as extraordinarily meaningful. The art work is a concrete whole which stands out for its striking sensibly perceptible form.

Within the realm of intuitive symbols, what is distinctive of the art work? First, it differs from most other intuitive symbols by the perfection of its form. Men are forever producing intuitive symbols, but few of these are works of art. The art symbol has what Langer called "significant form": form delivered from what is irrelevant, to stand out in bold relief, unmistakable in its meaning. It has that "splendor of form" which long ago was identified with beauty. It is recognized for its excellence.

There is a second distinctive characteristic which is necessary to note if we wish to distinguish the art symbol from all other intuitive symbols. Its form is set in an imaginary world, in which it has its meaning. Gifted men and women speak and act gracefully, beautifully, with a perfection of form, in their daily living: yet they are not "acting", and their actions are not properly works of art. Rather they are outstanding examples of excellence in real, everyday action. A graceful or powerful, highly significant gesture, or a thought beautifully expressed, or a facial expression or cry which reveals deep emotion, has its meaning in the setting of real life. The work of art is different. It is here to behold or to hear, but it belongs to another world than the here and now in which the observer lives. It is an image, a likeness of some aspect of one of the worlds in which man lives, or of some human feeling. But every beholder sets it in his or her own imaginary world of thought and feeling, in which it has unmistakable meaning. For the artist who produced it, it stood out against his total personal field, objective and subjective. No other person has the same personal field. For every beholder, the wondrously formed work is meaningful: it resonates in him or her, in another uniquely personal imaginary world. For the artist and for all who will ever behold the art work, it has the same significant form, delivered from all that was irrelevant in the original experience into which the artist had his insight, projected and standing forth now in its own existence (in the case of the works of plastic arts) or repeatedly renewed in its fleeting mode of existence (in the recitation of a lyric, the playing or singing of music, the performance of a drama). In a sense, the form is the same for all, but its setting is unique for every one: for the world of the imagination is a uniquely personal world, and this form has its full meaning only as it is set in such a world.

(2) *The creative process.* What I propose here is not a summary of artists' accounts of what they do in the creation of their works; much less is it an account of my personal experience. It is an attempt to provide a reasonable intelligible account of the artist's creative process as one can locate it within the structure of human experience which we have elaborated.

The artist's creative process begins with insight into some aspect of his world, objective or subjective or both. It is a vague grasp of relationships, of a pattern. In particular it bears often on some aspect of human feeling, of the human potential: what man can conceive of, feel, dare to do, achieve, suffer. Beginning with such an insight or succession of accumulating insights, the artist seeks to elaborate an image of what he has grasped. He does not stand back from his experience and seek to elaborate a conceptualization of the relationships grasped. Rather he works with images, likenesses of what he has grasped. One could say that he has a sense of analogy: a vaguely grasped similarity of images, whether in perception or in memory or in imagination. I suggest reserving *analogy* for a similarity of intelligible relationships which have been grasped and conceptualized. Corresponding to this in the artist's experience is a sense of *isomorphism*: likeness of sensibly perceptible forms, with some vague grasp of the intelligible relationships which can be discerned in what they hold in perceptible or imaginable configuration. I realize that *isomorphism* is used much more widely, for any likeness of intelligible form or relationship. What I am proposing, therefore, is simply a particular use of the word in this present context, to suggest the distinctive feature of the world within which the artist operates.

What do I mean, then, by this sense of isomorphism in our present reflection? It is a vaguely sensed, vaguely grasped likeness of form or pattern in the images of perception, memory, and imagination, and in the body image in which we somehow sense our emotions and motor impulses. For example, a whirling movement with a distinctive rhythm may suggest the pattern of feelings which we have experienced. That pattern may be suggested subsequently by the movement of music, or of dance, or of gesture, or especially by marvelously supple dream imagery. In dream we may have images of grace and beauty, of freedom of flight, far beyond the possibilities of representation by the movement of our bodies in waking consciousness, beyond the range of the suggestive power of music.

Since the variations of such vaguely similar images is endless, there is an endless variation of complementary isomorphism and suggestive power. Our bodily tone is vague and polyvalent, fitting many patterns of emotional, kinesthetic, and conative experiences. Countless images in our worlds of perception, memory, and imagination suggest that polyvalent pattern. Contrariwise, our bodily tone or body image may suggest any one or any series of images vaguely similar. Thus, in dream, there may be a succession of dream actions and patterns of dream symbolism linked with a single condition of the body at the moment.

The play of such isomorphism is fascinating, bewildering, completely unpredictable. One example remains vivid in my memory. I was presiding over a group discussion of a biblical text. After several had given their interpretations of the text, one woman said simply: "I feel spaciousness." It took me a long time to surmise what lay behind that statement. In what sense could she be understood to have given the *meaning* of the text for her? Surely it was not a sense of Scripture to be reached by any generally acknowledged manner of exegesis. Rather, she expressed in a vivid metaphor the "shape" of her feeling, her experience of the text in this setting. Having heard the text and others' interpretations, and being there with a deep sense of freedom and peace, she expressed her feeling at the moment, perhaps unwittingly, in a rich biblical metaphor, "spaciousness." She sensed a vague similarity of the sense of the text, the interpretations and the feelings expressed by others, the structure of the group experience, and the shape of her feeling.

Ultimately, in the consideration of such isomorphism, one faces the mystery of the fulness and the opaqueness of human being. The myterious continuity and interplay of symbolism is grounded in the continuity and interplay of all of the elements of man's humanly bodily being. Through all of man's conscious being there is an intellectual factor in the concrete totality of human experience. In the most vivid, concrete imagery, there is the grasp of an intelligible structure. The structure grasped is human. So too is the manner in which it is grasped: not by a spirit, nor by a brute, but by a man.

I said that the artist's creative process begins with insight into some aspect of his world, objective or subjective or both. How does he have insight into human feeling? Must he somehow have felt the emotion which he vaguely grasps and which he portrays in his work? Consistently with what I have said about our awareness and knowledge of feeling, I should affirm that the artist must have had some experience of the feeling which he portrays. How, in any other hypothesis, could one give an intelligible account of his insight into feeling? We *know* feeling by somehow grasping its structure, its "shape", as we experience it.[7] We are aware of our feelings. In that awareness, that subjective consciousness, we have a vague, marginal knowledge of its structure. It is marginal within the subjective field. From such marginal knowledge in the subjective realm, the philosopher and the artist proceed in opposite directions. The philosopher stands back to reflect upon the act, to determine its intelligible structure, and to conceptualize what he has understood. The artist as such is neither a philosopher nor a psychologist of any type. He does not seek to conceptualize. He seeks to elaborate an image of the feeling which he can project in an intuitive symbol. He moves from a particular subjective experience, vaguely understood, vaguely sensed to be similar in shape to many other images which he has from perception, memory, imagination, or dream, to a concrete work existing apart from himself now in the objective world, shaped to be recognizable unmistakably as an image of the feeling.

How could an artist have insight into a feeling which he himself had in no way felt? He need not have felt it as fully as other men and women whom he has encountered, and whose feelings may have inspired his work. But he must have shared somehow in the emotion; he must have empathized, registered something of what his fellow man has felt. Grasping somehow the meaning of another person's feelings, reverberating somehow with a sense of the structure of those feelings, is part of experience of our intersubjective world, and of that interpersonal play which is an original, irreducible, properly human experience. How could the artist project the image of a feeling which he had in no way shared? Feeling is not a thing which has a perceptible form: it is an experience within the conscious life of a person. I have a first-personal awareness and knowledge of my own feelings. I have some awareness of second- and third-personal feeling: the feeling of those with whom I stand in a

_____

[7] Cf. above pp. 121-123; 153-158.

personal relationship. There is an isomorphism of our feelings, and an isomorphism of feeling and the image in which it is projected. Without knowing from experience the shape of a feeling I could neither recognize it in another person nor project its image in a symbol.

Does the artist, then, express his own feelings in his work? I think that some distinction is necessary. His work may be inspired by experience or knowledge of the feelings of others, feelings which surpass any which he has experienced. Moreover, with regard to his own feelings, he does not express them directly and spontaneously in fashioning his work, as he may have expressed them in full normal interpersonal relationship. In most cases, writing lyric poetry is not the only way a poet has expressed his love. Yet, allowing for differences of degree and of mode of expression, I should say that in fashioning a work which portrays human feeling the artist is portraying what he himself has somehow felt.

What, then, does the artist do? With an insight which commands his whole effort, and monitors his shaping of the sensuous medium in a sort of running critique,[8] he draws on his own resources of perception, memory, imagination, and dream, to fashion an image by giving it significant form. It is this power to fashion, to shape his medium, to give it significant form, which is the artist's unique gift. The form is no mere copy of anything which he has seen or imagined or dreamed. It is like many other forms, but it is unique as it is realized in this medium. Though his work is individual, concrete, it has its own mode of abstraction: a form delivered from all that is irrelevant, a form which portrays better than persons and things and actions in daily life what the artist has grasped of the world and of human life.

The art work, thus formed, has a multiple isomorphism: a likeness of form with what the artist experienced in the objective and subjective world, and a likeness of form with what the beholder has experienced in his own objective and subjective worlds. The art work stands out, projected by the artist, to be contemplated by others. It is a point where worlds meet. It has its full meaning only as it stands out from the artist's whole experience, objective and subjective, and as it stands out in every beholder from his unique total personal and interpersonal ground.

---

[8] Cf. above, pp. 155-156.

The art work has meaning, but it is a meaning which the artist conveys without discoursing on it. He exhibits it, shows it forth, in a striking intuitive symbol. Its total meaning is beyond the artist's comprehension: for it takes on new, further meaning as it is set in every beholder's imaginary world. The work alone, standing out in the world, or renewed in a fleeting performance, figures perceptibly in the physical and interpersonal world. It has its meaning only for the beholder who sets it in an imaginary world which he must supply. Michelangelo's *Moses*, not very happily situated physically in the church of St. Peter in Chains, is not looking up to the wall or ceiling of the church. His gaze is fixed upon a scene which we must imagine, with the help of the Biblical account which the artist had in mind. Usually there is not even such an account to guide us.

(3) *Differentiation of the arts.* The artist creates an image of a world. Arts differ according to the kind of image which is created. In part, or remotely, this difference is due to the materials, the sensuous medium, with which the artist works. Principally and immediately, it is due to the differences of the kinds of form which the artist abstracts, and which he projects in the formed sensuous medium.

The world which is imaged, the total setting, is the imagined world, some aspect of the world. especially of human action and feeling. This is the setting of the whole image which is created. An important distinction must be drawn here. One can speak of figure and ground, of image and setting, in two senses. Within the art work itself, for example a painting or a sonata, one element stands out momentarily or permanently as figure against ground. Yet the whole work, the whole image, stands out as figure against the ground or field or world of imagined human thought and feeling which it suggests. This ground, field, or world is not part of the visible or audible formed sensuous image. It *is* in the imagination and memory and feelings of the artist originally, and then of the beholder or listener: it is the world suggested by the painting or sonata.

Taking *world* in this second sense, one can say that the same world of thought and feeling can be projected differently by different arts, with different kinds of images. Thus, the little world of a family, relatives, and friends, can be portrayed in a series of short stories, as in Joyce's *Dubliners*. It could be projected in a poem, or in paintings, or music, or drama, or even ballet. In every instance, one would have a different sort of image or set of images. In a sense, one could say that several arts could afford different openings upon the same world of thought and feeling.

I shall attempt to work out the differentiation of the principal arts, and then reflect on their interrelationship: how is it that various arts, with different forms and different images, can somehow image the same world of feeling?

(a) Painting is done by the elaboration of two-dimensional static visual forms. Limited by its materials (surface and paints), painting creates its image, the scene, which exists for the eye alone. When one walks into a real garden, he experiences it in a manifold perception: by a constant play of the eyes, by touch (feeling the temperature, moisture, and breeze), by hearing (sounds near and distant, approaching and receding), by moving into its space. When one sees a painting of the corner of that garden, the total effect must be achieved by sight: coolness and moisture, depth, and movement. The illusion of depth is achieved by a play of elements which enter into the creation of the image: lines, light and shadow, and colors in contrast. It is an illusion of depth, of a three-dimensional scene: you cannot walk into the space it represents; you cannot walk around it, as you could walk around a statue or a building. The illusion of movement is effected by figures of men and women or animals portrayed in an instant of mid-motion, or on the verge of moving: they are forever fixed in the painting, but forever suggesting the total movement prior to and following upon that instant. It is an illusion of movement, for only in the imagination of the beholder do these figures move. There is an illusion of life, of action, of feeling. All this the painter achieves by the elaboration of two-dimensional static forms, forms abstracted from real life and from imagined movement, delivered from all that is irrelevant to the thought and feeling which he seeks to project. Every figure must be depicted as caught at the right moment; the blend of figures in the artist's composition must suggest the action and feeling in the interplay of persons; staggered illusory planes must suggest depth; color must convey what in full real experience would be felt. The two-dimensional visual image is *there*: but it is set in an imaginary world in which all else has been suggested by the image. The world portrayed by painting is not just virtual space: virtual three-dimensional space is part of the illusion. The world is one of thought, feeling, and action: a human world in which the depicted figures and the total scene are set.

(b) The sculptor creates his work by elaborating the surface form of three-dimensional solid matter, or in some recent
art by the illusion of such continuous surface form. In classic
sculpture the artist carves or molds the figures of one or more
persons or animals. In some works of art, the form is not that
of a living being, but an abstract form, whether carved or molten
or wrought by patterns of taut wires: a form which somehow
conveys the shape of the feeling which the artist sought to
convey.

The work of sculpture is entirely visual: if you touch it,
you spoil its effect. The whole image is created by the treatment of the surface form of a body. Elements of the image,
which have their meaning in the whole, and which contribute
to the effect of the whole, are the posture and the treatment
of individual parts of the body. The sculptor's gift is that of
expressing all that he means by the surface form of his figures:
seeming life, thought, feeling, will, movement; the physical and
interpersonal world in which the figure seems to be, to which
he seems to be responding, and into which it seems that he
would move. In a great work of sculpture portraying a man
in his world, one can read the whole history of the man, caught
at this crucial moment of his life, and his project as he seems
to thrust into his future. All of this is part of the world which
is suggested by the image, the imaginary world in which the
image is set.

(c) The architect works differently with solid matter, and
creates a different kind of image by the elaboration of three-
dimensional surface form. He works to create buildings or
other enclosures of human life and activity, and by the shape
which he gives to his work he creates an image of the world
which is enclosed and sheltered. In a sense one can say that
all designing of buildings and enclosures creates images of a
human world, a culture, a way of life. Even the poorest of
such designs, purely pragmatic, are images of a world, of a sense
of the shape of human life, however lowly and dreary. Wretched
hovels of the abject poor, barn-like factories where men work
like poor machines, and the jungle of modern cheap apartment-
house tenements: all are images of the human world which they
enclose. Great works of architecture are a function of several
factors: the development of a way of life more worthy of man,
the vision of the shape of the life of family and community in
the world which it aspires to create, and the gift of projecting
that shape in an image which is created by the treatment espe-

cially of the exterior and interior surface of the buildings and complementary enclosures which contain it. As the surface form of a body expresses the shape of life and feeling in a work of sculpture, so in architecture the inner and outer surface of buildings express the shape of the life of the family or larger community which they enclose. The image is the meaningfully shaped building or cluster of buildings. The world imaged is the whole of the life and culture whose shape is shown forth in the shape of the buildings. Even when they are empty and silent, they symbolize the life which they are meant to contain. Even when they are filled and throbbing and ringing with life, they are images of a greater reality, a greater world, of a whole history and a vision of the future.

(d) The poet and other literary artists create a verbal, basically audible, image of a world, especially a world of human life, thought, feeling, and action. Though they use living language, and consequently are limited to a successive, discursive projection of their image, still they do not "discourse" on their world, but attempt to exhibit its image. Most of all in lyric poetry, but to varying degrees in all types of literature, the artist exploits the full resources of speech: quality of vowels and consonants, rhythm, and cadence, to heighten the suggestive power of his shaped sensuous medium. His pattern of words inevitably expresses concepts; yet he does not attempt to conceptualize or theorize about his world. He exhibits it in a prevalently intuitive symbol, a meaningful concrete image. In a sense his task is more difficult than that of the plastic artist (painter, sculptor, architect) since he cannot present a directly visible image. The form which he abstracts is the pattern of the life which he seeks to present. Only one of the elements of his image is perceptibly similar to an element of the real life into which he has had his insight: speech, the words uttered by the poet himself in a lyric, or the words which he fashions and presents as spoken by his characters. In both cases, living language is fashioned to express thought and feeling, and to exhibit in the very form of speech the characters who are portrayed. As speech is the most supple and most expressive of symbols in real life, so in the artistic creation of an image of life the speech of the characters is the most effective manifestation of their inner worlds, and of the interplay of persons in the intersubjective world which is shown forth.

For the rest, the elements which contribute to the total poetic or literary image are more abstract. The artist does not exhibit scenes, actions, and events: he narrates and describes, gradually building up the pattern which the reader must imagine for himself. Most of the elements of literature, therefore, do not exhibit a form which is comparable to the visual form in plastic art: a form which is perceptibly like what can be seen in nature. By the very nature of verbal symbolism, the pattern of words in narration and description have a certain isomorphism, a certain likeness of structure, with the reality which they are intended to depict.

In this case, therefore, imagination not only supplies the world in which the total image is set, but contributes to the gradual elaboration of the image itself. As the words succeed one another, the author's thought, imagination, and feeling find expression; and his image takes form fully only in the mind and imagination of his reader.

In poetry and literature generally, therefore, the abstracted form, which is the pattern or shape of the world portrayed, is complex. Only the words spoken by the poet in the lyric, or the words attributed to characters in dialogue, bear a directly recognizable resemblance to an element of human action in real life: speech. The rest of the form, elaborated by narrative and description, is built up in the mind and imagination of the reader. The total form, the abstract pattern bearing a likeness to the pattern of the world which is imaged, is verbal and audible; but it has varying degrees of abstractness, of remoteness from the full reality of the world which is exhibited.

(e) Drama, with a form that is visible and audible, verbal and bodily, is, I should say, the least abstract of the arts. It too is abstract, for human action and speech is delivered from the irrelevant, and appears on the stage "bigger than life". Yet the image is elaborated by a combination of action and speech, both of which are perceptibly similar to everyday life. Reflection on this characteristic of the form of drama can clarify what may have seemed obscure in my account of the complex form of poetry and literature generally. When drama comes to life in actual performance, scenes and action are not described, to be imagined by a reader: they are enacted before him vividly, as they cannot be in a work of literature.

(f) Dance creates its image of a world with all of the riches and suppleness of bodily movement and gesture. Its form is that of the full bodily realization and expression of thought, emotion, will, and motor impulse. In itself it is visible but not audible. More abstract than drama, since it is speechless and

even in ballet has only a tenuous link with a text, it exploits
the resources of bodily movement to the fullest, and far surpasses drama in its expressive bodily action. Usually inspired
by music, it projects a vivid visual image which music must
leave entirely to the imagination. Surpassing music in this mode
of expressiveness, it cannot approach the adequacy of music
in its own sphere, for music has a richness, complexity, suppleness and grace, power, imaginative suggestiveness, and expression of emotion which cannot be matched by the greatest dancing.

(g) Music, I should say, is the most mysterious and the
most effective of all the arts: it is the art of arts. Its form is
the felt form of human thought, emotion, will, and motor impulse, most of all the felt form of feeling. I say the *felt* form:
the form of feeling is not visible or audible or palpable: it is
felt as one feels emotion and willing and impulse to action.
It is grasped by the vaguest of marginal subjective knowledges
in our awareness of feeling. It is the felt dynamic shape, rhythm,
and quality of our feeling. The musical artist grasps that form
and projects it in an image made of patterns of vocal and
instrumental sound, simultaneous and successive, extremely varied in quality, in harmony and discord, with sound and silence,
variety of speed and rhythm. The musical image is audible,
but it is the image of a form of complex inner sense of thought,
emotion, will, and action which is not audible. Hence music
is the most abstract of arts. In it the artist, with an insight
into the felt shape of feeling, projects in an audible image a
form which is in no way audible. He does not abstract as
other artists do: rendering one perceptible aspect of a total
experience, heightening it, and projecting it concretely so as to
suggest all of the other factors of the experience which are
left to the imagination. Form in the musical image is the most
extreme instance of isomorphism: here the likeness of form is
in no way directly perceptible. The artist divines the aptness
of musical form to feeling, and the measure of his success is
the degree to which an audience attuned to his art senses the
meaning of his music. In music the story is not the thing,
nor a definite visual imagery, nor a particular personal experience. What is expressed is a pattern of feeling, a pattern which
is beyond verbal description, a particular pattern, yet one which
is recognized by every hearer as somehow being the pattern of
his or *her* experience, indeed of several experiences recalled or
imagined. The isomorphism of musical form with the form of
feeling is subtle and seemingly infinite. A single musical work

can suggest to each listener many scenes and experiences, all linked by the same deeply sensed form. Music is the most abstract, the most intimate, the most subjective, and the most widely appreciable art.

Having considered the differentiation of the principal arts, I should suggest three complementary reflections: first, on the degree of abstraction in the arts; second, on the unity of the arts in spite of all differences; third, on the differentiation of types of artists involved in the various arts.

First, then, one can arrange the arts in the order of increasing abstractness. Every art abstracts some form, delivers it from the irrelevant, and projects it in an image of a world. Some arts find their form in the realms of perception, memory, imagination, and dream: some visible or audible form, static or dynamic, which has been perceived, imagined, or dreamed. The art work is given a shape which is recognizably similar to a perceived or imagined form. Other arts create an image which is visible or audible, but which has a form which could never have been perceived. Keeping this basic difference in mind, one can make out the order of abstractness of the arts.

I should say that drama is the least abstract of all. It draws on the dynamic form of human action, visible and audible: it is closest to real life. Next, dance draws on the full range of the visible dynamic form of human action and gesture. Then painting and sculpture could be regarded as roughly equal in their degree of abstraction. Both depend entirely on visible static form, but they have resources and limitations which perhaps balance out. Painting has all of the resources of complex composition of line and color, but it must devise ways of creating the illusion of depth. Sculpture cannot present the fulness of scene or color, but it has three-dimensional form. Both painting and sculpture can draw on forms perceptible in experience. I should list poetry and the literary arts next. They are more abstract than the plastic arts, because they do not exhibit a form directly, but mediate it through words. However imitative and intuitive language may be, it still relies on a subtle sensuous metaphor, or sensuous isomorphism: by the sound and structure of language it conjures up the form to be imagined. Architecture is hard to judge in this regard. Though it is a plastic art, and relies on visible static form, still it is more abstract than painting and sculpture. Architecture creates an image which has the shape of the life, the culture, which it encloses. Life and culture have no visible shape: they involve a vast network of relationships which are not perceptible, but which are at least vaguely understood. The architect must divine that network, and by a sense of isomorphism create an image which can suggest it to the beholder. A higher degree of abstraction is involved in any so-called abstract art, painting, sculpture, and music: in various ways they leave the resources of forms which can be drawn from nature, and rely on a subtle sensuous isomorphism to create original forms which somehow shape an image of a world of feeling. Finally, for the reasons which I have indicated above, music as a whole, with varying degrees, is the most abstract of arts; for all music projects an image which has somehow the felt form of feeling, a form which could be neither perceived directly nor suggested by any discursive symbol.

What is the sense of an "order of increasing abstractness" in the arts? I should say that reflection on intuitive symbols generally, and art symbols especially, leads to two new conceptions which complement more traditional notions of abstraction and abstractness. It has been a commonplace in philosophical thought to conceive of the abstraction of form from matter, and to recognize the movement from initial intuitive thought and speech to increasingly abstract conceptual thought. In such a process of knowledge one comes to general, universal concepts, with a formal content which can be recognized in individual instances. What are the two new conceptions concerning abstractions? The first is that which Langer pointed out in her differentiation of discursive and non-discursive or presentational or metaphorical symbols.[9] The abstraction which is involved in the elaboration of non-discursive symbols is not a generalizing abstraction. Rather it is the deliverance of significant form from the irrelevant, and projection of that form not in a general concept but in a striking concrete image.[10] The second new conception is that which I have just suggested, that of an increasing order of abstractness. I know of no one who has spoken or written of this, but it seems to me that it is a clearly recognizable pattern which emerges from the reflection on the differentiation of the arts. What occasions this insight is the determination of the principle of that differentiation: the

---

[9] Cf. above, pp. 8-9 and 186-192; and for an ample synthesis, my article "Symbol According to Cassirer and Langer," *Gregorianum* 53 (1972) 615-634.

[10] Cf. above, pp. 186-194.

arts are differentiated according to the type of form which they abstract and project in the images which they create.

Recognition of an order of increasing abstractness in the arts suggests further reflection which brings out more clearly the unique role of intellect in the artistic creative process. There are two opposite directions of order of increasing abstractness. The first is that which is commonly considered. It is the order of stages in the process from intuitive to more conceptual thought and symbol. As abstraction increases, the proportion of the intuitive element in thought diminishes. The scientific, mathematical, and philosophical thinker moves continually farther away from images of the type which can be experienced in perception, memory, and imagination. One might designate this movement as being toward the supra-perceptual. The other order of increasing abstractness is contrary to the first. It is the order of stages in the process from images which originate in perception to forms which are increasingly remote from perception. The movement is toward the infra-perceptual.

What, then, does this imply concerning the role of intellect in artistic creation? Consider the types of knowledge which are involved in the two contrary processes. In the first, there is a movement towards an ever-increasing sharpness of the grasp of relationships, and of the concepts in which they are fixed and formulated. In the second, there is a movement farther and farther away from discursive thought and sharp conceptualization. As they increase in abstractness, the arts recede even from perceptual images which might initiate a process of conceptualizing thought. In the extreme cases, the artist moves in the realm of the ineffable, even of the unimaginable. He has the vaguest of intimations of the felt shape of feeling, and a grasp of sensuous isomorphism which enables him to create an image in the likeness of that feeling, an image which reaches the level of the perceptible. Artistic creation is perhaps the most dramatic illustration of the permeation of all conscious life by intellect. Here in the realm of the extremely marginal, and of the threshold of consciousness, primordial insight and understanding initiate the artistic creative process, and monitor the creation of the image, with an uncanny running critique of its adequacy.

The second complementary reflection concerns a certain unity of the arts which prevails despite their differences. Take the example which I have already cited: Michelangelo's *Moses*. It is a sculpted image of Moses' feeling as he saw his people committing idolatry. Michelangelo himself, master of other arts, could have created an image in a painting. Other artists, with an insight into the same world of feeling, could have felt its form and projected it in other art works: in narrative, drama, poem, or symphonic musical poem. Despite differences of type of image, and of degrees of abstractness, such works of art would somehow project images of the same world of feeling. How is this possible? At least three factors contribute to an understanding of this unity. First, the experience into which the artists have insight is a complex unity, with a blend and continuity of many elements, in all modes of intentionality. Second, any symbol presents part for the whole, and it has its full meaning only as it is set in the full world which it represents. An art symbol is an image which has its meaning only as it is set in the imaginary world of thought, feeling, and action into which the artist has had his insight. Third, there is an endless variety of forms which artists can sense to be like the felt form of the feeling which they are seeking to project. Isomorphism, in this case a likeness of sensuous form, is limitless. Every art work which would capture and project Moses' feeling would have its full meaning only as it suggested the full reverberation of the original experience in all of its dimensions. The several works would differ in their medium, in the abstractness of their form, in the perceptual imagery which they fix by their very nature. All would be similar in their isomorphism with the original experience, and with the artist's sense of its felt form. Like peaks rising from the same mountain range, they would be so many peaks rising from a single range of experience: every one evoking a sense of the whole.

Third, any reasonably full reflection on the differentiation of arts calls for a complementary differentiation of artists. In some arts, one artist alone creates the work, which is projected and given its independent existence once for all. This is the case in painting and sculpture. In other arts, the original artist, the creator, depends on the eventual collaboration of other subordinate artists for the production of the final work. This is the case in one way in architecture, in which the architect seldom builds the finished work. Yet even here, once the building is completed, it endures for some time. The collaboration of other artists is more striking in the performing arts, in which many artists complement the creator's work to bring forth the full, living work of art: director and singers and instrumentalists in the performance of music; director and actors in the performance of a play; choreographer and dancers in ballet; and more rarely the reciter of a poem or other literary work which comes to its full life only in actual recitation.

Langer points out the example of drama. By reason of its materials and its basic abstraction, drama poses difficulties for the playwright, and raises interesting questions concerning the sense in which he creates the play. More than any other art form, drama depends on choices made by the performing artists. Hence, the playwright has a special difficulty: he must establish a commanding form which is clear and powerful, able to hold the imaginative minds of director, actors, and designers to one essential conception, the poetic core. Yet the creator must allow scope for the interpreters, for their roles complement his.[11]

In drama, music, dance, and I should say lyric poetry and as far as possible other literary forms, works of art come to consummation only in their performances by great artists. That leaves a great realm of creativity to the performing artist, and every great performer gives a rendition of a work which is unique, and which may far surpass any performance in which the original creator might have sought to bring his work to full life. I include lyric poetry and other literary art forms here. To the extent to which they are truly great, they exploit as far as possible the riches of living language, and they come to full life only in a recitation in which the beauty and full range of the human voice enables the performer to bring the image to its perfection. The poet himself may have had a flat voice, and may have known the potential beauty of his poem only with the "inner ear". I should say that a poem is appreciated fully only by the man or woman who can recite it most beautifully and meaningfully, feeling the shape of the original poetic experience—or of a richer experience evoked by the same insight—as he or she shapes the living sound of the voice.

d. *Symbols in ordinary life*. All human conscious life involves continual symbolizing, and a succession of symbols of many kinds; for symbols are the meaningful sensuous terms of human conscious operations in all modes of intentionality. Obviously all forms of internal symbols are involved. All elementary external symbols too are blended in normal life. What I have said of the importance of speech and of language is true first of all concerning ordinary life: for it is from ordinary life

---

[11] *Feeling and Form*, 314.

that men rise to achievements in highly developed conceptual symbolizing or in the arts.

What is to be said, then, of developed external symbols as they figure in ordinary life? I dealt first with two orders of symbols which could be called paradigms of relative perfection: conceptual symbols in science, mathematics, philosophy, and theology; and works of art as intuitive symbols. Given the basic division of conceptual and intuitive, one could say that all symbolizing in ordinary life tends towards the ideals realized relatively in two orders: highly conceptual thought, and the arts. But what do I mean by "ordinary life"? I should set its limits by a series of negations: it is not the realm of dream, nor of mere imagination, nor of hallucination or any other pathological condition, nor of highly conceptual knowledge, nor of the arts, nor of the transcendent intersubjective (religion), nor of play. It is the life of waking consciousness; of the verifiably real and existing in an intersubjective world, as contrasted with the purely personal creations of imagination or the private spectacle of the victim of hallucination or other mental disorder. It falls short of the highly developed conceptual thought of science and related knowledges: the only way to achieve that type of perfection is to be a scientist or exact thinker of some other type; and that is not "ordinary". It usually falls short of the formal perfection of the arts, and it does not set its images in an imaginary world. I have not treated religious symbols, nor symbols in play; but I shall do so at least briefly, and then the contrast between them and the symbols of "ordinary life" will appear.

If it is difficult to classify symbols generally, I should say that it is impossible to define and classify the symbols which figure in ordinary life. Suffice it to say that they are generally blends of intuitive and conceptual symbols of all kinds, which usually fall far short of the perfection of both exact thought and art. It would be more exact to say that they always fall short of the conceptual type symbols of exact thought, and usually fall short of the formal perfection of the intuitive symbols created by the arts. I should say that in its intuitive element symbolizing in ordinary life differs in two ways from that of the great works of art. First, the images created in ordinary life have their setting in the many worlds of "real", continuing interpersonal life: not in the imaginary world in which the art image is set, and in which it has its meaning. That is the reason for my approach to the art symbol by reflecting on our experience of a work of art: an experience which stands out from the rest of our daily living. Second, intuitive symbols in ordinary life usually fall short of the formal perfection of art symbols: usually, but not always. There is what is called the art of living, and great men and women act in real life with a perfection of form which the most consummate actors cannot surpass.

e. *A religious symbol: the Christian sacrament.* Although my principal concern in this book is to contribute to a basic knowledge of man, a philosophy of man, any treatment of man and of human symbolizing must be open to the further reflection upon what is unique in man's operation within the transcendent interpersonal world, and what characterizes religious symbols. Before I conclude this book I shall indicate symbolizing which is more than merely human, and show how our present process of thought opens upon properly theological problems. Yet, just as I had to indicate the transcendent ground of human operation, or the transcendent intersubjective world,[12] so I think that it is necessary here to give some indication of a kind of symbol which has its setting in that world. Here, as elsewhere, I give an example, not a summary general treatment. The example which I give is the one which I know best. It is not the only one, obviously. It may be enough to remind us to hold our reflection open to a realm of symbolizing and of symbols in which further factors are involved. Religious symbols are part of a world which is in no sense "unreal": rather it is a real world which involves more factors, more dimensions, than the "ordinary" real world which we have indicated. Finally, I should explain what I mean by "the Christian sacrament". Here as elsewhere I am giving an example from a particular point of view, that of the experience of a Roman Catholic theologian within the Christian tradition. For Roman Catholics there are seven Christian sacraments. When I say "the" Christian sacrament, I am using the word *sacrament* as it may be applied analogously to all seven. In this section I am adapting what I have written earlier in preparation for this book.[13] I am seeking to set forth what is proper to the Christian sacrament, and in part I do so by contrasting it with the work of art.

---

[12] Ch. V, pp. 134-135.

[13] WILLIAM A. VAN ROO, S.J., " Symbol in Art and Sacrament," (Studia Anselmiana, 64 [1974]) 159-171.

The Christian sacrament can be understood only in its
setting, as an element in an extremely complex reality. Two
approaches to this reality help to situate the sacrament: an
account of one of the Christian sacraments, baptism, in its full
biblical setting; and a description of the concrete whole in
which baptism occurs in Christian worship.

First, baptism figures in a number of New Testament texts
which bring out its meaning by situating it in the full dynamic
pattern of the history of salvation.[14] These are the principal
elements in the texts: (1) The sequence of actions: preaching,
faith, repentance, turning to God, baptism, and a commitment
to a way of life. (2) Who acts in baptism? Little is said of
the external, visible action of the man who baptizes. The role
of the Church as a whole is only implicit. The preponderant
concern of the New Testament writers is the action of Father,
Son, and Holy Spirit, described in many texts which bring out
nuances of the roles and relationships of the Three. (3) What
is demanded of the person who is baptized? Besides the faith,
repentance, turning, and commitment already mentioned, all of
the texts which describe the effects of baptism implicitly indicate
the role of the baptized. God's saving action comes to term in
the full human response, and the divine action in baptism and
in all of the Christian sacraments comes to its term in man's
full response to grace. (4) What are the effects of baptism?
This is part of the question concerning the meaning of baptism:
in part this symbolic action signifies what it also effects in the
person who responds to grace. With a wealth of interwoven
figurative expressions the New Testament describes what happens to the person who is baptized: salvation, union with Christ,
union with one another in Christ, deliverance from sin, death
to sin, burial, resurrection, washing, consecration, sanctification,
new creation, gift of the Spirit, manifold relations to Father, Son,
and Spirit, and the beginning of a new life which looks to a
future final fulfillment.

Peter's sermon on Pentecost, as recorded in *Acts* 2, suggests
the way of discovery of the meaning of baptism. The immediate
baptismal text, *Acts* 2.37-42, not only sets baptism in the immediate context of a series of actions to be performed, but
also in the larger context within which alone baptism can be
understood: proximately, what God has done in Jesus; and

---

[14] I have commented on these texts in *The Mystery* (Rome: 1971)
195-238.

remotely, the prophecies and promises which have been fulfilled
in Jesus, and which refer back to the full history of salvation.
If one asks, then, what baptism means, the full answer involves
the whole history of salvation. In a sense, it was in answer
to the question concerning the meaning of baptism and the other
Christian sacraments that I wrote the book which I have mentioned, *The Mystery.*

The second approach to an understanding of baptism is
the description of the action as it is set in the liturgical action
of the Church. Here in Christian worship the essential saving
action is surrounded by a rich complex of persons, complementary ritual actions, and a multiple symbolism of sacred art,
all of which contribute to expressing the meaning of this event,
and to heightening the full Christian experience.

If one approaches baptism and the other Christian sacraments thus—allowing for the fact that biblical data for most of
the sacraments are meagre, and that the living faith and tradition of the community of believers is more important here than
in many other aspects of Christian faith—I believe that the
attempt to define the Christian sacrament involves two steps.

First, in the larger context of the history of salvation and
of the mystery of Christ, the sacrament is a moment in the
continuing process in which the saving action of Father, Son,
and Holy Spirit reaches this man or woman here and now, in
in the setting of this visible worshipping community within the
whole Church. Viewed in this setting, the Christian sacrament
is a complex symbolic action in which and by which the saving
God shows forth what he is offering to, and realizing in, this
man or woman.

Secondly, if the sacrament is considered in the narrower
context of the pattern of human action in which the divine
saving action is realized, the sacrament may be defined as an
act of worship performed by Christ in and through his Church
and minister. In this setting, I should define thus: the Christian sacrament is an act of public worship by which Christ,
through his Church and minister, representing the mysteries
of his human life, especially the Paschal mystery, signifies the
sanctification of a person, and when the person is properly
disposed sanctifies him or her by the very act performed.

Two things must be kept in mind in considering such a
definition: a general theology of worship, of Christian worship
in its entirety; and the full liturgical pattern of Christian worship. The sacrament is not the whole of Christian worship,

even though it is an important element. Moreover, in the particular sacramental event, the roles of both the so-called essential rite and the surrounding complementary rites must be considered. The definition regards the essential sacramental action. It should be complemented by an account of the other elements in the whole cult event. In the line of the essential action, Christ, through his Church and minister, honors the Father by consecrating and sanctifying this person, this community. Here the role of the Church and of the minister is instrumental, in the so-called descending line of the divine saving and sanctifying action. In the other elements of the whole act of worship, Christ is also acting in his Church and with her, but here there is question of her approaching in faith, receiving the divine gift, and responding fully. Christ and his Spouse, in the Holy Spirit, honor the Father with a full, rich, varied worship, and under the impulse of the Spirit the Church as Spouse sings the praises of both the Father and Christ her Spouse.

Any satisfactory treatment of the symbolism of the Christian sacrament must take into account the complementary roles of all the symbols involved: those of the essential sacramental action, those of the rites in which it is set, and all of the symbols of sacred art which further enrich the worship.

Some further understanding of the Christian sacrament may be gained from a comparison and contrast with works of art.

First, like the art symbol, the sacrament prevalently is intuitive, not conceptual. Moreover, like many art symbols, the sacraments are highly complex intuitive symbols, employing a multitude of symbolic elements to realize and express in a single concrete image a momentous divine-human action and an extremely rich human experience.

One of the sharpest differences between symbols in art and sacrament regards the importance of perfection of form. In art symbols excellence is measured entirely in terms of the perfection of the form, both in the original work of the creator and in the rendition of the performer. For such perfection in art there is no substitute. On the contrary, beauty of form may be almost completely lacking in an extremely rich act of sacramental worship. Here excellence is measured in terms not of beauty but of holiness, not of gracefulness, but of grace.

Like the art symbol, the sacrament is characterized by a certain condensation, an intensification due to a fusion of forms which heightens the emotional quality and suggests the complexity of the experience which is being expressed. In view of the difference which I have noted concerning the perfection of form, I should say that condensation or intensification is achieved differently in the art work and in the sacrament.

In the art work condensation seems to be due to the perfection of a single commanding significant form, which completely rules the fusion of symbolic elements into a significant whole. Condensation in art, then, seems to be linked with perfection of form.

In the sacramental celebration the matter seems to be different. Here there may be a manifold of symbolic elements which hardly can be said to be ruled by a single significant form, yet which contribute to a total expression and impression. Biblical words and phrases alluding to details of the pattern of salvation history, other symbolic elements adapted from universal religious experience and given a properly Christian sense, and the supporting symbolism of place, architecture, painting, sculpture, and music: all may contribute to the heightening of a single effect, to the expression of a meaning and a feeling which is not spelled out in discursive language, but presented whole for contemplation.

I include the symbolism of place, and a word of explanation may help to make clear what I mean. I am not referring to a sense of sacredness of place due to a sort of cosmic symbolism, in which, for example, the east has a certain sacredness associated with light. Without disregarding the impact of such deep symbolism, I suggest the importance of more particular associations with place in the history of the worshipping community. A particular church or chapel—or even an open field— may be full of meaning not only because of the people who now fill it and animate it with their worship, but also because of the memory of others who have worshipped there similarly, and beyond that because of associations with a richer past. It may be a place of great suffering, achievement, witness: a place of martyrdom, of the life and work and death of a great religious founder, or of other significant events in the history of the believing community.

Is there any law which governs the fusion of such elements and their contribution to the heightening of a single effect? It seems that there is, and that in the whole worshipping community there is a sort of basic insight, a sort of commanding form, which rules the development of an authentic worship: that is, worship which remains true to the very structure and basic law of the religious experience of the community. What is the guarantee of true development and heightening of effect? What safeguards against deviation and distortion? I think that the commanding form is the analogy of faith as sensed in Christian experience. It is only the sense of the faithful, the sense of the Church, which renders the judgment that a given symbolic element fits or does not fit. Having said that, I should add that such a sense of the faithful must be consistent with variations of judgments in different cultural situations: what is fitting for Christians of one culture, and completely consistent with true Christian experience, may seem strange to Christians of another time or place or culture. If this is true, there are no easy solutions to problems concerning the development of Christian worship. The sense of the Church is the sense of the whole Church, and the task of discernment will never be easy.

Two further considerations are suggested by the manner in which condensation is achieved in the sacramental symbol. Both considerations regard conditions for the perception of the full meaning of the sacrament; for the Christian sacrament does not have a meaning which is evident to any casual observer, nor even to an attentive observer who seeks to grasp the full meaning simply by contemplating the celebration. First, the meaning can be grasped only to the degree to which one has penetrated the Christian mystery itself. Bits of symbolism in the whole celebration have their full import only for one who understands them in their context in the whole history of salvation, especially in the complementary play of biblical images. This condition concerns a general preparation for the understanding of Christian worship. It suggests the indispensability of a rich catechesis and a continuing personal study and meditation. A second condition regards a certain preparation which is necessary for the perception of dimensions of meaning which a sacramental celebration may have in a particular worshipping community. Any community which lives a rich Christian life has its particular tone, a function of the blend of the lives of persons in community. Only an increasing familiarity with such a community will bring one to sense more fully the meaning of its celebration.

With regard to the distribution of roles, there is a certain analogy between the sacraments and some works of art. As we noted, there is a difference among the arts with respect to the artist or artists who contribute to the production of the full art work. In some cases, notably in plastic arts, one artist alone creates the art work. In others, the original artist, the creator, depends on the eventual collaboration of other subordinate artists for the production of the final art work, the living work of art.

Art forms of the second general class, in which there is a distinction of roles of creator and performers, suggest some notable similarities and differences in comparison with the Christian sacraments. In Christian belief, Christ has a role analogous to that of the creator of the art form: he originated the Christian sacraments, imposing their commanding form. To varying degrees the Church through the centuries has had a supplementary role in the further elaboration of the symbolism of the sacraments. Further, in the actuation of the sacrament in the living worship of the Church at any moment, there is an important personal and community contribution to the modality and tone of the worship. Yet, beyond all analogy with the influence of the artist's commanding form on successive performances of his work, there is a unique presence and influence of Christ and of the whole Church in every actuation of a Christian sacrament. In all public worship of his Church—indeed in all Christian worship borne by the grace of Christ—Christ is present and acting, in a variety of modes and degrees, but always really. He is not absent, not "past": he is worshipping in and through the whole Church, the local worshipping community, and the minister and participants. Moreover, in a derived manner and degree, the whole Church is present and active in all of its public worship, which is implemented only in the action of the minister(s) and participants in the local community.

Finally, the greatest difference of all between art work and sacrament is the setting in which it has its meaning. The art work is set in an imaginary world. The sacrament is set in the world which for the Christian is most fully real and counts for most: the transcendent world of the Christian mystery, in which Father, Son, and Holy Spirit continue their saving, sanctifying, transforming action, and in which the Christian lives in them, already sharing in eternal life. This is real, though its reality be grasped by faith alone. There is a difference between belief and make-believe.

f. *Symbols in play*. One can hardly afford to neglect play in any reflection on the full range of human operations, for most men, women, and children spend much of their time in various types of play. A rough definition of an extremely wide-ranging class of activities is this: any human activity engaged in for amusement, diversion, or pleasure derived from operating in a world different from that of ordinary life. If one reflects further on play, he or she may recognize that it pertains to the mystery of human transcendence, albeit in a humble sort of way. It is one of the ways of going beyond, or escaping from, the routine of ordinary life, where "ordinary" means what is of regular occurrence for a person. What is ordinary for one could be a thrilling new adventure for another: driving a car or truck, or piloting a plane. In the element of going beyond the ordinary, play has something in common with discovery in the pursuit of knowledge, creation of a work of art, experience of a work of art, or any great achievement in which a person somehow carves out a new world. What is proper to play, and differentiates it from these other kinds of transcendence, is its modest scope and humble place in the scale of values of most men: its purpose is amusement, diversion, enjoyment. Though excellent performance in some types of play gives pleasure from the exercise of considerable skill, still play as such hardly ranks with art or scientific discovery as a mode of human activity which involves pleasure in the exercise of a great power. I say *play as such*, allowing for professional performance, which could be considered a kind of art. Even though play be engaged in for its benefits to health and general wellbeing important for the pursuits of ordinary life, in itself it is another world.

The symbols of play are the terms of operations which have their meaning in one of the many particular worlds of play: from a child's play in a sandbox to a deeply thoughtful man's move on a chess board. Here, as everywhere, every symbol has its meaning as it is integrated into a whole. The kinds of symbols vary as do the kinds of play, with blends of intuitive and conceptual elements. Play is an imitation of life, an imitation of the operations which are proper to the world which is imagined and imitated n play. Competition, the desire for victory, and the passion of aggressiveness are hints of some of the sorts of worlds of activity which are imitated: the symbolism of the pieces on the chess board suggest that chess is a sort of war game. Play can be the "poor man's" science, art, industry, finance, politics, war, or any other realm in which he dreams of excelling. It does not involve new kinds of symbols, but countless worlds of make-believe, whose symbols are shadows of those which count in the world which is imitated.

* * *

These, then, seem to me to be the principal kinds of symbols. I should make two brief observations on what we have considered in this chapter. First, although symbols can be differentiated, and differences stand out clearly in many cases, still one must recognize a certain continuity of symbolizing and of symbols. As there is a unity in continuity of human operations, and an ever-varying blend of the many elements of human operation, so too there is a certain continuity in the world of symbols. Language, arts, science, philosophy, and religion develop slowly, and stages in human process cannot be marked off sharply and unmistakably. Second, as I noted at the outset, it is important to recall now that the differentiation of symbols has been worked out in terms of their cognitive function. The many kinds of symbols are so many kinds of terms of the process from insight to the realization and projection of what has been grasped somehow in knowledge. That is not the whole of symbolizing, as knowledge is not the whole of human life. To restore something of the fulness which we should demand of any account of symbols, we must turn now to consider more fully the functions of symbols.

Chapter IX

FUNCTIONS OF SYMBOLS

Let us pause for a moment to consider the process of our thought to this point, our goal, and our immediate task. After an initial description and reflection upon structures of human experience, we discerned and differentiated several human operations, elements of that experience. That differentiation of operations, the subsequent treatment of the sphere which is the total setting of human operation, and further reflection on the roles of intellect constituted our basic reflection on man.

Dealing with symbolizing and symbols in the last two chapters, we began our reflection on the aspect of human being which is our special concern in this book. Symbolizing, I have said, is a properly human operation, and symbols are human works.[1] We have considered three elements in symbolizing: its beginning in insight; two sets of modes, tendencies, and elements: conceptual and intuitive; and the worlds in which any symbol is integrated and has its full meaning. In the last chapter we worked out a rather complicated differentiation and classification of symbols, taking for the moment a nominal definition of symbol as a human work in which the sensuous is somehow meaningful.

With regard to what we have done thus far, one possible misunderstanding should be forestalled. When I speak of symbolizing as a properly human operation, I am not introducing another operation, different from those which we treated in the first part of this book. Symbolizing is properly human, and it is an aspect of all human conscious operations. Since human operation is human, it is bodily in a human way, and it comes to its term, its fulfillment, in a work which is sensuous and meaningful. In reflecting upon symbolizing, therefore, we have concentrated on a characteristic of all human conscious operation: in a variety of ways all these operations

---

[1] Above, ch. VII, p. 183.

terminate in works, within the person who is operating, or outside him. The works, sensuous and meaningful, are symbols, as we take *symbol* in the context of our thought.

Our goal is a more accurate definition of *symbol*, a further reflection on questions concerning symbol and meaning, some indication of more than merely human symbolizing, and some further questions which remain to be answered in the effort to understand human being.

Our immediate task is to consider the full range of functions of symbols, as a last step in the approach to the definition of symbol. All human conscious operation is symbolizing: not only cognitive operations, but emotive, volitional, and motor operations as well. Having recognized a cognitive factor in all symbolizing and symbols, we have worked out our classification of symbols on the basis of variations in that factor. Before proceeding to a definition of symbol, however, we must recall the other dimensions of human operation, and consider all of the functions of the symbols in which human operations terminate. Only thus can we hope to formulate a definition which may be fairly adequate.

Considering how human persons are in the world, and how by the interplay of their operations they come to a relative fulness of perfection, we may reflect on three sets of functions of symbols. The first regards the roles of the symbol in the conscious life of the symbolizer: in a variety of ways he or she comes to a relative fulness of being in the symbols in which his or her operations terminate. The second is what could be called the revelatory or representative function of the symbol. Any symbol, internal or external, stands out as figure against ground, and it somehow reveals or represents the total subjective and objective field in which it is known. This revelatory or representative function is analogous, and must be differentiated. The third regards the efficacy of symbols in the human world, personal and interpersonal.

The very mention of the interpersonal world should be enough to remind us of a set of problems which we have avoided since the beginning of chapter VII, on symbolizing. At that point I indicated that I would hold in abeyance a number of matters, to concentrate on the process of symbolizing in the individual symbolizer, and on symbols as his works. We cannot proceed farther without considering the bearing of three of those factors on our treatment of the functions of symbols, and consequently on our attempt to define the symbol. The three factors are these: (1) the role of the community in the creation of symbols; (2) the continued use of symbols, as distinguished from their creation; (3) the non-cognitive functions of symbols.

What, then, is involved in this chapter? First, I am concerned with three sets of functions of symbols. Second, I am restoring three factors involved in symbolizing and symbols. How do I propose to accomplish this twofold task? I shall proceed by dealing with the three sets of functions, introducing at the place where it is pertinent whatever must be said of the three factors. This will involve some complement to what has been said in chapters VII and VIII, in which we concentrated on the cognitive factor as the basis for differentiation of symbols.

ACTUALIZING THE SYMBOLIZER

Symbols function immediately in the actualization of the symbolizer. What does this mean?

First, the actualization of the human person is the realization of some degree of his or her potential: the achievement of some further degree of the perfection of human being which is possible. Not being fully perfect from the outset of life, a human person transcends his or her limited being at any stage by acting, operating. As we have seen in our extended reflection on human operation, all such action is performed within the matrix of the twofold basic human intentionality: cognitive and emotive/volitional/motor. Knowing is a way of *being*: advance in understanding and in truth is a heightening of one's being, an achievement of greater perfection. So too emotional, volitional, and motor operations which tend to what is really good for the person, or withdraw from what is really bad, improve the quality of life, heighten the degree of being or perfection. Such operations are *real*: they *count* in the intersubjective world and in the universe. They are part of the mystery of human transcendence.[2]

What is the role of symbols in such actualization? They are the formed, meaningful sensuous term in which human acts come to completion. We need not repeat our reflection on the variety and blend of human operations in all modes of intentionality. All that we have considered in this regard bears upon our present reflection on symbols. As human operations may

---

[2] Cf. ch. V, pp. 135-140.

involve a blend of several modes of intentionality, so a given symbol in which an operation terminates may function simultaneously in many modes. A word or gesture, or a combination of the two in a composite symbol, may be purely cognitive: it may be simply the formulation and expression of what I think. But in other situations a single symbol may function in several ways: expressing thought (what he is like), emotion (admiration or disgust), will (love or hate), and the corresponding motor action, of which it may be a part.

Actualization of the symbolizer, then, is the realization of his or her potential in intentional operations of all kinds: not only cognitive, but also emotive, volitional, and motor. To this point, therefore, we have restored one of the factors from which we had abstracted: the non-cognitive dimensions of human operation and human symbolizing.

Even so, our reflection remains severely abstract. We have reflected solely on the process within the symbolizer, and on his works. If we were to do no more, our thought would be stunted and wretchedly distorted. One could not treat adequately even the first of the three functions of symbols, actualization of the symbolizer, without recognizing the importance of the interpersonal world in which he or she is, and in which alone he or she comes to a certain fulfillment.

We are not solitary symbolizers. We are not alone, and we could not be alone for long. It would be vain, therefore, to speculate on some hypothetical solitary man, his symbolizing, and his symbols. It would be vain even to discuss whether such an hypothesis is impossible, contradictory. We are together, sharing one world, sharing one another's lives, whether we desire it or not. Our opportunity and our task are to enrich one another, to live together, to make our lives fuller and happier. The intersubjective world is the womb and cradle, the school and field of action, of symbolizing man and woman. Symbols are created by men and women, not born with them. They are created by persons who share a world, who together strive to cope, who follow their own hunches and hints from the actions, the glances, the manifest intentions of others. Symbols are created in the intersubjective world, and they function in it.

We must reflect further, therefore, on the actualization of the symbolizer as it regards his or her being in an interpersonal world. This will involve some complementary reflection on both symbolizing and symbols.

(1) *Insight.* All symbolizing begins with insight.[3] What we must recognize now is that insight occurs within a human community, and that the human community has a role in the total process of the actualization of the symbolizer.

A simple example may serve to suggest the role of community in the insight which occurs, both in the creation of symbols, and in their understanding and further use and adaptation. Suppose a group of men and women who know one another quite well, and who are familiar with personal traits and patterns of actions of individuals in the group. They have a vague sense of implicit networks of relationships, and of personal characteristics. At a given moment, as John is acting in a manner familiar to all, Bob has a flash of insight, and touches off John's trait with the word: "The hawk!" All understand what he means. All had a vague sense of the characteristics of John's action. Bob, with a quickness of wit and a knack of hitting things off with an appropriate word or gesture, catches and formulates a concept which all understand. It is life in the community which has occasioned Bob's insight, and which makes it easy too for others to grasp his meaning. Insights, from the humblest to the most brilliant, occur in the setting of an interpersonal world. The one who gets the insight and formulates the relationship which he has grasped acts as a catalyst in the life of the community. Both symbol-makers and symbol-users act against the same ground. The experience of insight, in both the creator and the users of symbols, stands out as figure against the ground of the everyday life of a given community, in a given culture.

So it is that the artist, the scientist, the revolutionary thinker, and the creator of a new style in any aspect of human living, gets his or her insight within a given culture, in recognizable continuity with that culture. Some novels and films could have been created only against the ground of the depression years in the United States. A revolutionary theory of society could have been conceived only as a result of insights into the plight of an oppressed people. In all these cases, and in many others which could be imagined or cited from history, it is the setting of a community, the vaguely sensed patterns of its life, which occasions the insight. And the symbol has a resonance in the community, because the creator has

---

[3] Cf. ch. VII, pp. 184-186.

grasped and formulated and projected for all to behold what many had vaguely surmised.

The relationship of creative insight to the community life which is its occasion and its setting is an aspect of the mystery of human being. Another aspect, closely linked, is the relationship of seeing and hearing in the total process of discovery and of learning. For a deeper understanding of the dependence of insight upon community I suggest a reflection on the importance of hearing and of the spoken word.

We cannot come to know much alone, by our unaided individual effort—if indeed we can be said to have learned anything alone. It is not only by seeing that we come to insight into what we see: we do not see relationships; nor is seeing the only sense experience within which normally we come to grasp relationships, to understand. We begin life learning by listening as we look: the spoken word and the pointing gesture guide our visual perception, and the seen and heard work together in our experience. We can share, and grow together in understanding, principally through the word: formulating, expressing, and sharing what we have grasped.

Beyond the question of an immediate primacy of seeing over hearing in our perceptual world, it is the mystery of the word which explains most of our learning: primarily the word in living speech, and then the word in the stored wisdom of written thought. We see first, or at least vision figures most prominently in much of our experience; but often it is only as we look and listen that we come to insight into what we perceive, and we come to know things and their names together. What we have perceived and understood we hold best of all in words which give form to our thought. We talk a lot, and living speech is like the great sea of primordial experience, within which islands of explicit acts emerge. Within the vastness of living speech the written word seizes and fixes forever some relationship which has been grasped. The insight which occurred, and the concept which has been formulated in the written word, can be understood as they are set in the life of a people. Eventually the written word will present problems of understanding, when the voices of that people will have been silenced. For the symbol, and the original insight, are intelligible only in the setting of the culture and the community in which they occurred.

(2) *Elaboration.* Not only in getting his insight, but also in elaborating his symbol, the individual symbolizer draws upon

and adapts the resources of his community and his culture. Clever as he may be, he is not a pure creator. His turn of phrase and his nuance of meaning are intelligible and striking precisely because he is operating with the resources of a known language, and his linguistic symbol stands out from common usage, but is close enough to have a recognizable meaning. His composite symbols expressing emotion and will, personal though they be in style, and vivid and fresh as they may be, are expressive and meaningful because they adapt symbolic elements known within his culture. Inventiveness in arts and in science and in full human living is a matter of striking out boldly from a known position; it is not an absolute creation from nothing, nor a sudden appearance from nowhere. The mathematician or scientist or philosopher who is creative must adapt a known idiom, lest the value of his discovery be lost to all of his peers, and be unintelligible for all posterity. The artist who creates in a new style cannot spring too far beyond known art forms, lest he find himself alone in the appreciation of his work.

(3) *Use and adaptation.* One can distinguish two stages of symbolizing activity. The first is primary, creative: it is the work of the symbol-maker. The second is receptive, utilizing, and adaptive: it is the continuing activity of symbol-users. What we have considered thus far in the process of symbolizing and the variety of its works regarded mostly the first stage. We must complement that consideration by a reflection on the second stage, in which most symbolizing occurs.

First, there are many similarities in the operations in the two stages. In both stages there is a succession of experience: primordial and explicit; a succession of explicit perceptions against a ground, in the setting of a field or world; and a succession of insights. At both levels, symbols express varying degrees of insight, and (in the case of symbols which terminate a multiple intentional operation) varying degrees of feeling, will, action, and full sharing of the total original experience. The difference between the creator and the user or adapter of symbols is not necessarily a difference of experience. Though there are instances of rare experiences which occasion a deep insight and a creative symbolizing, and though there is always a difference of perspective, still in a sense the same world is at hand for both creator and user, a world involving an implicit network of relationships in the continuum of experience. In a given experience, for both the eventual creator and the eventual receiver and user, the relationships are vaguely grasped in the perceptual field. The difference between creator and user is generally a matter of quicker intelligence and the knack of hitting things off with an apt word or gesture.

As the creator of symbols is situated in a cultural world, and his symbols stand out from the ground of that culture, and have meaning for men who share that culture; and as he must create in continuity with the culture which alone renders his symbols intelligible; so too the user and adapter of symbols must respect certain bounds, especially in a sort of secondary creative adaptation of symbols. He too must symbolize in the setting of his culture. Moreover, he must respect cultural and personal context in his interpretation of symbols. We cannot cut across a text, take a single word in any arbitrary sense, and affirm that this is the meaning of the text. In speaking or in interpreting the speech or written thought of another, we must acknowledge the fund of words in the constituted language of our culture, and acknowledge too the sense of a word in any sentence, determined by the context.

The distinction is often drawn between living, original speech, and dead, constituted language. It does not quite correspond to the distinction which I make here between creators and users or adapters of symbols. It is true that the poet, the writer, the artist of any type, stands out from the multitude, and in his finest moments he creates. But what of the rest of us, who do not have the same creative talent? Are we destined to shuffle the dead remains of what really lived only for a moment in the act of the great man's creation? No. There can be a continuing life and vitality, a continuing appropriation and re-creating, in the life of symbolizing man. One who truly appreciates a poem or any great symbol may rise to a moment when the symbol lives for him, and serves to formulate an insight and a feeling, a total experience, which is full, living, true, and which may surpass the quality of the insight and feeling and total experience of the original artist. As meaning is communicated, it is transformed. A poem, a psalm, a prophetic word, a word of St. Paul, a liturgical prayer, may mean something new and something richer than the reality imaged by the one who first spoke the word. The richer the life, the richer the symbolism.

Symbols are made and re-made, created and re-cycled, daily. Some symbols languish and die, when the reality which they imaged, the living reality of man, the living bond between men, the world which they made together and shared—when all this languishes or dies. Some symbols live long and gather vitality and fulness, for they image a truly human reality, and in the living interplay of persons both the creator and the user of symbols enrich the world of meaning.

(4) *Internal and external symbols.* In this series of reflections we are considering the function of symbols in actualizing the symbolizer with special reference to his or her living in an interpersonal world. In this regard, some distinctions must be drawn between what I have called internal and external symbols.[4] Internal symbols are within subjective conscious experience. They are not expressed or projected. They have no existence or consistency outside the subject, and they cannot serve to communicate meaning in an intersubjective world. Among such symbols we have included images in perception, memory, imagination, and dream; conceptions, reasonings, and judgments which remain unexpressed; emotions, acts of the will, and motor impulses which remain incomplete, unexpressed, unexecuted; and the body image. External symbols, on the contrary, are manifest to others, and they function in an intersubjective world. What, then, must be said of these two classes of symbols in so far as they regard the actualization of the symbolizer?

In so far as a man or a woman is concerned solely as a person, or solely as he or she stands in God's presence, one can recognize a certain full actualization in an inner act, terminating in one or more internal symbols. Even in conceiving of such an act, however, we must avoid the illusion of a full inner act which would involve no symbol, no sensuous factor. Every human intentional act involves a sensuous factor, which by its very nature is in continuity with the external sensuous realm, sensibly perceptible.[5] Moreover, though a man or woman can come to a certain relative fulness of being in such an inner act, the human person by nature is meant to live in an interpersonal world; and men and women live fully only when their minds and hearts are revealed in acts which affect other men and women. The gauge of our love of God is our love of our brothers and sisters, a love which must be shown in word and deed.

Considered as they live in their interpersonal world, men and women cannot function in community, and cannot come to their relative fulness of being, except by acts which reach

---

4 Cf. ch. VIII, pp. 222 ff.
5 Cf. ch. VIII, pp. 219-220.

fulfillment in sensuous, perceptible terms. The first function of symbols, therefore, is that of actualizing the symbolizer as a person living among other human persons.

Two more observations are necessary here. First, actualizing a human person precisely with regard to his or her living among other persons is not just adding a plus-value, a further perfection without which he or she could do quite nicely. One cannot live fully as a human person without opening upon the interpersonal world. Any man or woman who tried for long to live closed in upon himself or herself, with all thought and feeling unexpressed, would be in danger of serious personal derangement, and eventually in need of special care.

Second, I should emphasize that this whole reflection regards the actualization of a person in the *interpersonal* world. The heightening of perfection which is involved is specifically human. The value is real, it counts, it is significant only for other human persons. It is not measured in terms of physics or chemistry, though it always involves bodily factors which can be thus measured. It is not a matter of the relationship of human symbolizing to animals or plants. Investigation of such matters does not pertain to our present concern.

REVEALING THE SYMBOLIZER AND HIS WORLD

A symbol is the immediate term of a process which began with insight. The process may be multiple, with cognitive, emotive, volitional, and motor elements. The symbol is an *immediate* term, not ultimate: for symbols continue to function in the life of the symbolizer and in the lives of others in an interpersonal world. As an immediate term of a process, a term which is relative, not absolute, the symbol is a certain actualization of the symbolizer: in it he achieves a certain relative fulness of being. This is the function which we have considered. Since the symbol continues to function in the life of the symbolizer and of others, we move on now to consider two other sets of functions. One regards the symbol considered in relation to the process which preceded it, the process which it terminates. The other regards its further functions in affecting the life of the symbolizer and the lives of others.

It is the first of these further sets of functions which I have called "revealing the symbolizer and his world". In what sense is it a function of the symbol in relation to what has preceded it?

The symbol is a meaningful sensuous term of an operation. What it shows forth, what it projects, is a shaped sensuous image which has its total meaning only as it is set in the whole field, the ground from which it stands out as figure. That ground is the full world of the symbolizer, subjective and objective.

If the symbol is a gesture and word combined to express anger, it is a particular formed sensuous image in which an act of strong emotion comes to its fulness. The word and gesture are meaningful as they stand out from the flood of passion in the symbolizer, and their full meaning could be grasped only by one who knew the mystery of that person, of the injury suffered, of the world which he or she faced. If the symbol is a sentence expressing profound understanding, it is a revelation not only of that thought, but of the wisdom of the thinker, and of the world in which he or she has labored in the elaboration of scientific or mathematical or philosophical or theological knowledge. If it is a work of art, a statue or a symphony, by the mystery of a multiple isomorphism its form reveals the form of the artist's commanding idea and the form of the feeling into which he had his insight.

Every symbol, then, functions as a revelation of the symbolizer and of the world in which he had an insight and to which he responded in one or more of the modes of human intentionality. It is meaningful as *his* act, springing from a unique personal world, subjective and objective.

To whom does the symbol make its revelation? Allowing for the full range of symbols which we have differentiated in Chapter VIII, we should have to answer by distinguishing between internal and external symbols.

Internal symbols function within the conscious life of the symbolizer, in which he or she is aware of an objective world experienced from a unique perspective, and of an utterly unique personal subjective world. In my blend of perceptions, memories, imaginings, dreams and dreams recalled, understanding, judgment, emotions, will, and motor action, I have symbols which reveal my world to me, and reveal me to myself. Every one of them stands out as figure against ground, against the full ground which is uniquely mine, objective and subjective.

External symbols are perceptible to another person, and they can reveal the symbolizer to other human persons. Such symbols, then, are the "face" of the symbolizer in his interpersonal world, the meeting point of two worlds, that of the symbolizer and that of the perceiver. They mediate the symbolizer's impression on other persons, and his influence upon the interpersonal world. Immediately they reveal him and his world to the perceiver. Standing out as figure against ground, they have their meaning for the perceiver in so far as he or she is able to divine the ground from which they stand out. Every such symbol is representative: the part stands for the whole; the individual is integrated into the whole in which alone it can be adequately understood. The concept expressed is grasped as it is set in a whole movement of thought. A single act of love expresses a full life and play of emotion. A determined act of will expressed in a command or a decision is a thrust of a free man or woman shaping a world. A poised body, or a single movement, stands for a whole action about to begin or underway: the whole race is symbolized in the tense body of the sprinter poised against the starting blocks, and in every stride along his course, and in the final thrust with which he hurls himself against the tape.

The external symbol is a meaningful sensuous term of a human act, and its meaning is gathered to the extent to which the perceiver can read the full setting of the act, its full meaning: cognitive, emotive, volitional, and motor. In its revelatory power, the external symbol is in continuity with the realm of internal symbols of the symbolizer: the wealth of his inner world, of his response to the world in which he lives, is sensed in his external action. In the words and actions of strong men and women, rich in understanding and strong in emotion and will, we sense the depth of the person, and the reserve of power not fully expressed.

Affecting the Human World by a Manifold Efficacy

Revealing the symbolizer involves at least two persons: the symbolizer who is revealed, and the perceiver to whom he or she is revealed. In our preceding reflection we were concerned with the person revealed. Reflection on the other persons to whom the revelation is made introduces our third set of functions. Revelation to another person is communication of knowledge, and this is one of the set of functions which we can include under our present title. Symbols *affect* the human world: they are *effective,* and they have not only many effects, but many kinds of effects. It is this that I mean to indicate with the expression "affecting the human world with a manifold efficacy."

Here too, consistently with the pattern of our treatment of symbols, we must distinguish internal and external symbols, and consider the manifold efficacy with which they affect the human world. Before we attempt to deal with either, however, we must consider three elements which are involved in our reflection: reality, actualization, and causality. In part we shall be recalling previous reflections; in part, going beyond them.

First, with regard to reality, I simply recall and briefly summarize what I have developed earlier.[6] Whatever *is* in any way is *real*. The total reality of the universe is the existing universe in all of its concrete fulness. Within that universe of persons and things there is a continual interplay. The persons and things are real; their operations are real; the effects of the operations are real, and so are the relationships which are the consequences. Beyond all aspects of reality which are susceptible to measurement by physical and chemical methods, there are orders of properly human operations in the interpersonal world: the interplay of persons by all manners of intentional acts. Properly human operations, of knowledge, emotion, and will, are real, and their effects are real, both in the persons who act and in those upon whom they act in the kind of interplay which is specifically human. Because we are not fully perfect, and strive to achieve a greater degree of our potential relative fulness of being, we act, and by the quality of our acts and their effects we heighten or lower our degree of being and goodness. Knowing and loving are modes of being, within the mystery of the whole human way of being; and when we come to understand and judge truly, and when we come to love what is truly good, especially in our fellow men and women, we *are* more fully.

We are, and are real; and our properly human works are, and are real: they *count*, they are of value, in the universe of being. Symbols, then, as the meaningful sensuous terms of our human operations, *are*. The thought uttered or written, the emotion felt, the decision made, the agreement reached between two or more persons, the marriage union established, the statue carved, the symphony played, all of the works of man in arts and crafts, mathematics, science, and philosophy, religion and

[6] Cf. ch. V, pp. 135-140.

theology: all of these *are*, they *count*, in the various worlds in which men are and operate.

Actualization, as we have seen, is the realization of a greater degree of potential relative fulness of being.[7] In unique ways in human being it is part of the mystery of transcendence: going beyond the initial stages of our human being, realizing an ideal "self" in a richer life of knowledge and love, coming to a greater fulness of truth and goodness in our personal and interpersonal life.

Causality is influence upon the actualization, and hence upon the degree of fulness of being, of another. In the continual interplay of persons and things in the universe, they affect one another: one has its effects on the being of another. Some aspects of this interplay and influence fall within the observation and measurement of the empirical scientists. Others do not, but they are no less real. Physics and chemistry are themselves human achievements in the order of knowledge, highly abstractive, verifiable within their limits and by their own methods. They are particular human achievements, and it is beyond their range to rise up against the human thinkers who fashioned them, and to forbid any further developments of human knowledge, to say nothing of other human pursuits. As sensuous, symbols figure in the interplay of persons and things in a bodily universe. As meaningful by reason of a form given to them by a human symbolizer, symbols play upon others in a manner which can be grasped only by a study of the properly human modes of operation which are involved in symbolizing, in giving meaningful form to a sensuous medium. Symbols have a meaning given to them only by human symbolizers and perceptible and intelligible only by human persons in the interplay of the interpersonal world. It is by virtue of their meaning that they play unique roles in that world, and have an influence which can be called properly causal.

The third set of functions which we are considering now is properly causal. Presupposing our notions of reality and of actualization, we are concerned here with modes of causality of symbols in the interpersonal world: how they *affect* men and women, how they have *effects* upon them in various ways.

First, then, let us consider internal symbols, and what may seem to be a paradoxical efficacy, causality, influence upon the actualization of *another*. The paradox lies in this: that any

---

[7] Cf. ch. V, pp. 125-126; ch. IX, pp. 271-272.

influence of internal symbols, in accordance with the very notion of internal symbols, is within the conscious subject, the symbolizer. It is only because he is composite and complex in his human way of being bodily that one element in his conscious life can have an influence upon others.

It is far beyond my scope here to undertake a complete reflection on the human act, on all of the internal factors which in any way influence human action. I have used the rather indefinite words *affect* and *influence*, and I deliberately avoid attempting to distinguish satisfactorily various kinds of principles: conditions, occasions, and causes of different kinds. For our present purpose it is sufficient to acknowledge that the many kinds of internal symbols which we distinguished in Chapter VIII [8] are not simply terms of operations, but affect the life and conduct of the symbolizer. Anyone can reflect on his or her own experience, and recognize the incalculable variety of interplay of these factors: images in perception, memory, imagination, and dream; conceptions, reasonings, and judgments; emotions, acts of will, and motor impulse; and body image.

All of my conscious acts stand out against the ground of all that I have been and am at the moment of action. No one could give a completely satisfactory account of all of the elements which can enter into a human act, and of all of their possible blends. With regard to any particular action, no one can trace it back to all of its antecedents, judge the delicate balance of factors influencing decision and action, and pronounce with absolute certitude on the quality of his act. It is enough to recognize that the human person *is* in such a way that his or her action proceeds from varying blends of all of these elements in conscious life, and that internal symbols affect subsequent action in many ways.

With regard to external symbols, one can affirm from the outset that they affect other persons in many ways, and from the outset too one can acknowledge that it is impossible to spell out all the varieties of their influence.

First of all, symbols which are prevalently cognitive communicate knowledge. This is true especially of highly conceptual symbols, in relation to persons who are capable of grasping their meaning. But all kinds of intuitive symbols also can communicate knowledge, and communicate more effectively to those

---

[8] Cf. ch. VIII, pp. 222-227.

persons who are not trained in science, mathematics, or philosophy. What sort of influence is involved? The symbolizer,
and his symbol which has been given an existence outside the
symbolizer and a possibility of affecting other persons, are not
the sole cause of others' knowledge. When I read a book, or
listen to a lecture, I am undergoing an influence, I am affected
by a play of forces which is properly human, a meaningful sensuous influence. But it is I who perceive and perform all the
other intentional acts which follow. Without attempting to
work out a full theory of knowledge, accounting for all of the
factors involved in a highly complex field of relationships, we
can simply recognize that the symbolizer and his symbols do
play a role in the eventual genesis of other persons' knowledge.
Otherwise the scientist's or philosopher's passion, and their labor
in hope of communicating and making a difference in the lives
of their fellow men and women, would be utterly vain. Teaching
too would be the most futile activity, as well as one of the most
thankless! Symbolizing in a prevalently cognitive mode makes
sense, because the symbolizer and his or her symbols do something in the interpersonal world: they count, they make a
difference.

Not only prevalently cognitive symbols communicate knowledge. Every symbol is a meaningful sensuous term of human
operation: its has an intelligible structure which can be grasped.
Just as I can perceive things and events in the world, so I can
perceive meaningful human actions, and I can grasp their sense.
We learn more of human nature from our observation and insight into human action than from treatises on human action.

Beyond the communication of knowledge, symbols affect
the interpersonal world in countless other ways which are properly human. Just as I can gain insight into things about me,
and estimate their value, and respond in all the modes of intentional operations, so I can gain insight into all of the kinds of
external symbols by which I am somehow affected in the interpersonal world, and I can be influenced by them in all the
modes of my response. Here we find further aspects of the
mystery of isomorphism. As in the experience of the original
symbolizer there is a manifold isomorphism of persons and
things in his objective world, of all of his internal symbols, and
of his external symbols; so in the experience of the perceiver
of external symbols there is a continuation and extension of
the isomorphism in his internal and external symbols.

To some extent in our knowledge of things, and in our

response to them, we learn directly from things, and respond to them according to our estimate of value reached by direct experience of them. Yet for the most part we learn by listening as we look: living with other persons, we learn in the matrix of community, and what we know of things comes partly from personal observation, partly from others who communicate meaning by symbols of all kinds.

In the world of persons the matter is quite different. All of our knowledge of persons, and all of our response to them, is mediated by symbols. We have access to persons, and can come to insight into them, only as they appear to us, or as they affect us through the symbols which we perceive. In either case, it is only through the meaningful sensuous terms of their operations that we know them, and, consistently with the whole thrust of our reflection, that means knowing them through their symbols. When we come to know a thing by direct contact with it, we symbolize in a succession of operations. When we come to know a person, whether by direct interpersonal contact, or by perception of the symbols which are his works, or by the symbols by which others report their direct knowledge of him, we are coming to know another symbolizer. The original experience, somehow the fountainhead of all knowledge of persons and response to them, is interpersonal in the full second-personal mode.[9]

Whether they represent persons or things, symbols mediate to the perceiver something of the world of the symbolizer, subjective and objective; and the more effectively they represent that world, the more they mediate in the perceiver a share in the symbolizer's original experience. The more intuitive the symbol, the more vivid the meaningful sensuous form, the richer will be the variety of experience which the symbol mediates. Intuitive symbols stimulate memory, imagination, emotion, desire and decision, and action, because in a striking way, more adequately than is the case in ordinary, everyday experience, they present a rich, fully charged image of a personal response to a world.

What is the secret of the manifold efficacy of intuitive symbols? I suggest that the answer may be indicated by reflection on the comparison of two ways of knowing and responding to a person. The first is based on reading a dossier, without

---

[9] Cf. above, the differentiation of first-, second-, and third-personal acts, pp. 125-132.

ever meeting the man or woman in question. Anyone who has
served on a committee screening applications for a position
will be familiar with the type of knowledge which can be gained,
and the response which is elicited on the basis of such knowledge. Unfortunately for some applicants, decisions are often
made solely on the basis of such knowledge. It is presented
in highly abstract form, in answers to set questions regarding
factors which are considered significant for the judgment of
qualification for the position. It is highly conceptualized, and
strictly cognitive. When there is question not of admitting grad-
uate students to a department, but of recommending a man or
woman for a high position, the search committee usually will
not be content with such knowledge and response. One or more
of the candidates who seem best qualified on the basis of their
dossiers will be invited to come for an interview with the committee, and often with other groups whose judgment is to be
considered. When the person, or the two or more persons,
appears, the knowledge gained from full personal contact, and
the response to the person, may be quite different from the
original impression, and the choice will be made finally on the
basis of such personal knowledge and response. The knowledge
is no longer purely abstract: here the committee members face
the full reality of the person. The response is no longer purely
cognitive, no longer a judgment based on a process of weighing
a number of abstract factors: it is a full human response to
a person whose qualities could never be adequately held in an
abstract, technical discursive account.

What I have proposed is not just a comparison, but an
example of the difference between conceptual and intuitive symbols, and the range of their efficacy. In the two kinds of knowledge and response we have illustrations of experience involving
the two kinds of symbols. In general, conceptual symbols are
abstract, accurate in fixing an intelligible relationship, unmistakable in their meaning as they are set in the highly abstract
world of science, mathematics, philosophy, technology, or ad-
ministration. They mediate an experience which is purely cognitive: understanding and judgment. On the contrary, intuitive
symbols do not isolate a single intelligible relationship from
the total human reality in which it is enfleshed. They project
a meaningful sensuous form, concrete, individual. They are
abstract only in delivering that sensuous form from all that is
irrelevant, to make it more striking and richer in its suggestive
power. Usually they are not prevalently cognitive in function:

presenting a vivid sensuous image of a reality whose intelligible structure is vaguely surmised, they evoke a manifold response, perdominantly emotive, volitional, motor. They are highly efficacious, for they resonate in the full personal experience of the perceiver, evoking a flood of images of memory and imagination, a multiple emotional response, will, and action: they *move* men and women, who are not disembodied intellects.

In great intuitive symbols, in art and in life, there is a complementarity and a striking isomorphism of the experiences of the symbolizer and of the person who perceives and responds to the symbol. I should say that our reflection on the creative process in the experience of the artist has a bearing on the process of the person who perceives and responds to a great intuitive symbol.[10] With a vague insight into the shape of human feeling, the artist plunges into the depths of his own infra-perceptual experience, and with a sense of isomorphism of sensuous form he fashions an image of the feeling. He captures and expresses a shape which fits endless variations upon experiences which somehow have the same felt shape. His image has its power of suggestion because it plunges the perceiver into the same depth, with the sense of the felt shape of feeling. His own personal history is unique, and the particular experiences which for him have a similar shape are his very own. In art, and in great intuitive symbolizing in real life, the story is not the thing: what counts is the feeling which is expressed, and the essential experience is of the shape of the feeling. The flood of particular images, memories, feelings, insights, will, and motor impulse will be unique in the personal response of every man or woman.

I should distinguish between what I intend to effect in others by my symbol, and what it may effect in them beyond my intentions. In some respects, I may affect others far less than I intend; in other respects, far more. That is true even of the spoken word or gesture, with its fleeting existence. It is true more strikingly of symbols like the written word or the work of art, which are given an existence and a potential efficacy independent of the symbolizer. In all cases, in varying manners, this difference witnesses to the manner in which we affect one another by our symbols. The symbolizer and his symbol affects—or acts in such a way that he or she may affect—other persons; but symbols function according to the laws of

---

[10] Cf. ch. VIII, pp. 243-247, and ch. VI, pp. 152-158.

the interplay of persons in the interpersonal world. Symbols
are meaningful, and they have a potential efficacy, but their
actual influence depends on the manner in which they are
received by another symbolizer. This is a particular instance
of the old philosophical adage: whatever is received, is received
in the way which is proper to the recipient. It is an illustration of the perspectivism and selectivity of our perception and
all of our knowledge, and of our total response in all modes
of intentional acts. The actual influence of symbols occurs in
events in which the recipient is active, and every person acts
in function of his or her total personal ground, in an act which
is uniquely personal and unpredictable. Symbols are effective
only in the interaction of persons.

They tell of Ignatius of Loyola, contemplating the heavens
in the silence of the night from his little inner-court balcony
in sixteenth-century Rome, and feeling alone with God. How
human ingenuity has changed the world since then! If one
can still gaze at the heavens in relative silence today, he can
return to his room, turn on his radio, and hear hundreds of
messages crowding those silent heavens, seeking listeners, and
seeking to change the world. Men have changed the universe
with the great means of communication, but the changes are
meaningful only to men, harmful or beneficial as they may be
to the rest of creation.

Beyond the efficacy of symbols in their immediate impact
on men and women, it is by symbols that men and women create
their human worlds, the settings of their most important daily
actions, the networks of relationships which to them are most
real. In his power to transcend the initial stages of his human
being, and to realize more and more of his potential, by imagination and understanding and deliberate project he creates worlds
in which he lives more fully. From the earliest pact between men,
through the development of communities and nations, to world
organizations and international law, by symbolizing men and
women affect the interpersonal world, constitute realities which
really count, which are the invisible realms grounded upon symbolic acts and meaningful only to symbolizing men and women.

But when all of the far-reaching efficacy of symbols would
have been traced, the most important influence of symbols is
that by which from the outset of human life men and women
have found their uniquely human interpersonal fulfillment in
mutual knowledge and love.

I have differentiated three sets of functions of symbols.

Here, as in our reflection on the differentiation of human operations in the first part of this book, it is important to note how the various functions are blended in concrete human experience, personal and interpersonal. Symbolizing and the response to symbols can be a wonderful, indescribable blend of insight, feeling, will, and motor activity. I take two illustrations from personal experience.

The first is an experience which I had daily for long periods during the years of my study of philosophy as a young Jesuit preparing for the priesthood. At eight o'clock each morning, as an anonymous "voice" on the Sacred Heart radio program, I spoke to and prayed with a radio audience which at one time was estimated to number 150,000. Distant and invisible though they were, I felt a sense of intimate contact with them. Praying with them, and speaking to them for seven or eight minutes, knowing many of them from their letters, I felt not only a heightening of my own religious experience, but also a union with them and an impact upon them: many had written beautiful letters telling of what the program meant in their lives.

In the other experience, during the same period, I was responding to another's symbolizing. I was listening to a great preacher in the Church of St. Francis Xavier, the "College Church", in St. Louis. My total reaction included insight into his message, thrill at the beauty of his eloquence, deep emotional religious experience, and a manifold reverberation: my own further insight into the truth, my feelings beyond what he was feeling and expressing, my own religious response, and a strong motor impulse: a feeling of eloquence, a tremendous desire to preach, and in preaching to reach and embrace and draw others to Christ.

Living speech, true creation of symbols, truly personal use of language and "constituted symbols", can be a great peak experience both for the one who fashions the symbol or uses it in a new, personal way, and for one who hears and responds. There is a twofold transformation, enrichment, actualization in the moment in which the symbolic action is accomplished: the speaker, writer, actor, singer, or player has a unique new experience; in the person who sees or hears, the word or song or gesture is transformed as it is received: it has a meaning and a full resonance which it never had before. Both symbolizer and receiver are carried beyond any previous experience which they have known, and each experience is personal, utterly unique, set against the ground of a total personal world. The blend of the two experiences is a sort of magic moment, possible only in the human interpersonal world.

One sad complementary note must be added. I have spoken of the ways in which symbols function in affecting the human world, personal and interpersonal. From the whole tenor of a discourse which began with the function of actualization, heightening the perfection, of the symbolizer, one might be led to think only in terms of the positive influence of symbolizers and their symbols. Unfortunately this is not the case, as anyone will quickly recognize. So we must add explicitly the acknowledgment of the contrary set of effects. Men and women can and do act also in such ways as to harm themselves and others. Their operations come to term in symbols which diminish their degree of being, reveal their misery, and harm others. Men and women can act in ways which improve the physical and the interpersonal worlds. They can act too in ways which pollute either or both of those worlds.

I like to quote a verse in Psalm 115 which suggests a closing reflection on this matter. In verses 4-7 the Psalmist has described idols, and then in verse 8 he declares: "Those who make them are like them; so are all who trust in them." The idol-maker, and all symbol-makers and symbol-users, express not just a concept, but much of their whole character, feeling, way of life. So too men and women who find in certain symbols the expression of a feeling akin to their own reveal much of what they are. Symbols are a measure of the culture, the whole way of life, the spirit of those who create them, and of those who resonate to them.

Chapter X

A DEFINITION

We have come to the climax of our long process of reflection: the attempt to formulate a definition of symbol, and in doing that to complete the task of conceptualization. As I understand understanding, it is an operation of human intellect which comes to term in a concept, more or less inadequate, never quite definitive. Some at times have objected to the whole notion of definition, rejecting out of hand any effort to define. The best answer to any such objector is to ask: "What do you mean by *definition*? Either you can tell me, and so define *definition*, going against your own repugnance to the process; or you cannot, and you really do not know what it is that you are rejecting.

The situation is somewhat like that of the dialogue with one who denies the existence of God. When he or she tells me what "god" is denied, usually I agree with the denial: in that sense I too would be an atheist. But that is not what I mean by *God*. With regard to definition, the difficulty lies with some objectionable notions of definition, which quite reasonably are rejected. Having rejected them, however, one could remain open to acknowledging the reasonableness of other notions of definition, and of some efforts to define.

As I have indicated in treating conception as a cognitional operation, I propose a very modest concept of conception. The effort to understand comes to a relative term in a concept; and when we can give a reasonably adequate answer to the question "What is it?" we have defined the thing which we were seeking to know. I have no illusions regarding the perfection of my concepts or the definitiveness of my definitions. In seeking to understand, we are involved in a process whose ideal term would be complete knowledge, complete understanding. With regard to persons and things which exist in this universe we never come to realize that ideal. But we do understand something: we grasp intelligible relationships, and we fix persons and things in a field of such relationships. We understand them better as we succeed in grasping and holding more significant relationships, and locating the person or thing in the field in which he, she, or it is somehow understood. With regard to our present task, the definition of *symbol*, I have formulated many definitions over the last nine years. None of the definitions has stood up against the pressure of further questions. As I begin this chapter, quite frankly I do not know exactly what my definition will be. Surely it will not be the same as that which I last proposed in print.[1] The development of my own thought in the course of writing this book has forced some further reflection, and will occasion a different formula. What at last I shall propose in this chapter will be the best that I can manage, given my present understanding of the matter, and my relative success in elaborating a conceptual symbol. This definition, like those which preceded it in my earlier efforts, will not be final, comprehensive, a complete grasp of the "essence" of symbol. But I should be ready to defend it on its merits. At every stage of a long process over the years, I have formulated a definition which represented some advance over its predecessors, some further understanding which came in answer to further questions.

I could approach my present task, and illustrate the definition which I must now formulate, by retracing my steps, recalling previous efforts to define, pointing out the insights which they held and the further questions which called for further answers and more adequate formulae. That, however, would be too long a process, and it would necessitate explaining the context of my thought at every stage. Life is too short for that. The definition which I shall present here has been prepared by the whole course of the reflection done in this book. The book to this point is the setting in which the definition should be intelligible.

Having taken *symbol* in a very broad sense, I must formulate a definition which fits all symbols, and nothing but symbols. Consistently with my notion of definition, I must attempt to define symbol by setting it in its intelligible field. The symbol itself is a meaningful sensuous term of a human operation. The significant relationships in its intelligible field regard two sets of terms: (1) the multiple acts which the symbol itself terminates, intentional in many modes; and the total sub-

---

[1] In my address, "Man the Symbolizer," *Proceedings of the Catholic Theological Society of America* (New York: 1977) 109-112.

jective and objective field of the symbolizer; (2) what they tend toward in their multiple functions in the interpersonal world.

In this chapter, therefore, I shall propose a definition and explain it, consider whether or not all human operation is symbolizing, and examine the relations of this notion of symbol to what might be proposed as a "natural" or "essential" symbol. Within the limits of this work, I deal with symbol as it figures in purely human operation. I am not concerned with what might be said about something analogous in animals, nor with what transcends merely human symbolizing. I shall say something about the latter in chapter XII, "Beyond Merely Human Symbolizing."

Three elements of our earlier reflection must be kept in mind as we attempt now to formulate a definition: (1) the nominal definition proposed as a criterion for the classification of symbols; (2) the full classification of symbols; and (3) the functions of symbols. With regard to the second and third, our definition must be applicable to all kinds of symbols, and must account for the full range of their functions. Since we have taken *symbol* in a very broad sense, we may expect our definition to be analogous: it will be applicable to various symbols in a variety of modes. Since the functions of symbols too are various, and are performed in various blends and to varying degrees in different symbols, here too there will be a broad analogy allowing for many modes.

The principal difficulty, as I see it, is the shift from the nominal definition to a sharper conceptualization which fixes the basic analogous concept. Our nominal definition was this: *a human work in which the sensuous is somehow meaningful.*[2] Another formulation suggested by the course of our reflection is this: *a meaningful sensuous term of a human operation.* Since there are many meanings of *meaning* and of *meaningful,*[3] and since *sensuous* includes both what is within the consciousness of the symbolizer and what is externally manifested or distinct from him,[4] the problem of determining the basic analogous concept is not easily solved.

My solution is the concept of *image,* whose advantages outweigh its disadvantages. I shall attempt to make clear the basic meaning, to forestall some possible misunderstandings, and to

---

[2] See ch. VIII, pp. 215, 218.
[3] See ch. VIII, pp. 220-222.
[4] See ch. VIII, pp. 219-220.

work out its analogous sense. The principal difficulty will come with regard to these symbols, which I classified as internal: emotions, acts of will, motor impulses, and body image.[5]

The definition which I propose, therefore, involves a shift from *meaningful sensuous term of a human operation* to *sensuous image*, and an elaboration of its intelligible relationships based on its three sets of functions.

A symbol is a sensuous image which terminates a human intentional operation, represents the imaged reality, and may affect the human world with a manifold efficacy.

A symbol is a *sensuous image* ... An image is a likeness, which has a similarity of form with that of which it is an image. The similarity may be sensibly perceptible: a similarity of configuration, static or dynamic, which may be recognized in both. Within perceptual experience, however, it is by an intellectual operation that one grasps at least vaguely the likeness of form. This vague grasp of likeness of form is one of many roles of intellect permeating perceptual experience. I do not perceive my perception. Nor is it by perception that I compare two perceptions, or compare a perception with some other image, to judge their likeness. All grasp of relationship is a function of intellect. Sensibly perceptible similarity characterizes symbols which are prevalently intuitive. In conceptual symbols, on the contrary, the tendency is toward an image in which one recognizes a likeness of intelligible structure.

No image in human experience is a perfect likeness of that which it images: it is not a full replica of the imaged reality. Rather, the imaged reality is filtered, so to speak, in the operations by which a human person encounters and responds to the world. First, the full reality of persons and things and their continual interplay is registered in the range of human sense, and only those concrete configurations which can be received by the individual senses and somehow held together in total perception result as the terms of a multiple sensuous filtering. To recognize the limitations of such sensuous imaging, it is enough to recall some of the characteristics of human perception. Our perception is always realized from a particular momentary personal perspective: it holds a limited partial configuration of reality from that position, and it differs not only from other persons' perceptual images at the same moment, but also from our own successive images as we move in our

---

[5] See ch. VIII, pp. 226-227.

world. At any moment, for any person, perceptual experience is roving, and it affords a continual succession of fleeting, shifting images. At any moment at which we deliberately halt the fleeting, roving perception, what we hold in an image at the focal point is a tiny portion of the whole object, held as figure against ground, with the whole object itself set in a field which for us is less and less sharply registered as it is more remote from the focal point. Other internal symbols, in so far as they pertain to the order of sense knowledge, have similar limitations: the sensuous factors in the images of memory, imagination, and dream are even more remote than perception from the full concrete reality which is imaged.

Analogously, our concepts, and the reasonings and judgments in which they figure, are imperfect likenesses of the reality which we have grasped. We do not grasp and conceptualize the full reality of any person or thing. In any concept we fix a relationship or set of relationships which we have determined. Far from being the whole reality of the thing known, such relationships are not even parts of it. Our concepts and their objects are elements of our knowledge of things, not elements or parts of which the things themselves are constituted in their basic being. All of our principles are principles of knowledge, not of the basic being of the things which we know. Our concepts are accurate, and our judgments are true, in so far as things *are* in such a way as to ground the relationships which we observe and affirm. The likeness of concept to thing is an analogous oneness of form or structure. The thing is in such a way as to ground the intelligible structure which we elaborate in knowledge. Analogously, our judgments have a similarity of structure: in their composition and affirmation of being they somehow reflect the structure of the actual being of the thing known and affirmed. Here again, more obviously than in the case of likeness of sensibly perceptible configurations, it is the role of intellect, permeating all conscious experience, to grasp the similarity of form of image and imaged reality.

Continuing to note variations of the modes in which internal symbols are images, we may take together a set of symbols which differ from sense images and from internal intellectual symbols, and which have a certain affinity in the manners in which they too are images. Emotions, acts of the will, motor impulses, and our body image, in so far as they may be individuated in our conscious experience, stand out as peaks, as

relatively intense or sharply defined phases of a continuous
condition or process.   An individual act of love or anger, a
throb of pain, a renewed intention of will, a suddenly sharp
sense of body image in a particular situation, is a sort of part
of the whole condition or process.   It is an image of the whole,
standing out as representative of the whole.   Its likeness of
form with the whole of which it is part is more evident: it is
of the same structure as the whole, and it stands out as a
particularly striking moment in a continuous experience.   Consistently with what we have worked out concerning our consciousness and knowledge of these acts and their terms,[6] we
must attribute to intellect the grasp of the sort of likeness of
form which is involved in these symbols.

It is only by the rich variety and continual play of internal
images in our conscious life that we are aware of our world
and of ourselves in that world, and of the mysterious interplay
of elements within our personal being.   Every image, according
to its kind, is set in its context: our multiple perceptual field,
our emotional tone, the decisions which have given shape and
direction to our life, our bodily tone and sense of our situation
in the world.   In the whole play of conscious experience we
have a running estimate of our situation in the world and of
our personal condition, and we recognize a succession of familiar
images and the familiar relationships which they suggest.   Immediately, images are like other familiar images, and in our
normal circumstances they suggest the full realities which they
somehow represent.   The importance of our normal circumstances, of the familiar setting of our lives, strikes us when we
find ourselves alone in the dark in a strange place, or, to a
lesser extent, alone in any strange situation.   Our internal symbols, images of all sorts in which our many kinds of intentional
acts terminate within us, are essential for our own personal
conscious life.

We face the world, and we enter into the play of the interpersonal world, by the external symbols which in their own
proper modes are images.   Most immediately by our posture
and gestures and facial expression, and all the ways in which
we shape our bodies and our bodily action, we complete our
many intentional operations in acts which are sensibly perceptible and meaningful to other persons.   On the analogy of

---

[6] See pp. 151-158 for the reflection on emotion, volition, and motor
action.

our internal symbols in emotion, will, motor impulse, and body image, our gestures and our total bodily expression are images, likenesses, as the part is somehow the image of the whole. These symbols are meaningful to other persons because in our culture they are recognized as the perceptible aspect of a total act and attitude: they show the shape of the symbolizer's experience, cognitive, emotive, volitional, and motor. They are not the full reality of the symbolizer's experience: they are imperfect likenesses which are enough to suggest relationships. They suggest the shape of the symbolizer's experience, and its meaning as it is set in his total world, subjective and objective. The more we know of that world from long, intimate interpersonal relationship with the symbolizer, the more meaningful his or her gesture or glance will be.

In all other external symbols, in which we shape an external sensuous medium and produce a symbol which for at least a fleeting moment has an existence apart from us, we can recognize more easily how all symbols, every one in its own way, are images. Intuitive symbols, by their sensibly perceptible form, resemble the reality which they image. Conceptual symbols, fixing relationships which we have understood, in their own way resemble the imaged reality by a likeness of intelligible structure which is not perceptible in itself.

Fixing the notion of image as the first element of a definition of symbol, we are holding that multiple isomorphism which we have found in the whole range of symbols. Any attempt to spell out the isomorphism which is involved traces only a short series, a segment of a continuous whole which runs through the interpersonal world. Merleau-Ponty, discussing properly human, symbolic behavior, gave one very limited illustration. Reflecting upon what is involved in an organist's reading of musical notation and playing the music, he observes that the organist does not inspect the organ, part by part. Rather he recognizes in the space in which his hands and feet will play sectors, guiding directions, curves of movement, corresponding not to definite ensembles of notes, but to expressive values. The adjustment of motor excitations to visual excitations occurs by their common participation in certain musical essences. The correspondence of musical sign, movement, and sound is conventional: several systems of musical writing are possible, and several keyboards. But these three wholes, between which there exist only fortuitous correspondences of term to term, considered as wholes communicate interiorly. The sound of the melody, the graphic configuration of the musical text, and the development of the movements participate in one and the same structure; they have in common the same core of meaning. The relation of expression to the expressed, which in the parts is a simple juxtaposition, is interior and necessary in the wholes. The expressive value of every one of the three wholes with regard to the other two is not the effect of their frequent association: it is the reason for it. The true sign represents the signified, not according to some empirical association, but in so far as its relation to other signs is the same as the relation of the object signified to other objects.[7]

The likeness of structure which Merleau-Ponty illustrated in this example is what I have been calling isomorphism; and its range extends far beyond the three wholes distinguished by Merleau-Ponty. There is an isomorphism, a likeness of world with feeling, the composer's perception of that feeling expressed in word and action, his own feeling, his sense of patterns of sound which express the shape of the feeling, the musical notes which he writes, the player's reading of the notes, his sense of the shape of the movements which correspond, his action in playing, the patterns of the music being played, the patterns of the perception in the listener, his or her feeling, and the shape of that feeling as it is set in the personal world of the hearer. There is no end to the process, and no end to the variations upon a likeness of structure. It is confined, however, to the human interpersonal world; for it is an aspect of properly human experience.

All symbols, intuitive and conceptual, are somehow *sensuous* images. Just as it is impossible that there be a human act without a physical, bodily element, so it is impossible that any human intentional act terminate in an image which is not somehow sensuous. Man *is* bodily in a human way, and all of his operations, all of his works, are proportioned to his manner of being. Every symbol is elaborated by the shaping of a sensuous medium, the figuring of some intelligible relationship; but the manner in which the sensuous element pertains to the symbol is different, varying as the symbol is more or less intuitive or conceptual. Although scientific and mathematical symbols reduce the intuitive factor to a minimum, no imageless concept is possible in either. Scientific and mathe-

---

[7] M. MERLEAU-PONTY, *The Structure of Behavior* (Boston: c. 1963) 121-122.

matical thought must be expressed in spoken language or in written language or special symbols; and even prior to its expression it must be elaborated in a process in which images of words or symbols play a part.

Having insisted first of all that a symbol is a sensuous image, one should forestall some possible misconceptions. There is no question of a sort of picture-thinking, or of a copy theory of knowledge. In its cognitive function, a symbol is not an image produced in some manner comparable with a photographic or stamping process. Nor is our concept of symbol limited to functioning in a theory of knowledge: the symbol is an image in all of its functions, cognitive, emotive, volitional, and motor.

Symbolizing, imaging, is rooted in a particular function of intellect. To avoid some misunderstandings of isomorphism, it is important to note both elements of that statement: imaging is rooted in intellect; it is rooted in a particular function of intellect. What do I mean by this?

All understanding is a grasp of intelligible relationship. Symbolizing, imaging, involves a grasp of one type of relationship: the likeness of form which I have called isomorphism. This calls for some explanation.

First, understanding is a grasp of intelligible relationships of all sorts. In a cognitive act directed to some person or thing and focussed on one aspect of the object to be understood, I grasp any one of several possible relationships which are intelligible: cause-effect, succession, simultaneity, position in space, likeness of any sort of quality, equality or difference of any sort of quantity. In any other type of intentional operation, which may be predominantly emotive or volitional or motor, I have a marginal awareness and knowledge of the relation of act to object, and of the shape of the experience; and I can reflect on the act and its object, and come to an explicit knowledge of any one of several possible relationships which may be involved in my conscious life.

Whatever may be the type of relationship which I have grasped directly in a cognitive act, or which I have grasped vaguely and marginally in an act which is predominantly emotive or volitional or motor, when I symbolize I produce an image which is *like* what I have grasped. Whatever may be the variety of known relationships in the original experience, one type of relationship alone is relevant in the production of the symbol: the image is *like* the known structure of the imaged reality: it has a likeness of form, an isomorphism, with what has been grasped in the imaged reality.

An example may help. As I approach a street corner, I notice an excited crowd; and as I draw nearer, I see that there has been an accident. At the center of the crowd, beside the damaged cars, two men are arguing heatedly. As one man pours out a flood of words and gesticulates furiously, I get his version of what happened. Words and vivid gestures present the image of the collision and of the action of the other driver who was at fault. What the speaker has grasped is the cause-effect relationship between the other driver's act and the consequences in the collision. What he feels is explosive anger. What he projects is an image of both what he thinks and what he feels. He expresses both the structure of the cause-effect relationship and the shape of his feeling. He speaks and gesticulates with a running sense of the suitableness of his words and gestures to complete his acts of thought and feeling in an apt symbol. From the loftiest works of art or philosophy to the most banal acts of daily experience, symbolizing involves a monitoring function of intellect: the symbol is the known image of what has been grasped. Immediately the only relationship which is relevant between symbol and symbolized is a certain likeness of form.

As an imperfect likeness of the imaged reality, the symbol represents what it symbolizes. Its representative function can be undertsood by considering two aspects of the imperfection of the image. First, because it is a limited, imperfect likeness, the image can be understood only as figure against ground, or as a sort of part related to a whole. Its meaning cannot be grasped without a grasp of its setting. Second, precisely because it is intelligible as figure against ground, or as part in relation to whole, the image can represent the whole: it has a suggestive power to make the whole imaged reality somehow present to the perceiver. It stands for the whole imaged reality: the whole human experience, implicit and explicit, of a reality which is itself part of the experienced world. As the imaged thing or person or event or action is inseparable from the world in which it is, so the image is integrated into a whole human experience of that reality set in its world. It is enough here to note this representative function of an image. We shall elaborate it more fully in our further reflection on the meaning of our definition.

Since imaging is rooted in a function of human intellect, images are meaningful only for human persons. Within personal conscious life, internal symbols have meaning only for the symbolizer. They are inaccessible to anyone else. They cannot be reduced to those aspects of human bodily being which can be isolated by the abstractive empirical methods of physics, chemistry, physiology, or any other "objective" empirical science. External symbols have meaning for other human persons, and only human persons. We mean something to one another. Our experience of one another is something specifically human, something absolutely original in human experience, not to be explained as somehow grounded upon an encounter with things. It is only in the human interpersonal world that symbols make sense, because only human persons symbolize, as they share their world with other human persons. By the laws of their nature they are together, they are for one another, as they can never be together with things, or be for them.

Because all symbols are imperfect images, they are forever inadequate to express their meaning, which is itself only partial. As we live humanly in space and time, and can never live fully at any moment, so all of our symbols are the relative terms of limited human acts. Every one of us lives at the center of a personal sphere, enclosed in the reality of a universe which cannot be completely probed. Every probing is linear, and at every point it opens upon other veins, other directions to be probed. No one can probe in all directions at once, or ever grasp the whole. Nor, consequently, can anyone respond with full personal potential to the fulness of the reality in which he is immersed. In all of its dimensions, cognitive, emotive, volitional and motor, human experience is utterly inadequate; and all symbolizing is like the cry of jubilation, an inarticulate cry of mingled joy and anguish. In all of its dimensions it is an expression of an inadequate human response, and of a sense of inadequacy and frustration as well as of ecstasy in the presence of the overwhelming. All symbolizing is a partial thrusting, a carving out of worlds, a clutching for and moving toward a whole which can never be fully embraced by knowledge or held in full union by love.

Thus far we have considered the symbol as a *sensuous image*. This is the more difficult part of our explanation of the proposed definition, involving a shift from the nominal definition to a sharper conceptualization of this element of our formula. What remains to be explained simply re-formulates what we have worked out in the preceding chapter concerning three sets of functions of symbols. The symbol as sensuous image can be understood in its field of intelligible relationships, grounded on those three sets of functions. We may set forth these relationships briefly, since they simply follow from the full development of the sets of functions.

A symbol is a sensuous image *which terminates a human intentional operation,...* This element of the definition marks one set of relationships of the sensuous image: to the operations which come to term in the image. We have considered this implicitly in elaborating the function of symbols in actualizing the symbolizer. All symbols of both general classes, internal and external, are human works, and a certain realization of the human potential of the symbolizer. Considered, then, in relation to the operations by which they are produced, which are completed only as they come to term in a sensuous image, and which mark a relative fulfillment of the symbolizer's potential, the symbol is said to terminate a human intentional operation. The modes of intentionality, and their blend, vary, as we have noted often.

...represents the imaged reality,... Treating the functions of symbols, I formulated the second set of functions as *revealing the symbolizer and his world.* Reflecting in this chapter on the imperfection of the likeness of the image, I spoke of its representative function. I attempt to hold all of this in the formula *represents the imaged reality.*

What is it that the symbol reveals or represents? Since it is an imperfect image which has its meaning only as it is set as figure against ground, or is regarded somehow as part related to whole, the image somehow reveals or represents its whole setting: the whole of the symbolizer's operation and its setting in his full personal world, subjective and objective. It reveals or represents a human person responding to his world: his multiple intentional operation and the world which is its object or term. The *reality* imaged and represented is the total reality, subjective and objective, imperfectly imaged in the symbol.

To whom does the symbol represent this reality? We must distinguish again according to the class of symbols which is involved. All internal symbols function within the conscious life of the symbolizer. They represent to the symbolizer his or her own subjective and objective world in so far as they figure in conscious life. External symbols represent the imaged reality to other human persons.

...and may affect the human world with a manifold efficacy. All that I have written in the preceding chapter concerning

the third set of functions is covered by this last element of our definition. Here I say "*may* affect" for we must recognize that a symbol cannot have any effects if it is not actually perceived by a person. Moreover, the variety and the degree of its various effects depend upon the variety of the persons who actually perceive a symbol. Resonance in the understanding and feeling and total response varies according to the capacities and dispositions of the persons upon whom the symbol plays in the interpersonal world.

I say "the *human* world," not the *interpersonal* world, for here again we must recognize the distinction between internal and external symbols. Both have multiple influence, efficacy; but internal symbols can affect immediately only the conscious person in whose life they figure, whereas external symbols may influence any other persons who perceive them. The human world of which I speak, then, is both intrapersonal and interpersonal.

Set as it is against the ground of the whole of our preceding reflection, the definition should be intelligible without further explanation. I raise two further questions here. One regards apparent implications of the definition: is all human operation symbolizing? The other takes up a matter which I have mentioned before, but whose consideration I reserved for treatment here: what is to be said of the notion of a *natural* or *essential* symbol?

Is All Human Operation Symbolizing?

I have insisted often upon two characteristics of human experience which are essential for the theory of symbolizing and symbol which I have proposed. The first is the *continuity* of human experience: a continuity within every mode of intentional operation, and among the many modes of intentionality which are blended in total human experience. The second is the *figure-ground structure* and the other metaphorical expressions of the basic analogy of human operation: the setting of a particular act or object in its *field*, within its *horizon*, in its *world*, in the personal *sphere*.

Since we have recognized a certain continuity of the conscious and the non-conscious in the person, with the many worlds in whose interplay he or she is involved; and since the figure-ground structure can be found through all kinds of human operation, down to the firing of a single nerve cell, one might suggest that my theory implies that all human operation is symbolizing.[8] It seems that the same structure pervades human experience, that every least operation comes to a relative term which stands out as figure against ground, and which should be recognized as a symbol, a meaningful sensuous image.

I should reply that all human operation is *symbolic*, but that only conscious, intentional operation is *symbolizing*. What do I mean?

Consistently with the intelligible structure which we have found in the whole range of human symbolizing, I should say that all symbolizing is an aspect of human conscious, intentional operation. Symbolizing begins with insight, and through the whole range of symbols the process is intelligible only as a function of intellect, which permeates all intentional operations, grasps at least vaguely the analogy or isomorphism which underlies all formation of symbols, and monitors the process of forming the meaningful sensuous image of what has been grasped in the pattern of conscious life.

Our basic strategy in the study of human being has been to seek to determine the structure of those operations in which a human person is most fully human, operating in manners in which a relative fulness of perfection is achieved. Our whole concern has been with the variety and blend of intentional operations and their works.

What, then, is to be said of the implications of this study concerning other operations which are human, in the broad sense in which I have taken *human*:[9] every operation from that of a single cell to the most complex conscious act, exhibiting a structure which is specifically human, and uniquely personal. As we have indicated in the reflection on the total setting of human operation, there is a continuity of the total conscious field and the nonconscious ground, which is part of the total personal setting of conscious operations.[10] Every conscious operation and its term stands out as figure against that total ground. Moreover, by observation of the perceptible movements of another person who is unconscious, and especially by scientific

---

[8] I myself held this for some time, though I made distinctions which have occasioned further reflections and my present thought on the matter. For an expression of an earlier phase of my thought see my address, cited above, p. 292.

[9] See above, pp. 106-107.

[10] See above, pp. 123-124.

observation of patterns of nonconscious operations, one can recognize that the principles of continuity of operations, and of the figure-ground structure, can be observed in such nonconscious operations. What has been observed first in the reflection upon structures of conscious experience is recognized in a broad analogy running through all human operations.

Does that mean that a human person is symbolizing even in his or her nonconscious operations? Certainly not. It takes a conscious human person to observe the structures of such operations whether by objective observation of the movements of the unconscious person, or by scientific observation of acts which occur far below the level of consciousness. It is only another symbolizer who can observe such structures, recognize likenesses, and project what he has grasped in a symbol of some sort. Relationships and intelligible structures are grasped by intellect, in conscious operations.

One cannot say, therefore, that all human operation is symbolizing. I have suggested, however, that one could say that it is symbolic. I mean only that we can recognize patterns of action which run through the whole of human being and operation, conscious and nonconscious. We can determine many rhythms in human nonconscious operation, and a given moment or segment of an operation can be regarded as figure against ground. It can be projected to represent the whole movement, to suggest the whole rhythmic action.

That is a broad sense of symbolic, which fits into the whole theory which I have proposed. Analogously, symbolizing itself can be said to be symbolic. The pattern of symbolizing, projected in a theory of symbolizing man, represents the mystery of human being, of human striving for transcendence, of the continual thrusting to achieve a greater measure of potential fulness of being, of the carving out of new human interpersonal worlds.

To reinforce this distinction of symbolizing and symbolic, and this limitation of symbolizing to conscious intentional operations, I should recall that relationships, patterns, and structures are human concepts, fixed in acts of understanding, and functioning in human knowledge. They are principles of knowledge, not of being. Things are not made of relationships, patterns, and structures. They *are* in such a way that they ground the relationships which human observers discern and fix in their mode of being and operating. With regard to human being, and human operation at levels below consciousness, the same

is true. Such basic being and operation is not constituted of
relationships, structures, likenesses, images, symbols; nor does
it project images and symbols by being and operating. Men
and women *are* in such a way that relationships and patterns
in their operation can be observed and fixed, either by reflection on structures of conscious operation or by objective empirical study. Both modes of study produce works, symbols,
elaborated by men and women in conscious, intentional acts.

What is to be said of "Natural" or "Essential" Symbols?

My second question, like the first, is a test of the adequacy
of the definition of symbol which I have proposed. In my conception, symbolizing and symbols figure only in human conscious, intentional operation. The first question regarded a possible challenge from someone who would extend symbolizing
to operations which are completely below the level of consciousness, whether waking or dream. The second question could
be put from another position, and could suggest a more radical
challenge of my definition. The question is this: is there a
natural or essential symbolizing, and a kind of natural or essential symbol, which are part of the mystery of the basic being
of things and persons in the universe, independently of the
process of symbolizing which I have developed in the course
of my long reflection?

The question could come from one or two quite different
conceptions. One would be the notion of natural sign as opposed to conventional sign, which in a variety of forms runs
from the dialogues of Plato through a long western school
tradition of philosophy, strongly influenced by Augustine. A natural sign has a natural resemblance to another thing or person
or event, and so when it is perceived it brings that other thing
to mind. The relation between sign and signified is not arbitrary
or conventional, but natural. Another conception is that of a
symbol which is the very appearance of the thing: it is a natural,
essential symbol of the thing, which comes to its fulness of
being by making itself manifest in an appearance. The appearance is somehow distinct from the thing appearing, yet
is the very appearance of the thing, a sort of natural or essential
emanation from the thing.

I deliberately abstain here from any attempt to work out
the details of any one elaboration of such a concept. Consider-

ing a pair of "pure positions", I propose a series of reflections upon them, and I leave to others the confrontation of my position and that of any other individual thinker.

What is really at stake in the discussion of both questions is this: how are symbols constituted, and in what "world", or what order of "reality" are they to be located. In my theory, symbolizing is a properly human operation, and symbols are human works, products of conscious, intentional operations. The questions regard two other hypothetical accounts of their origin, and their status in the universe of being. In considering these questions, and thus dealing with hypothetical alternatives to my theory, I distinguish between things and persons.

First, things in nature, in their basic being in the universe, are not symbolizing, nor are their "appearances" symbolic, independently of the process of human symbolizing which I have elaborated. Consider a number of "things" which might be regarded as naturally symbolic: waves of the surface of a large body of water, a mountain called "Camel's Back", the sun, water, light, darkness. Apart from the formidable difficulty of saying in what sense these are "things" in their basic being in the universe, independently of the manner in which they figure in human perception and other intentional operations, it is obvious that in their total natural reality they are not naturally symbolic, nor naturally sending out "appearances" which are natural, real, "inner" symbols by which they come to their fulness of being in their very manifestation of themselves.

How is it that waves can be symbolic of vital movement and rhythm? Not, surely, by the whole of their "basic, natural reality." Nor is any other symbolism of water a matter of its total natural being manifesting itself. Waves are symbolic as they are perceived from a certain point of view: not *any* point of view whatsoever. The symbol is not the whole reality of the moving body of water, but the image formed by a human person, who grasps a likeness of form, an isomorphism. For him, from his point of view, as it is set in the context of his experience of life and of the shape of human feeling, the dynamic shape of the waves is symbolic, meaningful.

When "light", or the sun, is a symbol of the sacred, of a life-giving power, it is not the "nature" of light, nor the physicist's light, nor the "sun in itself", nor the sun from any point of view in the universe, nor from no point of view whatsoever. The sun is symbolic as it is perceived and grasped in the pattern of its rising and setting through the changes of seasons, in its function of lighting and warming, giving color to nature, calling forth life, growth, fruitfulness, giving a feeling of cheer and well-being. The sun is symbolic in manifold ways as it figures in the whole range of human conscious life.

A body of water may be symbolic, not by virtue of its "whole reality manifesting itself", not as water "in itself", nor as the chemist's water, nor water in the midst of the Pacific ocean a hundred feet beneath the surface. A given body of water may be symbolic for me: Lake Michigan. It is not the whole lake in itself, nor any portion of it whatsoever, but the lake as I knew it from a short stretch of its west shore: always to the east, over the rise in Wisconsin Avenue, where one sensed the cool lake air, or at the end of a country road running east from highway 141, or below Lake Park, in its particular aspect in the morning sun, or with the afternoon's sun at one's back along the bluff, or along the beach, or in a plunge into its surging cold waves. That set of experiences of that limited portion of that particular body of water is symbolic for me, but the mystery of the symbolism is that which we have worked out in the whole course of our reflection. I have a set of images which are symbolic as they are set in the whole context of my early life in Milwaukee. They represent "home," and any one of them is enough to make me feel at home. Any other body of water, suggesting any of these images as it is perceived by me from a particular point of view, can suggest to me the familiar scenes of boyhood. So it was that when I saw the sea from Siracusa, there at last sea was where it ought to be, as Lake Michigan had been for me: lying to the east.[11]

So it is with the "natural symbolism" of things: things are symbolic only as they are held from a given point of view in a given setting in the whole of human conscious experience. "Home" is what is involved for every man or woman in terms of a house of a given shape, on a north-south or east-west street, on the east, west, north, or south side of the street, in a given neighborhood at a given period of its development, with trees at a certain stage of growth, and all the memories of climate, persons, activities, and all that went to make up a life.

Things in themselves, in their basic being in the universe of bodily being, are not symbols. Nor are their natural "appearances" symbols. They do not radiate images, likenesses,

---

[11] See above, p. 22.

manifestations of themselves, as they come to the fulness of their being in their very external appearance. Everything in the universe of bodily being is involved in the interaction of all, and there are countless radiations which can be detected and measured by natural scientists. Men are continually affected by such radiation. Yet the appearance which things have for men is not a function simply of such natural radiation, or "emanation." What is sensibly perceptible for men is confined to the range of human sensory receptivity. The sensuous, the sensibly perceptible, is a function not only of the play of natural forces in the universe, but also of the selectivity of human receptivity and response. The configurations which figure in images of perception, memory, and imagination are the products of specifically human operations. They are sensuous, specifically human, though they are grounded in the way in which things are and act upon men. They are meaningful, because human intellect finds in such configurations not copies of things, but intelligible patterns of things interacting and involved in a number of intelligible relationships. The perspectivism of human perception and of all human knowledge, the variety of figure-ground structures, and the meaning of symbols as set in their total human field, objective and subjective, would be unintelligible in any hypothesis of symbols as a sort of natural emanation of appearances from things. Moreover, the implicaitons of such a hypothesis would include a crude notion of knowledge, a sort of copy-theory, in which we would know things as a result of passive impression of images emanating from things. Symbols are intelligible only as human works, terms of human conscious, intentional operations. They *are*, and they function, in human worlds of meaning.

So much for "things". As for men, they do symbolize " naturally": but they do so in the marvelously complex process which we have been elaborating throughout this book. Symbolizing is specifically human, and in every case uniquely personal. Moreover it is intelligible only in the interpersonal world. We meet one another, and have meaning for one another, as fellow symbolizers. It is by the wondrously complex process of symbolizing that we understand one another, respond to one another, and share in the continuing creation of properly human worlds.

Symbols *are*, they are real, and they function with a manifold efficacy; but their whole being and functioning and efficacy are in the human worlds of meaning, taking *meaning* in the full sense. They are the terms of human intentional operations of all sorts, by which men and women come to their relative fulness of being together in their interpersonal world. This is the unique realm in which symbols have status in the universe of being: they are human works, and they have meaning and value only for human persons.

CHAPTER XI

MEANING, VITALITY, AND INTERPRETATION

I gather in this chapter a number of questions which arise from the very nature of human symbolizing, and from the paradox of human symbols: their infinite potential meaning, and their severe limitations, precarious life, and bewildering mystery.

MEANING

From the whole course of our reflection it is clear that symbols are not merely cognitive in function: they do not merely give form to, and communicate, a conception. Their meaning is, or can be, multiple: cognitive, emotive, volitional, and motor. The blend of these functions is richer in intuitive symbols than in those which are almost exclusively conceptual. Yet, in the flesh and blood reality of the living symbolizer, conceptual symbols often are set in a total experience which has its own keen passion, driving zeal, and thrill at the beauty of the truth discovered. At times, too, the wary reader or listener may discern between the professed objectivity and detachment of the scientist or scholar and the all too evident feelings of the crusader. Conceptual and intuitive symbols as such, however, present different problems regarding their meaning. The more purely conceptual a symbol is, the more its meaning is purely cognitive, and is to be determined by mastering the total context of the thought in which it is set. The more intuitive the symbol, the more its meaning is set in the mystery of total human experience, personal and interpersonal. I am concerned in this chapter mostly with the latter types of symbol.

First, the more intuitive the symbol, the greater is its potential variety of meaning. Or, even more radically: since the matter is not that of a symbol regarded in itself, but of a symbol as set against a total personal and interpersonal ground, one could say that symbols have an infinite potential variety of meaning.

Every symbol has some cognitive meaning, some conceptual factor, however vague it may be. Part of the potential variety of meanings of symbols is a consequence of the inherent limitation of all human conceptualization.[1] What we understand and fix in a concept is an intelligible relationship, or a cluster of relationships. Even at its best, in its sharpest fixing of the relationship which has been grasped, a human concept is severely limited. The sharper it is, the more its achievement is symbolic of its limits: it is always abstractive. It holds a relationship, part of what the symbolizer has understood: not part, much less the whole, of the reality of the thing itself. Things are not made up of intelligible relationships. Concepts fix things more or less sharply in our understanding, and enable us to maneuver in the process of reasoning. Where human knowledge concerns things existing in the universe of being, it holds its limited achievement against the ground of the rest of the thing to be understood in its total field of intelligible relationships. The potential variety of meaning of the symbol is based in part upon the variety of vague intimations of the mysterious remainder. Those intimations may vary from symbolizer to symbolizer.

The potential variety of meaning of intuitive symbols is beyond calculation. The cognitive factor is vague: it is not sharply fixed, but suggested by the isomorphism of a sensuous image. The feeling, will, and motor impulse is unique in every case, for it is set against the total personal ground of the symbolizer. Both the intelligible field and the emotive, volitional, and motor action are qualified by the vaguely sensed structure of the larger field, both human interpersonal and transcendent. What a man or woman means by a given symbol is affected by his or her whole personal history, setting in community, and perhaps personal relationship with God. Nor does the matter end there, with an indication of factors in the symbolizer which heighten the potential variety of meaning. Meaning is transformed as it is communicated, for it is perceived and understood and responded to by another person, for whom it is set in another personal and interpersonal world. What Shakespeare meant by a sonnet is one thing. What the sonnet means to you is another. For every person who perceives the symbol,

---

[1] See above, pp. 71-72.

it has a unique message and it evokes a unique total personal response.

Considering the range of possible variations of meaning, the degrees to which any two persons share their worlds, one can ask whether, apart from the most abstract mathematical or scientific thought, any symbol is truly univocal? If a symbol has its meaning only as it is set in its full context, I should say that the answer to the question is clearly negative.

Yet we do not end in absolute subjectivism and relativism, in the complete dispersion of meaning, beyond all hope of communication and real interpersonal influence. Any such conclusion would be absurd: all symbolizing would be vain, and this study of symbolizing and symbols an exercise in utter futility. What saves us from it?

First of all, let us get the problem in focus. I am not denying all univocal concepts. In mathematics and in the exact sciences, to the extent to which they achieve almost purely conceptual symbols, those symbols have a clear meaning which can be grasped by anyone who masters the body of knowledge in which they are set. I say "to the extent to which they achieve almost purely conceptual symbols", because some of what is proposed as scientific thought calls for rigorous critique and purification. To cite one area as an example, I should say that the broad field of psychologies of various kinds presents serious problems in this regard. It is enough to consult a standard dictionary of psychological terms, to come to some awareness of variations of meanings of technical and scientific terminology.[2] As examples of initial work of critique and purification in the same area, I should cite some of the work of Langer and Merleau-Ponty.[3] As for philosophical and theological thought, only those who have devoted long serious study to works in these fields can estimate the magnitude of the problems of meaning and interpretation.

Allowing for whatever measure of univocal meaning may be claimed for conceptual symbols, I am concerned here prin-

---

[2] See H. B. and A. C. ENGLISH, *A Comprehensive Dictionary of Psychological and Psychoanalytical Terms* (New York: 1958).

[3] See SUSANNE K. LANGER, "Idols of the Laboratory," in *Mind: An Essay on Human Feeling*, Vol. I (Baltimore and London: 1967), p. 33-53; and MAURICE MERLEAU-PONTY, *The Structure of Behavior* (Boston: 1963) and *Phenomenology of Perception* (London and New York: 1962). Further critique of the works of both authors could be fruitful. And if the present critic's work is published, it too will be liable to similar treatment.

cipally with predominantly intuitive symbols. By definition they
do not involve sharp conceptualization. Hence it should not
be shocking to affirm that they are not truly univocal: they
do not, and cannot, mean exactly the same for any two persons.
When God is called "Father," the full reverberation of that
symbol is unique in every man and woman. What is involved
in the variations of meaning is not simply the cultural setting
of a society which is more or less patriarchal or matriarchal,
or more or less affected by contemporary feminist thought, or
by any other strong cultural influence. Nor is it simply the
structure and quality of a given family that is decisive. Within
all such larger fields, for every man or woman the meaning of
the symbol "Father" is affected by a unique set of personal and
interpersonal relationships to his or her own father.

A second distinction is necessary in our effort to get the
problem of meaning in focus. The first distinction regarded
the difference between conceptual and intuitive symbols. The
second regards the different senses in which we speak of the
meaning of symbols with reference to their cognitive roles on
the one hand, and their emotive, volitional, and motor roles
on the other.

In so far as intuitive symbols somehow give form to an
understanding of a relationship or set of relationships, they
have a cognitive role: they express and can communicate some
conception, however vague. When a man is shouting angrily
about what another has done to him, and trying to break free
from those who are restraining him from attacking the other
to punish him, we can distinguish the roles of his symbols.
The cognitive element is the intelligible relationship which he
formulates and expresses, with greater or less adequacy: we
get the idea of what he is talking about, what the other man
has done to him. That is the conception which he communicates
by the cognitive dimension of his symbols. At the same time,
by his tone of voice, gesticulation, bodily agitation, and struggle
to free himself, he is acting in the other three modes of intentionality, emotive, volitional, and motor. He is not telling us
what anger is: he is acting angrily, and his symbols are the
sensuous, perceptible elements of his passion. Similarly, he is
trying to carry out his will, and to complete the motor action
which is being prevented. We read the relationships of his acts
to their objects: we sense vaguely the shape of his emotion,
his will, his motor action.

To return now to our problem and our question: how do

we avoid absolute subjectivism and relativism? How do we succeed in communicating and influencing one another? I should say that the answer can be given only against the background of our long reflection on the structure of human experience in the first part of this book, culminating in the reflections on the role of intellect, in chapter VI.

All human conscious experience is perspectival, but it is *conscious*, and consciousness is part of the mystery of intellect. Though we perceive from where we are, and understand within our unique personal spheres, all of our conscious life is permeated by the massive primordial existential affirmation and vague understanding which is most characteristic of our human way of being. We have a vague sense, a running estimate, of our situation in our world. Imperfect as our grasp of intelligible relationships may be, and inadequate as our symbolizing must always be, we do understand something, and we succeed in giving form to what we have understood. We respond to what we have known as good or bad for us, and we are aware of the shape of our response in emotion, will, and motor action. We sense from the outset of our conscious life that we share our world, and more and more we can come to understand one another, not only communicating our knowledge, but grasping more and more surely the shape of our full human experience. Most of all in full second-personal relationships we can come to understand one another in spite of all the shades of difference of meaning of all sorts.

We face one another, and together we face a world. Facing that world together, we are aware of the perspectivism of our perception and of our total grasp; yet we share the world and probe it together: our world is *ours*, not the private spectacle of the victim of hallucination, but a shared world, in which we can compare our slightly different readings. Because we take readings on the same world, aware of our differences, we can make allowances for the differences, and come to share clusters of meaning. So we can communicate our conceptions with relative adequacy, as we progress in understanding and in the art of communicating. So too we can come to read more adequately one another's feelings and will and motor impulses.

Recognizing the limits of human symbolizing, and the infinite potential variety of meanings of our symbols, we settle for being human. Recognizing the special tantalizing indeterminacy of our intuitive symbols, we do not hanker after some non-human pseudo-cartesian existence, with nothing but clear and distinct ideas. We might conjecture what such ideas might mean to some sort of hypothetical pure spirit, but our conjecture would not help us to understand and appreciate our human condition.

We settle for being human. Moreover, within the realm of human being, if we are wise, we do not hanker after a life in which we would have nothing but sharply conceptual symbols. They may be razor-sharp. They are also razor-thin. They fix a relationship or a set of relationships. They have a certain reality, for they are the terms of human acts of understanding, which are real. But their reality is that of a particular, abstractive human operation, which leaves untouched more than it grasps of the world in which we live. A man or woman who would live almost exclusively in a world of highly abstract technical or scientific symbols would be in danger of stunted growth as a human person.

For all their lack of sharp conceptualization, intuitive symbols have the great merit of giving intimations of the full concrete reality which is only vaguely surmised. They hold us to the contemplation of that full reality. They do not foster the smugness of one who is complacent in the firm grasp of a set of abstractions. They communicate some knowledge, some insight and grasp of relaionships. Beyond that they give us a sense of full human experience, more than merely cognitive.

Finally, and most important, symbols have meaning which can be shared because they are created in the matrix of community, and they are essential to the very development of persons in community. The problem is not that of isolated symbolizers, who develop their symbols in solitude, and then at some point in their lives seek to communicate. Sharing their world, living together in their own community and culture, men and women strive together to cope. With all of their personal differences, they have a massive primordial sense of their situation in their world, and the creation and use and adaptation of symbols occurs within that shared experience. Your symbol has meaning for me because it fits a world which I share with you, and because in a sense I was close to the insight which you had as an original experience, and which you succeeded in holding in your symbol.

It is the role of community which explains both the possibility of sharing the meaning of our symbols, and the varieties of meanings of symbols from one community and one culture to another. Community itself is not a single mold in which human life is cast in all places through all ages. Every community has its own character, its own tone. The vast variety of communities is itself a consequence of the very law of human being, for every community has something of its character from all of the persons who have shared their lives in it; and as the variety of persons is infinite, and every person is unique, so too the variety of communities is endless, and every one is unique, since every blend of unique persons it itself unique. To the extent to which we share our lives in community, we have a certain common ground against which all of our symbols stand.

Gradually, living in community, men and women come to a deeper sense of the full concrete richness of the life of the community, and enter more fully into their interpersonal world. Here too there are personal differences: varying degrees of understanding and response. To the extent to which we share understanding and respond as we should to what we know to be good or bad for us as a community, we are better men and women, living a richer, fuller human life.

As personal differences set problems regarding the sharing of meaning in a given community, so differences of communities and cultures set more formidable problems. I shall return to these problems later in this chapter, dealing with interpretation of symbols.

Reflecting here on the human mystery of meaning shared in community, I have said nothing of what is unique in Christian community. The reason is simply that I am concerned with a basic reflection on human being, a reflection which may be a preparation for probing the Christian mystery. I shall indicate in the closing chapter of this book how this reflection opens upon the further questions raised by the Christian mystery as a particular instance of a transcendent world which involves more than merely human symbolizing.

Vitality

Like the men and women who make them, symbols are fragile, and their life is precarious. The fulness or emptiness of symbols, their life and death, are functions of a law based upon their very nature. Symbols always involve the integration of a particular into the whole in which it has its full meaning. Live, meaningful symbols are held in a full human

setting. They stand out against the full ground of the symbolizer; they are set in his total world, subjective and objective.
They are held in an interpersonal world in which men and
women share somehow the life and insight and feeling and
will of the symbolizer. In such a world symbols can communicate their meaning, and they can have a manifold influence.
When, for one reason or another, symbols lose their full human
setting, they lose their meaning and efficacy.

Conceptual symbols are live and meaningful when they are
set in the context of a full living thought, or the work in which
it terminates. They may lie for centuries without being understood, but they are intelligible, and there is hope that some
day they will be meaningful again for a man or woman who
masters the thought in whose context alone they have their
meaning. Words detached from that context in which they
once functioned as symbols, rattling now in an incoherent discourse, or lying in print in a meaningless maze, are no longer
conceptual symbols. They are relics, or empty shells, put together without meaning in pseudo-scientific, or pseudo-philo-
sophical, or pseudo-technical discourse. This happens at times
in a school tradition, in which the original master's understanding has been lost, in which stylized solutions are given to problems which are no longer real, and a formalistic façade awaits
the bulldozer of the merciless wrecker. Conceptual symbols
live and continue to gather meaning in a living tradition of
vigorous intellectual life. They are not the greatest of human
achievements, but they are great, and the conditions for their
life and progress are indispensable: intelligence, intellectual
vigor, and intellectual honesty.

In the case of intuitive symbols also, their vitality, meaning, and efficacy depend on their being set in the full human
reality in which alone they can function. They vary in quality,
intensity, and efficacy as the life of the community varies. Since
symbolizing is properly human, it is part of the mystery of
man: a mystery of light and darkness, riches and poverty, love
and hate, virtue and vice, fulness and emptiness, peace and
violence. Symbolizing begins with insight, reaches its immediate term in the elaboration of a multiple response to the
world into which insight has been gained, and affects the interpersonal world with a manifold efficacy. Some reflection on
the varieties of insights and of total responses suggests a distinction between vitality and power of symbols. They may be
more or less adequate, more or less powerful; but being in-

volved in the mystery of light and darkness, of life and death, of love and hatred, those symbols which have a great destructive power could hardly be called *vital*. I should reserve *vitality* for a fulness of meaning which is life-giving and truly enriching.

I am not interested in trying to work out here all of the ways in which symbols can be powerful and effective for evil, set as they are in human worlds in which a number of erroneous value judgments propose pseudo-values as supremely worthwhile: the satisfaction of lust, avarice, craving for power, pride. Men can work powerfully to attain such pseudo-values, and ruin their lives and the lives of others. The study of their symbols and of their efficacy would be a study in pathology.

What I am concerned with is the vitality and efficacy of symbols which are the flowering of rich human living, and which function in the dialectic of human progress. The basic law here is dialectical: our symbols are as rich as our lives, and in the dialectic of growth and progress the enrichment of both goes apace. We grow in understanding by every act of understanding. We grow in love by loving. Acquiring truth, we heighten our level of understanding and our probabilities of deeper insight and understanding. Loving the good, we are better men and women, and capable of a greater love.

Since we share our world, and together gain insight into it, and together strive to reach a greater fulness of life, the quality, vitality, and efficacy of our symbols are at once a gauge of the richness of our life in community, and the most important factor in its continuing enrichment. A gesture as simple as the handshake can be such a gauge and heightening of life when it is the unmistakable mutual expression and experience of esteem, love, fellowship. It can on the contrary, be utterly meaningless, and worse than no gesture whatsoever.

All that contributes to mutual understanding and love in the family, the local community, and the larger societies in which we live, can contribute to the enrichment of our symbols; for it is within our lives shared in these communities that we come to our insights, elaborate our symbols, and affect one another continually. All that contributes to our sense of our identity in these communities, our sense of the historical process in which we have come to share our lives, and of solidarity in our present life and aspirations for the future, enriches the human setting in which alone our symbols have meaning.

What, then, is the fulness of life which can foster deeper

insight, more adequate symbols, and their continuing vitality
and efficacy? I should say that it includes at least these elements: openness to the mystery and wonder of nature about us,
of human life, of our communities, larger societies, and nation,
the treasures of art and the record of great human living, and
the transcendent world of God and human relation to God which
penetrates, transforms, and enriches all human living.

First, we can enrich our lives by opening ourselves to the
wonders of nature: to the trees and plants and animals, the
landscape, the rhythms of the seasons, the growth and flowering
of plants, the blossoming of trees and bearing of fruit, the first
signs of autumn and then the leaves swept by the winds, sky
and lake or sea, dawn and sunrise, sunset and dusk, the heavens
at night. Much of contemporary life in many nations makes
such openness difficult. Too many men and women and children
live in drab areas of vast cities where little natural life can be
experienced, where access to parks and countryside is almost
impossible. Too many spend their increased leisure hours with
their eyes fixed on television sets, in rooms which are like Plato's
cave. What is lacking in their lives is not images: they are
jaded by an endless succession of images on the screen. They
lack experience of real life which would make some of the
images more meaningful and rewarding.

More important, we can live our lives with a greater awareness of one another as persons, being loved and loving, sharing
our meals with a sense of fellowship, celebrating our birthdays
or name days with special considerateness, marking with special
solemnity, joy, and reverence the great turning points in the
lives of every member of the family, living through the mystery
of sickness and compassion, of failure and support, of death
coming to a loved one.

We can live with a wholesome awareness of, and pride in,
our community and nation. We can hold and treasure the
works of art and history.

In all of the many worlds in which we live, we can be
aware of the rhythms of life, of the importance of peak experiences in which the meaning and value of life stands out clear and
unmistakable. We can come to a deeper sense of the structure,
the shape, of human living, to an insight into the isomorphism,
the vague analogies which run through all of nature and human
life as they are grasped by men and women. It is this keener
sensibility and insight which makes possible the creation of

symbols, and our understanding of them, and use and continuing adaptation of them.

Once again, although I am not working as a theologian in this book, I mention the transcendent world: the reality of God, of his action in the world and in the lives of men and women, of a fulness of life to be found in interpersonal union of knowledge and love. I do so because I am trying to give an account of structures of human experience, and of the full range of human symbolizing. Part of the record of human experience through the ages is man's life in relation to God. Some of the richest and most profound symbolism holds the reality of the Christian Mystery. And concern for the vitality and continuing efficacy of that symbolism is supreme for many men and women. It is also for me. I mention it here briefly. I have written a book which sets forth the Christian Mystery, the meaning and value of life in the Christian view.[4] I hope to write another book dealing with the principal Christian symbols, the sacraments.

Obviously what I am proposing here as a way of promoting the vitality of our symbols is a way of life, a project for individual men and women, families, communities, societies. As a way of life which is possible only for persons in community, it calls for individual effort, for sharing of insights, for the search of better ways of living together, for a sort of initiation and education. It calls not for an absolute beginning, but for a continued and intensified effort: for in our time many men and women, young and old, sense a greater need of sharing their lives in community, and have found a richer, fuller, more whole and more wholesome life. Though the malady of our time may be the fragmentation of persons and communities and the secularisation of human life, the remedy is at work in the world, and many are finding a greater wholeness and richness of life. They witness to a possible achievement which can be extended. In their lives the great, life-giving and enriching symbols are full of meaning.

Vitality of symbols is a problem especially in the broad areas of the arts and of religion. In both there is the question of how to communicate the meaning of symbols which have been recognized as highly significant and precious, but whose meaning is not immediately accessible to many contemporary

---

[4] WILLIAM A. VAN ROO, S.J., *The Mystery* (Rome: 1971).

men and women and children. Older poetry and literary classics
and even classical music require a certain education, and societies
which esteem them willingly undertake the expense and effort
involved in making them meaningful, for they enrich the lives
of those who come to appreciate them.

The problems of vitality of traditional religious symbols
are even greater. First, they were elaborated long ago, with
insights into things and actions which were familiar in another
culture, but which do not figure prominently in present-day life.
Fire, water, oil, bread, and wine, and the actions by which they
were produced or used or consumed, were part of the daily
lives of those for whom some Christian symbols were elaborated.
They do not figure in our lives in the same way today. Raising
wheat, making flour, and baking bread are not generally parts
of the life of a family. Yet insights into such things and actions
can be fostered quite easily by ingenious teachers, and such
insights are necessary for the understanding of traditional symbolism of both the arts and religion.

The major problem with religious symbolism is another.
The meaning of Christian symbols was not evident even to the
ancient peoples to whom they were first proposed. Neither in
the first centuries of Christian life nor now can the meaning
of baptism or the Eucharist be grasped by simply looking and
listening. Baptism is not any plunging into water whatsoever,
nor any symbolic death whatsoever. Nor is the Eucharist just
any sort of sacrificial meal, much less any sort of common meal
as a symbol of fellowship. From the outset the symbolism of
the Christian sacraments had to be explained, for it is not just
a "natural" symbolism: it is not to be grasped by insight into
things and actions in nature and in ordinary human life. Such
insights function in Christian experience, for there are many
levels of meaning, some of them shared in wide-ranging religious
experience. But there is a proper, specifically Christian sense
of sacraments and sacrifice, and it can be grasped only when
these symbols are set in the context of the history of salvation
and the mystery of Christ. The symbolism of the Christian
sacraments is largely biblical, and it is communicable and effective, as many men and women can testify today.

As I see the matter, these are the principal problems regarding the vitality of religious symbols, with particular attention to Christian symbols. I am not impressed by another sort
of objection: that the bread of the Eucharist is not *real* bread,
or that in another culture it should be substituted by rice. If

rice should be substituted in the Orient, then in the United States it would be equally reasonable to demand hamburgers with a choice of coffee or coke. If bread can still be a symbol of a meal, even in western countries in which it is no longer the staff of life, then it need not be an ordinary loaf, much less whole wheat as opposed to white bread. There is question of a symbolic meal, of a part for the whole. The symbol is understood as it is set in its full context, and the context involved here is principally the Christian mystery.

Allowing, then, for the difficulties of some kinds of symbolism which are precious, but whose vitality is precarious, I should return to my principal thesis: there is a reciprocal influence of vital symbolism and fulness of life of the community in which the symbols are set. Fully meaningful symbols are the works of men and women who are fully alive, and they have meaning and value for others who are alive. In the case of religious symbolism, deepening insight into the Christian mystery and the response of deeper faith and more fervent love find expression in a richer act of worship. By that act the worshippers themselves are further enriched, and so are others who witness and participate in their worship, for they sense and respond to the depth of the religious life which animates this community at worship. The whole process occurs in community, and in every community the life of worship has its unique tone. Within the mystery of the Church there are many particular ways of life and holiness, and every one has some characteristic mode of self-expression. True community worship is truly interpersonal, for the "we" of shared prayer expresses the union of persons who sense real interpersonal I-Thou relations with their fellow worshippers in this community. We learn more deeply, and teach others, the meaning of our symbols by the living reality of our worship in community.

The full setting of these symbols is not just the community gathered visibly for worship, but the whole of their lives, enriched by the Christian mystery, especially the mystery of Christian love. That love is symbolic: by it men will recognize them as disciples of Jesus (Jo 13.35); because of the way in which they are one in their love, men will believe that the Father has sent Jesus (cf. Jo 17.20-21). When people see the way these men and women love, if they know of the promise, they will know that it has been fulfilled in the sending of Jesus and in the love of those who live in Him.

INTERPRETATION

I propose here a number of corollaries or further conclusions from the whole course of our reflection. They bear upon two areas of thought in which many specialists have labored well, and I propose them for the consideration of men and women who know far more than I about either or both fields: hermeneutics and inculturation. What I say here will be meaningful only in the setting of the whole of the thought which I have worked out in this book. For those who have not done such a reflection for themselves, it may be stimulating and profitable to consider these conclusions, to weigh the intelligibility, coherence, and consequences of this line of thought. Both hermeneutics and inculturation demand a rich interdisciplinary collaboration, and they cannot be developed adequately without reflection upon the basic structure of human experience and the human way of being.

(1) Symbols can be understood only to the extent to which the perceiver has shared experience of the imaged reality. Again I distinguish what this means with regard to conceptual and intuitive symbols. Conceptual symbols can be understood to the extent to which a reader or listener has mastered the world of thought in which they are set. With continuing effort and continuing insight such understanding progresses. The task is arduous, but it is rather easily defined. The matter is more complicated with regard to intuitive symbols, and most of what I have to say concerns them.

Intuitive symbols project a concrete image of the shape of a full experience. They are elaborated with a vague sense of isomorphism, likeness of the image to the shape of the experience. Their meaning can be divined only by those who have had some personal experience of a similar shape, and recognize in the image the reality which both the symbolizer and they themselves have experienced, every one in his or her own personal mode. Perception of the symbol effects a reverberation in the perceiver, and perhaps the vividness of the symbol occasions a deeper experience of similar form. Without such a vague sense of the shape of a shared experience, no one can get the meaning of the symbol. As the symbolizer cannot project the image of a feeling which he or she has not known, so the perceiver cannot get the sense of an image of a feeling or total experience which is totally unknown. Symbols are meaningful within a community or culture in which men and women live in the same world, are "on the verge" of insights within their massive primordial grasp of their world, and recognize the import of a symbol whose sense thus is within their grasp. Understanding intuitive symbols, then, involves a certain participation in the experience: both a vague prior experience and a renewed experience in the response to the symbol. Since intuitive symbols have a multiple meaning, understanding them involves experience of their full meaning: not merely cognitive, but also emotive, volitional, and motor.

One must note an important conclusion concerning the therapeutic value of intuitive symbols for contemporary men and women, fragmented by the modern scientific and technical mind. For one suffering from that malady, cut off from vital contact with full concrete reality of nature and of human life, intuitive symbols cannot be applied like patent medicines for a quick cure. The therapist must awaken in his patient a sense of personal and interpersonal relationship, an awareness of the insight into concrete reality. To the extent to which such rehabilitation progresses, signs of a normal human response to intuitive symbols, and of their efficacy in the life of the patient, may be recognized. Here, as in the advance into any world of meaning, progress is gradual.

In short, we understand any symbol, conceptual or intuitive, only to the extent to which we respond to it in an experience of the imaged reality. Conceptual symbols are empty or dead in a "tradition" which has lost its life, its sense of the problems which moved a great thinker, and of the sense of his thought. Intuitive symbols have their full meaning only for those who are truly alive, sharing in community, and sharing experience of the imaged reality.

(2) Intuitive symbols cannot be translated or transposed in any way into another image with the same meaning. Least of all can they be reduced to conceptual symbols in a discursive account. The attempt to do so is futile: the full meaning of an intuitive symbol cannot be held in conceptual symbols. Yet the attempt is often made, with the illusion that one is "interpreting" the symbol. Instead, one is emptying it, or flattening it out.

Consequently, I suggest some reflection upon, and critical evaluation of, accounts of intuitive symbols as they are often given in studies of comparative religion. Individual symbols are described in a discursive account. Generalized classifications flatten out all individual differences, and leave the reader or listener with the illusion of understanding symbols which could never be understood except by one who was immersed in the culture and the particular community in which they live or once lived, and who came to sense their full meaning as he or she truly participated in the symbolic action.

(3) Since interpretation of symbols is impossible without participation of the reality which they image, there can be no hermeneutic which would provide a system for deciphering symbols. Even if the meaning of intuitive symbols were merely cognitive, it would not be amenable to deciphering, for it is not sharply conceptualized, and it has no exact conceptual equivalent. Much less can its emotive, volitional, and motor charge be rendered in a process of such deciphering. A theory of symbol, or of man the symbolizer, is not a manual for the quick and sure interpretation of symbols. Such a theory, like any hermeneutic which would be located within a larger theory of man, can only suggest how one must approach interpretation, and counsel the sort of initiation into a community experience in which alone such symbols can be understood.

(4) Inculturation, a relatively new concept, is as difficult as it is necessary, and the success of the process which it names could never depend on purely human factors. As it has been defined recently, *inculturation* is a properly theological term, used uniquely in regard to a process concerning the Christian Church. The definition given is this: "the inculturation of the Church is the integration of the Christian experience of a local Church into the culture of its people, in such a way that this experience not only expresses itself in elements of this culture, but becomes a force that animates, orients and innovates this culture so as to create a new unity and communion, not only within the culture in question but also as an enrichment of the Church universal."[5]

Though the process of inculturation thus defined involves the use and adaptation of symbols, it transcends merely human symbolizing, and I shall indicate in the next chapter how our reflection is related to it. For the moment it is enough to indicate some of the difficulties involved, and in what sense it involves more than merely human factors.

The notion of inculturation supposes that there is a properly

---

[5] ARY A. ROEST CROLLIUS, S.J., "What is so New about Inculturation?", *Gregorianum* 59 (1978) p. 735.

Christian experience, identifiable as such, and verifiable as authentically Christian in any of the symbols in which it is projected in any culture. Though the Christian message may be said to be somehow above all particular cultures, it is not to be found except as it is formulated in the symbols of particular cultures. It involves both conceptual and intuitive symbols, both of which types must be understood as they are set in the concrete Christian experience in which they are found through history and in the Church today. Moreover, Christian life and the Christian message include the conviction that there is a normative experience, and that there are normative teachings concerning the structure of that experience. There is, further, an authority vested in qualified members of the Church for the interpretation of that teaching and the judgment of the authenticity of any symbolic projection of the experience as properly Christian. The whole of authentic Christian experience and of its authoritative interpretation and verification is grounded upon the will of Christ as founder of the Church and the abiding presence and operation of the Holy Spirit within it.

Inculturation, obviously, involves serious difficulties. It cannot proceed without preserving biblical symbolism, for the Bible as interpreted in the full teaching authority of the Church is indispensable. It cannot dispense with a considerable body of symbolism, both conceptual and intuitive, which are essential to the faith and the life of the Church: professions of faith, and sacraments and sacrifice. A considerable amount of alien symbolism must be integrated into any culture, and the symbolic elements taken from that culture must be transformed in such a way that the process results in an enrichment of the life of the whole Church, not its deformation or extinction in this local church.

All of this involves much more than merely human symbolizing. Christ's intuition, the normative experience of the Apostles, the biblical formulation of the Christian message and of its Old Testament preparations, definitive formulations of faith, the abiding presence and guidance of the Holy Spirit, and the unfailing judgment of competent authority regarding authentic Christian experience are the principal factors which transcend merely human operation.

(5) A balanced judgment of conceptual symbols recognizes both the limitations of their functions and the importance of their role in a developed culture. They do not exhaust the meaning of intuitive symbols. Nor do they locate that meaning

in a fully conceptualized intelligible world. Rather they discover intelligible relationships within the concrete reality which is imaged, and they hold these conceptualized relationships within an intelligible structure. They are abstractive: within the total concrete reality they fix those relationships which have been grasped in further reflection, and which have been fixed in conceptual symbols.

Conceptual symbols are an achievement of a different order, and they play a role which complements that of intuitve symbols. They hold what has been understood and affirmed truly of the reality first vaguely grasped. Abstractive and partial though they be, they are solid achievements, and firm points of reference for the critique of other efforts to image the reality which has been experienced in the community. Any new intuitive symbol, or any new affirmation, must fit into or harmonize with what is affirmed as truly proper to the reality experienced by the community. Thus conceptual symbols and propositional truth play an important role in the normative judgment. In civil society they enter into the interpretation of law by the courts which are competent. In the Church they function in the judgment of what is consistent with the "analogy of faith": the full intelligible structure of what must be affirmed by faith concerning the Christian message and the structure of authentic Christian experience. That judgment can be rendered surely only by those qualified members who in the mystery of the structure and life of the Church are competent.

CHAPTER XII

BEYOND MERELY HUMAN SYMBOLIZING

As I stated in the introduction to this book, my scope and method in this whole reflection are philosophical, not theological. I do not intend here suddenly to extend the scope and change the method. However, since I have recognized that human experience, as witnessed by many men and women, includes an experience of the transcendent, and in some cases an interpersonal relationship with God, I have been aware that the mystery of human transcendence includes an openness to fulfillment in such experience. In a purely philosophical reflection on structures of human experience, human operation, and the proper mode of human being, one cannot affirm more than such a method justifies. Yet one's account of human being and operation, of human transcendence, must be open to the possibility that the witness of some men and women must be taken seriously. If there is an interpersonal relationship with God, and indeed with the revealing and saving God of first Israelite and then Christian tradition, the effort to understand such testimony and the reality to which it bears witness will be theological, not philosophical. Theology as an intellectual activity is the effort to understand within a life of faith. It begins with truths revealed by God and affirmed by faith, and it involves a continuing reflection upon structures of experience within a life of faith and love and hope grounded in the gift of the revealing and saving God. It achieves some fruitful understanding of the truths affirmed by faith, and of living experience of the reality of the Christian mystery. One comes to such understanding not only by discovering and formulating intelligible relationships among the revealed truths which are believed, but also by working out analogies with what can be known about man and the world and God by the work of pure human reason.

Without attempting such a theological work here, I wish to close this book by indicating how it opens upon properly theological problems, and how the theological work which I hope to continue elsewhere is in continuity with what we have done here.

Human symbolizing is analogous, and the many symbols which we have considered can be treated in a single reflection because there are basic analogies running through the whole of man's symbolizing and his symbols. When I say that, I do not forget what I have said about analogy. Properly speaking, analogy pertains to the realm of metaphysics, basic philosophy, concerned with being, one, true, and good. There is analogy in human symbolizing and human symbols because they develop within the matrix of the basic twofold intentionality which characterizes human being: cognitive and emotive-volitional-motor. They are aspects of the mystery of human being, and of human transcendence. The human person strives to realize his or her potential, to find a greater degree of fulfillment, a higher degree of being. Operations within the structure of cognitive and emotive-volitional-motor intentionality regard fulfillment in understanding and truth, and in union with what is known to be good. All symbolizing, in all of its modes and blends, is part of human striving for such fulfillment, such transcendence. It is analogous, as being, one, true and good are analogous. Symbolizing man is enriched in his or her own personal being, and realizes a greater unity or integration of personal being, as he or she comes to a richer share in truth and in the good, and affects others proportionately in the interpersonal world.

Human symbolizing and human symbols, then, are analogous. How does the analogy of properly human symbolizing afford resources for the further work of the theologian? In what way does the theologian find a deeper understanding of Christian truth and Christian experience by reflection upon the analogy of human symbolizing, and by extension of the analogy into the realm of properly theological truth?

I should indicate two lines of consideration, or perhaps more properly two phases of a single complex analogous conception. They may be given in answer to two questions. First, could one say that God somehow symbolizes, and if so how is his symbolizing analogous with that of man? Second, does man participate in a transcendent symbolizing which is an aspect of the divine? If so, what does it involve?

In sketching an answer to these questions I am like a man seated in a jetliner with a friend, trying to point out features of his native region as they move swiftly at a great height. I can do no more than trace an outline, mention some prominent features. But it is a land through which I have walked, in which I have lived, and which I have contemplated lovingly.

First, then, one can say that God symbolizes, and that the range of his symbols is beyond our grasp. Yet, in saying that, and in attempting to sketch the range and variety of divine symbols, one must reckon with the tormenting problem of all human thought and speech about God. Every human concept and word about God must be purified in a process which leaves it forever inadequate, but less grossly so than ordinary human speech. The human words which Christians regard as divinely inspired in the Bible are figurative and non-technical. They afford some understanding of the mysteries which can be grasped only in part, but they must be held together in the whole complex of what we affirm and deny about God. The carefully wrought concepts of theology are the result of a process in which such affirmation and denial serve to reduce even more the inadequacy and inaccuracy of our thoughts and words. When we speak of life and being, of knowledge and truth, of love and good, of operations of intellect and will, of procession and term, of interpersonal relations, we must do so with a constant sense of analogy. This is true of any human thought and speech about God. It is all the more necessary when one passes from the realm of a so-called natural knowledge of God to the effort to understand what God has revealed about himself: truths which no effort of mere human reason could discover, and which even when revealed surpass all human grasp.

All that I say in the following paragraphs, therefore, must be taken with the realization that I am not doing a theologian's work here, but sketching in a most inadequate way some of the elements of revealed truth which he affirms and whose intelligibility he seeks to probe.

The supreme truth affirmed by Christian faith, and the most profound mystery probed by theologians is that of the Holy Trinity, of Father, Son, and Holy Spirit who are one God. Though the approach to that mystery is through Jesus Christ, the Incarnate Word, and though some theologians insist on the dominantly Christological character of all Christian theology, I should agree with others who hold that all Christian theology is grounded ultimately in the mystery of the Holy Trinity.

Though theologians normally have not spoken of symbolizing in their elaboration of trinitarian theology, there is a sense in which one can find an analogy of symbolizing and symbol in the mystery of the "inner life" of the Trinity. The Son is the image of God (cf. Col 1. 13-15). Though exegetes differ, taking the statement as referring to the Son as God or as the God-man Jesus Christ, one of the most familiar elements of patristic trinitarian thought is that it is the Son as God who is the perfect image of God, the Father. Less common, but not to be disregarded, is the affirmation of some Greek Fathers that the Holy Spirit is the perfect natural image or likeness of the Son, his seal, his exact representation. God's knowledge and wisdom and love are revealed, and theologians have sought to understand the distinctions of Father, Son, and Holy Spirit, as well as their perfect likeness and oneness of "nature", by "processions" in "operations" of "intellect" and "will", and by the resulting relations.

On the analogy of man's highest operations of intellect and will, then, and of the symbolizing and symbols which are the terms of human intentional operations, it is reasonable to speak of a sort of eminent symbolizing in the very procession in the Holy Trinity, and of Son and Holy Spirit as being symbols. There is a purification of the whole notion of symbolizing and of symbol in such a process of analogous conception. The Son and the Holy Spirit are the terms of divine operations, not human. They are perfect natural symbols, not the ever-inadequate images in which all human symbolizing terminates. They "function" in the eminent interpersonal life of the Holy Trinity.

"Outside" the mysterious "inner life" of the Trinity, in the manifold divine operation, in the procession of all things from God and their return, there is a manifold symbolizing, and a wide range of symbols. All of them are imperfect, yet all show forth something of perfection of the God from whom they proceed, and whose operations they terminate. All of them can function in the human interpersonal world, for man alone can read their meaning and respond to the reality of his interpersonal world, both human and divine.

Though only man is said in the Bible to have been created in the image and likeness of God (Gen. 1. 26), God is the Lord of the universe as of all human history, and in the wonders of nature the glory of God is shown forth. The whole physical universe, then, is the work of a symbolizing God, whose operations terminate in sensibly perceptible works, all of which are somehow imperfect images, or "traces" of the total reality of their source. Man, contemplating the universe in which he is, need not go beyond it to discover the transcendent. If he reads it right and ponders its meaning, he finds the transcendent at the very core of persons and things. The universe is intelligible only as it is grounded in the source of all being and the goal of all striving.

Within human experience of intimations of the divine, and variations upon human conceptions of the sacred, of a god or gods who are the source of all, and whose symbols fill the world, there is witness to another experience, richer and more profound. Israel of the Old Testament witnesses to the encounter with a revealing God, who promises a fulfillment exceeding mere human conception and desire. He is the Lord of the universe, and he is at work in human history. He is at work in the choice of a people and the gradual fulfillment of his promises in them and through them. In the light of Old Testament revelation and Israelite faith, human history and the course of the universe is read as the history of salvation. The symbolizing God is showing forth the mystery of his saving action, in the accomplishment of the design which he reveals. As Christian theologians read that mystery, God's saving action is "sacramental": somehow sensibly perceptible in the signs which he gives, and effective of his purpose in the human world.[1]

Christian tradition bears witness to faith in a further revelation and a deeper and richer fulfillment than Israel could have expected. "In many and various ways God spoke of old to our fathers by the prophets; but in these last days he has spoken to us by a Son, whom he appointed the heir of all things, through whom also he created the world. He reflects the glory of God and bears the very stamp of his nature, upholding the universe by his word of power ..." (Heb 1.1-3). According to Christian faith, Jesus Christ is the eternal Son of God, become man, truly God and truly man. As the divine Son, he is the perfect natural image of the Father. As man, in the whole of his human being and operation, in all that he did and suffered, in the whole mystery culminating in his passion and death, resurrection and glorification, he is the revelation of the Father. His human love in his offering of himself in sacrifice for sinful men is the supreme revelation of the love of God: "While we were yet

---

[1] For a treatment of some of the principal themes of Old Testament salvation history, see WILLIAM A. VAN ROO, S.J., *The Mystery* (Rome: 1971) 1-105; and for the notion of the sacramentality of God's saving action, pp. 99-113; 178-186; 347-353.

helpless, at the right time Christ died for the ungodly. Why, one will hardly die for a righteous man—though perhaps for a good man one will dare even to die. But God shows his love for us in that while we were yet sinners Christ died for us ...." (Rom 5.6-8). In the whole mystery of his human being and operation, from the Incarnation to the full Paschal mystery, Jesus is the supreme revelation, the symbol par excellence, the prime sacrament, of God's love and saving action and of the fulness of life in union with Father, Son, and Holy Spirit. As the greatest of all symbols, the prime sacrament, he shows forth the full reality of the Christian mystery, and in and through him the Father accomplishes his work.[2]

In the continuing realization of the Christian mystery, God's unique symbolizing continues. Baptism is a symbol. Who is symbolizing as it is performed? If we look and listen, we should be apt to say that the man or woman performing the act and pronouncing the words is the agent, the one symbolizing. That is not the way the New Testament writers speak of baptism. If we look in their works for the answer to the question Who is baptizing? we find that they say little of the visible human agent, or even of the Church as somehow active. Their principal answer is that the Father, and Jesus, and the Holy Spirit are acting.[3]

Not only in the beginnings of Christian life, nor merely in the peak experiences, especially the celebration of the Eucharist, but in the whole of Christian life, God is symbolizing. The Christian is to be a symbol, a sacrament, showing forth the reality of the Christian mystery, and affecting the human world by mediating God's saving action to others. Here, however, we will do better to go back to the second question which I proposed at the beginning of this chapter: Does man participate in a transcendent symbolizing which is an aspect of the divine? If so, what does it involve?

God's operation in the whole of creation is symbolizing. All of his works show forth something of the full reality of

---

[2] For Christ as the Mystery, and the convergence and transcendence of themes of salvation in him, see *ibid.*, pp. 107-186; for Christ as sacrament of eternal life, pp. 178-186. For the role of the resurrection of Christ in particular, see WILLIAM A. VAN ROO, S.J., "The Resurrection of Christ: Instrumental Cause of Grace," *Gregorianum* 39 (1958) 271-284.

[3] For a commentary on New Testament texts regarding baptism, in which one can gather elements of the answer to the question about who is acting, see VAN ROO, *The Mystery*, 195, 199-202, 203-242.

the divine symbolizer: his wisdom and goodness and power. The mystery of the universe is one of the continuing sustaining operation of God, operating in the operations of all things, as he holds them in being. The world and all that is in it is symbolic of its transcendent ground. Of all that can be perceived in the universe, man is the greatest of the symbols, the greatest of God's works, made in God's own image and likeness. In his very human operations, then, man participates in a transcendent symbolizing.

Old Testament salvation history revealed a deeper sense in which men and women participate in divine symbolizing. In that process, in the revelation and realization of a higher destiny and a richer fulfillment, God's saving action comes to its term only in the full human response: in faith and love and the union which is the goal of the whole process.[4] God is at work in the lives of his people: they have known his work in the past, and they pray for its continuation: "... thou hast wrought for us all our works ..." (Is 26.12); "Let thy work be manifest to thy servants, and thy glorious power to their children. Let the favor of the Lord our God be upon us, and establish thou the work of our hands upon us, yea, the work of our hands establish thou it" (Ps 90.16-17). Yet they are to be a sign to the nations: he will show forth his glory in them, and they will draw other nations to worship him.[5]

In Jesus Christ human participation in divine symbolizing reaches its peak. Sent by the Father, he came to reveal the Father and his love. In his human nature and all that he did and suffered as man, and in his resurrection and glorification, he is the Prime Sacrament, the most perfect manifestation of God's saving action coming to term in the full human response, the symbol which shows forth that saving action directed to all men, and which is the instrument by which all grace is given to others.

Christ as man continues to function as the unique instrument of God's saving and sanctifying action for all time. It is he who acts, as God and as man, in and through his Church. The Church is his Body and his Spouse, and men and women come to fulness of life by faith in him and by baptism uniting

---

[4] See the chapter "Personal Response," *ibid.*, 59-69. The theme which runs through my book *The Mystery* is that God's saving action comes to term in the full human response: in Old Testament experience, in Christ, and in the Christian.

[5] On Israel as a mediator of salvation, see *ibid.*, 44-49.

them with him. In the Church's worship there is a blend of elements: Christ honoring his Father through the continuing worship which he offers in and through his Church; and the Church honoring her Spouse as she sings his praise.

In the public worship of the Church, the whole Church is active, sharing in the divine symbolizing. Her action is concentrated in the designated acts of her qualified members who act ministerially. In the action of the minister of sacrament and sacrifice there should be a rich blend of elements. That action is no mere official, "instrumental" action. Part of the mystery is this: one Christian comes to fulness of life in a worship which is itself sacramental. The minister does this in a unique way. His act should be a full act of personal worship, in the fulfillment of his role in the Church. Acting ministerially, he comes to his own fulfillment in an act which mediates grace and fulness of life to others. He has a unique share in the continuing divine symbolizing.

Nor does the sharing end with the minister. Every Christian, in every act borne by the grace of Christ, comes to a greater degree of personal fulfillment in an act which is itself also sacramental. All Christians share in the divine symbolizing. Their acts are symbolic: terminating grace-borne human intentional operations, representing the full reality of the Christian mystery realized here and now in this man or woman, affecting the interpersonal world with an efficacy which is more than that of merely human symbolizing.

Looking back now at this brief reflection on the many ways in which God symbolizes and men and women share in his symbolizing, one all-important distinction stands out, between the unique divine symbolizing in the Holy Trinity, and all symbolizing in which creatures have a part. Only the eternal Son and the Holy Spirit are perfect images, perfect symbols, transcending completely the limits which we have recognized throughout our reflection upon human symbolizing and symbols. The Son and the Spirit terminate divine processions, not human operations; and obviously they transcend all sensuous likeness. All symbolizing and symbols in which creatures share are imperfect.

If we consider God's symbolizing in and through his creatures, then we can say that God himself cannot symbolize perfectly in any of them: it is absolutely impossible for any creature to be the perfect image of God. Even Jesus as man, God's supreme work, is only the most perfect human revelation of divine love. One aspect of the inadequacy of all creaturely symbolizing is this: not even God himself can show forth the full divine reality in such an image.

Another aspect is this: all human symboizing, even when men and women share in the divine, transcendent symbolizing in the Christian mystery, is forever inadequate. Even this symbolizing is itself symbolic of the human condition. The human person strives for fulfillment, and in all symbolizing which tends toward the ideal of a greater truth and goodness there is some realization of the human potential. Yet, in all of the worlds in which we live and seek a greater fulness of life, all of our acts are painfully limited. We cannot probe at once in all directions, understand at once all mystery, embrace and hold in union all good. All symbolizing is like the cry of jubilation: a thrust, a half-joyful half-frustrating clutching, a forever indaquate human response to a reality which is overwhelming.

So, with Paul and all Christian mystics, the Christian must sense that the Christian mystery draws us to a quest which never ends in this life, and which can never bring us to embrace the fulness of God with a knowledge and love which are perfect only in the Son and the Spirit. Paul's prayer is for the Ephesians and for us: "... that Christ may dwell in your hearts through faith; that you, being rooted and grounded in love, may have power to comprehend with all the saints what is the breadth and length and height and depth, and to know the love of Christ which surpasses knowledge, that you may be filled with all the fulness of God" (Eph 3.17-19).

PROSPECT

If I have understood anything of symbolizing and of symbols and of symbolizing man, much remains to be done. For this book itself is a symbol, the term of a sustained effort to understand. Like all symbols, it is inadequate. Many more questions arise, much more probing and reflection remain to be done, and the task will never end.

I should indicate two areas in which more is to be done. One is the properly philosophical reflection on human being. I regard this book as a contribution to a continuing effort to understand. I have not engaged in a dialectic of opinions. I have not indicated how my thought, as it has developed in this book, differs from the thought of others, and indeed from my own previous thought. I have begun with description of some examples of human experience, and I have reflected upon it and found what seem to me to be intelligible structures. If others can reflect on their own experience and find that this account is intelligible to them, their reflection and their understanding is one bit of evidence which contributes to the verification of what I have elaborated. The only kind of verification which is relevant and possible for such thought comes in such reflection and understanding. If this account of man the symbolizer accounts for the significant data, and if it affords an intelligible structure which can hold the answers to further questions, it stands. The further questions of a philosophical nature are many. Those which I have in mind concern principally what could be called the human a priori. If man *is* and operates in the manner which I have worked out here, then questions concerning human nature and powers can be put and answered without some of the misunderstandings which mar much past controversy. I do not foresee my own effort to continue along this line. But I did not foresee most of what I have done in this book, and it is quite possible that I be drawn into what may be a fruitful further development.

The other area is theological, and I hope to continue to work out the implications of this book in the two areas in which I have worked most for several years. One is sacramental theology, and I hope to return to the effort to do the book *The Christian Sacrament*. I began it in 1967, and I interrupted it twice, to do two other books, *The Mystery* and this. The other area is the basic theological reflection on God. At present I plan to continue a work which may be entitled *God and Theology*. In its present tentative form it deals with biblical conceptions of God and then goes on to consider how and why theologians go beyond such biblical conceptions. The book probably will be both a basic theological treatment of God and a running commentary on the nature and method of theology, as illustrated in the actual development of the thought. What I have done in this book has considerable significance for both the theological treatment of God and the reflections on the nature and method of theology.

These, then, are the prospects.

One last bit about man the symbolizer. It is something which struck me a few years ago, and which I have shared with many. As I prayed the thirty-fifth Psalm one day, I was struck by verse ten: "O LORD, who is like thee ..." I stopped and reflected: what be the effect if we replaced the capitalized "LORD" with the name for which it stood? But in what form? If God, speaking of himself, said that his name is "I AM", and if the sacred writers, writing of him in the third person, wrote the name 6000 times as "He IS ", then, when I address him directly, the name should be "YOU ARE". It is a simple, two-syllable linguistic symbol. How it transforms that prayer! "O YOU ARE! Who is like you?" "YOU ARE!" It is a massive affirmation of the fulness of being of the Beloved. All else that I can say of him or to him merely retails the wonders of that name. It is a massive affirmation, full of wonder, love, joy. It expresses the full thrust of symbolizing man, who would burst the bonds of language, who tends toward a knowledge and love whch will not terminate in any image fashioned by man. He stretches for a moment and yearns to fly—and still is standing on his toes.

BIBLIOGRAPHY

ARNOLD, MAGDA, *Emotion and Personality*, 2 volumes. New York: Columbia University Press, 1960—London: Cassell, 1961.

CASSIRER, ERNST, *The Philosophy of Symbolic Forms*, 3 volumes, translated by RALPH MANHEIM. New Haven—London: Yale University Press, 1953, 1955, 1957.

DE WAELHENS, ALPHONSE, "A Philosophy of the Ambiguous," foreword to the second French edition of M. MERLEAU-PONTY, *The Structure of Behavior*, translated by ALDEN L. FISHER. Boston: Beacon Press, 1963.

ENGLISH, HORACE B. and AVA CHAMPNEY, *Psychological and Psychoanalytical Terms*. New York: David McKay, c. 1958.

FINANCE, JOSEPH DE, S.J., *Essai sur l'agir humain*. Rome: Gregorian University Press, 1962.

———, *Éthique générale*. Rome: Gregorian University Press, 1967.

GOLDSTEIN, KURT, *The Organism*. Boston: Beacon Press, c. 1939, 1963.

KLUBERTANZ, GEORGE P., S.J., *The Discursive Power*. Sources and Doctrine of the *Vis Cogitativa* According to St. Thomas Aquinas. St. Louis: The Modern Schoolman, 1952.

———, *The Philosophy of Human Nature*. New York: Appleton-Century-Crofts, 1953.

LANGER, SUSANNE K., *Feeling and Form*. A Theory of Art. New York: Charles Scribner's Sons, c. 1953.

———, *Mind: An Essay on Human Feeling*, vol. I. Baltimore—London: Johns Hopkins Press, c. 1967.

———, *Philosophy in a New Key*². New York: New American Library, c. 1942, 1951.

LONERGAN, BERNARD J. F., S.J., *Insight*. A Study of Human Understanding. London—New York—Toronto: Longmans, Green and Co., 1957.

———, *Method in Theology*. London: Darton, Longman & Todd, c. 1971.

MERLEAU-PONTY, MAURICE, *Phenomenology of Perception*, translated from the French by COLIN SMITH. London: Routledge & Kegan Paul—New York: The Humanities Press, 1962.

———, *The Structure of Behavior*, translated by ALDEN FISHER. Boston: Beacon Press, 1963.

MULLER-THYM, BERNARD J., "The Common Sense, Perfection of the Order of Pure Sensibility," *The Thomist* 2 (1940) 315-343.

POLANYI, MICHAEL, *Personal Knowledge*. New York: Harper & Row, c. 1958, 1962.

RICOEUR, PAUL, *Philosophie de la volonté*, [Tome] I. *Le Volontaire et l'involontaire;* [Tome] II. I. *L'Homme faillible;* II. II. *La Symbolique du mal*. Aubier: Éditions Montaigne, 1963.

ROEST CROLLIUS, ARY A., S.J., "What is so New about Inculturation?" *Gregorianum* 59 (1978) 721-738.

VAN ROO, WILLIAM A., S.J., "Law of the Spirit and Written Law in the Spirituality of St. Ignatius,» *Gregorianum* 37 (1956) pp. 417-443.

——, "Lonergan's Method in Theology," *Gregorianum* 55 (1974) 99-150.

——, "Man the Symbolizer," *Proceedings of the Catholic Theological Society of America* (1977) 102-113.

——, *The Mystery*. Rome: Gregorian University Press, 1971.

——, "The Resurrection of Christ: Instrumental Cause of Grace," *Gregorianum* 39 (1958) 271-284.

——, "A Study of Genus in the Philosophy of St. Thomas Aquinas," *The Modern Schoolman* 20 (1943) 89-104; 165-181; 230-244.

——, "Symbol According to Cassirer and Langer," *Gregorianum* 53 (1972) 487-534; 615-677.

——, "Symbol in Art and Sacrament," *Studia Anselmiana* 64 (1974) 159-171.

INDEX

Actualization: 271-278, 282.
Analogy: 141-142, 330-337.
Analogy of faith: 264, 328.
Appropriation: 43-45.
Aristotle: 152, 158.
Arnold, M.: 87, 90, 92, 93, 152.
Attention: 106.
Awareness: 106 (see: consciousness).

Behavior: 83.
Blending of conceptual and intuitive in symbolizing and symbols: 192-193.

Cassirer, E.: 1-5, 188, 191, 193, 196-201, 203-204, 205-207, 216-217, 218-219, 232.
Causality: 282-290.
Cogitative sense: 152.
Cognition, cognitive: 31-33.
Commemoration: 43-45.
Common sense: 155, 160.
Community: role in symbolizing: 272-278, 316-317, 318-323.
Conception: 64-75.
Conscious, consciousness: 13, 106, 111-132.
Continuity of human operations: 24, 81-82, 105.

Definition, notion of: 291-292.
De Waelhens, A.: 144.
Differentiation of operations and terms or effects: 31.
Discernment of operations: 31.
Discernment of spirits: 169.
Discursive power: 152.

Emotion: 84-93.
Elements in symbolizing and symbols, conceptual and intuitive: 186-194.
English, H. B. and A. C.: 313.
Experience: 32.

Field: 11-13, 110.
Figure-ground: 13, 38, 40, 105.
Finance, J. de: 94-98.

God, natural knowledge of: 213.
Goldstein, K.: 28, 137.

Ground: 109-110.

Hermeneutics: 324-326.
History: 44-45.
Horizon: 110.
Human experience: 17-30.
Human intersubjective world: 125-134.
Human operation: 106-107, 304-305.

Ignatius of Loyola: 288.
Imagination: 47-56.
Inculturation: 324, 326-327.
Insight: 57-64, 184-186, 273-274.
Intellect, roles of: 143-181.
Intellectual operations: 57-82.
Intentional, intentionality: 13, 26-27, 84, 115-116, 139-140.
Interpersonal, intersubjective: 13, 272-278.
Isomorphism: 172, 192-193.

Joyce, J.: 247.
Judgment: 75-76, 79-80, 167-169.

Klubertanz, G.: 88, 152, 159.

Langer, S.: 5-9, 30, 31, 153, 188, 217, 232, 254, 257, 313.
Leibniz: 205.
Lonergan, B.: 65, 107, 115-116.
Love: 99-103.

Mean, meaning, meaningful: 216, 220-222, 311-317.
Memory: 41-47, 54-56, 147-149, 164-165.
Merleau-Ponty, M.: 11, 31, 34, 77, 83, 108, 110, 144, 169, 297-298, 313.
Metaphor and analogy: 141-142.
Metaphysics: 209-213.
Method: 28-30.
Michelangelo: 247, 255-256.
Modes of symbolizing: 186-194.
Motor action: 103-104.
Muller-Thym, B.: 155, 161.

Non-conscious personal ground: 123-124.